THE LIFE OF
HENRY BROUGHAM
TO 1830

HENRY BROUGHAM
From the portrait by Gambardella in Lincoln's Inn, London

THE LIFE OF
HENRY BROUGHAM
TO 1830

BY

CHESTER W. NEW
EMERITUS PROFESSOR OF HISTORY
MCMASTER UNIVERSITY, HAMILTON

OXFORD
AT THE CLARENDON PRESS
1961

Oxford University Press, Amen House, London E.C.4

GLASGOW   NEW YORK   TORONTO   MELBOURNE   WELLINGTON
BOMBAY   CALCUTTA   MADRAS   KARACHI   KUALA LUMPUR
CAPE TOWN   IBADAN   NAIROBI   ACCRA

PRINTED IN GREAT BRITAIN

PREFACE

IT is thirty years since the publication of my biography of Lord Durham. Even at that time I had thought of writing a biography of Lord Brougham, for I had come to feel as I made my way through the Durham project that Brougham was the most vital personality of that period and that his efforts in many directions effected more real progress for Britain and the British world than did those of any other person living in those fruitful years. While the earlier task supplied me with some material, that proved to be a very small amount indeed compared with what I acquired later.

Of the tributes written immediately after Brougham's death, one of the most apt was the comment of the *Daily Telegraph*: 'He is done marching, the old *drum-major* of the army of *liberty*.' He initiated and maintained by his energy and enthusiasm so many movements, and they were nearly all, as the *Telegraph* suggested, in the direction of liberty—freedom for the slaves, for the uneducated that they might have schooling, for the poor that they might have good books, freedom for a university education in a university that was open to all, freedom of the press, freedom for every man to worship God as he pleased without prejudice to his political rights and opportunities, or to his right to learn and to teach, freedom for Dissenters, for Catholics and for Jews, free trade and a free course for justice for the poor as well as for the rich, freedom from the old system of trafficking in boroughs, and for all who paid taxes freedom to vote. This volume is largely about these and his many other enthusiasms, and about the antagonisms encountered and the conflicts he had to wage. At first I sympathized, as I do still to some extent, with those who sneered at Brougham and were occasionally disgusted. The faults of his character always stood out clearly and certainly they are not omitted here, although I have refrained from retailing what was purely the malice and spite of enemies who were injured by liberty for others. But having lived so long with Brougham I can now see more clearly the greatness shining through. This volume ends with his becoming Lord Chancellor. I hope to publish another volume in a few years covering the remainder of his life.

Brougham, who for so many years was more talked about than any public man in Britain, was at the end of the century hardly talked about at all, and although he looms large today in the minds of students of history, to the general reader he is little known. Some of the reasons for this are obvious enough. Brougham's most sensational popular triumph was won in conducting the defence of a British queen on trial for adultery. It is not surprising that that most exciting and important historical event escaped the school history books. Various other reasons have been suggested, but one of the most significant is simply the fact that Brougham was too successful. A generation before his death the Negro slaves had found their freedom and slavery was no longer an issue. Within two years of his death the Forster Education Act was passed, embodying principles which Brougham had been the first to advocate half a century earlier. It clinched the victory for universal education for which Brougham had worked so hard and pleaded so passionately. At the same time an era of law reform which he had inaugurated was reaching its completion. Two years before Brougham's death the Second Reform Bill established the electoral franchise which Brougham had always advocated and the British working man had the vote at last. When he died the University of London, of which he had been principal founder, was firmly established; and a chain of new universities open to all, and which he alone had first advocated, was extending across England. The Dissenter was enjoying equality with the Churchman, the Catholics had been emancipated for many years and the Jews for more than a decade. All Brougham's enemies had been driven from the field. His causes had all succeeded.

While there has been no full biography of Brougham (his own autobiography is extremely unreliable) there have been a number of shorter sketches. The earliest filled half of the last volume of Lord Campbell's *Lives of the Chancellors*. It has been too readily dismissed as 'spiteful' in intent and character—it was said that when Jack Campbell came to write on Lyndhurst and Brougham he would add a new terror to death—but certainly resentment and disappointment prevented Lord Campbell from doing anything like justice to Brougham. The book does contain a considerable amount of apparently sound information, which cannot be found elsewhere, but it is often distorted and inaccurate. Atlay's sketch in his *Victorian Chancellors* is good within limits, but not a biography; secondary material was well used but there was no research in manuscript sources. Professor Aspinall's *Lord Brougham and the Whig Party* was a painstaking and masterly treatment of that aspect of the subject and my indebtedness to it will be obvious from the many references to it in my political chapters. G. T. Garratt's *Lord Brougham* published in 1935 was slight, sometimes fanciful, and contained many errors. Mrs. Hawes's *Henry Brougham* (1957), a brief introduction to a large subject, is of all the biographical sketches of Brougham one of the most accurate. All biographical accounts, however, have been confined almost entirely to Brougham's political career, to the consequent neglect of his great fight against slavery, for education on many fronts, and for law reform. I have attempted to give the latter topics their due consideration and corresponding space in this book. (Law reform belongs mainly to my second volume but is not neglected in the first.)

Brougham's activities were so varied and so much material has been made available to me that selection has been difficult. There is an embarrassing wealth of Brougham's correspondence in the private manuscript collections to which I was afforded access, as well as in unexplored stretches of the public manuscript depositories. The most valuable of all was the collection of manuscripts preserved by Brougham himself and cited here as Brougham MSS. They were purchased a few years ago by University College, London, and except for details related to particular subjects, have not been previously employed. They constitute one of the largest of historical manuscript collections and contain valuable material for a great many subjects. The work of arranging and indexing them has been going on for some time and is now nearing completion. The greater part of this volume was written originally before I saw the Brougham manuscripts, but practically all of it was rewritten in their light.

Very few of Brougham's countless letters in many collections are dated by anything more than the day of the week. In many cases I have dated his letters, confidently, placing my dates in square brackets in my footnotes.

So many persons have helped me that in tendering my thanks I hardly know where to begin or where to stop. Professor Trevelyan, Lady Cecil, and Professor Aspinall have taken a kind interest in my work and they, as well as others, wrote letters of introduction that were essential for the use of private papers. The following, now deceased, very kindly afforded me access to their family papers: the Third Earl of Durham, the Fourth Baron Hatherton. I am very grateful for similar permission to use their manuscript collections to the Duke of Devonshire, the Duke of Wellington, the Marquess of Lansdowne, Earl Grey, Earl Spencer, and Sir Fergus Graham; and to Sir John Murray for access to the transcripts of the Creevey MSS. I also desire to express my gratitude to Lady Eleanor Langham for making the Horner MSS. available to me through Professor Fetter, whom I also thank. The late C. K. Ogden kindly afforded me a limited access to the Brougham manuscripts when they were in his possession and recommended full access later. My thanks are due to the librarians and library staffs of many libraries in the United Kingdom, the United States, and Canada. The librarians have displayed everywhere a most helpful interest and generosity. I am also grateful for the university library-loan facilities of the United States and Canada. Whatever rule there may be in regard to naming individuals in this respect, I feel that I must make exception in three cases. Mr. Joseph Scott, Librarian of University College, University of London, was not only very generous in giving me full access to the Brougham manuscripts after their purchase by University College but he was the soul of kindness and friendship in facilitating my work with them. Miss Margaret Skerl, while she was devoting her experience and skill to the arrangement of those manuscripts, turned aside very often to render me assistance that was invaluable. She gave to me much of the information in regard to the *Edinburgh Review* lists which I have embodied in the early pages of my appendix, as well as sending me important microfilm. Miss Dorothy Davidson, Associate Librarian of McMaster University, has been a friend always at hand, generous, informative, and untiring.

Professor Bellot kindly read two chapters on Launching London University and suggested some valuable amendments. Dean Allan Leal of Osgoode Hall Law School, formerly an

Honour History student of mine, gave me material assistance for the chapter on Brougham's Law Reform speech of 1828 and on various points of law throughout the volume.

I wish to express my gratitude for financial assistance from the American Social Science Research Council for two grants, the Canadian Social Science Research Council for one grant, and McMaster University for two grants.

C. W. N.

McMaster University
Hamilton, 1960

PUBLISHER'S NOTE

Professor New died before the publication of this book, but he did have the satisfaction of seeing the complete text in proof. Although the research had all been done, he had not yet begun to write the second volume to which he several times refers here. The materials gathered in the course of thirty years of research have been placed at the disposal of another scholar and from these it is expected that the life of Brougham after 1830 will eventually be written.

CONTENTS

CHAPTER I

Childhood and Youth

In the year 1777 an English squire, whose fiancée had died on the eve of their projected marriage, travelled north, seeking consolation in a change of scene. On his arrival in Edinburgh he was advised to live at a 'genteel' lodging-house kept by a Mrs. Syme, the widow of a clergyman and sister of the Principal of the University. Within a few months he had married this lady's daughter. The newly married couple moved to No. 21 St. Andrew's Square and there, on 19 September 1778, Henry Peter Brougham was born.

On the father's side, we know little enough that is significant. In later life, Henry Brougham made elaborate claims to an ancient lineage of high renown, and entertained his guests at Brougham Hall with tales and mementoes of his crusader ancestors. They were the more entertaining because they were not believed. In a candid moment, in the writing of his memoirs, he spoke of the 'respectable mediocrity which seems to have characterised my many ancestors, none of whom so far as I have been able to discover, were ever remarkable for anything. Many, no doubt, were fighters, but even in that career of doubtful usefulness were rather prudent than daring.'[1] To this there is little to add, except that there was a streak of insanity among the Broughams, which was recalled at times as a possible explanation of some of the actions of the greatest of the family.

While Henry Brougham's father and his forebears had held land in Westmorland and Cumberland for a number of generations, there was no landholding tradition on his mother's side. There was nothing there but brains. The girl brought up in the Edinburgh lodging-house belonged to an aristocracy of intellect. Her ancestors had been ministers of the Kirk, professors, poets.

[1] *The Life and Times of Henry Lord Brougham, Written by Himself (1871)* (usually known as *Memoirs* and henceforth cited as such), i. 7–8.

The most illustrious member of his mother's family was Robertson, the historian. This great-uncle exercised a direct and powerful influence on Henry Brougham. He provided the inspiration for Brougham's humanitarian drive. His *History of Scotland* had been acclaimed with enthusiasm. Then came the Principalship of the University of Edinburgh, a position which he held for twenty years. A year after he became Principal, he was elected Moderator of the General Assembly. His next book, *Charles V*, gave him a European reputation. Although scholarship has seldom been esteemed in any country as it was in Scotland at the end of the eighteenth century, it was not to scholarship alone that Robertson owed his position in the Kirk and in Edinburgh. He had given successful leadership to the moderate party in the Assembly by virtue of statesmanship, eloquence, and debating power. The pride in his abilities that stimulated the boyish ambitions of his grand-nephew expressed itself fifty years later in the statement that he 'directed the ecclesiastical affairs of Scotland for more than a quarter of a century with unexampled success'.[1] In politics he was a moderate Whig. He ardently championed the cause of the American colonists and was one of the earliest writers who declared boldly that slavery was inconsistent with Christianity. A man of intense industry, he left his problems in his study, and in his social contacts he was lively, humorous, and full of decorous fun. He was remarkable for his tolerance of the opinions of others. He had strong emotions under a dignified and usually placid exterior. He was very much of a Scot withal. When asked if he had noticed how superficial was the Anglo-Saxon part of Hume's history, his reply was, 'Why, yes, I have, but the truth is . . . he was paid for it before he wrote it'.[2]

The character that young Brougham was to develop was different in many ways from that of his great-uncle, but all and more of the latter's humanitarianism, eloquence, debating power, liberal outlook, energy, good nature, and fun can be found in it. The boy was only fifteen when the great man died, but pride and ambition were running high in his mind long

[1] *Works of Lord Brougham*, 11 vols., 3rd ed. (1856) (henceforth cited as *Works*), ii. 240.

[2] Ibid. ii. 284. See *Collected Works of Dugald Stewart*, ed. Sir William Hamilton, 11 vols. (1854–60), x. 101; *The Works of William Robertson*, 6 vols. (1851); *Edinburgh Review*, Apr. 1803, p. 229; *Works*, ii. 231 seq.

before that. His education had been directed and carefully watched by the Principal. He had treasured his companionship and frequently listened to his sermons. One in particular made a deep impression. It was on the eve of the French Revolution and it included a sympathetic prophecy of the struggle for liberty that was to come.[1]

A more intimate influence was exercised by Dr. Robertson's sister, the boy's grandmother. 'To her', Brougham wrote in his old age, 'I owe all my success in life. . . . Remarkable for beauty, but far more for a masculine intellect and clear understanding, she instilled into me from my cradle the strongest desire for information, and the first principles of that persevering energy in the pursuit of every kind of knowledge, which, more than any natural talents I may possess, has enabled me to stick to, and to accomplish, how far successfully it is not for me to say, every task I ever undertook.'[2] 'An ardent love of liberty and hatred of oppression seemed part of her nature.' 'Humanity was a constant topic.'

Brougham's mother was less intellectual in her interests, but possessed a great deal of practical ability and canny common sense. She was a wise counsellor to her brilliant son who was so frequently lacking in judgement. The activities of her second son, James, were inextricably linked with Henry's career; he jackalled for him all his life. Henry was constantly sustained by his affection and gave of his own without stint.

In childhood, as in manhood, Henry Brougham was always bubbling over with life. A servant, who had a propensity for breaking things, always had the ready excuse, 'Sure, ma'am it was crackit before'. One day Master Henry fell downstairs and his mother cried, 'Oh, did you break your head?' 'No, no, Mother,' the boy called back, 'it was crackit before.'[3]

At the age of eleven Henry Brougham at the Edinburgh High School entered the class of the Rector Alexander Adam, one of the rare great teachers. Adam had fought for his education against hunger and bitter want and made of himself a distinguished classicist. He frequently recounted his struggles

[1] Ibid. ii. 243 seq.; *Memoirs*, i. 26 seq.
[2] Ibid. i. 11–12.
[3] George Harris, *Memoirs of Lord Brougham* (1868), reprinted from the *Law Magazine and Law Review*, Aug. 1868.

to his boys when he was inculcating the importance of industry and self-reliance. One of those boys was to develop an industry that was untiring and stupendous and was to rely on himself too much. Adam also urged his pupils to acquire a breadth of knowledge and of intellectual interests. In the early days of the French Revolution he frequently talked to them about the changes that were going on in the world and his liberalism blazed out in the expression of strong democratic sympathies. A few years later he was to find himself under fire on that account.

This teacher had a strong faith in the power of education to exorcise all the evils of society and there is reason to believe that that trend in Brougham's mind had its origin in these High School days.

Adam placed a great emphasis on the importance of public speaking. He not only studied with his boys the great orators of the ancient world, but he went out of his way to make practical suggestions to them and to encourage an interest in debating. Young Henry Brougham availed himself fully of this help. So far as interest was concerned, he needed little spur. From his infancy he had been fond of addressing imaginary audiences and it was probably before he came under Adam that he amused his mother by placing an imaginary prisoner on trial and proceeding to examine witnesses, cross-examine, sum up the evidence, and pass sentence. His mother and grandmother apparently gave him every encouragement in this direction and the latter urged Chatham upon him as a model of eloquence.[1]

He was subsequently to study not only 'the oratory of the ancients' but that of every public speaker of renown who visited Edinburgh, and he organized a debating society called the 'Juvenile Literary Society' with which Francis Horner was associated. By the time he was sixteen he and his friends were debating such topics as, 'Are there any innate ideas in the human mind? . . . Does the establishment of small states or extensive empires tend most to the good of society? . . . Is trial by jury proper in civil cases as well as in criminal cases? . . . Would it be more for the advantage of this country if the East India trade was open to every one, instead of being (as it

[1] *Memoirs*, i. 36, 43–44.

is at present) confined to a chartered company? . . . Has the philosophy of Aristotle been ultimately of advantage to Science?'[1]

We have a picture of Brougham as a schoolboy from the pen of a distant relative: 'The first time I was introduced to him he was about twelve years old and was on one of the bridges of Edinburgh, with a huge quarto under his arm which proved to be a work of LaPlace in the original. I wondered what sort of lad this must be who not only studied mathematics for pleasure, but through the reading of a foreign tongue.'[2] Among his fellow pupils at the High School were Henry Cockburn, John Murray, later Lord Advocate of Scotland, and Francis Horner, who had been his playmate since infancy. Brougham graduated in 1791, but it was felt that he was too young to proceed to the University and from August 1791 to October 1792 he was at Brougham Hall in Westmorland, the ancestral home, with his father and a tutor.

In the autumn of 1792, at the age of fourteen, not an unusual age at that time, he entered the University of Edinburgh. There he attended classes in nearly all the subjects of a general arts course. It is difficult to say what influence the various professors exercised over him. Of Dugald Stewart, Brougham had very little to say in later life. He admired him as a lecturer, but Brougham was brimming over with questions about everything that could be known, and Dugald Stewart had no time for conversations with his students. Playfair had and it was to him that Brougham turned. They talked mathematics together by the hour, fraternized in various ways, and wrote to one another about mathematical problems until Playfair's death in 1819.[3]

Brougham also developed a great admiration for Black, whose class he attended when the latter was at the height of his fame as a scientist. George Birkbeck, who was to become the founder of the Mechanics' Institute movement, which Brougham did so much to energize and popularize, was a fellow student in this class. How intimate Brougham and Birkbeck were at this time we cannot say, but at least a basis was laid for a valuable co-operation later.

[1] Brougham MSS.
[2] Lord Campbell, *Lives of the Chancellors*, viii. 225, 3rd ed., 8 vols. (1848–69).
[3] *Memoirs*, i. 65–68; Henry Cockburn, *Memorials of His Time* (1856), 1878 ed., pp. 31–32; Brougham MSS.

He added considerably to his reputation as a prodigy by writing at the age of sixteen a paper on Optics which was accepted by the Royal Society and read on 28 January 1796 when he had just turned seventeen. Whether it really made the 'addition to the Newtonian doctrine' which it claimed to do is open to serious doubt, as is also Brougham's statement of seventy years later that the omission of certain parts in the printing of the paper withheld from humanity for decades the secret of photography. Encouraged by the success of this paper, he had another ready for the Royal Society in the following year on 'Further Experiments on the Application and Properties of Light', which was accepted, read, and published in due course. These papers attracted the attention of Professor Prevost of Geneva, who criticized them for lack of precision. Another Royal Society paper by Brougham—on Porisms this time— appeared a year later.[1]

In 1796 Brougham completed the four years in 'Humanity and Philosophy', and began the study of law. Although his father advised against it he had his eye on the English Bar, for as he wrote in a letter to Horner the Scottish Bar was 'a miserable object as an *ultimate* object'.[2] It is also clear from this letter that he hoped one day to sit in the House of Commons. His ambitions were already taking shape. It is not surprising that the figure of Francis Bacon appears to have been very often in his thoughts at this time; a legal and political career adorned by literary and scientific triumphs was to be his. During the next eighteen months he was 'constantly engaged in historical and political reading'.[3]

In November 1797 he was elected a member of the Speculative Society and in 1799 he was one of its four presidents. This was not only the most important literary and debating society of the University, it was one of the most famous of Scottish institutions. For all the distinction of its history, it is doubtful if its membership ever comprised such a remarkable group of men as at this time. Walter Scott, although no longer at the University, continued to attend its meetings. Its more active

[1] *Transactions of the Royal Society*, lxxxvi. 227–77; lxxxvii. 352–82; lxxxviii. 378–96; *Memoirs*, i. 68–71.
[2] Horner MSS., Brougham to Horner, 21 Sept. 1796.
[3] Ibid., 27 Mar. 1797.

members included Francis Jeffrey, who was to be the greatest of Scottish reviewers, John Alexander Murray, later Lord Advocate of Scotland, Charles Grant who was to become Lord Glenelg, and Henry Petty, later Lord Lansdowne, who was to be associated with Brougham in the advancement of education as well as in the leadership of the Whig party. Brougham's old friend Horner was voted in at the same meeting. Henry, later Lord, Cockburn and the inimitable Sydney Smith joined a few years later.[1]

Here were just the stimulus and the opportunity that Brougham needed and he was very much in his element. Seldom had even the Speculative seen such energy, and his eloquence developed so rapidly that Cockburn, writing fifty years later, said that Brougham in the Speculative was as good a speaker as he ever was. Brougham himself would have said later that that was nonsense and that he learned a great deal about speaking during his first two years in Parliament. We can follow Cockburn more readily in his statement that not only in the Society itself, but even to half a dozen of its members, Brougham 'could abandon himself to his subject and blaze as if he had been declaiming against Cicero in the forum'.[2] Speaking at the seventieth anniversary dinner of the Speculative Society in 1834, Jeffrey referred to Brougham as the man whose name 'has for many years been more before the public than any other name in this country' and he recalled Brougham's days in the Speculative—'the versatility of his talents . . . his power of illustration and that ardent, somewhat ferocious, eloquence in which he scorched and blasted and overthrew all those who dared to give him battle'.[3]

Although he was working very hard both at his study of law and in preparation for the weekly meetings of the Speculative, he found time for activities of a very different kind. Sir Thomas Dick Lauder wrote: 'Brougham's companions consisted of two sorts, viz., intellectual men, such as Jeffrey, Cockburn, and Murray, and fellows of dissipation, fun, and frolick.'[4]

[1] Cockburn, *Memorials*, pp. 76 seq.; Lord Cockburn, *Life of Lord Jeffrey* (1852), i. 46 seq.; *Memoirs and Correspondence of Francis Horner*, ed. Leonard Horner, published in 1843, 1853 ed., i. 56.
[2] Cockburn, *Memorials*, p. 78.
[3] *History of the Speculative Society of Edinburgh* (1845), pp. 209–10.
[4] Quoted in Campbell, viii. 230.

Brougham himself wrote:

I cannot tell how the fancy originated; but one of our constant exploits, after an evening at the Apollo, or at Johnny's, was to parade the streets of the New Town, and wrench the brass knockers off the doors, or tear out the brass handles of the bells. No such ornaments existed in the Old Town; but the New Town, lately built, abounded in sea-green doors and huge brazen devices, which were more than our youthful hands could resist. The number we tore off must have been prodigious; for I remember a large dark closet in my father's house . . . which was literally *filled* with our *spolia opima*. . . . Looking back to those pranks reminds me of the inexhaustible fund of spirits we possessed, and how that *capital* foundation of never-tiring energy and endless restlessness enabled some of us to work on with unfailing strength to the end of life; and even now, writing at nearly 90 years of age, I can recall those, not boys' but young men's freaks with pleasure and even exultation.[1]

It was probably at this time that Brougham went one day with a lad named Pillans (later rector of the High School and one of Scotland's greatest educationists) to the Edinburgh Theatre to see a new play. It proved to be dull. Every attempt at fun missed fire. Four acts dragged out. The curtain went up on the fifth with the stage set for a dinner party. The gentleman in the chair flourished his glass and asked for a toast. Young Henry Brougham stood up in the pit and said, 'I humbly propose, "Good afternoon"', which was then the customary toast for concluding a party. He turned, walked toward the door, and waved his hat for the audience to follow him. With laughter and cries of 'Good afternoon', they streamed out of galleries, pit, stalls, and boxes. That was the first of Henry Brougham's countless *public* speeches. Many of them were to be equally successful, but few had the same merit of brevity.[2]

One of Lauder's stories of Brougham's student pranks was related by Lord Campbell as follows: He went one day at this time to a meeting of the Caledonian Hunt at Dunfries. He offered to bet everyone at the table d'hôte that none of them would write down in a sealed packet the way he (Brougham) meant to travel next day to the races a few miles away. He then

[1] *Memoirs*, i. 89–91.
[2] Lord Campbell (viii. 225–6) placed this story in Brougham's High School days, but the dates associated with this play and its author make that impossible.

sealed up his proposal and placed it with the others. It stated that he would go in a *sedan chair*. He won his bet and a great crowd accompanied him. That evening at dinner he repeated the bet. They thought of all sorts of fantastic locomotion; he wrote down that he would go in a simple carriage and won again.[1]

In August 1799 Brougham went off with his friend Charles Stewart on a tour of the Western Islands. Their boat soon came to be known as 'the mad brig'. At one place Brougham invaded the bedroom of the owner of the hotel in the middle of the night, announced that he was a messenger from Hell, and shot a cat. A story having been circulated (probably on Brougham's own initiative) that he was a kinsman of Mr. Pitt, he commanded a great respect among the natives of St. Kilda's, who must have been greatly puzzled at the conduct of the great man's relative.

In the early months of 1800 he was working hard preparing for his final law examinations. They were passed successfully and on 10 June he became a barrister.[2] A month and a day later, at San Salvadore, his brother Peter fought a duel with the second mate of the *Queen* and was killed. 'I was nearly distracted', Henry wrote later. 'Indeed I verily believe that my mind was for a time unhinged for I left Edinburgh and wandered about I know not where.'[3]

[1] Ibid. viii. 230–1.
[2] Ibid. viii. 236.
[3] *Memoirs*, i. 224–5.

CHAPTER II

Barrister Without Remuneration: the Founding of the *Edinburgh Review*

BROUGHAM's first cases were well scattered and any success they might have brought was negligible. But failure did not impair his high spirits. He signalized his arrival at the Jedburgh Assizes by charging in his one-horse chaise through the judge's stately procession. His daily jokes in the court-room seem to have been almost as broad and quite as annoying. Sir Thomas Dick Lauder, commenting on them, said 'Brougham continued to persecute my poor old relative, Lord Eskgrove, whom he nearly tormented to death; about this time his [Brougham's] conduct was so eccentric that he was supposed to have shown a slight tendency to insanity, and his friends were very uneasy about him.'[1]

Brougham was not the only brilliant, ambitious, and restless young man in Edinburgh whose prospects seemed dim. Several of his closest friends were in the same position. Out of that restlessness was born the *Edinburgh Review*. Jeffrey, Sydney Smith, Brougham, and Francis Horner were its founders. Three of the four were young lawyers of markedly liberal views, to whom every path of advancement was closed as long as Scotland submitted to the Tory domination of Henry Dundas, who ruled the country with a smiling face and an iron hand, and delivered it bound and gagged to successive governments at every mock-election.

Francis Horner, the son of an Edinburgh merchant, was born in the same year as Brougham, played with him as a child, was a year behind him at the High School, and succeeded him as 'dux' of the rector's class. They went through the University together, were voted into the Speculative Society on the same evening, and were closely associated in the ensuing years. Horner made a deep impression on that Edinburgh group of

[1] Campbell, viii. 241.

brilliant men, as he did later in Parliament, whether or not he was the first real economist in the House of Commons. Like Brougham he possessed a tremendous capacity for intellectual labour. Yet he was a strange companion for Sydney Smith and Brougham, for he was as lacking in humour as a man could be and yet live. A year before the *Edinburgh Review* began, his fortunes and outlook at the bar were indicated by an entry in his diary, 'I am creeping into a little business, which gives me the shadow and fancy of occupation'.[1]

Francis Jeffrey was five years older than Brougham and Horner. He went through the High School four years ahead of Brougham, then studied at Glasgow and Oxford, returned to Edinburgh for a law course, and was in the Speculative several years before Brougham and Horner joined. These three became its great debaters. He was a fairly liberal Whig. He was constantly writing essays on all sorts of subjects, as well as a good deal of poetry. In 1802 he was already extremely opinionated, filled with a zest for the truth, merciless in his criticism. Although he had been practising law for seven years, Jeffrey's prospects were no brighter than those of Brougham and Horner. He was married a few months before the *Review* was contemplated. 'We trust to Providence, and have hopes of dying before we get into prison [for debt].'[2]

While Jeffrey, Brougham, and Horner were lawyers without briefs, Sydney Smith was a clergyman without a parish. At Winchester he and his brother had won all the prizes possible and he was head of the school as Brougham and Horner were at Edinburgh. His career at Oxford was a distinguished one. His father, who had been a merchant of Eastcheap had come into some money and, according to Sydney, was in process of 'buying, altering, spoiling, and then selling about nineteen different places in England'.[3] But none of the money came Sydney's way. The father, having insisted on his being a clergyman, further insisted on his shifting for himself. After a few years as a curate in an obscure village, he engaged to tutor a rich man's son and in that capacity, in 1798, the man who was

[1] Francis Horner, i. 135.
[2] Cockburn, *Jeffrey*, ii. 52, Francis Jeffrey to John Jeffrey, 1 Aug. 1801.
[3] *A Memoir of the Reverend Sydney Smith* by his daughter, the Lady Holland, with selections from his correspondence, 2 vols. (1855), i. 14.

to be considered the greatest English wit of the nineteenth century, this genial fat man 'with a mouth like an oyster and three double chins', 'his faunlike face a sort of promise of a good thing when he does but open his lips', came to Edinburgh.[1]

Possibly Smith's own choice of the law as a profession, which had been surrendered to his father's choice of the Church, influenced him in seeking out in Edinburgh the company of young lawyers rather than that of young clergymen. Sydney Smith immediately set himself up as guardian angel for Jeffrey. Sometimes he merely chaffed him. Writing to the little man, he said, 'Magnitude to you must be such an intoxicating idea that I have no doubt you would rather be gigantic in your errors than immense in no respect whatever'.[2] On other occasions he was more serious. 'If you could be alarmed into the semblance of modesty, you would charm everybody.' Jeffrey's attitude to life, he suggested, could be summed up as, 'Damn the solar system! bad lights! planets too distant, pestered with comets. Feeble contrivance! Could make a better with great ease.'[3]

Sydney took life easily, and Brougham was a dynamo of energy. That probably influenced Brougham's later judgement on Sydney: 'He was an admirable joker; he had the art of placing ordinary things in an infinitely ludicrous point of view. I have seen him at dinner . . . drive the servants from the room with the tears running down their faces, in peals of inextinguishable laughter. But he was too much of a jack-pudding.'[4]

It was Sydney Smith who spoke the words that brought into being what was not only the greatest literary review, but one of the most liberalizing, humanizing, and beneficent forces of the century.

Towards the end of my residence in Edinburgh, Brougham, Jeffrey and myself happened to meet in an eighth or ninth story or flat in Buccleuch Place, the then elevated residence of Mr. Jeffrey. I proposed that we should set up a review; this was acceded to with acclamation. I was appointed editor; and remained long enough in Edinburgh to edit the first number. The motto I proposed was, 'Tenui musam meditamur avena'—We cultivate literature on a

[1] Reminiscences and Correspondence of Henry Crabb Robinson, 2 vols., 3rd ed. (1872), ii. 175; C. H. E. and S. M. Brookfield, Mrs. Brookfield and Her Circle (1906), p. 122.
[2] Osbert Burdett, The Rev. Sydney Smith (1934), ii. 50.
[3] Memoir of Sydney Smith, ii. 33.
[4] Memoirs, i. 247.

little oatmeal. But this was too near the truth to be admitted, and so we took our present grave motto from Publius Syrus, of whom none of us had I am sure ever read a single line. . . . When I left Edinburgh, the Review fell into the stronger hands of Jeffrey and Brougham, and reached the highest point of popularity and success.[1]

Brougham insisted later that the house in which Jeffrey lived was not eight or nine stories high. There was no house of more than three stories 'in Buccleuch Place or in that portion of the new town'. Horner apparently was not the only one who could not understand Sydney Smith's jokes at times. The fact Brougham was at such pains to point out was probably what prompted Sydney to catch at the humour of giving the five-foot Jeffrey a ninth-story residence. He probably no more intended the 'eighth or ninth story' to be taken literally than he did the statement that he never read a book before he reviewed it—'It prejudices one so'.

Brougham was not at first a member of the committee of editors because Sydney Smith complained of his 'indiscretion and rashness' and that he was 'violent and unmanageable'. It was suggested that Brougham resented Smith not letting him have his own way. Certainly Brougham insisted on Jeffrey having complete control and, with Jeffrey as editor, Brougham, as Jeffrey said, 'was admitted after the third number and did more work for us than anybody'.[2]

In the months that intervened between the proposal of the *Review* and the appearance of the first number in October, Brougham was for the first time attacked by the disease that makes men write books. But he was constantly changing his mind as to what the book was to be. The plan which he outlined in December 1801 in a letter to Loch was abandoned. In a letter written in February he referred to the proposed book as 'my Politics'. Then in the spring he thought of writing on the West Indies. He dropped that on the appearance of James

---

[1] *Memoir of Sydney Smith*, i. 31; *Works of Sydney Smith* (1844), Preface.

[2] Cockburn, *Jeffrey*, i. 110; *Life, Letters and Journals of George Ticknor*, 2 vols. (1877), ii. 150; Hesketh Pearson, *The Smith of Smiths* (1934), pp. 46–47; *Memoirs*, i. 249–50. Professor J. Clive's excellent *Scotch Reviewers, the Edinburgh Review, 1802–15* (1957), appeared after this chapter was written. Professor Clive made a painstaking and thoughtful study of the *Review* to 1815. His account of the founding is, of course, fuller than this and it provides a much richer background, but his findings do not clash in any important manner with the conclusions stated here.

Stephen's book on the West Indies, and proposed to write 'a small work upon the subject of "The Colonial Policy of Great Britain in the present Crisis" '. The 'small work' became two volumes, *An Inquiry into the Colonial Policy of the European Powers.*[1]

The first number of the *Edinburgh Review* appeared in October. Approximately three-quarters of the articles were written by Jeffrey, Smith, Horner, and Brougham. Each of these, following the policy which was to be pursued throughout the history of the *Review*, was not so much a book review in our sense of the term, as an extended article based on a book and frequently departing from it. The *Review* was an immediate success. The sale and the applause exceeded all expectations. A publication undertaken by so able a group had unlimited opportunities. No first-class review existed in Great Britain. As Lord Cockburn said, 'the learning of the new journal, its talents, its spirit, its writing, its independence, were all new'.[2]

Sydney Smith's summary of the great causes served by the *Review* and the need for the reforms it advocated has been frequently quoted. A number of others might be added, such as criminal-law reform, the development of popular education, the amendment of the poor laws, and municipal reform.

Brougham probably wrote six articles for the first number. That on Wood's *Optics* appears to be a good straightforward review, well written and just. That on Acerbi's *Travels* was, in its severity, in general harmony with the character of the *Edinburgh Review* in its early years. This clever young man was here sharpening his powers of sarcasm for later use. 'His [Acerbi's] information, though arranged in chapters, is . . . devoid of lucid order. . . . Most of his anecdotes seem to have contained a little humour or singularity at some distant period; but to have lost all pretentions to these qualities in passing through Mr. Acerbi's memory.'

His review of *The Crisis of the Sugar Colonies* was a very serious matter. Here was the subject which Brougham had of recent months taken particularly to his mind. He had been intending to write a pamphlet or a book on it and had been pestering his

---

[1] *Brougham and his Early Friends*, ed. R. H. M. B. Atkinson and G. A. Johnson, 3 vols. (1908), i. 285–9, 299, 349, 362. Brougham to Loch, 23 Dec. 1801, 9 Feb., 4 Sept., 7 Nov. 1802.

[2] Cockburn, *Jeffrey*, i. 106.

friends to help him to secure a great deal of information on the West Indies. Now appeared this book on the subject, published anonymously but written, as Brougham knew, by James Stephen, one of the most active champions of the movement for the abolition of the slave trade. Brougham probably disagreed sincerely with Stephen on some matters of opinion, but the article would have been unduly severe even if its young writer had spent more months on the study of the West Indies than Stephen had years. Almost the only points on which he agreed with Stephen were that the slave trade must be abolished, and that that action must be taken by the British Parliament, whatever the supposed rights of the colonial legislatures might be.

In the last paragraph of this article there appeared something of the soul of this ambitious, sarcastic, and argumentative young man, something of that genuine humanitarianism which he had learned from his grandmother and her distinguished brother. This article shows us Brougham at grips with a subject which commanded all his powers and it is his first contribution to the anti-slavery movement. Brougham was to use the *Edinburgh* skilfully and effectively from first to last in the interests of that great cause.

Brougham's longest article—thirty-seven pages—in the second number of the *Edinburgh* was a history and critique of the balance of power, ponderous at first, spirited as it advanced. But most of his articles in this number were on mathematical and scientific subjects and two of them had a tragic sequel. In the light of history Thomas Young stands out as one of the greatest scientists of that age. In the Bakerian Lecture on 'The Theory of Light of Colour' he suggested a doctrine of the interference of light which proved to be epoch-making in its significance. Young Brougham, critic of politics and mathematics and would-be scientist, did his best to retard the epoch.

Brougham's articles afforded little information as to what Young's theory was and consisted almost entirely of abuse, disdain, and homilies on the folly of publishing hypotheses without adequate experimentation. Young, unaccustomed to such treatment, felt the criticism keenly. He was chagrined to find that after this condemnation no one would take his theory seriously, but Young's exposition must have been unsatisfactory or it would not have been damned by these two reviews. He proceeded, however, to prove his point by a simple experiment. Brougham in another article in the ninth number of the *Edinburgh* said that Young must have made a mistake in performing the experiment. Young then published a pamphlet, in the course of which he paid his respects to Brougham. 'Conscious of the inability to explain the experiment, too ungenerous to confess that inability, and too idle to repeat the experiment, he is compelled to advance the supposition that it was incorrect.' The *Edinburgh Reviews* containing Brougham's articles sold about 3,000 each. Of Dr. Young's pamphlet only one copy was ever sold. French scientists were to take up Young's work with very important results, but that was years later.

Before the *Edinburgh Review* had completed its first year the group that launched it had begun to break up. Horner, making the plunge on the brink of which Brougham was hesitating, left for London and the English Bar in March of 1803, and Sydney Smith left Edinburgh for London in August. John Allen, who was on the circumference of the group, had preceded Horner, having attached himself to Lord Holland as physician. They gave Horner a farewell banquet at Fortune's Hotel and, as a fitting climax to so great an occasion, made their way in the dead of night to Manderson's druggist's shop, which boasted one of the grandest bronze signs in Edinburgh. They hoisted Brougham on the shoulders of the tallest of the company, from where he climbed to the top of the doorway and 'twisted off the enormous brazen serpent which formed the explanatory announcement of the business that was carried on within'. The attention of the city guard was apparently aroused and the founders of the *Edinburgh Review* 'had a hard run for it'. But fortune still smiled upon them. It was a grand *coup*.[1]

For the third number of the *Review* Brougham wrote five articles and part of another.[2] Of the article on Ritson's *Essay on the Abstinence from Animal Food as a Moral Duty* Sydney Smith said: 'Brougham and I sat one night over our review of that book, looking whether there were a chink or crevice through which we could drop one more drop of verjuice.'[3] The jocular

---

[1] *Memoirs*, i. 90.
[2] *Early Friends*, ii. 67; Brougham to Loch, 19 June 1803.
[3] Harriet Martineau, *Biographical Sketches* (1869), p. 394. See also *Memoirs, Journals and Correspondence of Thomas Moore*, 8 vols. (1853), vii. 13.

Sydney Smith was in those early days of the *Edinburgh* as brutal as Brougham. It is probable that, seven years older than Brougham as he was, he was the latter's tutor in invective. There is a letter from Smith to Jeffrey, written while the first number was being prepared, which asked for Dr. Parr's head with something of the intensity with which Herodias sought that of the Baptist, but instead of intriguing for it he put it all to Jeffrey squarely with fierce candour.[1] As the years passed, however, this habit of ruthless invective slid from the fat shoulders of Sydney Smith. With Henry Brougham the habit grew and was developed at times to the point of genius. It helped him to do some of his best work, notably in the destruction of great abuses, and it inevitably made for him many of his worst enemies.

After the appearance of this third number, Jeffrey was officially appointed editor of the *Review*. At that time there was a decided lack of unity between the three of the original four whose friendship had founded the *Review*. Horner was strongly displeased with the type of reviewing developed by Brougham and Sydney Smith and the latter two were at odds over Sydney's efforts to continue the exclusion of Brougham from the inner counsels.[2] On 30 May (1803) Horner wrote:

> With regard to Brougham I had suspected what you told me from a letter he wrote me some days ago in which he throws out indiscreet hints and threats of a *rival* review and an *opposition*. . . . I do not want to know anything more particularly about Brougham's intrigues, for I have no interest in such pitiful anecdotes and I do not wish to have any reason to think more lowly of Brougham in some respects than I have been forced to do for some time past, in spite of old habits of intimacy.

This letter also states that Horner had not written to Brougham since the former had gone to London.[3]

There is nothing to indicate whether or not Brougham had given any offence to Horner beyond the character of his reviews and his incipient revolt against the *Edinburgh*. Certainly the spirit of that letter is such that it indicates a cooling of the friendship between Horner and Brougham long before the time when Lord Holland's *Reminiscences* blames Brougham for break-

---

[1] *Memoir of Sydney Smith*, ii. 16–17. Sydney Smith to Jeffrey, June 1802.
[2] Horner MSS.
[3] Ibid., Horner to Jeffrey, 30 May 1803.

ing it off. Brougham on his side was writing to Horner in as friendly a spirit as ever and pouring out to him the tale of his troubles with Sydney Smith.

On 27 June he wrote to Horner about his relations with Sydney Smith:

The most perfect good humour has all along subsisted between us two, a constant interchange of visits and walks and letters, while in our reviewing capacity we have been reviling each other, I dare to say, as cordially as if we had been poets, or players, or women.[1]

About the same time Brougham's book *An Inquiry into the Colonial Policy of the European Powers* was published. To speak of it, as one writer has done, as 'the first of his great works' is clearly absurd. But it is no more absurd than Lord Campbell's flattering suggestion that had the gifted Brougham been willing to have devoted sufficient time to it, he might have written a work which would have been as epoch-making as Adam Smith's *Wealth of Nations*. His magnificent gifts were very different from those of Adam Smith. To say 'had he taken the time' is merely begging the question. He lacked the patience that makes for great scholarship. What he always sought was the effect of the moment. The effect of the moment, the power to move men to resolution and to action is the true test of oratory and Brougham was in everything the superb orator. That he talked so well and wrote so poorly was a matter of natural aptitude of essential character.

His books, nevertheless, attracted some attention and had some influence in their day. This first one was, on the whole, well reviewed. But the *Colonial Policy* proved quite clearly that Brougham, for all his clever and drastic criticism of others in the *Edinburgh Review*, did not know how to construct a book.[2] He would have been very much surprised in this summer of 1803 to know that it was what he had written about the slave trade that was to give the book its only significance for history and for him. The champions of a great cause made him almost immediately one of their leaders, and to that cause and its sequel, the abolition of slavery, Brougham was to give the best that was in him. The *Colonial Policy* had been written to attract

---

[1] Horner MSS., Brougham to Horner, 27 June 1803.
[2] For an excellent analysis of the *Colonial Policy* see A. Aspinall, *Lord Brougham and the Whig Party* (1927), pp. 7–9.

the attention of the diplomats. It won the attention of the 'Saints'. (The name given to the Evangelists associated with Wilberforce in giving leadership to the parliamentary movement against the slave trade.)

In this month of June 1803 the Friday Club was inaugurated. It was a select company of the literary lights of Edinburgh. Starting with sixteen, elections were to be made slowly and carefully until a complement of thirty was reached. Jeffrey said that the idea was Walter Scott's. 'All his friends are included and all ours.' Of those already mentioned in these pages, Brougham, Jeffrey, Sydney Smith, Murray, Cockburn, Dugald Stewart, and Playfair were among the original members, as was also Thomas Campbell, the poet. They met for supper every Friday and sat 'chatting until two o'clock in the morning'.[1] On one of their first Fridays the talk turned to medicine among the Greeks and the work and character of Galen. And that in turn led to a bronze head of Galen over the door of Gardiner's apothecary shop. It was high and apparently secure, but since Brougham, with the aid of some of this company had captured Manderson's serpent, even Galen's head might be a possible prize. Brougham particularly seemed keen for the adventure, and under the inspiration of his famous punch, 'a beverage of rum, sugar, lemons, marmalade, calves foot jelly, water and more rum', Professor Playfair, Sydney Smith, and Thomas Thomson (Clerk of Sessions and one of the regular contributors to the *Edinburgh Review*) sallied forth with Brougham. The professor (Brougham's beloved professor of mathematics) tried to hold Sydney Smith as steady as possible while the Clerk of Sessions climbed on to his shoulders. Thomson had 'almost reached the prize', when they saw the watch stealing toward them and with the men of the watch was—Brougham, wearing a broad grin, and his trick nose, no doubt, twitching with amusement on his homely face. Professor, clergyman, and Clerk of Sessions made for safety, but without Galen's head.[2] For Sydney Smith 'the battle of Galen's head' as he called it was the last Edinburgh exploit. He departed for London on 8 August.

Brougham had at last decided for the English Bar and was

[1] Cockburn, *Jeffrey*, i. 118 seq.
[2] *The Book of the Old Edinburgh Club*, iii. 110, quoted in Aspinall, p. 5; Pearson, pp. 42–43.

reconciling himself to the prospect of waiting five long years before he could qualify for it. Henry Brougham's name was entered at Lincoln's Inn on 14 November of this year (1803), although he did not move to London until a few months later. By that time three more numbers of the *Edinburgh Review* had appeared, for each of which Brougham wrote a number of articles. The way in which Brougham used the *Review* to serve the great causes which he led, particularly the anti-slavery movement, popular education, and law reform, the difficulties that developed over party politics in the forties and the final dramatic break, must be left to later chapters.

CHAPTER III

Crusading Against the Slave Trade

THERE is a great deal of confusion in the popular mind about the British abolition of slavery. The later movement for the abolition of slavery itself is constantly confused with the earlier one for the abolition of the slave trade. The trade was abolished in 1807, although the enforcement was not effective until 1811. The movement for the abolition of slavery may be said to have begun in 1822 and ended in 1838 (not 1834, as usually supposed). The confusion is particularly notable with regard to Wilberforce, who is so often acclaimed as the man who freed the slaves. Wilberforce and Clarkson were the great leaders of the movement against the trade, and public opinion hailed Wilberforce as its hero. As the hero of the first movement he lent prestige and encouragement to the second. But the freeing of the slaves was achieved by other men. Brougham made important contributions to the first movement. He was one of Wilberforce's inner cabinet and he delivered two telling blows at critical moments in its closing years. Of the second movement which freed the slaves, he was one of the three great leaders.

It was Brougham's *Colonial Policy* that brought together the orator of the first movement and the orator of the second. Just how Wilberforce and Brougham met we do not know. But shortly after Brougham arrived in London at the beginning of 1804, Wilberforce was introducing this young man of twenty-five to his friends as 'a fellow-labourer in the vineyard', and almost immediately he was made a member of the central committee.

A good short account of the evils of the slave trade is given in a few pages of Professor Coupland's life of Wilberforce.[1] The wars and raids and treasons in Africa to make slaves, the panic that prevailed when a slave ship appeared, the terrible middle

---

[1] Sir Reginald Coupland, *Wilberforce* (1923), pp. 71–74.

passage in the most torrid of climates with the slaves packed together on shelves, the indescribable conditions during a storm, fever and disease and lashing, the women and children the victims of the brutality of the crew—it is all told without sentiment or homily with the deadly accuracy and objectivity of the historian. The report of a Privy Council Committee in 1789 showed that of the slaves shipped to Jamaica, $12\frac{1}{2}$ per cent. died in the crossing, $4\frac{1}{2}$ per cent. on shore before the day of sale, and about 33 per cent. in the 'seasoning', a total of 50 per cent. The figure for the whole of the West Indies was not so high —but so far as Jamaica was concerned, one Negro was done to death for every new labourer secured for her plantations.

With all of this, it was a most profitable business. It has been estimated that over a long stretch of years the average annual profit on the capital invested was 30 per cent. Half of the total slave trade came to be centred in Liverpool. The statement that Liverpool was 'built on the bones of African slaves' was sentimental nonsense, but certainly its development as a port owed a great deal to the slave trade.

An awakening of practical humane Christianity found an intense application to social reforms in that extraordinary group of Evangelicals, Anglicans indirectly influenced by Whitfield, not Wesley. With the single exception of Brougham, all of the great leaders of both the anti-slave-trade and the anti-slavery movements were Evangelicals. Their motives were deeply religious. Their letters are saturated with a sense of being responsible to God and His children for every moment and for every thought. The Quakers, who had been in the field against the trade before the Evangelicals, and who supplied the movement with leaders of the second rank, displayed a similar zeal and piety.

Into this company of 'saints' came Henry Brougham. He was not pious in their sense and he did not speak their language. He *did* share their humanitarian enthusiasm. The sincerity of that they never doubted. They admired him greatly and always spoke of him in the highest terms. And Brougham himself never praised any man in such unstinted terms as he praised Thomas Clarkson and Wilberforce. The former was the leader of the movement outside Parliament, who ran down every vestige of evidence against the evil, even to the extent of pursuing one witness through ports in every sea and finding him on the three-hundred and seventy-ninth ship which he searched.

Clarkson, when a student at Cambridge, won an essay prize open to the university. Nobody had won it twice. Clarkson was ambitious to do so. That second year the topic assigned was, 'Is it right to make men slaves against their will?' (selected by Vice-Chancellor Peckard, who was an anti-slave-trade 'crank' before the organized movement began). Young Clarkson won his prize a second time, but before that happened the subject had eaten into his soul and kept him awake at nights, shocked and shamed by what he read. Was this really going on and no one doing anything about it? Travelling home after that term Clarkson broke his journey for a few moments of prayer in which he dedicated his life to the abolition of what a chosen few regarded as the greatest of human curses. He led the movement outside Parliament as valiantly as Wilberforce led the parliamentary movement. And everywhere he went running down evidence, the paid ruffians of the slave trade sought to run *him* down; he narrowly escaped being pushed off the end of a pier one dark night in Liverpool. He should be bracketed *with* Wilberforce as the hero of the movement to abolish the slave trade. Brougham came to be more closely associated with Wilberforce, but with Clarkson he maintained a tender friendship which lasted throughout Clarkson's life.

That great-uncle, Robertson the historian, who first inspired Brougham's humanitarianism, was one of the first to raise his voice against the slave trade and against slavery. Both, he said, were incompatible with Christianity, and had no place among Christian peoples.[1] It may be assumed that Brougham's original intention of writing his first book on the West Indies brought to him a considerable amount of information about the trade and stimulated his antagonism to it. His book *Colonial Policy* carried him into the inner circle of the opponents of the slave trade. In the concluding chapters of *Colonial Policy*, Brougham took the position that the worst features of the West Indian system were the bad treatment of the slaves and the large proportion of recently imported Africans.

[1] F. J. Klingberg, *The Anti-Slavery Movement in England* (1926), pp. 54–55; William Robertson, *The History of the Reign of the Emperor Charles the Fifth* (Prescott ed., Philadelphia, 1902), i. 264–8.

Arguments in favour of the trade were refuted one by one. The following examples may illustrate Brougham's style in dealing with them:

A traffic which at the utmost never employs more than five thousand seamen has been called the pillar of the British navy. A traffic which destroys more sailors in one year than all the other branches of trade put together destroy in two; a traffic which is in fact the grave of our ablest seamen, has been extolled as their best nursery. . . . But we are told that if the British were to abolish the slave trade, the French and Dutch would take it up. . . . May not the same argument be used in France and Holland to oppose the abolition? . . . So that a trade of iniquity and shame is to be supported to all eternity because each of the parties engaged in it may say that the others might continue it![1]

Those who were called 'abolitionists' at that time were advocating *only* the abolition of the trade. The 'abolitionist' leaders, with the single exception of Granville Sharp, went out of their way to assert that they were not suggesting the abolition of slavery. On the very eve of victory over the trade, Wilberforce opposed in the strongest terms a motion for the abolition of slavery. That was to some extent a matter of tactics. To admit that there was any possibility of the slaves being emancipated would have antagonized many who supported the movement for the abolition of the trade. Some of the leaders envisaged in their minds, no doubt, the ultimate disappearance of slavery by evolution, not by legislation, while others contented themselves with believing that the abolition of the trade would be followed by the disappearance of the worst evils associated with slavery.[2] In his *Colonial Policy* Brougham predicted that if the slave trade were removed, slavery in the West Indies would develop into a sort of serfdom and that in turn would give way to personal freedom in a manner similar to the breakdown of medieval serfdom. It may be assumed that Brougham did not expect the abolition of slavery itself to take centuries, but he would have been very much surprised in 1803 if any one had foretold that thirty-five years later he himself would lead the final drive which would end slavery in fact as well as in name. Throughout the last section of the *Colonial Policy* slavery appears as an essentially

---

[1] H. Brougham, *Inquiry into the Colonial Policy of European Powers* (1803), pp. 487–90.   [2] Klingberg, p. 73.

intolerable system. At the suggestion of its defenders that 'Christianity itself approves of the institution' Brougham blazed out. If that were so 'I hesitate not to declare that there is an end of all rational faith in Christianity; for what can more decisively disprove the divine origin of any system of belief than its inculcating or sanctioning the slavery of the West Indies?'[1]

The good reception which the *Colonial Policy* received indicates that Brougham's treatment of the slave trade must have had considerable influence. It also brought Brougham into the movement at the most critical stage of its history. Its leaders had been hopeful of success in 1789 and again in 1791 and 1792. But the French Revolutionists had included the abolition of the trade in their humanitarian programme and as the tide of feeling in England turned against the Revolution, it carried with it everything that was being suggested in France. After the outbreak of war between England and France there developed a tendency to postpone all reform; it could wait, all efforts must be bent to the prosecution of the war. Even Pitt's interest in the abolition of the slave trade fell off. In 1793 Clarkson saw nothing but black despair. The Abolition Committee met on only two occasions in 1795 and 1796 and then did not meet at all until a few months after Brougham's book was published. Wilberforce who had valiantly introduced resolutions year after year ceased to do so after 1800. Every voice was stilled. Then in 1804 the movement suddenly came into being again. Brougham's *Colonial Policy* which attracted to him the attention of its leaders had been published in the previous summer, and before Wilberforce made his next motion on 30 May 1804 Brougham was a member of the Abolition Committee which was again at full steam ahead.

Since feeling in France, the land of the enemy, was swinging back in favour of the slave trade, feeling in Britain was free to revert to enthusiasm for its abolition. Encouraged by awakened energy among his old supporters, Wilberforce planned to bring the abolition of the slave trade before Parliament again. At this point Brougham's alertness and energy, which were to amaze English public life for half a century, asserted itself. In a few weeks he wrote a pamphlet which presented the facts and arguments for abolition of the slave trade in a brief and incisive form especially adapted for busy parliamentarians, and he—or rather

[1] *Colonial Policy*, pp. 486–7.

the Abolition Committee—had it in the hands of every member of Parliament when Wilberforce made his motion.[1]

It was constantly asserted by the defenders of the trade that the Negroes were better off in America than they would have been in Africa where some were convicted criminals and all would be subject to the risks of war. Brougham's answer to that was to show that many of the so-called convicted criminals were the victims of charges trumped up by the trade, and that the most potent cause of wars in Africa with all their sufferings was deliberate attack to secure slaves for a profitable market. He followed that up by figures to prove that half of the Negroes taken from Africa were killed by the trade itself. Then he described the sufferings of the slave after sale, and refuted the popular fallacy that the slave trade was a valuable nursery of British seamen.

One of the strongest arguments for the continuation of the trade was that without it the stock of Negroes in the West Indies could not be kept up and the plantations could not be cultivated. Brougham insisted that that depended on the humanity of the planters and its relation to natural increase. The abolition of the trade would also greatly improve conditions in the West Indies by reason of the fact that the importation of new Negroes had always been one of the main causes of disturbances and insurrection.

On 30 May (1804) Wilberforce made his motion for leave to introduce an Abolition Bill and it was carried by a substantial majority. It was a great night for the old crusaders and the new recruits. Wilberforce, who was a merry soul, celebrated at his house in saintly fashion, and there among the inner circle discussing the details of the bill to be prepared was young Brougham.

The bill met its great test, the second reading, on 7 June. Pitt spoke with Brougham's pamphlet in his hand. George Rose, one of the leading defenders of the trade, urged a postponement of the vote on account of the undue influence of this pamphlet recently published and circulated among the members of the House. Wilberforce replied: 'Was the House to be supposed to be taken captive by that book so as to require another week to enable them to recover their judgment?'[2] After a spirited debate the bill was carried at two o'clock in the morning.

[1] *The Correspondence of William Wilberforce*, ed. his sons, 2 vols. (1840), i. 328.
[2] *Hansard*, 7 June 1804.

On 8 June Francis Horner wrote to Murray: 'He [Brougham] is more with Wilberforce and the Thorntons at present than in any other society and has been a very active member of their committee for conducting the Abolition Bill.' Horner adds in his sober and, shall we say, Whiggish fashion that he does not think this connexion a valuable one for Brougham. 'The Saints are not properly a political set of men; and their character is so entirely cast from their religious zeal that there can be little community of sentiment between them and Brougham when the object that at present brings them together is once gained.' Nor did Horner altogether like Brougham's pamphlet although everybody praised 'its distinctness and good sense'.'Brougham could not write on such a subject without much information and much argument, and he ought (to please us) to have taken more pains with the manner.'[1] Again that querulous note in Horner's letters in contrast to Brougham's generous friendliness at that time.

The bill passed its third reading 27 June and on the following day Brougham wrote to Horner: 'I am just come home from Wilberforce's after the final victory of that great cause. . . . A letter has been received from Lord Grenville . . . promising his support and offering to conduct the bill [in the House of Lords], but suggesting that if it comes from the government it may be better received.'[2]

Brougham was over-confident and the 'abolitionists' were fated to another two years of disappointment. Wilberforce was informed that it was too late in the session to take the bill to the Lords and it was too dangerous to the cause to risk defeat there; it would be better to wait until the next year. Pitt told Wilberforce definitely that the Cabinet had discussed the matter and agreed 'that the subject be hung up till the next year'. The Lords would insist on evidence and it was too late in the session to submit evidence. Certainly the opposition to the measure in the Upper House was strong and included leading members of the Cabinet.[3] Wilberforce did, however, secure from Pitt a definite promise that the slave trade to the conquered colonies would be abolished by royal proclamation. Brougham was one

---

[1] Horner MSS., Horner to J. A. Murray, 8 June 1804.
[2] Ibid., Brougham to Horner, 28 June 1804.
[3] Coupland, *Wilberforce*, pp. 309–11; Klingberg, p. 124.

of the six men whom Wilberforce took into consultation on this matter.[1]

Brougham had already moved the *Edinburgh Review* into the battle against the slave trade and it seems probable, from his correspondence with Jeffrey, that it was he who induced Wilberforce to write a very trenchant article in the *Review* in October 1804.

In the meantime Brougham was off to Holland, partly to secure further information on the slave trade and partly to help the abolition movement there. Wilberforce spoke of Brougham's 'enlightening the minds of the good people of Holland'.[2] He had interviews with a number of influential men. One means of enlightenment was a Dutch translation of his pamphlet summing up the case against the slave trade.[3] He was pleased to find that a number of the men with whom he talked were well acquainted with his book on *Colonial Policy*, though their confusion of 'abolition' of the trade with 'emancipation' of the slaves was a constant source of irritation to him.[4]

Brougham was back in Edinburgh in January 1805. A little later he was at work on a strong article for the July number of the *Edinburgh Review*. The book which he had selected for his fulcrum was a French work entitled *Examen d'esclavage* which presented in a consistent form the old assurances that some were designed by nature to be masters and others to be slaves, that taking Negroes from Africa to the West Indies was a work of mercy and that without the slave trade there could be no sugar and no West Indian colonies. In the first part of this article Brougham was concerned with citing passages in this book which provided evidence against the system it was defending. This, for example: 'In their own country, the negroes are surrounded by every kind of fear from the moment of their birth, the fear that their parents may sell them; the fear that kidnappers may carry them off.' And the following from the notes of a slave captain: 'Negroes brought to the factories, loaded with irons, galled with their ligatures, half killed with blows, scarcely able to walk . . . And from whom had they received this treatment?

---

[1] Klingberg, pp. 124–5, 125 n.; *Life of Wilberforce by his sons*, 5 vols. (1839), 2nd ed.
[2] Wilberforce, *Correspondence*, i. 328–30.   [3] *Memoirs*, i. 279–87.
[4] The author of the article on Brougham in the *Dictionary of National Biography* repeated that mistake in referring to this trip.

From their parents, from their friends, from their brothers, who brought them from the inmost recesses of the country, a distance of two hundred leagues (seven hundred English miles) to sell them at the factories on the coast.'

On which Brougham's comment was: 'Yet the slave trade is a blessing to those poor Negroes! And the existence of the factories [trading-posts] on the coast has no sort of influence on their lot! And it is quite indifferent to them whether they live at home, or are brought down this jaunt of pleasure to see a little of European manners.'

Brougham made much in this article of the evidence of the superiority of Negroes in the interior of Africa where there was no slave trade to those of the coastal districts where the trade flourished. When he came to comment on conditions in the West Indies themselves we catch a glimpse of the Brougham who was to be a leader in the movement for emancipation. 'When you place human beings in circumstances which necessarily subject every motion of their bodies to the control of another's will, felt at each instant of their lives, you deprive them of all the sentiments which make the human character what it is in ordinary situations.' In the last pages of the article he traced, as he had done in his *Colonial Policy*, a future evolution from slavery to serfdom and from serfdom to 'the total emancipation of the negro'. After this, in nearly every number of the *Edinburgh Review* there was a plea for the abolition of the slave trade in some article of Brougham's.[1]

The year 1805 was one of great activity by the abolitionists. It should have been the year of final triumph. But the exigencies of the political game were unfavourable.

On Pitt's death in January 1806 Grenville and Fox came into power and the hopes of the movement came to be centred on Fox. Wilberforce and most of his associates were political opponents of the veteran Whig leader. But the friends of young Brougham were Whigs. Just at this time Lord Holland, Fox's nephew, returned from the Continent and Brougham's old Edinburgh associates Allen, Sydney Smith, and Lord Henry Petty (later Lord Lansdowne) brought Brougham into the Holland House circle.

[1] *Edinburgh Review*, July 1805, no. 8; Oct. 1805, no. 13; Apr. 1806, no. 3; July 1806, no. 16 (a neat reference in dealing with a different subject); Jan. 1807, no. 3.

'On the slave trade, in general, we talked a great deal', wrote Brougham to Wilberforce of his first evening in Fox's house, with Lord Holland and Lord Henry Petty, and he reported the conversation in detail, promising to continue to try to influence them as best he could.[1] In his next letter to Wilberforce, Brougham said that he had lost no time in urging the matter on Lord Holland who promised to do his best with Fox. 'In the meantime, does anything more occur to you as possible to be done either publicly or privately for this cause?'[2]

On 10 June Fox moved in the Commons the resolution that led straight to final victory. It was passed by a large majority. A similar resolution moved by the Prime Minister, Grenville, was successful in the Lords.

Brougham's review of Pinckard's book on the West Indies in the *Edinburgh* for January 1807 shows that he felt that they were on the eve of victory. It is no longer enough to repeat the arguments against the slave trade: he is now concerned with conditions amongst the plantation slaves themselves. Cruel treatment had been the rule rather than the exception. Pinckard's facts proved that it was impossible 'to infuse into the common run of the West Indians the least idea that cruelty to a Negro is a crime'.

'If it pleases God to spare the life of Fox', Wilberforce had said in June 1806, 'and to keep him and Grenville together, I hope we shall see next year the termination of all our labours.'[3] Fox was dead within three months, but the legislation based upon his resolution was passed in the following year. On the eve of certain triumph, in the midst of Romilly's eloquent eulogy of Wilberforce, the House of Commons rose and cheered him to the echo, while Wilberforce himself 'sat bent in his seat, his head in his hands, and the tears streaming down his face'.[4] After the second reading his neighbours on Clapham Common went to Wilberforce's house to hold high carnival. 'Well, Henry,' said the gleeful host to Thornton, 'what shall we abolish next?'[5] What none of the abolitionists thought of abolishing was slavery itself.

[1] *Correspondence of Wilberforce*, ii. 77–78, Brougham to Wilberforce, n.d.
[2] Ibid. ii. 79–80, Brougham to Wilberforce, n.d.
[3] Coupland, *Wilberforce*, p. 333.
[4] Ibid., p. 341.
[5] Ibid., p. 343.

Nor was the slave trade really abolished. They were to learn that legislation is one thing, enforcement another. Punishment by fine could never check so profitable a trade. Henry Brougham entered Parliament in February 1810. Four months later he called attention to the extensive continuation of the slave trade and gave notice of legislation which he carried through Parliament in the following year, making slave trading a felony punishable by imprisonment for five years or fourteen years' transportation. It was not until the Felony Act that the abolition of the slave trade at last became effective.

CHAPTER IV

Whig or Tory? 1804–7: Attack on the Orders in Council 1808

URING the years 1804 to 1807, from his moving to London to the passing of the Abolition Act, Brougham was giving thought to party politics. All his expressions of opinion and his associations in his Edinburgh days had been liberal and in Scotland to be liberal meant to be aligned against the Tory rule of Henry Dundas. By every instinct of his youth and every political conviction of his manhood Brougham was at war with Dundas's system of government. That fact closed to him every door of preferment in Scotland and drove him to England to seek a career.

In England he was not surrounded and stifled by Tory despotism. The aristocratic conceptions of government which he had learned to hate were strong in the traditions of the Whig party too. If he were to be guided by personal interest and ambition, he might well ask himself: Who has risen to a position of leadership in the Whig party in recent years who had nothing but brains, and was not born in the aristocracy? They were few, and their path had been as steep as it was narrow. In the Tory party, on the other hand, it was relatively easy for such a man to rise. Eldon, Canning, and others had made their way from humble origins.

From the time he arrived in London Brougham was feeling his way. He was trying to secure some appointment, preferably a diplomatic one, from Tory ministers. At that time he was talking Tory to Horner and probably to others.[1] Four months later Horner said that Brougham was sure to make a name for himself in Parliament, but 'the choice of a party would perhaps give him some difficulty'.[2]

In these first six months in London, February to July 1804,

---

[1] Horner MSS., Horner to Murray, 28 Feb. 1804.
[2] Ibid., Horner to Murray, 8 June 1804.

Brougham associated himself with Wilberforce and his Saints, all, or nearly all, of whom were Tories. At the same time he joined the 'King of Clubs', the membership of which was almost entirely Whig. He was probably introduced to this 'conversation club' by Sydney Smith and Horner and in it he fraternized with Romilly, Mackintosh, and other prominent Whigs, and with James Mill.[1] Full of assorted knowledge and always a good entertainer, Brougham was bound to be a success at such gatherings.

We can readily believe Lord Campbell's statements that 'from his first introduction to men of the highest birth and the most distinguished position', he felt himself 'on an entire equality with them', and that 'without any approach to vulgarity or impertinence he treated them with the utmost familiarity'.[2] He warmed the great houses with his abounding humour. What he had later to discover was that these Whig grandees were as loath to allow a middle-class prodigy *political* privilege and opportunity as they were pleased to be entertained by his society. His standing was not improved when the Earl of Lauderdale, one of the proudest of the Whigs, wrote a book on economic theory. Brougham's attack on it in the July (1804) number of the *Edinburgh Review* was characteristically abusive. Sydney Smith said that the article was 'most able and the censure amply merited', but it raised a storm among the Whigs. It is not surprising, therefore, hovering as he did between Tory and Whig, that some people began to suspect that this brilliant young man was 'setting himself up for sale'. And when he entered Parliament six years later he carried with him a reputation for inconsistency and for what many regarded as lack of principle. It was a reputation he was never entirely to live down, even though his parliamentary record was to be one of consistency and of principle.

As has been previously noted, Brougham was brought in 1805 into the Holland House circle, where Lord Holland presided in his benignity, Lady Holland in her asperity, Sydney Smith was chief jester, and Luttrell, Rogers, and Brougham himself provided royal entertainment. Talk of scholarship, letters, and politics flowed in an endless stream. It was already a Whig salon, though not yet a shrine, for Fox had another year to live.

---

[1] C. G. Oakes, *Sir Samuel Romilly* (1935), p. 111.   [2] Campbell, viii. 251–2.

In January 1806 the 'ministry of all the talents' came in. It was dominated by Whigs and has been usually considered a Whig government. Immediately after its accession Lord Holland, who was a member of the new cabinet, suggested to Brougham that he turn his skill in caustic review against the foreign policy of the previous administration. The result was a pamphlet, published anonymously, entitled *An Inquiry into the State of the Nation at the Commencement of the Present Administration*. It was a drastic criticism of Pitt's whole foreign policy, the causes and conduct of the war, and particularly the mistakes of recent years. He also advocated extensive changes in Britain's colonial system, the abolition of the slave trade, the amendment of the navigation laws, a juster rule in India, attention to the grievances of the Irish Catholics, and reform in the parliamentary system at home.

Within a few days of its publication this pamphlet was attracting an attention which naturally bred speculation as to its authorship. When challenged, Brougham denied it. It has been suggested that Brougham wrote the eulogistic review of his own pamphlet in the *Edinburgh Review* for April 1806. The only evidence for that is the not very reliable Copinger list, which, in this case, may have depended on the loose talk of the day, talk indulged in, no doubt, by many who regarded the story as a good joke without believing it. Certainly Brougham was capable of puffing his own pamphlet, but would Jeffrey, knowing as he almost certainly did that Brougham had written it, have permitted him to review it, and would he have been so dishonest as an editor as to have Brougham disagree with himself explicitly and somewhat sharply in the latter part of the article? The disagreements there expressed, as well as the rest of the article, sound like Jeffrey's sincere convictions. They may, of course, have been expressed by another writer to whom Jeffrey assigned the review.

A few months later Brougham wrote a letter to the Tory Wilberforce which showed how closely he was studying the opportunities of getting into Parliament. Of the patrons of rotten boroughs the Tory Lowthers were among the most powerful. What Brougham wanted Wilberforce to do for him was to write to Lord Lowther (later Lord Lonsdale) asking that he, Brougham, should be named for the vacant seat in Westmorland, or failing that, for one of the Lowther boroughs.[1] The Government, though predominantly Whig, was supported by some Tories, including the Lowthers. It appears from a letter among the Horner manuscripts that Brougham informed Horner that he had the support of Fox, Lord Holland, and other Whig leaders in making this application, the Government to support Lord Lowther at Carlisle 'where his Lordship's interest is not quite secure' in return for Lowther's support of Brougham as a government candidate.[2]

Although Wilberforce the year before had on his own initiative sought to secure a diplomatic post for Brougham, writing to Pitt that 'You perhaps could not in the whole kingdom find any one in all respects so well qualified. . . . He is a man of uncommon talents and address . . .', his letter to Lord Lowther was anything but an unreserved endorsement of the application:

'Every man', he wrote, 'is open to requests which he cannot well refuse and which he feels a little awkward about granting. . . . The writer of the note is a man of very extraordinary talents and qualifications and knowledge for his time of life. . . . I ought to add that I have heard from common fame that he is the author of a pamphlet lately published on the state of the nation, and . . . I cannot but say that the language in which it speaks is not such as one should have expected from any warm admirer of Mr. Pitt. . . . Lest I should seem ungrateful to Mr. Brougham in refusing such a request . . . I think it best to transmit his note to you, and you will, I trust, receive it with your accustomed kindness.'[3]

Brougham had no reason to love the Whigs but he was always glad of the opportunity to be politically active. In August 1806 he received from them his first political appointment. He was made secretary to a mission to Portugal which was a complete failure. Then when Lord Holland placed him in charge of the Whig press campaign in the general election of January (1807) he responded with Broughamesque energy. With a very limited assistance from others 'in the course of ten days', according to Lord Holland, 'he filled every bookseller's shop with pamphlets, most London newspapers and all country ones without exception with paragraphs', and wrote and distributed to all the boroughs in the country handbills 'adapted to the local interests of the

[1] Hist. MSS. Com., *Lonsdale MSS.*, p. 184.
[2] Horner MSS., Horner to Murray, 2 June 1806.
[3] Hist. MSS. Com., *Lonsdale MSS.*, pp. 182 seq., 21 May 1806.

candidates'.[1] Lord Holland sent to Brougham paragraphs, headings, and other suggestions.[2] John Allen of Holland House wrote articles which he sent to Brougham, accompanied by reports of how pleased the leaders of the Whig party were with Brougham's work.[3]

The Whigs lost the election, but this association with the party strengthened Brougham's connexion with it. That was clinched by his leading the attack on the famous Orders in Council, an attack in which the Whigs followed Brougham, rather than Brougham the Whigs.

At this time Brougham's oldest friendship seemed to be in further difficulties. The following letter from the Horner manuscripts helps us to understand what had happened, at least so far as Horner was concerned. Francis Horner wrote to J. A. Murray, who was a close friend of both, on 26 May 1806:

There is no degree of confidential communication between him and me, and we only see each other when we happen to dine on the same day at the table of a common acquaintance. . . . I cannot much respect the man who could write both the review of Lord Chatham's letters and the late *State of the Nation*, who reviewed Lord Lauderdale and gives that author an opportunity of expressing his surprise at the familiarity of old acquaintance with which his critic now accosts him. There is a grievous want both of pride and principle in all this. . . . I must confess that there may be a shade of resentment mixed with my judgment of Brougham's public conduct. . . . I have not been strong enough to throw off a little indignation at the neglect with which he has treated me and the indifference with which he has appeared to me to sacrifice the intimacy of a life-time. Perhaps this jealousy, which still has a good deal of affection in it, inclines me to see things worse than they are. The subject has of late cost me some uncomfortable hours, both on account of the real loss I have suffered in Brougham's conversation which is so full of entertainment and instruction, and the disappointment of my plans of life which always included him.[4]

It does not seem to be particularly reprehensible that Brougham should praise Chatham's private character as revealed in his personal letters to his nephew and at the same time attack

---

[1] Lord Holland, *Memoirs of the Whig Party*, 2 vols. (1852–4), ii. 228, quoted in Aspinall, p. 15.
[2] Brougham MSS., 20, 21, 24 May, 2 June, n.d.
[3] Ibid., n.d., 2 June.   [4] Horner MSS.

the foreign policy of the Tory government of 1806. Perhaps Horner had not read both the documents and was the victim of gossip. Again Brougham was always ready enough to be friendly socially with a man whom he had attacked publicly. But Lord Holland, who was habitually honest and generous, also wrote of this matter later in terms of the strongest reprobation of Brougham. He said that 'he visibly estranged himself from his early friend and companion', appeared to be at pains to accentuate their differences, and that Horner 'disdained to court a friendship which he saw he could not preserve'.[1] Lord Holland ascribed the trouble in part to jealousy of Horner on Brougham's part.[2] But at the time the above letter of Horner's was written there was no apparent reason for Brougham to be jealous. A few months later he may have resented the Whigs bringing Horner into Parliament before they found a seat for him, but up to that time Brougham had attracted much more public attention and even Whig favour than had Horner. Surmise does not carry us far. We have already noticed that several years before this, at a time when Brougham was very friendly, Horner had been exceedingly objective and even severe in his comments on Brougham in letters to mutual friends who may not have been too discreet.

In Brougham's many extant private letters there is no expression of dislike for Horner or any adverse criticism of him. Ward, in the course of a general judgement on Horner, implied that he was anything but good natured and had become very impatient of contradiction. 'So much so that I find the people with whom he lives most find it necessary utterly to banish from conversation any subject on which they differ from him materially.'[3] This suggests one possible reason for Brougham avoiding Horner while wishing to remain on good terms with him.

In his determination to exclude British trade from the continent of Europe Napoleon had extended his 'coast-system' by forcing Prussia to close her ports to British trade. Great Britain's reply

---

[1] Lord Holland, *Further Memoirs of the Whig Party* (1905 ed.), pp. 45–46.
[2] Ibid., pp. 234, 257.
[3] *Letters to Ivy from the Earl of Dudley* (1905), p. 118.

to that, in the month of May 1806, was the 'Fox blockade' of the northern coast of Europe from the Elbe river to Brest. Then Napoleon crushed the Prussians at Jena, conquered Prussia and from its capital published his famous Berlin Decree on 21 November (1806).[1]

In the Berlin Decree Napoleon declared a blockade of the coastline of the British Isles. Napoleon's naval weakness prevented an actual blockade. But this gave Napoleon the excuse for doing something which he had the power to do. On the pretence of a blockade which did not exist he could in his own ports and those of his allied and subject states investigate neutral vessels and, on finding evidence that they had come from a British port, refuse them entry. The Decree stated specifically that no vessel coming direct from a British port or having been in a British port subsequent to the date of the Decree should be received in any continental port under his control and that any vessel contravening this provision by making a false declaration should be seized. All goods that were British either by ownership or origin were to be seized wherever they were to be found. And Napoleon in the enforcement of the Decree insisted that proof that goods were not British must be afforded by 'certificates of origin'. There were also provisions for seizure of British subjects and their property. The Berlin Decree was to be the foundation of that Continental System, that exclusion of all British goods from the continent of Europe toward which Napoleon had been working for years.

The British replied to the Berlin Decree with the Orders in Council. The first of these Orders emanated from the Ministry of all the Talents, on 7 January 1807 and was frequently referred to as 'the Whig Order in Council'. Its title describes it accurately. 'Order in Council, prohibiting trade to be carried on between Port and Port of Countries under the dominion or usurped control of France and her allies.'

In projecting his great Decree from Berlin immediately after crushing Prussia, Napoleon chose the dramatic rather than the

---

[1] For a general account of the events leading to the war of 1812 see especially A. L. Burt, *The United States, Great Britain, and British North America from the Revolution to the Establishment of Peace after the War of 1812* (1940). For the Continental System see E. F. Heckscher, *The Continental System* (1922), and F. E. Melvin, *Napoleon's Navigation System* (4 vols., 1919). My account here is necessarily concerned mainly with the British Orders in Council.

logical moment for initiating his Continental System. Drama to him was always as important as logic, but he never slackened his pace in acquiring the control of more and more European coastline, in order that he might acquire the power to impose a truly continental self-blockade. In the early months of 1807 he secured the consent of Turkey, Austria, and Denmark to his system, then he defeated the Russians at Friedland. In July Napoleon crowned his earlier achievements by the Treaty of Tilsit which secured the adhesion of Russia to the Continental System on conditions that were bound to be fulfilled. Addressing his soldiers Napoleon said: 'The Peace of Tilsit puts an end to the operations of the Grand Armée. . . . It is probable that the continental blockade will not be an empty word.'[1] There were still some gaps in the coastline of Europe—they would be filled up as soon as possible—but Napoleon now felt that he could proceed with the enforcement of his great Decree.

By autumn the Tories were again in power in Great Britain and in November they passed what may be called the great Orders in Council. These Orders have, in the broader sense, been much misunderstood. In their narrower sense, statesmen and parliamentarians at the time confessed their inability to comprehend their literal meaning. But a careful study of their text[2] and of the parliamentary statements of those principally responsible for them affords a fairly clear understanding of their main lines. They aimed at directing all trade with Napoleon's Europe, *through Great Britain*. They sought also to give British colonial products an advantage over French and Spanish colonial products and to help British manufacturers in West Indian markets. And the neutrals (including the Americans) were being told baldly that the only trade which Great Britain would permit them to carry on with Napoleonic European ports (trade through Great Britain) was the trade which had been forbidden to them by Napoleon. The Americans and other neutrals would have to take the risks involved.

The correspondence between Perceval and other cabinet ministers in the weeks preceding their proclamation indicates clearly that they understood the main object of the November Orders to be commercial rather than retaliatory, though they

---

[1] Melvin, p. 17.
[2] The text is given in *Hansard*, x. 126 seq., and in Heckscher, Appendix I.

emphasized the latter object in their parliamentary presentation.[1]

In a sense it may be said that Brougham began his attack on the Orders in Council before they were in existence. The public had had good hints of what was coming, some of them in editorials in *The Times* which was well informed and close to the Government.[2] On 2 October Brougham wrote to Lord Howick (later Lord Grey) that he was preparing an article on the subject for the October *Edinburgh Review*. In it Brougham argued against the Orders in Council in advance and predicted that if such measures were adopted and persisted in they would lead to a war with America. This article, appearing as it did immediately before the Orders in Council themselves, attracted a great deal of attention throughout the country.

In the January (1808) number of the *Edinburgh Review* Brougham had another long article on the Orders in Council. He refused to accept the main object of the Orders as being retaliatory. They aimed rather at forcing the neutrals 'to trade with France in a particular way profitable to ourselves'. He also refused to make any attempt to defend the Whig order of January 1807.

It should be noted in passing that this independent attitude toward the Whig party was quite sincere. He could play the Whig game well enough at times, but when embarked on any of his great causes, Brougham was always to let the party know that he was not going to them and that they must come to him. That was partly sincere devotion to a cause; it was partly personal pride. Both traits tended later to keep from him official leadership in the party and lessened his importance in the eyes of those who in political history can see only party leaders and prime ministers.

In this article Brougham argued that a prudent British statesman would aim to make the greatest use possible of the lines of trade which Napoleon could not impede—the carrying of British goods from Great Britain to neutral countries and from there to Napoleonic countries by neutral vessels. 'No certificate of origin, nor any other conceivable regulation, could have prevented a

---

[1] *Diary and Correspondence of Lord Colchester* (1861), ii. 134; Henry Adams, *History of the United States*, 9 vols. (1889-91), iv. 93-96.

[2] *The Times*, 29 Sept., 6, 17 Oct. 1807.

British cargo from finding its way by such a route.' And that is just what was prevented by the Orders in Council.

What do the *statesmen* whose system we are examining propose to themselves? They resolve at once to shut up the roundabout trade, which the enemy could least of all have effected himself; and they try to encourage the direct channel, which is the most under his control. . . . It is related that the Chancellor Oxenstiern said to his son when he sent him to a congress of statesmen, and the young man was struck with awe at the solemnity of the occasion, 'Go, my child, and see how little wisdom it takes to govern the world.'

This article was hardly off the press—Parliament had just assembled but had not got to the question of the Orders in Council—when the news reached England that the Government of the United States had placed an embargo on all American shipping and had put into force the Non-Importation Act, prohibiting the import of many classes of British goods, which had been passed in April 1806. The British Tories were quick to declare that the American embargo was not the result of their Orders in Council since it was dated 22 December and the news of the British Orders had not reached the United States by that date. Official notification had not reached the American Government but British newspaper predictions and private letters conveying a general description of the forthcoming Orders had. The Orders in Council permitted very little American trade that did not violate the prohibitions of Napoleon and that at great risk. The reply of the American Government was virtually, Very well, there will be no American trade at all. The object of the embargo was to force the British Government through loss of British–American trade to repeal the Orders in Council.

The evidence for the Orders in Council causing the embargo includes the original draft of the President's message to Congress and a dispatch of Erskine to Canning dated the day before the embargo was imposed. Jefferson, in part, thought of the embargo as a substitute for war. Relations between the United States and Great Britain had been bad enough before the Orders in Council, what with the search of American ships for deserting British seamen and incidents like the Leopard–Chesapeake affair.

The three systems—Napoleonic, British, American—were now complete. Napoleon's first Milan Decree laid down precise regulations for determining that a vessel had touched at a British port and substituted seizure of ship and cargo for mere exclusion as the penalty. The second Milan Decree was promulgated after Napoleon heard of the November Orders in Council. It declared that any vessel that had submitted to search by a British ship or paid a British duty had forfeited the protection of its flag and was lawful prize. It also extended the 'blockade' of the British Isles to all British ports in any part of the world.

When the debates on the Orders in Council in the British Parliament began on 27 January (1808) the news of the American embargo had reached England. The Tories had the better of the debate. There was a vague uncertainty about most of the Whig speeches. The Whig attack on the whole was neither acute nor well informed.[1] It was then that a number of London, Liverpool, and Manchester merchants who were opposed to the Orders in Council and anxious to have them repealed turned to the young lawyer who had made their cause his own and who was writing such clever articles in the *Edinburgh Review*. They engaged Henry Brougham as counsel and secured for him the privilege of pleading their case at the Bar of the House of Commons and presenting evidence in support of it.

The merchants of England were divided on the question according to their particular interests. Obviously the Orders in Council benefited the West Indian trade. It is equally clear that the trade with America was injured by the Orders in Council in any case and more than ever after the embargo and the operation of the American Non-Importation Act, which were the direct results of the Orders in Council. Those engaged in other trade were divided in opinion.

Brougham urged on the merchants the method of mass petitions, as many names and as many petitions as possible. On 18 March he spoke at the Bar of the House of Commons on behalf of the petitions of the London, Liverpool, and Manchester merchants against the Orders in Council.[2] A number of witnesses were examined by Brougham and cross-examined by Perceval and Stephen. On 1 April Brougham summed up the evidence in his first great speech to that forum in which he was to deliver so many.[3]

[1] *Hansard*, x. 150 seq.
[2] Ibid. x. 1183.
[3] The Speech of Henry Brougham before the House of Commons, 1 Apr. 1808,

The stopping of British trade to America could not, Brougham contended, be imputed entirely to the American embargo. The orders for the spring shipments always reached Great Britain before the middle of January. The news of the embargo did not arrive until 26 January. The evidence had shown precisely that a large deficit in the trade to America had occurred before that date; therefore it must have been directly due to the Orders in Council. One witness had testified that before he heard of the embargo he had, because of the Orders in Council, reduced the number of workmen he employed to a fourth of their former number; another that his pay sheet was reduced to a quarter of its previous amount.

If the Government had only had the wisdom to leave things alone! British goods were being successfully carried to Europe by American vessels in the face of the Berlin Decree. Brougham took the case of a Yankee captain carrying a cargo from Yarmouth into a Napoleonic port. Challenged by Napoleon's official he said 'From America' and produced false sailing papers, and all was well. But since the Orders in Council, 'the French prefect *knows* that the American vessel *must* have come from Yarmouth or some other British port'. Since the enemy 'must now be convinced that it was impossible that any considerable number of ships should elude our cruisers', American ships will be seized on principle as coming from Great Britain. Again the British Government had 'countersigned the enemy's edict'. Producing the evidence which we have already noted, Brougham proceeded to contend that the Orders in Council caused the embargo.

In conclusion he urged the immediate repeal of the Orders in Council. Then 'the lesson which the wisdom of parliament and, let me add, of the country, shall have given to its rulers, will . . . frighten any rash projectors from ever again presuming to take for the subject of his wild experiments the edifice of British commerce'.

The immediate effect of Brougham's speech, delivered as it was to a crowded House and crowded galleries, was that the Government decided to do what it had not previously contemplated—submit rebuttal evidence. For a period of three weeks Perceval and Stephen produced and examined witnesses and

in support of Petitions from London, Liverpool, and Manchester against the Orders in Council.

Brougham cross-examined. When it was all over and the plea of the petitioners was rejected, Brougham wrote to Lord Grey that 'the Liverpool and Manchester delegates . . . [were] all tolerably well satisfied'.[1]

Brougham was in high favour with a large section of the mercantile population. At the age of thirty he was now a national figure. There would be other battles on the Orders in Council. As history unfolded itself, this proved to be the prelude to his victorious attack in 1812.

[1] *Memoirs*, i. 399, Brougham to Grey, 21 Apr. 1808.

CHAPTER V

Rousing Byron: the *Quarterly Review*: Parliament at Last

URING the year of his first onslaught on the Orders in
Council Brougham was, in a negative manner, making
literary history. He almost certainly wrote two passages
in the *Edinburgh Review* one of which awoke the embattled genius
of Byron's *English Bards and Scotch Reviewers* and the other shocked
into birth the *Quarterly Review*.

No one has ever thought highly of Byron's *Hours of Idleness*.
There can be no wonder at these youthful efforts being received
unfavourably in the *Edinburgh*. The review is a good example of
Romilly's statement that 'the editors seem to value themselves
principally on their severity and they have reviewed some works
seemingly with no other object than to show what their powers
in this particular line of criticism are'.[1]

Byron had just finished reading this review when a visitor
called. One look at the poet's face brought the question, 'Have
you received a challenge, Byron?' A challenge it was. With
thoughts of 'rage, resistance and redress' he drank three bottles
of claret and felt better. He threw his feelings into twenty lines
of poetry and felt 'considerably better'. Then for a year he wrote,
remodelling a shorter poem that was to have been called *British
Bards*, adding his new theme, polishing, perfecting. On 16 March
1809 *English Bards and Scotch Reviewers* was published and a new
name appeared among the great poets of the English tongue.[2]
Brougham, whom Byron did not at first suspect of writing the
pages which started it all, escaped with two lines, probably
written late in 1808:

> Beware lest blundering Brougham destroy the sale,
> Turn beef to bannocks, cauliflower to kail.

[1] *Memoirs of Sir Samuel Romilly*, 2 vols., 3rd ed. (1842), i. 426. The evidence for
Brougham's authorship is so strong that we cannot accept his frequent denials.
On one occasion at least he acknowledged it.

[2] E. C. Mayne, *Byron*, 2 vols. (1912), i. 117–22.

The *Edinburgh Review* had at the outset eschewed party politics although it had sought to include occasional political articles of a non-partizan character. Before long it was understood that Brougham would do most of the political articles, while Jeffrey, the other prolific contributor, would give his attention mainly to literary criticism. As long as Brougham's own party politics were undecided, his political articles and the others which appeared were nicely balanced. Walter Scott and other Tory contributors were well content. But as Brougham swung toward the Whig party the *Edinburgh* took on more and more the complexion of a party organ. That was partly the work of Brougham's own pen and it was partly the result of his influence over the editor.

This development was bound to result in the Tories looking around for some means of off-setting the adverse political power of a review which circulated so widely. Scott urged Jeffrey to suppress Brougham and when the latter replied that that could not be done, Scott suggested that he himself should be allowed to try his hand at Tory articles of the Brougham type. But Jeffrey still demurred.[1] Then came Jeffrey's scathing review of Scott's *Marmion* in the April number of this year (1808). In the same number there was an article attacking the Government on the Orders in Council and puffing Brougham, Baring, and Erskine for their able opposition to them. Scott refused to contribute any longer. Brougham wrote a strong anti-Government article on Spain in the July number.

That was the situation when Jeffrey and Brougham collaborated to produce the 'Don Cevallos' article in the October number of the *Edinburgh*. It was generally believed at first that Brougham wrote it, but later it was suggested that Jeffrey wrote most of it. Jeffrey's own statements, variously reported at second and third hands, are strangely conflicting. Brougham wrote only the first or second paragraph. Brougham wrote 'a passage near the beginning'. 'The last pages were his own' (Jeffrey's). 'It was a *joint production*' was his statement to Macvey Napier who succeeded him as editor of the *Review*, and Napier was convinced that Brougham wrote the most obnoxious passage.[2] Most of the

---

[1] J. G. Lockhart, *Life of Sir Walter Scott*, 2nd ed. (1853), p. 210.
[2] *Selections from the Correspondence of the late Macvey Napier*, ed. by his son (1879), pp. 308–9 n. This note discussed the evidence of authorship.

article referred to developments in Spain and the last pages, which Jeffrey said he wrote, attacked the British Government for its Spanish policy. But the passage which gave most offence to so many people was five pages from the beginning of the twenty-page article. That passage is pure Brougham. And neither in its form nor in its matter does it sound at all like Jeffrey. By implication Jeffrey indicated to both Scott and Horner at the time that Brougham wrote the most 'mischievous passage'. The clinching evidence is in a letter from Jeffrey to Brougham, 12 July 1810, in which Jeffrey clearly blamed Brougham for it. 'I cannot consider you as not at all times blameless of this sort of imprudence, tho I certainly know no one who can unite such power and vehemence of invective with such skill in avoiding general offence. Cevallos, I think did exasperate some persons it might have been better to have had with us, and your last attack on Pitt has . . . had nearly the same consequence.'[1]

In this passage, variously regarded at the time as a highly dangerous piece of demagoguery and a courageous trumpet-call of liberalism, Brougham wrote:

The resistance to France has been entirely begun and carried on by the people in Spain . . . the middle and, above all, the lower orders. . . . Those who had so little of what is commonly called *interest* in the country,—those who had no *stake* in the community to speak the technical language of the aristocracy, . . . they who could not pledge *their fortunes*, having only lives and liberties to lose,—the bulk, the mass of the people, nay, the very odious many-headed beast, the multitude, . . . alone, uncalled, unaided by the higher classes . . . raised up the standard of insurrection,—bore it through massacre and through victory until it chased the usurper away. . . . Common justice demands such a change of government as will give the people, who have saved the state . . . a large share in its future management . . . and carry reform—change—revolution . . . salutary just and necessary revolution—over all the department of state. Such a system will have the full approval of the English people. And who then shall ever more presume to tell us that the people have nothing to do with the laws but to obey them, with the taxes but to pay them, and with the blunders of their rulers but to suffer from them?

[1] Brougham MSS. There is a good summary of the evidence in the article by Elizabeth Schneider, Irwin Griggs, and John D. Kern on 'Brougham's Early Contributions to the Edinburgh Review' in *Modern Philology*, Feb. 1945.

The Earl of Buchan placed this October number on the threshold of his front door, stepped back for a running kick and landed it well out into the street. Sydney Smith reported to Lady Holland who was on the Continent: 'The Review not only discontinued by many but returned to the bookseller from the very first volume: the library shelves fumigated, etc.'[1] The Tories dropped other political issues for the moment and turned their whole force against the *Edinburgh*. Their newspapers made daily attacks.[2] The shades of the French Revolution were evoked. One ardent Tory wrote to a bishop that the 'Don Cevallos' article contained 'the essence of Jacobinism' and an under-secretary of state wrote a pamphlet on *The Jacobinical Tendency of the Edinburgh Review*.[3]

It was not only the Tories who were offended. That passage in the 'Don Cevallos' article was not Whig doctrine. It was naked liberalism and to most Whigs flagrantly indecent. It was worse; it was that cursed thing called 'democracy'. Brougham himself wrote at a later date that the article offended the Whigs as much as it did the Tories.[4]

Francis Horner joined in the condemnation. He wrote to J. A. Murray:

I have not time to say all I would on Brougham's review of Cevallos; I think it most reprehensible in its tone and spirit, and very unworthy of his knowledge and judgment, not only in what relates to the actual history of the Spanish insurrection, but also in the application he makes to the constitution of our own country. Are all the fruits of a long continued study of politics, great opportunities of seeing both affairs and men very near at hand, and the best talents nature had to give, to be thrown away upon dashing declamations?[5]

It was the 'Don Cevallos' article that was the deciding factor in the establishment of the *Quarterly Review*. In the autumn John Murray, the London bookseller, heard that Scott had expressed some ideas of a rival publication. Murray went to visit Scott. He arrived just after the October *Edinburgh* with 'Don Cevallos'

---

[1] *Memoir of Sydney Smith*, ii. 57; *Letters of Sydney Smith*, 2 vols. (1953), i. 152, Smith to Lady Holland, 10 Jan. 1809.

[2] *Memoirs*, i. 420, Brougham to Lord Grey, 2 Dec. 1808. See *Thomas Moore*, viii. 71.

[3] J. B. Nichols, *Illustrations of Literary History*, 8 vols. (1817–58), vii. 197; Wharton, *Jacobinical Tendency of the Edinburgh Review* (1809).

[4] *Napier Correspondence*, pp. 308–9, Brougham to Napier, 27 Oct. 1839.

[5] Horner MSS., 9 Dec. 1808.

came out. Scott's first words to Murray were hot with indignation and on that basis they proceeded to formulate their plan of a rival review.[1] Scott took up the project with all his energy and wrote scores of letters to literary Tories, while Canning worked with the politicians who after 'Don Cevallos' needed little stirring up.

So, following closely the plan of the *Edinburgh*, but embodying political principles contrary to those which Brougham had injected into the former, the *Quarterly Review* came into existence. Throughout the century the rival Whig and Tory reviews were to have a remarkable history. Brougham had helped to establish one and had given it its political tone. He provoked the other into existence.

He returned to London on 25 November (1808) in the midst of the 'Don Cevallos' tempest. Three days earlier he had been called to the English Bar. When he went the Northern Circuit he was sorely disappointed to find how little business he could pick up, although according to Lord Campbell he added greatly to the life of the circuit in its convivial moods, and his general amiability made him 'very popular with his brother barristers'.[2] In his general discontent he apparently became more impatient than ever with the Whigs for not getting him into Parliament. He might have been partly consoled if he could have overheard the remark of the Whig leader, Lord Grey, to Creevey in September or October 1809, 'the first man this country has seen since Burke's time is *Brougham*'.[3]

In November 1809 Lord Lansdowne died. Lord Henry Petty, Brougham's old Edinburgh college-mate, succeeded to the peerage and his Camelford seat in the Commons was left vacant. The borough belonged to the Duke of Bedford and, at Lord Holland's request, the seat was offered to Brougham. Lord Holland wrote to him while he was hesitating: 'As you have the same advantage in activity as a cat has in lives over other mortals, possessing at least as much as makes up the stock of nine ordinary men, I do not see why Parliament should break in on your professional duties more than the *Review*, and I think that *you* will find yourself equal to all three occupations.'[4]

---

[1] Ibid., p. 237.   [2] Campbell, viii. 255–6.
[3] *The Creevey Papers*, ed. Sir Herbert Maxwell, 2 vols. (1903), i. 108.
[4] Brougham MSS., 4 Jan. 1810.

A month before this Brougham had ceased to go to Holland House,[1] and appeared to cut himself off socially from the man who had befriended him most heartily and who had most clearly discerned his value to the Whig party. Lord Holland said in his *Memoirs* that Brougham 'never assigned, nor, I believe, could assign any motive for dropping all habits and connection with me'.[2]

Brougham had apparently taken offence at some action or expression of Lady Holland. He wrote, in a letter to Lord Grey four years later:

Quarrel there was none, nor anything like it; but I was compelled no longer to frequent Holland House, and I ceased going there silently, without saying one word to any human being. When asked why . . . I always let it appear that Lady Holland had declined my acquaintance, not I hers.[3]

In a postscript to that letter, Brougham referred to an incident which can only be understood when it is borne in mind that on account of Lady Holland's having left her first husband to live with Lord Holland, as well as the fact that she was later divorced, many of the ladies of the aristocracy refused to go to Holland House. Brougham said that a friend of his had suggested 'the real cause of offence'. When the Hollands stopped to call at Brougham on their way down from Scotland, Brougham's mother had the courtyard barred to prevent their entering, 'saying that she herself was too old to be hurt by Lady Holland, or anybody of that kind, but that she had an unmarried daughter, then living with her, and therefore no Lady Holland should set foot in her house!' 'I remember my mother was immovable, and there was nothing to be done but that I should go out to the carriage, make any excuse I could invent and go on with the Hollands to visit Lord Thanet. On looking back . . . I cannot but give my friend credit for his sagacity in applying the circumstance to the long-continued and bitter spite with which I was favoured by Lady Holland.'[4]

It would be interesting to have Lady Holland's side of the story but we must be content with Lord Holland's mystification

---

[1] See *Letters of Sydney Smith*, i. 176, 199.
[2] Lord Holland, *Further Memoirs*, p. 45.
[3] *Memoirs*, i. 100–1, Brougham to Grey, 5 Jan. 1814.
[4] Ibid., pp. 101–2.

and Brougham's attempt at explanation. The end of the break came six years later. Lord Holland said: 'In 1815 or early 1816 Lady Holland and myself were asked if we would receive him [Brougham] without any explanation of his long estrangement. We answered "yes"; and he resumed the habits of familiarity and intimacy as if nothing had happened ... as if we had parted in the morning.'[1]

Brougham entered Parliament in 1810, and like Disraeli twenty-five years later he arrived with a reputation already made. There is a story, probably mythical, to the effect that he made a vow not to speak for a month.[2] Certainly that month of silence was looked back to as a matter of wonder during the fifty-four years of his parliamentary career. It is difficult to avoid the conclusion that his maiden speech was purposely devoid of fire, sarcasm, and rhetoric, and that it relied mainly on the learned exposition of a constitutional issue. But he was disappointed that it was considered so much of a failure and he wrote to Althorp in low spirits. Of the speeches that followed, until June, J. W. Ward wrote: 'He is not a favourite with the House, and there is a sort of hardness in his manner that does not take. It is very odd, for in private nobody is more popular.'[3]

Then on 14 June he made his first great parliamentary speech.[4] It embodied his proposal to make slave trading a felony and thus secure the enforcement of the 1807 abolition of the slave trade. It was a spirited attack on the slave traders and their evasions of the law, and a pungent argument that the British trade could be ended only by Parliament making slave trading a felony punishable by transportation or imprisonment. Further reference to this speech and to Brougham's Felony Act in the following year will be made in a chapter devoted to the cause of the Negro slaves. Except for a few brief and unimportant statements he did not speak again in Parliament until he successfully introduced his Slave Trade Felony Bill on 5 March 1811.

In the meantime he had had his first great law case. At that time the Government was very sensitive about criticism by

---

[1] Lord Holland, *Further Memoirs*, pp. 45 n., 234.
[2] Campbell, viii. 260.
[3] *Letters to Ivy*, p. 104, quoted in Aspinall, p. 22.
[4] *Speeches of Lord Brougham*, 4 vols. (1838), ii. 19–39.

newspapers. The records show that the Attorney-General, Sir Vicary Gibbs, had forty-two *ex-officio* informations for criminal libel filed in the three years 1808 to 1810, while only fourteen had been filed in the preceding seven years. These *ex-officio* proceedings were usually associated with a careful selection of special juries.

On 15 June 1810 William Cobbett was brought to court charged with seditious libel in publishing in his *Political Register* an article on flogging in the army.[1] He was sentenced to two years' imprisonment and a fine of £1,000.

In August, the month after Cobbett was sentenced, Drakard wrote for the *Stamford News* an article which Leigh Hunt reprinted in the *Examiner*. It attacked the Government and exposed the brutality of flogging. The Attorney-General immediately filed information against Drakard, the publisher of the *Stamford News*, and the Hunt brothers, proprietors of the *Examiner*, on charges of seditious libel.

The trial of the Hunts presented a clear issue. The friends of reaction, tradition, and established order on the one side and those of general liberty, liberalism, progress, humanitarianism, and a free press on the other, looked forward to this trial with the keenest anticipation and anxiety. And all realized that much would depend on the selection of the counsel for the defence. Leigh Hunt chose Henry Brougham. They were brothers-in-arms who understood one another thoroughly. One may surmise that Brougham, who believed that anything was within his power, looked forward to it with the greatest confidence. But in fact Brougham was an English lawyer of only two years' standing who had not had a great case in either Scotland or in England. In the *Edinburgh Review*, in the opposition to the Orders in Council, and in one session of Parliament Brougham had shown his mettle, but the test of a *cause célèbre* in a court of law was another matter.

The case came up on 22 February 1811. It proved to be a clash between two great advocates as well as between two conceptions of social order. Sir Vicary Gibbs had made his way to the top of his profession and was to close his career as Lord Chief Justice. Brougham was at his best when his feelings were deeply aroused, as they were in this case. He was as ardent in

[1] G. D. H. Cole, *Life of William Cobbett* (1947), pp. 155 seq.

championing the freedom of the press as Gibbs was inflexible in
its suppression. But before everything Brougham was a humanitarian. For him the matter of flogging in the army was a primary
issue. For both this was more than a case; it was a cause.

The following quotations are given from the article for the
publication of which the Hunts stood trial. After giving instances
of a sentence of 1,000 lashes, of another of 750, and yet another
of 800 lashes, the article went on:

> The Attorney General had said that mutineers were not dealt with
> as Napoleon would have treated his refractory troops. . . . His
> soldiers have never yet been brought up to view one of their com-
> rades . . . his back torn to the bone by the merciless cutting whipcord,
> applied by persons who relieve each other at short intervals that they
> may bring the full unexhausted strength of a man to the work of
> scourging; . . . they have never beheld a surgeon, with dubious look,
> pressing the agonized victim's pulse and calmly calculating to an
> odd blow how far suffering may be extended until in its extremity
> it encroach upon life. In short, Bonaparte's soldiers cannot form any
> notion of that most heart-rending of all exhibitions on this side of
> hell, *an English military flogging*.
> Let it not be supposed that we intend these remarks to excite a
> vague and indiscriminating sentiment against punishment by mili-
> tary law; . . . discipline forms the soul of an army, . . . the military
> code must still be kept distinct from the civil and distinguished by
> greater promptitude and severity.

The Attorney-General in his speech to the jury contended
that: 'The effect of this libel was obviously to excite discontent
and dissatisfaction in the minds of the soldiers . . . and to
disincline others from entering that service'; the comparison
with Napoleon's treatment of his troops was particularly mischievous at a time when Great Britain was at war with France.[1]

Brougham, in addressing the jury, said that the particular
question they must try was whether the article was written for
a wicked purpose.

> But . . . you are now trying a more general and important question
> than this. You are now to determine whether an Englishman still
> enjoys the privilege of freely discussing public measures. . . . Whether
> an Englishman, anxious for the honour and renown of the army, and
> deeply feeling how much the safety of his country depends upon the

[1] *The Times*, 23 Feb. 1811.

perfection of its military system, has a right to endeavour to promote the good of the service, by showing wherein the present system is detrimental to it.

Brougham referred to pamphlets written by two distinguished generals, Sir Robert Wilson and Brigadier-General Stewart, which had attacked the flogging in the army, representing it as acting as a deterrent to recruiting, effecting no improvement in the regiments, and weakening the spirit of the soldiers. Both had compared the British Army with the French Army in this respect in a manner unfavourable to the former. Brougham said that he was not, of course, arguing that one libellous statement justified another.

But it is because I hoped, and you must too, that those officers are incapable of a libellous intention; . . . were incapable of the design of sowing dissension among the troops, and deterring men from entering the army; . . . there are no two persons more attached to the country and the service. . . . If they could publish such things without the possibility of any man accusing them of libel, the mere fact of these things being published is no evidence of a wicked or seditious intention. . . .[1]

The Attorney-General maintains that it [Hunt's article] tends to excite mutiny and to deter persons from enlisting in the army. . . . The men therefore are to see their comrades tied up, and to behold the flesh stripped off their bodies, aye, bared to the bone! they are to see the very ribs and bones from which the mangled flesh has been scourged away,—without a sentiment of discontent. . . . Let their eyes devour such sights, let their ears be filled with the cries of their suffering comrades; all is safe; there is no chance of their being moved. . . . But have a care how, at a distance from the scene, and long after its horrors have ceased, you say one word upon the subject! . . . Above all take care how you say a word on the general question of the policy of the system . . . because a single word of argument . . . will rouse the whole army into open revolt. . . . Do not stop up their ears while the air rings with the lash. Let them read the horrors of the spectacle in the faces of those who have endured it. Such things cannot move a man, but description, remark, commentary, argument, who can hear without instantaneous rebellion?[2]

Lord Ellenborough in charging the jury referred to Brougham's speech as one 'of great ability, eloquence, and manliness',

---

[1] *Speeches*, i. 30–33.
[2] Ibid. i. 42–47.

but rather in the way of warning them against it. 'In the conscientious discharge of his duty', he had 'no hesitation in pronouncing this a seditious libel.'[1] The jury, after being out an hour and three-quarters, brought in a verdict of Not Guilty.

Of Brougham's old university circle, Murray wrote from Edinburgh immediately after the trial:

The exultation of your friends is great. . . . The accounts of your speech and the verdict . . . have given us more delight than anything that has of late happened in these bad times. . . . The prosecution of libels is carried too far and it is a great object that it should be checked. You are the first person since Erskine who has done so and you have now a much higher situation than any ministry could give you.[2]

Tierney wrote to Lord Grey:

Brougham has gained great reputation by his defence of Hunt . . . and he has a fine career open to him at the bar. What a narrow escape he had of being a mere politician instead of a distinguished lawyer.[3]

Jack Campbell wrote to his father:

His [Brougham's] speech was the best that has been made in the King's Bench these seven years, and from the extraordinary luck of getting a verdict against the Attorney-General and the Chief Justice in a case of libel he is a made man. If he chooses to stick to the law he is sure of getting its highest honours.[4]

Horner wrote to James Brougham:

Besides the pleasure which Henry's friends derive . . . it is with everybody a subject of congratulation on public grounds that at length some resistance is made to the indiscreet and oppressive prosecutions for state libels.[5]

Something of the edge was taken off the Hunt triumph by the fact that at Lincoln three weeks later Brougham failed to secure the acquittal of Drakard, the original publisher of the article which the Hunts reprinted. Brougham's argument was similar

[1] *The Times*, 23 Feb. 1811.
[2] *Memoirs*, i. 520–1, J. A. Murray to Brougham, 26 Feb. 1811.
[3] Howick MSS., Tierney to Grey, 24 Feb. 1811.
[4] Mrs. Hardcastle (ed.), *Life of Lord Campbell*, 2 vols., 2nd ed. (1881).
[5] Brougham MSS., 23 Feb. 1811.

to that employed in the Hunt trial and he felt that he made as great an effort, but ascribed the inconsistency of the verdict to the difference between the Middlesex jury and the Lincolnshire jury, which Lord Campbell described as one of 'old-fashioned, ultra-Tory, fox-hunting squires'. Actually, the Drakard jury was packed, since ten special jurors were planted in it, while there were only two in the Hunt jury. The sentence was eighteen months' imprisonment and a fine of £200. To a modern reader the most remarkable statement in the Drakard trial is one that occurs in the charge of the judge, Sir George Wood, who insisted that *parliament was the place for the discussion of the laws of the country, not newspapers.*[1]

In this same year, 1811, Brougham made several speeches in Parliament on flogging in the army, and on 15 April of the following year he cited a number of particularly bad cases in both the army and the navy.[2]

In this, his second session of Parliament (1811), Brougham gave much more of his strength to humanitarian causes than he did to party politics. He had continued his association with the Saints (the Wilberforce group), which Horner had considered so unfavourable to his political prospects. At the same time he was writing long articles in the *Edinburgh Review* during the year 1811 on Spain, the Russian Army, philosophical transactions, oxymuriatic gas, Parliamentary Reform, the slave trade, West Indian slavery, and a particularly good one on the education of the poor, which will be noticed later. There was also an article on the conduct of the war, which Brougham was constantly criticizing, while expressing hopes for peace, some of which were emotionally pacifist. This article was more optimistic about the outcome of the war than earlier ones.

Late in 1811 he learned that the Duke of Bedford was about to sell the borough of Camelford, which meant selling Brougham's seat in Parliament from under him. Rumours were rife that the Whigs had had enough of Brougham and were showing him the door. But one cannot read his letters at the time and arrive at any other conclusion than that he was sincerely convinced that the Duke was obliged to sell Camelford. He criticized freely in private and in public nearly every public man of the

---

[1] *The Times*, 18 Mar. 1811.
[2] *Hansard*, xx. 776 seq., xxii. 389 seq.

time, but he never had anything but good to say of the Duke of Bedford. The Duke did not fear Brougham's liberalism as some other Whig leaders did. Camelford was sold but Brougham was allowed to retain his seat until Parliament dissolved. During that time he was to lead the final and successful attack on the Orders in Council.

CHAPTER VI

Repealing the Orders in Council:
The Liverpool Election

BROUGHAM opened his new attack on the Orders in Council on 3 March 1812. Since his first onslaught in the spring of 1808, many strange developments had occurred in the ruthless three-cornered commercial warfare between France, Great Britain, and the United States. Each country probably suffered most from the restrictions it had itself imposed—it was a three-cornered duel with boomerangs.

The American embargo was so injurious to the United States that it was abolished on 1 March 1809. The Non-Intercourse Act, forbidding Americans to trade with Great Britain or Napoleonic countries so long as the latter continued their restrictions, was also unsatisfactory.

In the following month the British Government modified its system by a new Order in Council dated 26 April (1809). The Baltic and a number of Italian ports were now open to American vessels without the requirement of their entering British ports and submitting to the other regulations of 1807. Much of the spirit of the old Orders remained, but there was a real concession to the United States. Brougham, in an *Edinburgh Review* article for July, hailed this as a victory for the opposition to the Orders. After estimating the loss inflicted on British trade by the Orders in Council he said that the authors of the original Orders in Council now 'saw that to persist in it was ruin'.

The year 1810 was marked by striking changes in the American relation to this triangular commercial struggle. On 1 May the Non-Intercourse Act was repealed by a measure which at the same time authorized the President, 'in case either Great Britain or France shall, before the 3rd day of March next, so revoke or modify her edicts as that they shall cease to violate the neutral commerce of the United States', to impose non-intercourse with the nation that had not so acted.

Then on 4 August (1810) Cadore, the French Foreign Minister, handed to Armstrong, the American Minister at Paris, a letter which had been written almost entirely by Napoleon himself. Although the Cadore letter opened by saying that Napoleon's decrees 'are revoked' and that 'after the 1st of November they will cease to have effect', it was so worded that the effectiveness of this 'revocation' was conditional on one or other of two things, and both these were deliberately ambiguous. The English were 'to renounce the new principles of blockade' as well as revoking the Orders in Council. And the United States were to 'cause their rights to be respected by the English', which was so vague that it might have meant anything.

The terms of the American Non-Intercourse Act of May required that 'the edicts' of one belligerent should actually be inoperative before non-intercourse should be declared against the other. Yet President Madison proclaimed on 2 November (1810)—without even waiting to hear by sailing vessel across the Atlantic what Napoleon had done on and after 1 November —that France had complied with the conditions and if Great Britain did not do so within the intervening three months, the Non-Intercourse Act would go into effect against her on 1 February (1811). What Napoleon did on, and after, 1 November was to continue to seize and confiscate American ships and to tell his own men that the Berlin and Milan Decrees were the basis of his whole structure and must be enforced at all costs. It is true that he employed specious arguments at times to meet the anger of American ministers and to represent the seizures and confiscations as being grounded on causes other than the Decrees.

When the Cadore letter was brought to the attention of the British Government, the reply of the latter to the American authorities was that there was no public revocation of Napoleon's decrees and no satisfactory evidence that he was not enforcing them. As soon as such evidence was definitely presented, the Orders in Council would be repealed and not before. On 2 March 1811 the American Congress passed, not a non-intercourse act, but a non-importation act against Great Britain.

As a result of all this, from the summer of 1810 France and the greater part of Europe, Great Britain, and the United States began to suffer from a severe economic crisis. The crisis in Great Britain, marked by bank failures, bankruptcies, and unemployment from July 1810, was greatly intensified by the American Non-Importation Act of March 1811. British exports to Europe were also directly reduced by the tightening up of Napoleon's system in 1810. As the suffering became intense it was natural that many people should think of the Orders in Council as largely, if not entirely, responsible for it and of their repeal as the great cure. The wisdom of the Orders in Council had been questioned by many from the beginning. The merchants' petitions and Brougham's leadership had stirred up strong feeling against them in 1808, and this now asserted itself under all the goading influences of an economic crisis.

In March 1812 Brougham renewed his attack in Parliament. He prepared the way for the reopening of the campaign, as he did for nearly all his great undertakings, by an article in the *Edinburgh Review*. Appearing in the February number of this year, 1812, it was entitled 'Disputes with America'. The greater part of it dealt with the question of the *justice* of the Orders in Council, particularly in their application to the United States. It was written, as stated at the outset, 'from a conviction of the ruinous consequences of an American war'. He discussed briefly the right of search for deserting seamen but came quickly to the subject of blockade, giving a clear exposition of international law on the matter. If international law is thrown overboard by both belligerents, as was the case in the present struggle, 'if there be no limit to this right of blockade but the good pleasure of the belligerents, . . . then it is in vain to talk of neutral rights or of neutrality at all. In such a case a neutral in the position of the United States will inevitably despise the belligerent that is least able to enforce its decrees and will be drawn into the quarrel against the stronger power.'

She [Great Britain] endeavoured to monopolize, instead of retaliating. In answer to a decree saying no one shall trade with England, she said: Every one shall trade with England, or give up all trading whatsoever. . . . Both neutral and enemy might trade as largely as before, provided they chose to drive that traffic through the medium of British ports. . . . It is therefore quite impossible to defend the Orders in Council on the principle of retaliation. Their preamble states that principle, but only to abandon it. . . . Surely if an American war is so dear to our rulers,—if they must at all risks have a rupture with the only free people beside ourselves now left in the world, . . .

they may find some less revolting pretext on which to found their measure.

Brougham was to bring in his motion on 3 March. The Tories were in something approaching a panic. They feared Brougham and they feared the division. Rumours flew about the clubs and the lobbies. The Government would be deserted by Tory merchant members in large numbers.[1]

Brougham left a sick-bed to make his motion and a long speech. He moved for a committee 'for the purpose of taking into its consideration the present state of commerce and manufactures of the country, particularly with reference to the effects of the Orders in Council and the licence trade'. His vivid language seared into the minds of his hearers the distress in the country, which he related directly to the Orders in Council. Brougham refused to accept the Customs House figures as anything like a reliable indication of what the amount of exports had really been. The owners' valuation had been accepted and many owners liked to enhance their importance by exaggerating their trade figures. Much of the so-called exports to South America—as a result of the fortunes of war—were not exports at all. Large quantities of goods had gone out to South America in these years on a speculative wave and had either perished there without sale, or had been returned to England. Goods seized in the Baltic in 1810 had figured in the 'exports' of that year. There had been a very great decrease of exports in 1811. British shipowners were complaining of losses while the shipping of various little nations in northern Europe was greatly increased. He then discussed the substantial grievance which the Orders in Council afforded the United States. 'Let us conciliate America . . . let us not be falsely proud and refuse this inquiry from the weakest of all weak fears, the fear of acknowledging that we have formerly committed an error.'[2]

Brougham's first supporting speaker in this debate was Alexander Baring (later Lord Ashburton),[3] whom Brougham referred to as 'the greatest merchant in the world' and who had also played a prominent part in the attack on the Orders in Council in 1808. In reply to George Rose's argument that the Orders in Council prevented Napoleon getting raw materials and cotton

---

[1] R. Plumer Ward, *Memoirs*, 2 vols. (1850), i. 445–6. Diary, 3 Mar. 1812.
[2] *Hansard*, xxi. 1092 seq.   [3] Ibid. xxi. 1126 seq.

from America, he pointed out that according to the Order of April 1809 there was nothing to prevent those commodities going from the United States to the coasts left open by that Order and thence to France.

James Stephen followed Baring.[1] He admitted the distress but denied that it was caused by the Orders in Council. He stressed the increase of exports in 1809 and 1810 but omitted to mention that the United States withdrew its restrictions on British trade in three months of one year and eight months of the other.

In his reply Brougham said:

It became parliament to stand forward between the country and the ruinous effects of such a mean and profligate policy, and to save it from the last of the disasters, into which the Prince Regent's ministers were hurrying it,—a war with America. . . . If any man there was desirous of preserving peace with America he would vote for the inquiry; and every one who gave such a vote might go to his home and lie down with the consciousness that he had done his uttermost to avert the greatest evil with which the people of England could be menaced.[2]

Brougham's motion was defeated by a majority of seventy-two, which while it was considerably smaller than their normal majority, was larger than the Government had expected. On the following day Brougham wrote to one of the leading merchants of Liverpool: 'Our division is a good one, and by following it up with petitions an American war may be prevented.'[3] Directly and indirectly he urged merchants throughout the country to deluge Parliament with petitions, and to avoid all references to party politics, confining themselves rigidly to the matter of the Orders in Council.[4]

The cumulative effect of the flood of petitions made itself felt and on 28 April the Government gave way to the extent of consenting to an inquiry by committee of the whole House. Brougham urged that the House go into committee on this subject the very next day and continue from day to day, putting aside other business. This was, in part, sheer force of temperament, but although he did not fully know how critical and imminent was the drive toward war on the other side of the Atlantic, he does

[1] *Hansard*, xxi. 1133 seq.   [2] Ibid. xxi. 1162 seq.
[3] *Memoirs*, ii. 12, Brougham to Thorneley, 4 Mar. 1812.
[4] Ibid. ii. 8–11.

seem to have realized that he was fighting against time to avert war with the United States. It may be asked why he called witnesses for six weeks. The answer would appear to be that he realized that a strong case must be made out if the previous adverse majority of seventy-two was to be overcome. For Brougham's cause a premature division would be fatal. He secured the consent of the House to sit in committee the next day and every day, and a little later he succeeded in reserving for the inquiry all the time from four-thirty to ten o'clock of each day.

Brougham and Baring examined witnesses and carried on brief debates on the evidence on the one side, and Perceval and Stephen acted in a similar capacity on the other. In this matter of the Orders in Council there comes a tribute (a rather mixed one) from an unexpected quarter—Lord Campbell's contemporary, acrid, and somewhat spiteful biography of Brougham in his *Lives of the Chancellors*. Campbell said that in his attack on the Orders in Council in 1808 it was supposed that Brougham's ardour was stimulated by the high fees which he received from wealthy clients. 'But now [1812] that he was acting as a representative of the people from pure patriotism or love of fame, his zeal was still more ardent, and to gain his object he sacrificed much time which he might profitably have employed in his profession. To his honour be it spoken, that if he was liable to be misled by an inordinate love of notoriety, he was ever above the sordid influence of pecuniary gain. . . . From covetousness he was entirely free.'[1]

On 11 May, the Prime Minister not having arrived at the House, Brougham refused to wait for him. Brougham proceeded with the examination of a witness. A few minutes later he heard what seemed to him a muffled shot, as though a pistol had gone off in someone's pocket. He noticed a movement in the galleries toward the doors, but he proceeded without a pause. Then General Gascoyne came rushing up the House crying 'He is shot'. Brougham asked if it was Whitbread, whom he was expecting. 'No, Perceval; he is shot dead.'

Perceval had been one of the two principal authors of the Orders in Council. In his own government his influence had been the deciding force that had constantly stood between them and all suggestions for repeal. Now Perceval was removed by

[1] Campbell, viii. 267.

the bullet of a mad assassin, fired in the lobby of the House of Commons.

Out of respect for Perceval, as well as on account of the difficulties of arranging a new administration under a new Prime Minister, it was urged that the inquiry should be suspended, at least for a few days. Brougham would not consent to the delay of a single day. The motion had been 'from day to day' and 'from day to day' it must be. He was, he said, trying to prevent a war with America. Of Brougham's refusal to suspend proceedings Lord Holland said: 'He braved the censure of enemies and shocked the more timid and more gentle of his friends. ... To that wise and firm, but at the same time somewhat odious conduct, the country is indebted for the revision of a system, unjust to other nations and ruinous to itself.'[1]

At the same time Brougham's indignation blazed out at what he considered the inhuman treatment of Bellingham, Perceval's murderer, who was certainly insane. The court refused to give his counsel time to obtain evidence of insanity from Liverpool. After a summary trial (which presents a striking contrast to justice as it is administered today) he was sentenced to be hanged seven days after the crime and three days after conviction. To Brougham this was 'the greatest disgrace to English justice'. Apparently most men and women living in England at the time were inclined to view the matter more in the manner of Queen Charlotte who wrote to her son, the Prince Regent: 'I only grieve that the execution could not take place immediately after the condemnation, tho it must be owned that two days for recollection and preparation for the prisoner to go out of the world is a grant worthy a Christian and religious nation.'[2]

On the day of Bellingham's trial, Brougham was urging that the House sit till one or two in the morning to hear evidence against the Orders.[3] On one occasion, at least, it sat till four.[4] He finished with his witnesses a few days later and for several weeks after that evidence was presented on the other side, witnesses being examined by Stephen and cross-examined by Brougham.

[1] Lord Holland, *Further Memoirs*, pp. 131–2.
[2] *The Letters of King George IV*, ed. A. Aspinall, 3 vols. (1938), i. 77, Queen Charlotte to the Prince Regent, 17 May 1812.
[3] *Hansard*, xxiii. 221.
[4] *Creevey Papers*, i. 133, Brougham to Creevey.

At last, on 16 June, Brougham was permitted to sum up the evidence and to make his motion for an address to the Prince Regent requesting the repeal of the Orders in Council. As he rose to speak he was puzzled by a remarkable occurrence. James Stephen was not in his seat. Did it mean that the Government had decided to surrender? But if so, why permit a debate, why allow Brougham to sum up his case?[1]

In his opening remarks Brougham described in moving terms the distress in the manufacturing community. Over a hundred witnesses had been examined representing all the great manufacturing and mercantile districts. These witnesses had been unanimous:

Birmingham and its neighbourhood, a district of thirteen miles round that centre was formerly but one village, I might say one continued township. . . . In what state do you now find that busy hive of men? Silent, still and desolate during half the week; during the rest of it miserably toiling at reduced wages, for a pittance scarcely sufficient to maintain animal life in the lowest state of comfort, and at all times swarming with unhappy persons, willing, anxious to work for their lives, but unable to find employment. He must have a stout heart within him who can view such a scene and not shudder. . . . If you this night say 'No' to the petitions against the Orders in Council, you let loose upon the country thousands and thousands,—I will not say of riotous, or disorderly, or seditious, or even discontented people—but only of hungry men who must either find food or perish.

In Yorkshire, in the clothing country, similar conditions prevailed. In Kidderminster 'the great carpet manufacture is almost entirely destroyed'.

When the witnesses told the story of the sufferings of their workpeople . . . there was something in it which all the power of acting could not even imitate; it was something which to feel it as I now feel it, you must have seen it as I saw. The men to whom I am now alluding belonged to the venerable Society of Friends, that amiable body of persons, the friends indeed of all that is most precious to man, the distinguished advocates of humanity, justice and peace, and the patterns as well as the promoters of all the kindest charities of our nature. In *their* manner of testifying to this cause, there was something so simple and so touching, that it disarmed for a season the habitual

---

[1] *Memoirs*, ii. 20–21; *Speeches*, i. 413–14.

indignation of the father of the system [James Stephen] and seemed
to thaw the cold calculations of its foster parent [George Rose].

But let us merely pause upon the broad fact of the . . . amount of
the American trade [if it were restored by repealing the Orders in
Council]. . . . I would have you employ the glory which you have
won at Talavera and Corunna in restoring your commerce to its
lawful, open, honest course. . . . And if any thoughtless boaster in
America or elsewhere should vaunt that you had yielded through
fear, I would not bid him wait until some new achievement of our
arms put him to silence, but I would counsel you in silence to disregard him.

George Rose made a last desperate attempt to defend the
Orders. It was so weak that *The Times* expressed wonder that
they could ever have received the sanction of the ministry 'when
so little was urged on Tuesday night in their defence'.[1] Baring
made a strong speech in support of Brougham's motion. Then
Castlereagh rose to make a speech, the apparent intention of
which was to justify the Orders and at the same time to condemn
them to death. (He came both to bury and to praise.) He
admitted that Brougham had made out 'a grave case of national
distress'. If something were not done to open the American
market, that distress would become much worse. Yet, looking
back, he did not regret that they had adopted the procedure
embodied in the Orders in Council. All that was clear in
Castlereagh's statement was that in some form or other, at some
time or other, the Government was prepared to either suspend
or repeal the Orders in Council. Whatever it meant, it was
victory for the Whig Opposition at the end of a long struggle
and they broke into cheers.

Whitbread rose to state that he was 'unable to understand
the meaning of the noble lord'. Castlereagh stated that the
Government would not act until it had received a reply from the
United States. When Whitbread protested against this, Castlereagh in a third effort at explaining himself, said: 'He *never
meant that there should be any delay in suspending the Orders in Council.*
He meant that they should be suspended for a definite time, and
that this circumstance should be communicated to the American
government for the double purpose of ascertaining whether she
would in consequence abrogate her Non-Intercourse Act, and

[1] *The Times*, 18 June 1812.

also that she might apply to France to return to the ancient system of belligerents.'

Brougham was, of course, the great hero of the occasion. He would have been more of a hero to the members of that House if he had had the patience to sit back and sip with dignity the strong wine of victory. But that would not have been Brougham. He had to spring to his feet, jump on his prostrate foe, execute a veritable war-dance over his body, and gibe at the absent Stephen. 'His honourable and learned friend had not been able to bring himself to witness the death of his darling offspring.'

Ultimately, under pressure from Brougham, the Government decided to revoke the Orders instead of suspending them. On the 19th Brougham, impatient of delay, threatened to revive his motion on the 24th, thus presenting the ministers with a five-day ultimatum. On the day before it expired, 23 June, a declaration was made revoking the Orders.

This was the first Whig triumph for many a year. It was also the first parliamentary victory for the new industrialists who were remaking England. Brougham's praises were sounded on all sides, and merchants and manufacturers threatened to inundate him with presents. Among his letters of congratulation was a very cordial one from Francis Horner expressing the 'delight and pride' of 'all your friends'.[1]

Toward the end of July the news reached England that on 18 June, two days after Brougham's final attack and the Government's surrender, the United States had declared war against Great Britain. The sailing ships carrying the news of the declaration of war and of the repeal of the Orders in Council passed one another on the ocean. It has been suggested that if there had been an Atlantic cable at that time there would have been no War of 1812, no invasion of Canada, none of the glorious prowess of Canadian soldiers, no burning of the American capitol. As Professor Burt has said, 'that will always be a debatable question'.[2] Certainly war would not have been declared in June. President Madison said later: 'If the Orders in Council . . . had been repealed but a few weeks sooner, our declaration of war proceeding from that course would have been stayed, and negotiations on the subject of impressments, the other

[1] *Memoirs*, ii. 23.
[2] Burt, p. 316.

great case, would have been pursued with fresh vigour and hopes.'[1]

The news of the declaration of war brought an immediate offer from Brougham to the Government to proceed to Washington, without remuneration, for nothing but his personal expenses and that of one servant, to try to negotiate peace, in the hope that as the destroyer of the Orders in Council he would be a welcome envoy.[2] This was a redemption of a pledge made in Parliament and was urged by friends, including Alexander Baring. Whatever else may be thought of this offer, it was apparently as sincere as it was impulsive. The offer was made on 1 August and was graciously refused. Seven weeks later Castlereagh wrote a very friendly letter to Brougham in which he suggested that they should talk over together the whole American situation.[3]

There is a strange sequel to this violent struggle, led by Brougham on the one side and by James Stephen on the other. Forty-seven years later Stephen's son, Sir James Stephen, wrote to Brougham a letter in which he revealed some secrets about his father. In that letter he said: 'The Orders in Council which fell beneath an assault of your own, he himself at last admitted to have been an error'.[4]

'Brougham is at the height of human glory', Ward wrote to

---

[1] J. Madison, *Works* (9 vols., 1900–10), ix. 273.

[2] *Memoirs and Correspondence of Castlereagh*, ed. C. Vane (12 vols., 1848–53), i. 119–20.

[3] Brougham MSS., 19 Sept. 1812. These events have been described as they appeared to Parliament and to the people. It has been suggested recently, without supporting evidence, that Castlereagh had decided to repeal the Orders in May, and did so as soon, or almost as soon, as a stable government was formed. On 21 Apr. the repeated promise that the Orders would be repealed, *if* the Napoleonic Decrees were revoked, was fully confirmed. But Napoleon did not revoke his Decrees and it is difficult to believe that Castlereagh ever supposed that Napoleon would do so. In May the American Minister in Paris was presented with a document which purported to be a revocation and which was forwarded to Castlereagh. It was dated a year earlier and during that year Napoleon had continued to seize American ships. Castlereagh, who was not easily fooled, would not have been deceived by that. He said nothing about suspending the Orders in Council until a week after stable government had been resumed and then he did so only when faced in Parliament with a division in which the Government would have been defeated. He surrendered to Brougham. And suspension became repeal only when Brougham's further ultimatum had but one day to run.

[4] Brougham MSS., Sir James Stephen to Brougham, 19 May 1859.

Mrs. Stewart two weeks after the revocation of the Orders in Council. 'His notions of popular questions are not much to my taste, but I heartily rejoice at his prosperity. It is delightful to see the success of great talents and industry.'[1] In many such letters written all over the country, Brougham was hailed as one of the greatest parliamentarians in British history.

Overjoyed at the Repeal of the Orders in Council and believing that war with America had been averted thereby, the merchants held enthusiastic meetings in all the industrial cities and tried to heap presents upon Brougham. He consulted his friends (Lord Grey, Lord Holland, Lord Erskine, Romilly, and Baring) about the ethics of accepting presents for services rendered as a member of Parliament. It was agreed that he would be justified in accepting as a mark of appreciation of a great public service anything that he would not think of buying for himself. He was embarrassed in the summer of 1812 by a flood of services of plate for which he had no use. He acquired a collection of cups, and among other gifts was a pair of blankets which he turned over to his friend Whitbread for Whitbread's daughter who was about to be married.[2]

Of far more value than plate, cups, or blankets was an invitation from a group of merchants in Liverpool to stand as their candidate in the approaching general election. Since the borough of Camelford was being sold, this offered to Brougham what seemed to be his only chance of remaining in Parliament. It would also give him the satisfaction of continuing his parliamentary career as a leader of the commercial middle class with the prestige of representing the great city of Liverpool, the port of the Industrial Revolution.

In the three months and a half between the revocation of the Orders in Council and the beginning of the election, the ambitions of five men were centred on the parliamentary representation of Liverpool. The two sitting members, both anxious to be re-elected, were General Gascoyne, a dependable Tory and strongly attached to the corporation of Liverpool, and General Tarleton, too independent a Whig to please the party leaders, and equally unsatisfactory to the corporation. Another member of Parliament whose sights had been fixed on Liverpool for some time was Thomas Creevey, a native of Liverpool, of supposedly

[1] *Letters to Ivy*, p. 167.   [2] *Memoirs*, ii. 29–34.

middle-class origin, although there were rumours that he was the illegitimate son of a peer. A left-wing Whig, Creevey had been well introduced to the Whig aristocracy, and although usually hard up financially he was a frequent and welcome visitor in their homes, writing about them in entertaining and frequently censorious letters to his wife and stepdaughter, hoping as he did so that these letters would have a cash value for his family after his death.[1]

It was Thomas Roscoe, merchant, historian, and banker, who proposed Brougham to his fellow citizens in Liverpool and ultimately led the group who placed Brougham and Creevey in nomination. Immediately after the repeal of the Orders in Council, Roscoe had written to Brougham that in addition to having 'effected the relief of this country and prevented a war with America'. Brougham had done much for popular government. 'Such a victory of public opinion has never occurred in my time.'[2]

A meeting of Liverpool merchants who had been active in the movement for the repeal of the Orders in Council was held on 30 June. On the following day Roscoe wrote to Creevey, 'Liverpool seems to have risen from the dead. The Customs House and quays are crowded and the entries for export are immense.' He described the enthusiasm with which the suggestions of Brougham's candidature had been received and added: 'I know not how you stand at present, but I really think if you and he were to offer there is every reason to think it might succeed.'[3]

Two months later, on 4 September, a great dinner to Brougham was held at Liverpool. Roscoe, in the chair, insisted that Brougham had done everything that had been possible and would certainly have averted war with the United States if it had not been for the obstacles and delays interposed by the Government. Brougham, in his speech, emphasized the impor-

---

[1] His whole correspondence, including a great many letters from Brougham, possessing considerable political and social interest, lay buried from sight until they were discovered by the late Sir John Murray. A fraction of it was subsequently published in the *Creevey Papers* and John Gore's *Creevey's Life and Times* (1934). Apart from the two editors, the author of this book is the only person who has gone through the unpublished part of the correspondence which is many times greater than the published.

[2] Brougham MSS., 25 June 1812.

[3] Creevey MSS., 1 July 1812.

tant role that had been played by vast petitions to Parliament in the campaign against the Orders in Council and urged the repetition of that practice when great public causes emerged.[1]

Creevey's health was drunk at the Liverpool dinner and in Roscoe's speech his being a member for Liverpool was suggested. But there was no indication of any marked enthusiasm for Creevey. In the correspondence between Creevey and his wife a month later, just before the election, there was a good bit of suspicion and distrust of Brougham, speculation about Brougham's welcoming some arrangement that would exclude Creevey, fear of 'treachery'. There can be little doubt that this accounts largely for Creevey's frequent references to Brougham, from this time on, as 'Wickedshifts', 'Beelzebub', and 'The Archfiend', playfully as those terms were employed in his correspondence.

What justification was there for this distrust and suspicion of 'treachery'? Brougham and Creevey were not definitely invited to stand for Liverpool until 25 September. Some weeks *before* that, Brougham suggested to Lord Grey, and apparently to Lord Grey only, that he would prefer not to have Creevey as a running mate, made other proposals to Grey and implied that he would be willing to listen to different arrangements if they were initiated by others. In one letter to Grey, the Whig leader, he said definitely 'Creevey won't do'.[2] At the same time Brougham was telling Creevey that Liverpool was not keen for him, which was true, and that he would not consider any other arrangement unless his teaming up with Creevey was impossible, which was not true.[3]

Some of Canning's friends and some of Brougham's favoured an arrangement by which a united support would be obtained for Canning and Brougham, which would ensure their election, a member-each saw-off between Tories and Whigs. In September Brougham wrote to Creevey that his rejection of that had been 'instantaneous'. But actually he had written to Grey seeking for advice in the matter and Grey had replied unfavourably.[4] Brougham had then refused, but it may be doubted that he did so in the terms which he reported to Creevey. In fact Brougham's

---

[1] *Liverpool Mercury* (a weekly), 11 Sept. 1812.
[2] Brougham MSS., Brougham to Grey, 16 Sept., and n.d.
[3] Creevey MSS., 'Friday' [18 Sept. 1812].
[4] Ibid. 'Monday' 7 Sept. 1812; *Memoirs*, ii. 40, 10 Aug. 1812.

repeated affirmations, in his letters to Grey and Creevey in the following weeks, of his dislike for sharing Liverpool with Canning,[1] are open to suspicion. Brougham had in mind Lord Grey's persistent dislike and distrust of Canning. It is more than likely that if Lord Grey could have overcome these feelings for the moment and assumed even a neutral attitude to the Canning–Brougham proposal, that Brougham would have consented to it, and Liverpool would have been represented in the next Parliament by the two most brilliant members of the House of Commons, on opposite sides of the House.

Parliament was dissolved on the 24th and an invitation to Brougham and Creevey was sent by Roscoe's Liverpool group on the 25th. *After* that Brougham gave no consideration to any other arrangement, although the Canning–Brougham proposal from the other camp was repeated during the actual voting. It was during the period between the invitation and the beginning of the election that friends of Creevey who disliked Brougham tried hard to infect Creevey with suspicions of Brougham's 'treachery'.[2] At that time Creevey was making sure of his election at Thetford. With that in his pocket he wrote to his wife that he did not 'care a damn for Liverpool' although he would do his best there.[3] But Creevey was warm-blooded, during the actual election the not-caring-a-damn attitude evaporated and he became as ardent for Brougham's election as for his own.

Lord Grey was very much interested in Brougham's election prospects. There can be no questioning the sincerity of these words in a letter to him on the eve of the voting: 'There is no person with whom I feel a stronger desire to cultivate and secure the closest and most confidential connection, both political and personal, than with yourself.'[4] Immediately before the election began, Brougham and Francis Horner spent a happy time together at Brougham Hall. Of Brougham Horner wrote to Murray: 'Nothing could be more entertaining or in better humour. Indeed, since our old days of careless fellowship, I have never known him in so good a tone of mind as through the whole of our late visit.'[5]

[1] Brougham MSS. and Creevey MSS.
[2] *Creevey Papers*, i. 168–70.
[3] Ibid. i. 170, and Creevey MSS. for parts omitted in *Creevey Papers*, 5 Oct.
[4] *Memoirs*, ii. 59, 4 Oct. 1812.
[5] Francis Horner, i. 114.

It was Canning and Gascoyne, backed by the Tories and the corporation, against Brougham and Creevey, supported strongly enough by the most active Liverpool Whigs but not with any enthusiasm by the leaders of the Whig party as a whole, with Tarleton a lonely fifth wheel to the election coach. What turned the eyes of the nation on Liverpool in this general election and gave it fuller reports in the press than any other constituency was the contest between Canning and Brougham. Canning had been in Parliament for nearly nineteen years and Brougham for only three sessions, but Brougham was already rivalling Canning as a parliamentarian. They caught the imagination of the public as did no other men engaged in politics, largely because they were both highly imaginative themselves and both believed in bold strokes. That did not endear them to the ruling class, to which neither belonged. They were both mainly of middle-class origin and found their strength in middle-class support. Canning carried a particularly heavy handicap in that day because his mother had been an actress, but a man of the middle class found it much easier going in the Tory party than he did in the Whig party with its blue-blooded, exclusive leadership. Canning's energy and industry were almost as remarkable as Brougham's, but he was not so entertaining except when he was on his feet when he was a good match for Brougham in banter.

Brougham and Canning were the ablest parliamentary debaters of the first half of the century. They were the greatest of its orators. While both excelled in the grand style, Canning's eloquence was colder and more confined; he never reached, nor did he attempt, the heights of Brougham's passionate emotional appeal. As masters of invective they have seldom been rivalled. Brougham's invective was like a battering-ram with tremendous force behind it; Canning flicked his wrists and there was a rapier thrust that went deep. Both men overdid their supreme gift of invective to their own hurt. The statement that Canning never made a speech without making an enemy for life was, of course, caricature, but it was good caricature. The price that Brougham paid for his invective is part of the story told in this book. The marked individuality, so evident in both, accounts to some extent for the fact that neither worked well with colleagues. In 1812 that was a matter of record in Canning's case, and one of suspicion in Brougham's. The suspicion was fully justified when after his long years in opposition, Brougham's Cabinet colleagues of the thirties found it as difficult to work with him as it had been for Canning's team-mates in the early years of the century to work with Canning. Neither was supported strongly by anything approaching party unanimity at this or at any other time. Both were intriguants and as such were distrusted more than they deserved.

Nor were these the only respects in which these two were marked off from their contemporaries. They both appreciated the importance of the press to a degree not usual at that time, and in an age when public men were dominated by a spirit of oligarchy, both were liberals with a liberalism restrained by reason, and both believed in popular appeal which they practised with remarkable success. In this last respect Brougham at thirty-four already had a record behind him, while Canning, at fifty-two, was in this Liverpool election to put his belief in popular appeal into full practice for the first time, much to Brougham's surprise.

Although the older Canning might be supposed to be the better known in 1812 in Liverpool, Brougham's personality was more of an issue and a target. Commercial Liverpool loved Brougham for the revocation of the Orders in Council and hated him for being one of the leading opponents of the slave trade who had struck it the deadly blow of making it a felony only the year before.

In any classification of the boroughs Liverpool must be considered an 'open' constituency. But it was a freemen borough in which about 3,000 freemen of the borough had votes out of a population of 100,000. The 'influence' of the corporation was strong. The majority of the voters were working men, but with the open voting, every employer knew how his employees voted and the latter usually voted as their employer did. In Liverpool a small number of great merchants held a powerful position and an election tended to be more a duel of interests than a test of popular sentiment.

For those who looked forward to a bitter clash between two great masters of invective, neither of whom had shown any scruple in regard to personal attacks, this election was a disappointment. Brougham in his first speech stated that he would make no personal attack on his opponents, and Canning followed suit. Auditors could hardly trust their ears. Brougham and Canning discussed public questions throughout without personalities or any show of bitterness, and both devoted their remarkable energy and equally remarkable eloquence to direct popular appeals. Mobs clashed and drove one another back. Two men were killed and a few injured, probably as a result of mob crowding; one stone made a direct hit on Roscoe's son and in its flight grazed Brougham's ear. But for Liverpool it was a remarkably peaceful election. The interest, however, was keen, and Professor Ramsay Muir, in his *History of Liverpool*, was justified in writing: 'The great parliamentary election of 1812, the most exciting ever fought in Liverpool . . . was a duel between Brougham and Canning, the two most brilliant orators and most dazzling figures of their age. Seldom can any electorate, in any constituency, have been the auditors of oratory of such quality as these two great men poured forth daily.'[1]

During the eight days of voting, Brougham made 160 speeches, and Canning probably as many. During the daytime the speaking was from hustings and, after rival processions, from in front of Roscoe's bank, and from in front of John Gladstone's house, where a boy aged three years, William Ewart, looked on with unrecorded interest.

In the evenings the candidates made the rounds of the clubs. In one of his letters (strange that he had time for letters!) Brougham said: 'My nights are spent in the clubs. I visited 25 or 30 last night for 7 hours and spoke at length and drank at each. This is dreadful.'[2] Since Brougham never got tired of speaking, the last remark must refer to the drinking. Creevey wrote to his wife on Sunday, the 11th: 'I must say Brougham behaves as well as a man can possibly do, and I am every day more struck with the endless mine of his intellectual resources.' And later: 'I have been perfectly amazed during this campaign at the marvellous talent of Brougham in his addresses to the people.' To which Creevey added: 'Still, I cannot like him. He has always some game or underplot out of sight, some mysterious correspondence, some extraordinary connection with persons quite opposite to himself.'[3] Obviously the last remark does not

---

[1] Ramsay Muir, *History of Liverpool* (1907), pp. 238–9.
[2] Brougham MSS., Brougham to Grey, 'Tuesday' [6 Oct.].
[3] *Creevey Papers*, i. 170, 172.

refer to the election itself. It seems to be a reflection of his suspicions of Brougham's intrigues before the election. After the voting was over Brougham, in a public statement, said that in his campaign speeches he had discussed his own record in opposing and revealing the abuses of public expenditure, 'the appropriation by the crown of unconstitutional funds, . . . the increase of military influence, the corruption of the court, the imposition of unpolitic and unequal taxes . . . the dangers that menace our colonial system from misgovernment and injustice, the mischiefs that have befallen the constitution of parliament from abuses in the representation . . .'.[1]

In the voting, which began on Thursday, 8 October, Canning led throughout. On Saturday the 10th, at the close of the poll, Canning was 31 ahead of Brougham, Brougham 5 votes ahead of Gascoyne, and Gascoyne 8 ahead of Creevey. On Monday Brougham increased his lead over Gascoyne to 22 and on Tuesday night the vote stood: Canning 926, Brougham 892, Creevey 866, Gascoyne 864. On Monday or Tuesday the Tories proposed an arrangement that would secure the election of Canning and Brougham, which Brougham rejected, declaring, 'We are fighting it out'.[2] On Thursday night, the 15th, Gascoyne was in second place, 171 ahead of Brougham. Brougham made a vigorous rallying speech to his supporters, but Creevey wrote to his wife, in characteristic style: 'Well, my pretty, Diddy and Brog-ham are fairly done, beat to mummy; but we are to take the chance of some miracle taking place in our favour during the night, and are not to strike till eleven or twelve or one to-morrow. We had to do with artists who did not know their trade. Poor Roscoe made much too sanguine an estimate of our strength.'[3] On the following day, at noon, Brougham and Creevey conceded the election to Canning and Gascoyne and withdrew.

The general opinion of the Whigs outside of Liverpool was that Roscoe had made a great mistake in insisting on running Creevey, and that if Brougham had stood alone as a Whig candidate, he would have been elected. Tierney wrote to Grey

---

[1] *Liverpool Mercury*, 23 Oct.
[2] *Memoirs*, ii. 60, Brougham to Grey, 13 Oct.; *The Times*, 16 Oct. (report apparently written 13 Oct.).
[3] *Creevey Papers*, i. 171, where the letter is misdated 18 Oct.

(while the battle was still close) that he had heard that 'from the enemy's quarters'.[1] Brougham agreed with this but gave an additional explanation of his defeat in a letter to Lord Grey, written on the evening of the day on which he surrendered.

We ran them amazingly hard. On Sunday last they would have compromised; on Monday they thought themselves quite beaten, and on Tuesday; but on Wednesday things looked up, though Gascoigne only passed me yesterday at one o'clock. The fact is they all renewed their subscriptions, and said if £ 50,000 were required they were resolved to do it. They gave twenty and thirty guineas a vote. Our friends have not spent £ 8,000.[2]

This may sound like the statement of a disappointed candidate but wholesale corruption is not improbable in that period. Thirty guineas for his vote was for even a well-paid labourer in Liverpool as good as a third of a year's wages. Certainly in the last day and a half Canning's vote was increased by 535, Gascoyne's by 323, and Brougham's by 95. In such elections votes were purposely held back, but if they had any ready reserve of votes it is difficult to understand the Tories proposing an arrangement to elect Canning and Brougham a few days before that remarkable increase began.

While the willingness of some wealthy merchants of Liverpool to spend so much money to defeat Brougham was partly due to their general dislike of his reforming politics, its principle cause lay in Brougham's successful efforts against the slave trade. On that score both they and Brougham were to have long memories. Thirty-one years later Brougham, writing to Peel, implied that the slave traders had defeated him at Liverpool in 1812 and had pursued him with their malevolence in all the intervening years. 'They detest me with a hatred hardly natural for branding them with the name and fate of felons.'[3] Half of the world's slave trade had been centred in Liverpool, and after Brougham's Felony Act of 1811 many Liverpool merchants who had been indirectly connected with it lost heavily, as well as the slave traders themselves. By 1812 Brougham was attacking the evils of plantation slavery, and John Gladstone, Canning's 'commander-in-chief', was one of the great plantation owners.

[1] Howick MSS., 14 Oct.
[2] *Memoirs*, ii. 61.
[3] Add. MSS. 40532, f. 172, Aug. 1843.

Years afterwards, speaking *in Liverpool*, Brougham said, obviously referring to this election: 'I never bribed in Liverpool, I never treated in Liverpool. I never either bought or sold the freemen electors.'[1] Which was quite exceptional for any party to an election in those days of lavish bribery and free beer.

In his victory speech on the hustings Canning complimented his opponents on their conduct. He knew them now 'better than he had done before. His friendship for them was increased.'[2] Brougham said in a letter written later than Canning 'conducted the contest fairly and honourably' and that as they 'met as friends at the beginning of the election', they parted at the end of it on the best of terms.[3] Brougham for some years had wished to know Canning better. The election achieved that. Canning wrote to Wellesley: 'There has not been such a struggle here for fifty years',[4] yet in the midst of their 320 speeches, Brougham and Canning managed to take time out to chat about various subjects.

On the afternoon of that day of acknowledged defeat, Brougham and Creevey rode on horseback the eight miles from Liverpool to Lord Sefton's Croxteth Hall. Creevey asked a man on the road why the church bells were ringing and the reply was 'the election'. That put it in Brougham's head to ask every man they met why all the church bells were ringing, what was going on. 'For the election.' 'What election?' asked Brougham, and each man in turn informed them about it. Then the inevitable happened. 'Why were the church bells ringing?' 'Why, the election.' 'What election?' 'Eh, Mr. Bruffam, Mr. Bruffam, is that you? Is that Squair Cravy that's rode on before you? Whay never moind, better luck another toime, you know.'[5]

[1] *Speeches*, iii. 598, speech at Liverpool in 1835.
[2] *The Times*, 20 Oct.
[3] Harris, p. 14.
[4] Add. MSS. 37297, f. 179, 17 Oct.
[5] Creevey MSS. Note by Miss Ord, telling the story as Creevey told it to her.

CHAPTER VII

Adviser to the Princess of Wales

IN 1795 Caroline of Brunswick married George, Prince of Wales. That marriage was to be the cause of the worst of the misfortunes of the Prince of Wales, including the ultimate entry of Henry Brougham as the leader of those who successfully sought to increase his bad repute.

As Caroline grew up she was shuttle-cocked emotionally between her lion-hearted father, her coarse-minded and loose-tongued mother, and her father's mistress. She learned quickly enough not to be shocked and was much too quick in her desire to shock others. She had plenty of spirit, and a vivacious superficial cleverness.

While bringing her to England, as the envoy of George III, Lord Malmesbury set down in his diary his summary of the Princess's character:

She has a ready conception, but no judgment; caught by the first impression, led by the first impulse; some natural, but no acquired morality, and no strong innate notions of its value and necessity; warm feelings and nothing to counterbalance them; great good humour and much good nature, . . . rather quick and *vive*, but not a grain of rancour. . . . She has her father's courage, but it is to her (as to him) of no avail. *He* wants mental decision; *she* character and *tact*.[1]

That was Caroline of Brunswick, Princess of Wales at the age of twenty-seven. These quotations will enable us to spare the reader a number of statements from those who later came to know the Princess in England. She changed very little. Throughout her unfortunate and pitiful career, for nine years of which Brougham was her principal adviser and, towards the end, her defender, she was the woman described here so clearly.

The Princess suffered her first British indignity before landing in Britain. Lady Jersey, the Prince's mistress in that year of

---

[1] *Diaries and Correspondence of the Earl of Malmesbury*, 4 vols. (1844), iii. 196–7. Diary, 10 Jan. 1795.

grace, was appointed one of her ladies-in-waiting. The words of Prince and Princess on their first meeting are well known: 'Harris, I am not well. Pray get me a glass of brandy. . . . I will go directly to the Queen.' 'Mon Dieu, est-ce que toujours comme cela?'[1]

At dinner the Princess had her innings. As described in Lord Malmesbury's diary:

I was far from satisfied with the Princess's behaviour; it was flippant, rattling, affecting raillery and wit, and throwing out coarse vulgar hints about Lady——[Jersey], who was present, and though mute, *le diable n'en perdait rien.* The Prince was evidently disgusted, and this unfortunate dinner fixed his dislike, which, when left to herself, the Princess had not the talent to remove; but, by still observing the same giddy manners and attempts at cleverness and coarse sarcasm, increased it until it became positive hatred.[2]

Throughout the remainder of that year Prince and Princess quarrelled violently. Exaggerated rumours of this further increased the Prince's unpopularity. They waited for the birth of their daughter, the Princess Charlotte, and then separated completely, finally.

After several changes of residence the Princess took a cottage at Blackheath, where she lived for some years, surrounded herself with her friends, entertained many of the most distinguished men of the time, Tory and Whig alike, and saw very little of the royal family. She thoroughly enjoyed the company of clever men and women, and under their stimulus displayed a great deal of wit and a certain amount of charm. She was a good hostess in the sense of doing the honours perfectly. But she wished to have none but clever persons about her. Lady Charlotte Campbell quoted her as saying: 'Mein Gott, dot is de dullest person Gott almighty ever did born.' While her English was far from perfect she did not speak the language in that fashion—that was one of Lady Charlotte's devices for gingering up her book for publication. But the substance of the remark is in character. The Princess prided herself, quite justifiably, on her ability to judge personality, and entertained all comers quite freely with the results of that ability. When she was not entertaining others, she entertained herself by writing in French

---

[1] *Diaries and Correspondence of the Earl of Malmesbury,* iii. 218. Diary, 5 Apr. 1795.
[2] Ibid. iii. 219. Diary, 5 Apr. 1795.

sketches of the men and women she met, which were said to be lively, concise, and discerning.

In October and November of 1801 gossip reached Lord Glenbervie from several sources to the effect that the Princess of Wales was pregnant. The Prince apparently heard the same stories.[1] A year later, in November 1802, the Princess, who was extraordinarily fond of children and was interesting herself in the care and education of several boys and girls of humble parentage, adopted a boy named William Austin, the son, presumably, of a dock labourer and his wife, who had been born in July 1802.

The Prince of Wales at first turned a deaf ear to all suggestions of his wife's misconduct.[2] Then, in December 1805, Lady Douglas came forward with her extraordinary story (which was later proved to be false).

The 'Delicate Investigation' which followed has, in all subsequent accounts, including recent sympathetic biographies of the Prince, been described as having been instigated by the Prince of Wales. According to Lord Moira, it was Lord Thurlow, the Lord Chancellor of the Tory government which resigned in January 1806, who in his last days of office urged that there be a thorough investigation of Lady Douglas's statement and of the conduct of the Princess. With the coming in of the Ministry of All the Talents in January 1806, Lord Erskine, the new Chancellor, wrote a letter to the King in which he stated that the Prince of Wales 'took no steps whatever to make it the subject of public investigation; but manifested on the contrary the greatest desire to avoid it if possible'.[3]

At the request of the Government the King authorized the appointment of four cabinet ministers to act as a commission of investigation. They very soon arrived at the conclusion that William Austin was really the son of Mrs. Austin and that the

---

[1] *The Diaries of Lord Glenbervie*, 2 vols. (1928), i. 255, 256, 258, 285. 4, 11, 14 Oct.; 15 Nov. 1801.

[2] A collection of letters and statements which were among the Home Office papers and have since been moved to Windsor. While they were in the Home Office papers the author was given special permission to examine and use them. H.O. 126. 2: statement by Lord Moira enclosed in the Lord Chancellor to the King, 29 Dec. 1806. In all references to this collection of documents I have given the original Home Office notation.

[3] H.O. 126. 2: statements of Lord Moira, Lord Erskine to the King, 25 Mar. 1807.

Princess had not been pregnant.[1] But the report of the commissioners did not stop there. It said:

Those declarations, on the whole of which your Majesty has been pleased to command us to inquire and report, contain . . . other particulars respecting the conduct of Her Royal Highness, such as must, especially, considering her exalted rank and station, necessarily give occasion to very unfavourable interpretations. From the various depositions and proofs annexed to this report, particularly from the examination of Robert Bidgood, William Cole, Frances Lloyd and Mrs. Lisle, your Majesty will perceive that several strong circumstances of this description have been positively sworn to by witnesses, who cannot in our judgment, be suspected of any unfavourable bias, and whose veracity, in this respect, we have seen no ground to question.

And what was the evidence of these witnesses whose veracity was declared to be unquestioned? It is difficult to think that anyone could read the evidence of Cole, Bidgood, and Frances Lloyd, three of the four named in the report, without concluding that these servants of the Princess believed positively that she had committed adultery with at least two of the men whose names were mentioned—if their evidence was honest. In fact it was indirect evidence of adultery. And the commissioners said that their 'veracity, in this respect, we have seen no ground to question'. Of the four named, Mrs. Lisle alone did not mention damning details and expressed a more lenient view of the conduct of the Princess, saying in effect that she was one of those women who just could not help flirting.

The Princess found able support among the Tory leaders then in Opposition. Perceval and Eldon hoped that by writing a

[1] But see *Letters of George IV*, ii. 282, 359, James Brougham to Henry Brougham, and James Brougham's Memorandum, for the story which the Princess told James Brougham in Italy in 1819, to the effect that 'William Austin' was the illegitimate child of Prince Louis Ferdinand of Prussia, smuggled into England by a German woman, adopted by the Princess, and passed off as the child of the Austins. The Princess had already told this story to Lady Charlotte Campbell. And Brougham said in his Memoirs that she frequently told Lady Charlotte Lindsay the tale of his German parentage and his being smuggled into England. It might look, on the face of it, like a tall tale by an habitual liar, but Brougham came to believe it after Lushington had picked up good supporting evidence from Germany. Brougham said that the substitution was made 'after a few years'; according to the Princess it was at some time before the investigation. See *Memoirs*, ii. 425. Lushington's letter repeating what he heard in Germany at Queen Caroline's funeral is in Brougham MSS., 27 Sept. 1858.

strong defence for the Princess, showing up the irregularities of the Whig commissioners and arguing that their conclusions were unjust, they could drive the Whigs from power. Perceval wrote the Princess's fervid letters of protest. One of these, a very long statement from the Princess of Wales to the King, dated 2 October 1806, later to cover 156 pages of print, was the main defence of the Princess.[1] It was a masterly piece of work by Perceval aided by Plumer and to some extent by Lord Eldon. When the Tories returned to power in March 1807 most of the printed copies of it were burned and Eldon, as Lord Chancellor, issued an injunction against its publication. It was no longer useful or desirable for them.

The Princess had been given no opportunity to defend herself, there had been no cross-examination of witnesses in her interest, and the evidence had been presented by the commissioners in the form of statements with no inclusion of the questions asked. When we add to this the fact that the demand of the Princess for a full and fair investigation, in which she would have full powers of defence, was refused by the Ministry of the Talents, it is easy to understand her insistence that she had been treated unjustly.

The new Tory government befriended the Princess by passing a Minute of Council on 22 April 1807, stating after dismissing the Douglas charges that 'all other particulars of conduct brought in accusation against her Royal Highness to which the character of criminality can be ascribed are satisfactorily contradicted or rest upon evidence of such a nature, and was given under such circumstances as render it in the judgment of your Majesty's confidential servants undeserving of credit'. (The *contrast* is sharp enough between the statement of the Whig commissioners 'whose veracity we have seen no ground to question' and that of the Tory Cabinet, 'evidence undeserving of credit', in regard to the *same* witnesses.)

Although since the Ministry of All the Talents in 1806 and 1807 the Prince had been gradually moving away from the Whigs, it was generally believed that he would nevertheless bring the Whigs in when he became Regent early in February

[1] *The Proceedings and Correspondence upon the subject of the Inquiry into the Conduct of the Princess of Wales*, London, 1807 (printed, but not published) pp. 24–182, and *The Book*, London, 1813, paged differently in various editions.

1811.[1] The Whigs ascribed his failure to do so to the restrictions placed on the Regency and believed that the Regent would call them to office when the restrictions were removed in February 1812. The news that he had still refused to do so came as a stunning blow to the fondest of fond hopes. Dreams of office, of loaves and fishes, of sinecures and pensions vanished in the clear dawn of disenchantment. High and low in the Whig party the vials of wrath were poured out. Lord Holland described some of it in a few sentences of his Memoirs:

> In conversations, speeches, and publications there was much personal asperity and some indecorous satire and invective. . . . We all incurred the guilt, if not the odium, of charging His Royal Highness with ingratitude and perfidy. We all encouraged every species of satire against him and his mistress . . . He retorted in language to the full as unmeasured, and in assertions much more unfounded.[2]

The poets took their turn with the vulgar rhymsters. And the Whigs were not lacking in poets. Though the absurd rhapsody of Byron over the tears of the Princess Charlotte, and Tom Moore's sarcastic attack on the Prince who had so generously befriended him, were joyfully received in those angry days, it may be doubted that the Whigs gained as much in poetry as they had lost in patronage. It was in these weeks of Whig bitterness that there was born what we have called the Whig legend of George IV. That legend of an utterly debased and worthless Prince Regent and King grew from month to month and from year to year, until it came to be the accepted view of millions who had never known him as Prince or King.

Certainly his decision to exclude the Whig party from control was a wise one. Professor Roberts, who made a very careful study of the subject of the Whigs and the war, says in the closing paragraph of a long discussion:

> Even granting that the Whigs in office would have been forced by the exigencies of the case to continue the foreign policy and military commitments of their predecessors, was there any reason to suppose that they would carry them out as satisfactorily? . . . A Whig ministry would have meant disaster in the Peninsula, for it would have taken them too long to realize and admit that their predecessors

---

[1] See Michael Roberts, *The Whig Party 1807–1813* (1939), pp. 337–9.
[2] Lord Holland, *Further Memoirs*, pp. 121–4.

had been in the right; and in the meantime the struggle [the Peninsular War] would have been over.[1]

This year 1812 brought to the Princess of Wales the ablest and most successful of her supporters and to the Prince the most deadly of his opponents. Cold calculation actuated Brougham's championship of the Princess. After a brief period of mutual attraction based on her admiration of his brilliance and his appreciation of her superficial cleverness, Brougham, from 1812 on, despised her in his heart more and more, while becoming ever more ardent in her support. The rest of the world might be deceived, but not the Princess. With all her folly she was astute enough to discern his real feelings.

In 1809 Brougham had entered the Princess's circle at Blackheath. Lady Charlotte Lindsay, that brilliant, witty, and eminently sensible daughter of Lord North, was one of the Princess's ladies-in-waiting. She was to be a life-long friend and admirer of Brougham and next to Brougham himself the most valuable champion of the Princess of Wales. Their team-work, however, did not begin until August 1812.

In 1811 the Princess of Wales and her daughter, the Princess Charlotte, consulted Brougham as a lawyer on Princess Charlotte's legal position. But legal advice was something very different from general and political advice. Early in November 1811 Brougham counselled Grey to write to Lord Grenville 'and the more influential Whigs in both houses' recommending 'forbearance, at least, toward the Prince'.[2] And in the same month, Brougham in the *Edinburgh Review* broke into high praise of the Prince Regent for his staunch and generous support of the Lancasterian work for popular education in which Brougham was so keenly interested.

Two months later, for no readily accountable reason, it was a different story. Brougham in the middle of his great speech on the Droits of the Admiralty, 21 January 1812, flung across the House of Commons a personal attack on the Prince Regent and his favourites. The attack fitted well into Brougham's main argument that there should not be in the power of the Crown a fund that was not controlled by Parliament.

With the wrath of the Whigs against the Regent after their

[1] Roberts, pp. 170-1.   [2] Brougham MSS., 9 Nov. 1811.

rejection in February and May, Brougham showed no sympathy. His private letters are full of the lack of unity in the Whig party. They were, he felt sure, not ready for power even if the Prince would think of letting them have it, and a coalition of any sort was undesirable.

In June (1812), after he had made his way through his political difficulties, the Regent employed the plenitude of his powers in placing a further restriction on the visits of his daughter, the Princess Charlotte, to her mother. The King had been sufficiently impressed by the Delicate Investigation to consent to the Prince's proposal to restrict those visits to once a week. Now the Princess Charlotte was to be allowed to visit her mother only once in two weeks.

Harsh as this was bound to appear to the public, this writer must confess to a great deal of sympathy for the Prince. Inept and frequently tyrannical as was his treatment of his daughter, whom he never understood, there can be no question of his devotion to her. Of his wife, of course, he believed the worst, and to his mind that went much farther than the gossip of the day or anything in the evidence of 1806. At all costs he felt that he must protect his daughter, now sixteen, against the evil influence of her mother. And apart from the state of the Prince's mind, there are the clear facts of the situation. The mother was frequently indecent and even coarse in her language, as her own mother had always been. She could discuss the morals of other women with great freedom and with anything but a lofty or even dignified conception of female virtue. The cleverness of her visitors was liable to be careless of youthful ears. One of her particular friends was a woman whose reputation for promiscuity was notorious even in that day; the paternity of her children was reputed to be so distributed that someone, punning on the family name of Harley, dubbed them 'the Harleian Miscellany' (a famous literary collection). Sir William Drummond, a frequent visitor to the Princess of Wales, was supposed to be an atheist. Certainly he was antagonistic to accepted religion and the general Christian view of the Bible, and at her mother's house he attempted to indoctrinate the Princess Charlotte when she was apparently no more than fourteen. He told her that there was no truth in 'scripture history'. 'It is all an allegory and nothing more.' He explained to her some of Tom

Paine's arguments against Christianity and told her that 'priests have always been the most corrupt and contemptible of mankind'.[1]

The young Princess had revolted against this in a characteristically high-spirited fashion, but when these conversations came to the ears of the King and he also heard that the whole Mary Anne Clarke scandal had been discussed in her presence at her mother's house, with her mother participating, he had laid down a rule that she should meet no one but her mother at these visits. An exception was made in the case of members of the royal family.[2] And when the King heard of a remark which the young Princess had made about one of her mother's reputed lovers, he had ordered 'that she never should be allowed to see her mother alone'; the lady who had accompanied her should always remain in the room.[3]

Complaints about the cruelty of this enforced separation of mother and daughter were exaggerated and to some extent affected. In our sources, including the letters of the Princess Charlotte, there is no hint of any great affection on the part of the mother. There is no reason to believe that she looked forward with maternal solicitude to these visits of her daughter. And the Hesse story shows how little she was concerned about her daughter's welfare.[4] Miss Stuart in her biography of the Princess Charlotte states that it was Brougham, in 1812 and 1813, who 'taught her [the Princess of Wales] to twang the maternal string with excellent effect'.[5] Of that there can be no doubt. As for the Princess Charlotte, the following are her references to these visits to her mother, written confidentially to her closest friend, Miss Mercer Elphinstone, in the months preceding the new restriction:

September 26 [1811]—'*My Duty* calls me to-morrow to Kensington.'

December 9—'I dined at [the] PSS.['s] on Saturday. . . . Generally she is not in a good humour. It is a distressing thing to entertain suspicions, but when things *have occurred* one cannot help having one's *ideas* upon *some things*; of course I would not be the person in the world to say such a thing except to you.'

---

[1] Hist. MSS. Commission, *Kenyon MSS.*, pp. 565–6. See *Letters of George IV*, i. 517 n.

[2] *Letters of George IV*, i. 517–18, 3–17 n.   [3] Ibid. i. 517.

[4] For the Hesse affair see *Letters of George IV*, i. 516 seq., and ii. 57 seq.

[5] Dorothy M. Stuart, *Daughter of England* (1951), p. 52.

December 20—'I am going to get into my carriage to carry me off to a very disagreeable diner [*sic*] at Blackheath, where I shall be most horribly tired.'

January 6—'I shall be . . . just in time to set off for the Black-heath dinner, which shall be *humdrum* enough.'[1]

The Princess of Wales nevertheless felt bound to make a protest and create an issue. And when she fought she always fought boldly. There had to be a highly emotional appeal. And the one man in England who could ring all the changes and pull out all the stops with precision and effect, in that sort of appeal, was Brougham. It is true that that was not so manifest in 1812 as it became later. But already his sincere and humane horror at the floggings of soldiers and his zeal for the freedom of the press had given the Hunts such a brilliant defence that the country rang with it. And in the cold and cautious House of Commons his moving descriptions of stark suffering in the manu-facturing districts had done much to sweep away the Orders in Council. That victory evoked overwhelming applause within a week of the order imposing the new restrictions on the meetings of the royal mother and daughter. Brougham was the lion of the moment. Moreover, although the Whig magnates might find a sensational campaign in favour of the Princess of Wales distasteful, Brougham at that time had nothing immediate to hope for from them. They had made no move, since it was known that Camelford was to be sold, to bring him into the next Parliament and a campaign on behalf of the two Princesses might have definite political advantages by giving the Whigs a demonstration of his powers. He was shortly to be nominated for Liverpool, but the nomination came not from the Whig party but from a group of merchants whom he had led in the battle against the Orders in Council. By once more marshalling the middle classes, who were not acquainted with the Princess as were the aristocracy, and by another dramatic campaign, Brougham might bring the Whigs to heel again. To change the figure, if, as Brougham believed, the supposed grievances of the Princess could be made the best card in the political game, the Whigs as a party would not neglect it indefinitely. In any case, a bold independent course suited immediately both his calcula-tions and his temperament.

[1] *Letters of the Princess Charlotte*, ed. A. Aspinall (1949), pp. 6, 16–17, 18, 22.

And there was the young Princess Charlotte. Impulsive, high-spirited and strong-willed, never at ease with her father, hating the Tories with true party spirit and regarding them as a pack of scoundrels, the Princess Charlotte in that summer of 1812 was in a particularly rebellious frame of mind. Her father had made the bad mistake of cutting off all correspondence and communication with the closest friend of her unhappy life, Miss Mercer Elphinstone. Brougham was, no doubt, well informed, and there was now the prospect of a campaign that would play up both wife and daughter against the Prince Regent. And for his political ambition the Princess Charlotte's cause offered quite as much as that of the Princess of Wales. The young princess was the heiress to the throne after her father, whose life was a bad risk. Established as Queen, she would certainly bring in the Whigs, and speculation on what she would do for the man who had championed her in the days of darkness was the stuff of which Brougham's dreams were made in the summer of 1812 and for some years to come. In her cause also he could carry his heart with him part of the way, for he was attracted to the younger princess as he never was at any time to her mother; in the later part of the period he felt a real sympathy with her in her sufferings.

Within a month of the imposing of the new restriction, Brougham was giving detailed advice to the Princess of Wales in regard to her conduct. Before he left London for the Northern Circuit in mid-August he cautioned her 'to have no communication with the Court except in writing'.[1]

The Princess was forbidden to visit her daughter at Windsor. She said that she would do so if she did not see her daughter once a week at Kensington. Between early in August and early in October the Princess of Wales made a series of excursions to Windsor with a view to on-the-spot negotiation and threatened gate-crashing, using a house of hers there as the base of operations. The prohibition was enforced and access to her daughter at Windsor prevented.[2] Brougham advised the Princess throughout, directing operations from his law circuit in the north. The

---

[1] *Memoirs*, ii. 147–8.
[2] Brougham MSS., Lady Charlotte Lindsay to Brougham, 7 Aug. [1812]; *Letters of the Princess Charlotte*, p. 30; *Memoirs*, i. 154, Lady Charlotte Lindsay to Brougham, 29 Sept. 1812.

Princess wrote to Lady Charlotte Lindsay about her 'warfare with the royal family' and the 'fun' she was having, keeping them in 'hot water', 'teazing and worrying them'.[1]

On 6 December John and Leigh Hunt, publisher and editor of the *Examiner*, were placed on trial for a libel against the Prince Regent, and Brougham was counsel for the defence. He had accepted the case before he decided to lead the Princess's campaign against the Prince. But it fitted into the campaign he was waging, and to the height of his powers he used his defence of the Hunts to discredit the Prince in the minds of the people.

With a sincere idealism Leigh Hunt had espoused all the reform proposals of his day. Those who disagreed with him were the enemies of humanity, as were all those who offended his sense of the fitness of things. He poured out his wrath upon the Methodists. With the most exemplary intentions, he was a thoroughly intolerant champion of liberty. When, in February 1812, the Prince Regent received his full power and retained his Tory ministers, Leigh Hunt lashed out at the Prince. On 15 March he published in the *Examiner* Charles Lamb's anonymous poem on the 'Prince of Whales'.

On 18 March the Tory *Morning Post* chided the 'ungenerous conduct' of some Whigs when the health of the Prince Regent was drunk at a dinner, and burst forth into this rhapsody addressed to the Prince: 'You are the Glory of the People, you are the Protector of the Arts, you are the Maecenas of the Age. Wherever you appear, you conquer all hearts, wipe away tears, excite desire and love, and win beauty towards you. You breathe eloquence. You inspire the Graces, you are an Adonis of loveliness.' In the next *Examiner* Leigh Hunt quoted that from the *Post* and, stung by the Whig feelings of the moment and this sickening Tory eulogy, he wrote in hot anger:

What person unacquainted with the true state of the case, would imagine, in reading these astounding eulogies, that the Glory of the People was the subject of millions of shrugs and reproaches! That this Protector of the Arts had named a wretched foreigner his Historical Painter in disparagement of his own countrymen! That this Maecenas of the Age had not patronized a single deserving writer. That this Breather of Eloquence could not say a few decent extempore words, if we are to judge at least from what he said to

[1] Brougham MSS., 12, 19, 28 Sept. 1812.

his regiment on its embarkation for Portugal! . . . That this Exciter of Desire (bravo, Messieurs of the *Post*), this Adonis of Loveliness, was a corpulent gentleman of fifty. In short, that this delightful, blissful, wise, pleasurable, honourable, virtuous, true, and immortal Prince, was a violator of his word, a libertine over head and ears in debt and disgrace, a despiser of domestic ties, the companion of gamblers and demi-reps, a man who has just closed half a century without one single claim to the gratitude of his country or the respect of posterity.[1]

It is easy to understand the rage of the Tories and the prosecuting zeal of Sir Vicary Gibbs, but when the Prince Regent consented to the indictment of Leigh Hunt and his brother John for libel on the basis of that editorial he made one of the worst mistakes of a career distinguished by imprudence. He raised it from a probable obscurity to a position of great influence. It became something of a classic text for the Whig legend of George IV and its last statement was repeated time and again for well over a century.

Hunt's outburst had been grossly libellous (and much of it was absurd). There could be little doubt of the judgement of any court. But Brougham welcomed the case with gusto. He wrote to Lord Grey, 25 November: 'I feel somewhat anxious about the verdict, but am fully confident of the defence and its effects all over the country. It will be a thousand times more unpleasant than the libel.'[2]

Brougham's general line of defence was to represent Leigh Hunt as a young man with high moral principles deeply concerned with the welfare of the country, a young man whose principal interests had been not politics but moral issues and social reforms. He had looked forward with hope to the coming of the Regency and the bringing in of the Whigs to whom the Prince Regent was deeply committed. When the Prince, after achieving full powers, retained his Tory ministers, who were opposed to all reforms, Hunt's hope was changed to 'black despair'. Immediately after that came this sickeningly extravagant eulogy in the *Morning Post*. It was the *Morning Post* he had attacked and the criticism of the Prince was incidental to his indignation at that type of journalism.

[1] *Examiner*, 22 Mar. 1812.
[2] *Memoirs*, ii. 72.

When he came to consideration of the public interest Brougham gave full rein to his eloquence:

My learned friend will talk to you of the danger of acquitting, and it is my duty to tell you that there may be some danger in convicting. Are you prepared to say, and if you are (in God's name) convict, that the immoralities of a Prince and his courtiers . . . are to have no check for the future . . .? Are you, twelve moral men, many of you fathers of families, prepared to say that we will no longer be guided by the virtues of our ancestors, we will no longer brand vice or laugh at folly? . . . If you are prepared to say this, you are prepared to open the flood-gates of immorality and to let loose upon after ages a race of monarchs, compared with whom the first Charles was wise and the second honest, and the most loathed monsters of antiquity were chaste.[1]

After the retirement of the jury, Brougham scribbled a letter to Lord Grey, which included the following:

I fired for two hours very close and hard into the Prince—on all points, public and private. . . . The jury's retiring is of itself a victory in the circumstances.

P.S.—Accounts just received that in twenty or twenty-five minutes (passed by court in great agitation) they found us *guilty*.[2]

The *Examiner* carried the fullest account of the trial, with a verbatim account of Brougham's speech. It was eagerly bought up and a few weeks later the speech was published in pamphlet form. The Hunts were sentenced to two years' imprisonment.

With the Hunt case off his hands, Brougham could give closer attention to the Princess of Wales's campaign. In its conduct his partner from now on was Samuel Whitbread, the most energetic, the most liberal, and the most independent of the Whig leaders in the House of Commons, and, with Brougham out of the House for the time being, the most eloquent, with the possible exception of Romilly. To Whitbread, every abuse was a challenge and he was a noble champion of reform. He was as rash as he was brave, his judgement was bad and too often he was ardent rather than astute. His conceptions of foreign policy were bogged down in sentimental and ignorant pacifism. To the other leaders of the Whig party Whitbread was a constant source of irritation. Most of them were too conservative and too cautious not to resent his liberalism. In the correspondence of the Grenvilles, both published and unpublished,[1] Whitbread is the *bête noire*. While that was the attitude of the leaders of the Whig party, the Whig left wing in the House of Commons (the Mountain) was more devoted to Whitbread than to anyone else. He had a strong following in the middle class. Whitbread was also a romantic who believed with a rather terrible sincerity that in a spirit of chivalry he was going to the rescue of a princess in distress.

Brougham gave a great deal of time and care to the preparation of a statement of the grievances of the Princess of Wales, and also of the Princess Charlotte in relation to the restrictions imposed upon them. This was to take the form of a letter from the older Princess to her husband, the Prince Regent.

When she received the letter from Brougham the Princess said that it was 'exquisitely perfect'.[2] She had it copied, signed it, dated it 14 January 1813, and sent it off. For several days the letter shuttled backward and forward, the Prince refusing to have any communication with his wife. Then the Princess, probably on Brougham's advice, wrote to Lords Liverpool and Eldon asking them to *read* the letter to the Prince. The communication would then be going through them and not directly to him. This time she waited over a week for a reply. On the 28th Lord Liverpool wrote to inform the Princess of Wales that her letter had been read to the Prince Regent. 'His Royal Highness was not pleased to signify any commands upon it.'[3]

At this point a study of certain dates reveals a significant aspect of the story. On 23 January the Princess Charlotte paid her regular visit to her mother (according to the once in two weeks rule).[4] Some time before 28 January the Princess of Wales's letter was read to the Prince. On Monday, 1 February, *nine days* after her last visit, the Princess Charlotte was permitted to dine with her mother.[5] Then the Prime Minister wrote a very gracious

---

[1] The principal published groups are the Dropmore Papers and the Fortescue Papers (Hist. MSS. Com.). The Grenville MSS. are a fairly recent accession to the British Museum, Add. MSS. 41851–8.

[2] Brougham MSS., 30 Dec.

[3] *Creevey Papers*, i. 177: copy of Lord Liverpool to Lady Charlotte Campbell, 28 Jan. 1812.

[4] *The Times*, 25 Jan.; *Autobiography of Cornelia Knight*, 2 vols. (1861), i. 197.

[5] Ibid. i. 205, 207.

letter to the Princess of Wales, conveying a message from the
Prince Regent asking whether Wednesday, 10 February, or
Thursday, 11 February, would be more convenient for her to
receive her next visit from her daughter. The Princess selected
the 11th, *ten days* after the last visit. There can be little doubt
that Miss Knight, lady companion to the Princess Charlotte,
was right in concluding that this sudden favourable break from
the once in two weeks rule was the result of the Prince having
had the Princess's letter read to him.[1] The letter had made much
of the once in two weeks. There is every reason to believe that
Brougham wrote it with a view to publication and popular
appeal. In the matter of publication, Brougham had now to act
quickly before anything like a once a week rule was established.
There is among the unpublished Creevey manuscripts a letter
from Brougham to Creevey written on the evening of Sunday,
7 February:

> There is a letter from Jenky [Lord Liverpool] rather civil, with a
> message from Prinny allowing young P. to dine on Wednesday or
> Thursday and desiring the mother to send for her and fix the day.
> This looks like the white feather again. Now, have you heard any-
> thing else, any universal cry *against* its coming out? Let me have a
> note on this point, as it is the last before firing the shot. The bearer
> will call in half an hour for your answer.[2]

Although the letter did not appear until Wednesday, Brougham lost no time that Sunday evening after getting his reply
from Creevey. There appeared in a London paper next day a
paragraph giving the public the first intimation that such a
letter existed and telling briefly the story of its comings and
goings. *The Times* and other papers reprinted the paragraph on
Tuesday.[3] On that day Brougham, with the full consent of the
Princess, sent the letter to the *Morning Chronicle* for publication
on the morning of Wednesday, 10 February.

The public hears the Princess of Wales speak to her husband,
the Prince Regent (in Brougham's words):

> It is with the greatest reluctance that I presume to obtrude myself
> upon your Royal Highness, . . . In the eyes of an observing and

---

[1] Cornelia Knight, i. 217.
[2] Creevey MSS., 'Sunday, Temple 7 o'clock', obviously Sunday, 7 Feb. 1813.
[3] *The Times*, 9 Feb. 1813. Earlier references to the proposed preparatory paragraph in Brougham MSS. and Creevey MSS.

jealous world, this separation of a daughter from her mother will only admit of one construction—a construction fatal to the mother's reputation. . . . He who dares to advise your Royal Highness to overlook the evidence of my innocence, and disregard the sentence of complete acquittal which it produced, . . . betrays his duty to you, Sir, to your daughter, and to your people, if he counsels you to permit a day to pass without a further investigation of my conduct. . . . Then let me implore you to reflect on the situation in which I am placed without the shadow of a charge against me, without even an accuser, after an inquiry that led to my ample vindication, yet treated as if I were still more culpable than the perjuries of my suborned traducers represented me, and held up to the world as a mother who may not enjoy the society of her only child.

. . . The irreparable injury which my daughter sustains from the plan at present pursued has done more in overcoming my reluctance to intrude upon your Royal Highness than any sufferings of my own could accomplish. . . . That her love for me, with whom, by His Majesty's wise and gracious arrangements, she passed the years of her childhood, never can be extinguished I well know; and the knowledge of it forms the greatest blessing of my existence. But let me implore your Royal Highness to reflect how inevitably all attempts to abate this attachment, by forcibly separating us, if they succeed, must injure my child's principles—if they fail, must destroy her happiness. . . .

I am, Sir, with profound respect, and an attachment which nothing can alter, your Royal Highness's most devoted and most affectionate Consort, Cousin and Subject, Caroline Louisa.

The Prince Regent submitted to the Cabinet and a select group of officials the question 'whether it is fit and proper that the intercourse between her Royal Highness, the Princess Charlotte and the Princess of Wales should continue under restriction and regulation'. All of the documents associated with the Delicate Investigation of 1806 and immediately subsequent to it were laid before this larger body.[1]

The newspapers were full of the Princess of Wales in the months following the publication of the letter. Perry, editor of the *Morning Chronicle*, the leading and most uncompromising Whig paper, would give no support to Brougham and took a position that was unfriendly to the Princess. In this he was following the party line, for it is a mistake to suppose that the Whigs as a party supported Brougham and the Princess. *The*

[1] Diary of Lord Colchester, 17 Feb. 1813.

Times deprecated the whole affair and in mid-February was distinctly unfavourable to the Princess. Part of its editorial of the morning after the publication of the letter might almost have been copied from that of the rampantly Tory *Courier* of the previous evening. But early in March *The Times* clearly swung with the tide of public opinion and was supporting the Princess. Barnes, not yet editor, told Brougham later that this change was occasioned by a serious drop in circulation and that circulation increased rapidly when *The Times* backed the Princess.[1] The *News* supported the Princess strongly from the day after the publication of the letter and in four weeks its circulation increased 27 per cent.[2] That was an indication of the effect on public feeling of the letter and of Brougham's earlier campaign.

Before the end of February the members of the Privy Council had completed and signed their report and submitted it to the Prince Regent. It stated that they had carefully considered the letter of the Princess of Wales to the Prince Regent. 'After a full examination of all the documents before us, we are of the opinion that under all the circumstances of the case it is highly fit and proper . . . that the intercourse between her Royal Highness, the Princess of Wales, and her Royal Highness the Princess Charlotte should continue to be subject to regulation and restraint.'[3]

With Brougham out of Parliament and immersed in his law cases on the Northern Circuit, it was Whitbread's turn to carry the ball. Always a forceful speaker and frequently a very effective one, Whitbread was at the height of his powers on 5 March. He made the most of the Cabinet minute of 1807 in which the ministers whom he faced had practically cleared the Princess of the charges and evidence of the year before. He held them in the trap which Brougham's letter had set in assigning the Delicate Investigation of 1806 as the reason for the restriction on the meetings of mother and daughter. The Prince and his

---

[1] *Memoirs*, ii. 276, where Brougham speaks of the change as occurring in 1814. The *Memoirs* are badly confused at times. The change occurred clearly enough in 1813. See Brougham's letter to Grey, 21 July 1814 (*Memoirs*, ii. 238) where the reference to 'the Princess of Wale's case' is obviously to something earlier than the time referred to in *Memoirs*, ii. 276.

[2] A. Aspinall, *Politics and the Press, 1780–1850* (1949), p. 307.

[3] This report is in *Hansard*, xxiv. 1107 seq.; and in *Annual Register, 1813*, Appendix to Chronicle, pp. 344–7.

personal advisers had asked the Privy Council to go back to that. And that awkward Tory Cabinet minute lay between the Delicate Investigation and the present report which recommended the continuation of the restrictions. Whitbread could ring the changes on Eldon and his Tory colleagues who had cleared the Princess in that minute of 1807 and now had the effrontery to repeat the old aspersions.

Castlereagh as government leader in the House of Commons had to make some reply to Whitbread. In actual fact the Cabinet minute of 1807 had been a matter of political necessity rather than a judicial verdict, but Castlereagh could not say that. His speech was almost as great a triumph for the Princess as was Whitbread's. He said that the recent Privy Council commission 'was not to inquire into and try over again Her Royal Highness's conduct, *which had been cleared by the former cabinet*; it was to advise the Prince Regent on a particular point'. He surrendered on the matter of the Princess's conduct and stated that the restrictions 'ought to be considered merely as a matter of regulation arising out of the unfortunate circumstances of separation [the separation of the Prince and Princess]'. A significant feature of the debate was that the Whigs gave no party support to Whitbread. Ponsonby, their official leader in the Commons, attacked Brougham and Whitbread for supporting the Princess, in such a manner as to emphasize as strongly as possible the fact that he spoke for the Whig party in fact as well as in form.[1]

On 10 March Brougham wrote to Creevey:

Snoutch [Ponsonby] seems to have been busy at his old trade of throwing people overboard. . . . I own it seems to me that the thing is overdone. The Princess so completely white-washed that *any thing* of any kind now must leave a stain. I am quite confident that the publication of the evidence [of 1806] would do so and am therefore anxious nothing should be done at all. . . . She is fated to destruction if she stirs and I fear she will. . . . begging my best thanks to Whitbread . . . for his glorious behaviour and speech.[2]

On 13 March the Prince published in the *Morning Post* and the *Morning Herald* 'the evidence' that Brougham so much feared, the 1806 depositions of Bidgood, Cole, Francis Lloyd, and Mrs. Lisle. The reaction to it in the weeks that followed

[1] *Hansard*, xxiv. 1148 seq.   [2] Creevey MSS., 10 Mar. 1813.

showed that, so far as the effect on the general public went, Brougham's fear had been greater than necessary. That move of the Prince's came too late. Public support was by that time so solid behind the Princess and against the Prince that most people either regarded the evidence of 1806 as a mass of perjury or concluded that even if it were true the Princess could be excused much by the way the Prince had treated her. Unlike the general public, however, the seventeen-year-old Princess Charlotte was profoundly shocked.

Brougham's reply to the Prince's publication of the depositions was the publication in the press of Perceval's 1806 defence of the Princess.[1] Before the end of March complete editions of 'the Book' were on the market, most of them extended to recent events and including recent documents, such as the letter of 14 January, the Privy Council report, and the Princess's letter to the Speaker of the House of Commons. Lady Melbourne, referring to the depositions, said that it was 'the fashion amongst ladies to burn their newspapers that the servants may not read such improprieties'.[2]

In the meantime Whitbread was continuing his battle in the House of Commons, now with singular indiscretion. His success had been too much for his vanity. On 15 March he went out of his way to point out that the Princess of Wales had disclaimed all knowledge of any intention to publish her letter of 14 January.[3] Brougham's comment on that, in a letter to Creevey from the Northern Circuit, was sharp: 'No kind of countenance should have been given to Mother P's d——d lie disavowing the publication. It might be very bad to contradict her in the present stage of the business, but no advantage ought to have been taken of so bare-faced a trick. . . . She knows that I have in my possession half a dozen letters under her own hand and Lady C. Campbell's urging the publication of the letter. . . . It is the only dirty thing in the whole case.'[4] Whitbread then launched a bitter attack against the commissioners of 1806.[5] With the exception of Lord Ellenborough, those commissioners were still prominent members of the Whig party; and Whitbread's attack was as regardless of justice as it was of mercy. Brougham deplored it as much as anyone. For Erskine, and for Romilly who had been secretary of the Commission, he was moved by a feeling of warm friendship. Towards the other commissioners there was no personal attachment. He had counted on the failure of the Whigs to support him in his campaign for the Princess. But his game was to force the Whigs to readmit him to a place in their leadership after he had won his personal triumph, and he had no desire to have his bridges burned. So he would have nothing to do with injuring the party. As he wrote to Creevey: 'One can't help regretting anything which damages not *Grenville*, but the *whole Whigs*. This should always be avoided if possible.'[1] He said that Whitbread had gone much too far and should try to withdraw.[2]

Popular feeling expressed itself in demonstrations whenever the Princess of Wales appeared in public. At this time also addresses from public bodies began to reach her. Brougham was soon writing the Princess's gracious replies to the addresses, with apt but not fulsome appreciation of the wisdom and sterling sense of justice of the British public. Brougham balked at a suggestion that he should write the address of the corporation of the city of London as well as the reply to it.[3] But he did make some suggestions about its contents.

On 20 July the Prince Regent staged a grand fête in Vauxhall Gardens to celebrate Wellington's success on the Continent. The Annual Register described it as 'an entertainment perhaps among the most superb, extensive and costly that was ever given in England'. Certainly it reflected the Prince Regent's love of the magnificent. On the day before, Brougham wrote to Creevey: 'Mother P. certainly goes to the *Tea Garden* tomorrow-night to meet her husband. It was her own idea but I highly approve of it on *his* account. . . . The consternation of Prinnie is wonderful. I'll bet a little money he don't go himself.'[4]

The Princess of Wales was 'much applauded by the crowd' outside the fête and was cheered by the guests within. Brougham wrote exultantly to Creevey:

[1] See *Creevey Papers*, i. 181, Brougham to Creevey, 'Monday' [29 Mar. 1813].
[2] Creevey MSS., Brougham to Creevey, 'Thursday' [25 Mar. 1813].
[3] Ibid., Brougham to Creevey, Apr. 1813.
[4] *Creevey Papers*, i. 182, 'Monday' [19 July 1813].

I send you some fragments relative to Mother P's last annoyance of 'our fat friend'. I really think it has been the severest thing of the whole. I am sure it has made him more laughed at. I have it from one of the stewards, who speaks most confidently of it, that P. expressed himself as beyond description annoyed, and declared he would 'give anything in the world that he had never thought of this damned fete' . . . P. poor wretch could not summon up courage even to go in the evening, so his benefit (as it was meant to be) has turned out to be hers.[1]

After this triumph of the Princess, Brougham decided to let matters rest so far as she was concerned, allowing public feeling, now so strongly in her favour, to consolidate itself. For the remainder of 1813 events on the Continent and the apparent termination of the war absorbed public attention. At the end of the year Brougham's interest and that of a number of other persons shifted to the Princess Charlotte and the proposal that she should marry the young Prince of Orange.

[1] Creevey MSS.

CHAPTER VIII

The Two Princesses

THE projected marriage between the Princess Charlotte and the Prince of Orange was a matter of high politics; it was designed to strengthen an alliance between Britain and Holland. The Prince Regent managed to get the young couple engaged on 12 December. Two days later, to her horror, the Princess learned that the Prince of Orange expected her to go to Holland with him after the marriage and go 'backwards and forwards constantly' between England and Holland. They were to have residences in both countries, spending a portion of each year in Holland and a portion in England.[1] The Princess had not thought of being required to leave England. She broke into a 'violent fit of sobs and hysterical tears'. In the confusion of the moment she apparently promised to go to Holland for short visits.[2] On 14 February she said that she wished to have any going abroad made dependent on her consent. 'My wishes would be certainly not to think of moving from England for a year at least after the event.'[3]

The Duke of Sussex, while approving of the marriage, wished to have the matter of the Princess's going to Holland discussed in Parliament. Brougham, anxious that the Princess should be kept in England, urged that on Lord Grey.[4] When the Princess turned to Lord Grey for advice, he said that her going to the Continent at any time should be entirely a matter of her own choice. But he was opposed to the matter being discussed in Parliament. In April he suggested that she should write to her father asking for a clause in the marriage contract that would make any leaving the country a matter for her decision.[5]

Early in March the Princess Charlotte applied to Brougham

---

[1] *Letters of the Princess Charlotte*, p. 93 : to Miss Mercer Elphinstone [14 Dec. 1814]; Cornelia Knight, p. 269.

[2] Cornelia Knight, pp. 268–9 *Letters of the Princess Charlotte*, pp. 93–94.

[3] Lady Rose Weigall, *Brief Memoir of Princess Charlotte of Wales* (1874), p. 85.

[4] See *Memoirs*, ii. 196–208.

[5] *Letters of the Princess Charlotte*, pp. 109–12, 7 Feb., 114–15, 10 Apr. 1814.

for advice. Lady Charlotte Lindsay acted as intermediary. The Princess promised to follow Brougham's advice in every respect and Lady Charlotte Lindsay placed letters from Brougham before her.[1] On 12 April Lady Charlotte Lindsay told Brougham that the letters of the Prince of Orange were very unsatisfactory, that he talked of her 'being forced to comply' and that 'she is now more firmly resolved . . . to break off the marriage if her leaving England is insisted upon'.[2]

The Princess's letter to her father, written 15 April at the suggestion of Lord Grey, blew up a storm. Brougham wrote a number of the Princess Charlotte's letters at this time. The spirit displayed was no doubt that of the Princess, but the turn and fine finish of expression and the cogency of argument were Brougham's. Throughout she insisted that she must receive an assurance that she would never leave the country except by her own consent and that she would not go to Holland immediately after the marriage. She wrote to the Prince of Orange on 9 May that if he could not exert influence successfully on the British Ministers to that effect, the marriage was off. Then Prince of Orange, Prince Regent, and Cabinet came to heel. And the Princess got her clause in the marriage contract, formally on 10 June, though she had received assurance of it some time earlier.

The overthrow of Napoleon was celebrated in England by a visit of allied princes in the month of June (1814). The lives of the Princess Charlotte, the Princess of Wales, and Brougham were all radically altered by that visit. Queen Charlotte, roused to greater social activity, planned two drawing-rooms for June. The Prince Regent immediately informed her that since he would have to be present at them, his wife would have to be absent. He would not meet her on any occasion either in public or in private.[3] That, of course, went much farther than the Queen's two drawing-rooms. It meant that the wife of the Regent would be barred from all social functions associated with the visit of the allied sovereigns.

The two princesses had not been on friendly terms for some

[1] *Memoirs*, ii. 192.
[2] Ibid. ii. 186. See also Cornelia Knight, i. 279.
[3] The Queen's letter to the Princess of Wales and the ensuing correspondence may be found in *Hansard*, xxvii. 10, 49 seq., in the Annual Register for 1814, State Papers, pp. 348–50, and in the current daily press.

time. The Princess Charlotte had not wanted to visit her mother. Although Lady Charlotte Lindsay wrote to Brougham that the Princess Charlotte 'seemed to be in despair about any possibility of reconciliation with her mother',[1] the edict about the drawing-room had the effect of bringing mother and daughter together again. Whitbread and Brougham wrote for the Princess of Wales letters of protest to the Queen, the Regent, and the Speaker of the House of Commons, and sent them to all the newspapers, for whom, of course, they were intended.[2] At this time Brougham was sending the Princess of Wales to the opera as frequently as possible to catch the applause of the people, while the Prince was greeted everywhere with hisses and groans.

During the visit of the allied sovereigns, the Princess of Wales talked fairly definitely about leaving England and living on the Continent. It had become apparent that in addition to being barred from all public functions, private calls on her by visiting princes were to be cut off and she was to be avoided as though she were a leper. One example of the Prince's thoroughness was his issuing what was practically an order to his sister-in-law, the Duchess of York, who was the sister of the King of Prussia, not to visit the Princess of Wales during the royal visit.[3]

This treatment by those who obeyed the orders as well as by him who issued them plunged the Princess of Wales into a fit of melancholy in which for once her spirit was broken. Whitbread knew of her talk of leaving England, but hoped that circumstances 'might change her mind'. When Whitbread knew of it, Brougham knew of it. And to Brougham this news came as a severe shock. The fact that if she went abroad she could no longer be used to stir up popular feeling against the Prince and the Government was the least of the dangers he envisaged. He believed that if the Princess of Wales left England for the Continent her conduct would be freed from restraint and she would play into the hands of those who would lay hold on anything that might provide evidence on the basis of which the Prince might obtain a divorce. A divorce might mean another marriage and the birth of a son, in which case the Princess

[1] Brougham MSS., 22 May 1814.
[2] *Memoirs*, ii. 216–18, Brougham to Whitbread and Whitbread to Brougham [24 May 1814]. Draft of the letter to the Queen in Brougham MSS.
[3] Creevey MSS., Brougham to Creevey [6 June].

Charlotte would not become Queen. And with that would go
the hopes that Brougham had built upon her reign. His own
fears were somewhat allayed by his realization of the difficulties
that in any case would confront the Prince in the matter of a
divorce. But when he put this up to the Princess Charlotte
immediately, he did so with full force. The eighteen-year-old
Princess was credulous enough to accept Brougham's predictions
without question when they confronted her suddenly with the
loss of the throne. Brougham easily persuaded her that if she
remained in England without taking the trip to the Continent
immediately after her marriage, her mother might well change
her mind about going abroad. And *everything* must be done to
change her mind. Brougham, no doubt, had hopes that a firm
statement by the Princess Charlotte that she would not go to
Holland after the wedding would break the marriage project.

Other motives than those suggested by Brougham also moved
her strongly in the next few days toward seeking to end her
engagement. One of these was her infatuation for Prince Augustus, cousin of the King of Prussia, whom she first met at a dinner
for the visiting notables at Carlton House on 8 June. The private
visits which followed, revealed by the recent publication of the
letters of the Princess Charlotte, could not, however, have
occurred before 11 June, when Brougham had already played
his trump card with the Princess. She was by then thoroughly
disgusted with the Prince of Orange. She said later that they
had not been on 'comfortable terms for some time'. She became
angrier and angrier because on only one day was she allowed
to attend the grand ceremonies of this royal celebration of
victory. On that day, the 9th, she was invited to a court held by
the Queen Mother and a dinner at Carlton House. From all the
other functions and parties she was as rigidly excluded as was
her mother, for a very different reason—her age. Yet she was
the heiress to the throne after her father and was old enough to
be married. While she chafed, on the outside of everything, her
fiancé, the Prince of Orange, in spite of her remonstrances, left
her at home and went everywhere. Lady Charlotte Lindsay
wrote to Brougham that the Princess was 'quite enraged' at not
being allowed to go to the Ascot races on the 10th.[1] The Prince
of Orange not only went to Ascot, but he made quite a day of it

[1] Brougham MSS., 'Saturday evening' [11 June].

and returned to London roaring drunk on the outside of a stage coach. The Princess Charlotte abhorred drunkenness. A day or two before that he had been drunk and disorderly at Carlton House. The young Prince Paul of Württemberg had got him 'into a scrape with the Princess Charlotte', according to the Queen of Wurtemburg (sister of the Prince Regent), who apologized later for her son's behaviour.[1] Brougham's account indicated that the Prince of Orange was drunk, and very drunk.[2]

The young Princess, with wedding preparations speeded up, no indication of a house being provided for her in England, and determined not to go to Holland after the wedding, asked for an interview with the Prince of Orange as soon as he got back from the royal junketings at Oxford on the 14th and 15th. They met on the 16th for the last time.

Although there was plenty of rumour and speculation about it, Lady Charlotte Lindsay's letter to Brougham is the only authentic account we have of that last meeting. It is trustworthy, because Lady Charlotte was so scrupulously careful to give the exact truth in her frequent reports to Brougham:

I am just returned from a three hours' visit at Warwick House, where I arrived at a most interesting and critical moment. When I came in, Princess Charlotte told me that she was very anxious to see me, for she had come to a resolution to have a thorough explanation with the Prince of Orange: that as no preparation was making for any house for them, she felt convinced that they meant to play her a trick, and get her out of England as soon as she should be married. She also told me that she found the Prince of Orange much changed in his language about her mother, and taking part more with the Prince Regent; that she was determined to support her mother, and felt that both she and her mother should remain in England, and support and protect each other. In all the popular applause she has lately received, her name has always been coupled with her mother's which seems to have had a great effect upon her. While we were talking the Prince of Orange was announced: she went to him, and desired that I should remain where I was, to hear the result of their conference, which has ended in her *positive declaration* that she *will not leave England now*, but will avail herself of the discretionary power promised her in the contract; and gave as her reason the situation of the Princess of Wales, whom she thought herself bound in duty not

[1] *Letters of George IV*, i. 457–8.
[2] *Creevey Papers*, i. 257, Brougham to Creevey, n.d.

to leave under her present circumstances. He appeared to be very unhappy, but seemed to admit that if Princess Charlotte adhered to this resolution, the marriage must be off. He begged her to reconsider it, and left the house in much agitation. All this proves that it was the intention to send them immediately to Holland, or to break off the match in the case of Princess Charlotte's availing herself of the power given her in the words of the contract. She seems quite resolved not to yield and has promised to let me know the moment this matter is completely ended. I wish you had been in my pocket to have given your advice.[1]

The final breaking off of the engagement and the statement of her reasons were embodied in a letter which the Princess addressed to the Prince of Orange that evening. The key sentence was:

. . . From recent circumstances that have occurred I am fully convinced that my interest is materially connected with that of my mother, and that my residence out of this kingdom would be equally prejudicial to her welfare as to my own. . . .[2]

When Whitbread showed to Creevey a copy of the Princess's letter, Creevey dashed this off to his wife:

By God! it is capital. And now what do you suppose has produced this sudden attachment to her mother? It arises from the profound resources of old Brougham and is, in truth, one of the most brilliant movements in his campaign. He tells me he had had direct intercourse with the young one; that he has impressed upon her the fact that, if her mother goes away from England . . . that then a divorce will inevitably take place, a second marriage follow, and thus the young Princess's title to the throne be gone. This has had an effect upon the young one almost magical.[3]

Neither Creevey nor Brougham knew anything about the sudden attachment of the Princess Charlotte to Prince Augustus, which was a carefully guarded secret. Yet it is altogether probable, in view of all the circumstances related above, that the marriage would have been broken off if the Princess had never met the Prussian prince. It should also be pointed out that it

---

[1] *Memoirs*, ii. 208–9, 'Thursday half past three o'clock' [16 June 1814].
[2] *Letters of the Princess Charlotte*, p. 117.
[3] *Creevey Papers*, i. 197–8, 21 June.

was by standing on her rights as secured by her marriage contract, and by refusing to go to Holland, that Princess Charlotte
broke the engagement.

The proposal of an annuity of £50,000 was not formally made
to the Princess by Lord Castlereagh until 29 June, but she and
her advisers were informed of it several days earlier. Brougham
felt sure that the Princess would get the money in any case, and
that the strong popular support which he and Whitbread had
won for her would be further enhanced by her refusing it in the
first instance. She must be very careful to make it clear that
she was not bartering any of her claims for a money consideration, nor giving up any sense of grievance against the Prince.

Brougham and Whitbread discussed the matter after the
House rose on the 29th and it was agreed that Brougham should
write a letter signed by the Princess and addressed to the Speaker
of the House of Commons, refusing to accept the money. Brougham probably wrote the letter that night. Early next morning
Whitbread sent a note to the Princess indicating its purport and
stating that he would submit it to her at Connaught House at
2 o'clock. But before 2 o'clock arrived Whitbread received a
communication from the Princess enclosing a copy of a letter
which she had written to Lord Castlereagh that day *accepting*
the proposal. The Princess had concluded her letter to Castlereagh with:

As no condition whatever, derogatory either to her rights, her
rank, or her honour, have been annexed to this act of justice, the
Princess of Wales accepts it unquestionably, in order to prove to
Parliament that she is never averse to any proposal coming from the
Crown to replace her in the proper splendour adequate to her situation, and to throw no unnecessary obstacles in the way to obstruct
the tranquility or impair the peace of mind of the Prince Regent.

When he had recovered from his amazement, Whitbread
went to Brougham, whose 'convulsions in consequence were
very strong', and to Lady Charlotte Lindsay who burst into
tears. Then he went to the Princess and told her that the last
paragraph of her letter had 'surrendered everything, and her
words would be retorted upon her whenever she wished to assert
the rights of her station'. She immediately said that she would
assert those rights by going to the great thanksgiving service

at St. Paul's a week later and Whitbread said that that 'might impair the tranquility of the mind of the Prince Regent'.[1]

On the evening of what she regarded as that unfortunate day, Lady Charlotte Lindsay wrote to Whitbread: 'She [the Princess] does not appear to me to be aware that she has been forfeiting all claim to your advice and assistance.'[2] Two days later Brougham wrote to Creevey:

I suppose you have heard of Mother P. bitching the thing so completely—snapping eagerly at the cash, and concluding with a civil observation about unwillingness to 'impair the Regent's tranquility'!! etc. . . . We are of course fully justified in giving her up. . . . However, tho' she deserves death, yet we must not abandon her, in case P. gets a victory after all.[3]

On Tuesday the 5th, Whitbread persuaded the Princess to inform the Government that she did not need £50,000 a year and would prefer to accept a smaller annuity.

Between 11 and 27 June, when the Prussian princes left England, there had been several secret meetings at Warwick House, where the Princess Charlotte resided, between the Princess and Prince Augustus. That handsome Prussian prince, the object of Princess Charlotte's infatuation, was a man of thirty-five, whose reputations for relations with women was apparently well known to all of the royal family except the young Princess herself. The Duke of Kent said that 'Prince Augustus was the only black sheep in his family'.[4] This was the romance in which Miss Knight, her lady companion, took such a busy interest. On one occasion when Miss Mercer Elphinstone arrived at Warwick House, Miss Knight informed her, with some trepidation, that Princess Charlotte and Prince Augustus were together in her room. Miss Mercer asked Miss Knight to interrupt them, and when the latter refused, Miss Mercer walked in and broke it up herself.[5] The Prince Regent would certainly

[1] The facts described in this and the preceding paragraphs are given in Whitbread's letters published in *Creevey Papers*, i. 199–201.

[2] Brougham MSS., 30 June 1814.

[3] This letter is given in part in the published *Creevey Papers*, where the editor discreetly changed 'bitching' to 'bungling' and misdated the letter, which was written on Saturday, 2 July. Creevey MSS., 'Saturday' [2 July]. Given in part in *Creevey Papers*, i. 201–2.   [4] *Letters of the Princess Charlotte*, p. 175.

[5] Greville's account of Miss Mercer's statement to him in 1832. *The Greville Memoirs: a journal of the reigns of King George IV and King William IV*, ed. H. Reeve, 3 vols. (1884), ii. 327.

have stopped these meetings if he had heard of them in time. After he did hear of them, Miss Knight could not have been greatly surprised at her dismissal from her position.

On the evening of 12 July the Princess was informed by her father that she was no longer to have her residence at Warwick House, but was to live at Carlton House with him for five days, after which she was to reside at Cranbourne Lodge, in the midst of Windsor Forest, where she was to have no visitors except Queen Charlotte once a week.[1] It was universally supposed at the time, and has been supposed ever since,[2] that these measures were taken with the sole purpose of intimidating the Princess into marrying the Prince of Orange. But the Prince Regent had heard of the meetings with Augustus, and the Princess's companion, Miss Knight, who had connived at them, was at the same time dismissed from her position, together with most of her other ladies-in-waiting.

The general association of these measures with the marriage project in everyone's mind was natural enough, particularly as nothing was known of the Princess's infatuation with Prince Augustus. There is, however, only one bit of real evidence to support it. Miss Knight said that the Bishop of Salisbury, who had been the Princess's preceptor, 'hinted to Princess Charlotte in a private conversation and to me *on paper*, . . . that unless Princess Charlotte would write a submissive letter to her father and hold out a hope that in a few months she might be induced to give her hand to the Prince of Orange, arrangements would be made by no means agreeable to her inclinations'. Whether or not the Bishop spoke on behalf of the Regent, that is evidence of an intention in the mind of the latter to bring pressure to bear on his daughter in relation to the Prince of Orange. And that may have played some part in the measures of 12 July. But a stronger reason for them existed in the knowledge which the Regent had acquired of the secret visits of Prince Augustus. Eighteen years later Miss Mercer Elphinstone (then Countess Flahault), who had been in the best position to know all the facts of the situation, stated categorically to Greville that the dismissal of the Princess Charlotte's ladies resulted from the fact

[1] Cornelia Knight, i. 304.
[2] I must here except Miss Stuart in her recent *Daughter of England*, with whom I agree without any doubt in the matter.

that the Regent 'somehow heard of these meetings', which were 'contrived by Miss Knight'.[1] Miss Knight in her own accounts would naturally wish to protect herself—and the Princess—in the mind of the public. She did say, however, in a memorandum made at the time that when the Prince Regent spoke to her on the 11th, he had mentioned the visits of one of the Prussian princes.

When Miss Knight asked the Prince Regent at the time of her dismissal what her offence had been, he refused to state it,[2] influenced no doubt by the danger of his daughter's name becoming associated with that of Prince Augustus. Certainly the measures which he adopted, harsh as they may seem, were, in the main, designed to protect her, as he had already protected her against her mother. He did not know all about the Hesse affair, with her mother's willingness seriously to compromise her, until five months later but he knew enough about it and about the visits of this rake of a Prussian prince to cause him grave apprehension.[3] He was too frequently tactless, inept, and arbitrary in his treatment of his daughter but his position was a very difficult one and it is deserving of sympathy.

Princess Charlotte herself still believed that the Orange match, now so hateful to her, was the cause of these developments. Miss Knight had said nothing to her about the Regent's statement in regard to Prince Augustus's visits and she believed that he was completely ignorant of them. After her father had outlined the new programme to her at Warwick House in the late afternoon of 12 July, Princess Charlotte came out of the room highly excited, spoke to Miss Knight for a moment, rushed into her bedroom where Miss Mercer was dressing for dinner, said she was going to her mother, grabbed a bonnet, ran out of the house, hailed a hackney coach, and was driven to her mother's house in Connaught Place, firmly determined to live with her mother and never return to her father. Her mother was at Blackheath at the time. The Princess Charlotte sent a messenger to her immediately and another to Brougham, summoning him to Connaught House.

Brougham, who was dining at Michael Angelo Taylor's, had worked on a law case nearly all the previous night and, thinking

---

[1] *Greville Memoirs*, ii. 327.   [2] Cornelia Knight, i. 305.
[3] For the Hesse affair see *Letters of George IV*, i. 516 seq., ii. 57 seq.

that the messenger was sent by the Princess of Wales, said that
he could not go. But he was informed that the message was
urgent and a coach was waiting for him. He slept all the way.
He stumbled up the stairs half-awake, to be greeted by the
Princess Charlotte, who ran to him, seized his hands and said
'I have just run off'. At Brougham's request she gave him a
brief outline of what had happened and said that the rest would
have to wait till after dinner, which she had ordered. Miss
Mercer was with the Princess, she and the Bishop of Salisbury
having been sent to her by her father as those most likely to
bring her to reason. The Bishop had returned to the Regent
with a proposal from the Princess that she would return if Miss
Knight and her maid were reinstated, and Miss Mercer was
permitted to visit her freely. She would *not* return unless those
conditions were fulfilled. The Prince had summoned a group of
advisers. Lord Eldon, the Lord Chancellor, and Lord Ellenborough, the Lord Chief Justice, explained the legal aspects of
the situation; the Prince had absolute authority over his eighteen-
year-old daughter. The Bishop was sent back with a statement
that the Princess must return to her father unconditionally.

Before the Bishop of Salisbury returned to Connaught Place,
the Princess of Wales arrived attended by Lady Charlotte
Lindsay, and the party sat down to dinner. When Brougham
protested that he had nearly finished dinner when the sum-
mons reached him, the Princess Charlotte said: 'But you may
eat a little bit with us, and at any rate you can carve.' Brougham replied that the only dish he could carve was the soup.
That set the tone for the dinner. They all assumed an air of
gaiety. The young Princess, according to Brougham, 'was in
high spirits, seeming to enjoy herself like a bird set loose from
its cage'.

When the Bishop of Salisbury returned he was not invited to
join the party dining on the first floor; he was shown into a room
on the ground floor where he had to wait. Lord Chancellor
Eldon, Lord Chief Justice Ellenborough, the Chancellor of
the Duchy of Lancaster and Leach, however, were even refused
admittance to the house. As the arrival of each in turn was announced at the dinner party, his exclusion was determined. The
Princess of Wales said that Lord Eldon was to stay outside,
which was highly pleasing to the Princess Charlotte who had an

old grudge against him. The Lord Chief Justice was to stay with 'Old Bags' (the Lord Chancellor). Leach and Adam arrived in hackney coaches. Although Lord Eldon and Lord Ellenborough were apparently in the latter's carriage, the belief or pretence of the party was that they were all in hackney coaches and the Princess Charlotte said that it would be good for them to become accustomed to that form of conveyance since she, as their future sovereign, had set the fashion for them. Brougham had sent for the Duke of Sussex, her favourite uncle, and he joined the party on the first floor.

The fun disappeared with the dinner dishes, and they settled to serious discussion, all turning to Brougham for advice. Brougham explained the law exactly as Eldon and Ellenborough had done at Carlton House. The Princess Charlotte must obey her father. She must return to him to Carlton House, and Brougham told her candidly that she should on no account spend the night under any other roof. She would have no choice except to return voluntarily or to do so under compulsion, for the Lord Chief Justice would not lose much time in issuing a writ of habeas corpus. (As a matter of fact, although Brougham was not aware of it, Ellenborough had a writ of habeas corpus with him. He was outside the fortress for the time being, but he sat entrenched in the law of the land.) Brougham's insistent advice was that she should return voluntarily.

Brougham said later that the young Princess 'was affected beyond description. I have told many a client he was going to be convicted, but I never saw anything like her *stupefaction*.' Her mother, the Duke of Sussex, Miss Mercer Elphinstone, and Lady Charlotte Lindsay all backed Brougham. He knew that the Regent would never consent to her retention of Miss Knight but he suggested that she write a note to her father asking if she might be free to see Miss Mercer and retain Miss Rawden. The Regent's position was still unconditional surrender.

The Duke of York arrived at three in the morning to take the Princess to her father. His Royal Highness was shown into the room downstairs where the Bishop of Salisbury was still waiting. The Princess had recovered her obstinacy and told Brougham tearfully that he had deserted her, when the people would have supported her. Brougham took her to a window to explain what an appeal to the people would mean.

I have but to show you to the multitude which in a few hours will fill the streets and that park, and possibly Carlton House will be pulled down, but, in an hour after, the soldiers will be called out, blood will flow, and if your Royal Highness lives a hundred years, it will never be forgotten that your running away from your home and your father was the cause of the mischief; and, you may depend upon it, the English people so hate blood that you will never get over it. . . . Through the rest of your life you will never escape the odium which, in this country, always attends those who by breaking the law occasion such calamities.

At last the Princess said that she would go with the Duke of York to her father. But before she did so she asked Brougham to draw up a minute to the effect that she could never willingly marry the Prince of Orange and that if such a marriage were announced, it should be made known that it was without her consent and against her will. All present signed the minute.[1]

Brougham and the Duke of Sussex had assured the Princess Charlotte on the night of her flight that her friends would support her. During the next few days they bent their energies on whipping up parliamentary discussion. Brougham urged Grey to come from Howick to speak in Parliament.[2] On the 19th the Duke of Sussex asked five questions in the House of Lords which were written out for him by Brougham.[3] Did the Princess Charlotte have that degree of communication with her friends which she had enjoyed before she left Warwick House? Was she as free to send and receive letters as previously and was she able to use pen, ink, and paper? Was she 'in that state of liberty

[1] This scene at Connaught Place is based on four accounts by Brougham, the only first-hand descriptions of it: a letter to Lord Grey of the following day, *Memoirs*, ii. 233 seq., and later accounts in the *Edinburgh Review*, Apr. 1838, pp. 31–35, the *Law Review*, xi. 280 seq., and *Memoirs*, ii. 226 seq. Miss Knight gave an account of her own movements during the evening (i. 304–60), but she was at Connaught House for only short periods. The window incident does not appear in the letter to Lord Grey and the dinner is described only in Brougham's last two accounts. There are slight differences in all of his accounts but no serious contradiction. Brougham said in his Memoirs that he showed what must have been his *Edinburgh Review* statement to the Duke of Sussex before it was published and that the Duke substantiated it, whilst making a few trifling corrections. Miss Mercer and Lady Charlotte Lindsay were living at that time and also in 1845 when the *Law Review* account was published. There is no record of any dissent. There is a brief account in the Creevey Manuscripts where a note by Creevey states that the Princess of Wales described the scene to him, apparently with no digression from Brougham. For the sake of the reader I have changed the tense where Brougham made a shift of tenses.   [2] *Memoirs*, ii. 236–7.

[3] Creevey MSS., Brougham to Creevey [23 July 1814].

which persons considered not in confinement ought to be in?'
Had not the physicians prescribed sea bathing for her? Was it
intended that she should have an establishment suitable to her
rank?[1] The effect on the public mind of these questions by the
brother of the Prince Regent, and of the reply of the Government that these were not matters proper for parliamentary discussion, may be readily imagined.

The popularity of the young Princess and the unpopularity of
the Regent reached a height that was unprecedented. Noting
the measure of his success, Brougham was all for letting matters
rest as they were on 21 July when he left for the Northern
Circuit. 'One sympton of success is *The Times* wheeling around
in a night just as it did in Mrs. P.'s case. This is a sign of almost
infallible certainty.'[2] Brougham had also learned that there
would be little help from the Whigs. Grey and Holland were
exceptions, along with the Duke of Sussex, Brougham, and
Whitbread (who, however, had nothing to do with this matter).
Although there was illness in his family, Lord Grey made the
long trip from Howick to support the Princess Charlotte in
Parliament. He made a good speech but he discovered that
Brougham was right about the rest of his party hanging back
and he concurred in Brougham's suggestion that the parliamentary discussion should be suspended.[3]

Brougham wrote to the Princess of Wales from York a last
desperate appeal, in which he repeated what he had frequently
said to her before, but in a somewhat blunter fashion:

. . . Depend upon it, Madam, that there are many persons who
now begin to see a chance [if she lives abroad] of divorcing your
Royal Highness from the Prince. . . . As long as you remain in this
country I will answer for it that no plot can succeed against you. But
if you are living abroad and surrounded by base spies and tools who
will be always planted about you, ready to invent and to swear as
they may be directed, who can pretend to say what may happen.[4]

In the meantime the Princess Charlotte was in the position of
a prisoner subject to restrictions that were humiliating and cruel
in effect if not in intention. But the suffering that they involved

[1] *Hansard*, xxviii. 7, 55 seq.
[2] Creevey MSS., Brougham to Creevey [23 July].
[3] *Memoirs*, ii. 243–6, Grey to Brougham, 26 July 1814.
[4] Ibid. ii. 253 seq., 30 July 1814.

was not nearly so great as that imposed upon her by hearing of her mother's decision. Miss Mercer Elphinstone wrote to Lady Charlotte Lindsay on 29 July a letter that has been preserved among the Brougham manuscripts:

I am just returned from Cranbourne Lodge. . . . I have long been of opinion that most of the Princess Charlotte's illness depends upon the state of her mind, and I am now more convinced of it than ever from the dreadful effect of her mother's letter announcing her departure from England had upon her. I really never can forget the distress and agitation she was in at the first moment, and even when I left her two days after, her pulse continued at 98. . . . Let me entreat you to use every exertion of your influence for Princess Charlotte's sake, to induce the Princess not to make a long absence, which would be so ruinous, both to the interest of mother and daughter.[1]

But heedless of all warnings the Princess of Wales sailed for the Continent on 8 August.

Meanwhile Brougham continued to befriend the Princess Charlotte, who wrote to Miss Mercer Elphinstone, 16 November: 'I cannot tell you what a support I feel B[rougham] is for my comfort, and delight at thinking too so able a person *still remains* my mother's *protector*. . . . This raises him higher than ever in my opinion, for certainly she does not deserve it of him, as her conduct has been anything but grateful.'[2]

The conduct of the Princess of Wales was soon giving rise to scandal. There were already spies at work as Brougham had predicted, though the campaign of the Prince's friends and employees did not come into full force until nearly a year later. But, in any case, they did not invent Bergami. He was engaged by the Princess as courier in mid-October of 1814. Whether or not his background was that of a 'good family' and he had come down in the world, certainly under the Princess's solicitous interest, he went up very fast in her service from waiting at table to chamberlain and frequent companion. Within a relatively short time she designated him 'Baron'. To say the least, the Princess made a complete fool of herself over this handsome courier. All sorts of honours were heaped on Bergami, several members of his family were taken into the Princess's service, his brother was promoted from the status of a servant to a place at the Princess's table, and his sister, a woman of no education, was, in May

[1] Brougham MSS., 'Friday' [29 July].   [2] *Letters of the Princess Charlotte*, p. 167.

1815, appointed as her lady-in-waiting under the title of 'the
Countess Oldi'. It was natural that a flood of gossip should
reach England from English gentlemen and ladies on the Continent. They suggested adultery before there was any *organized*
investigation by friends of the Prince. With one exception this
gossip need not be quoted here. Ward (later Lord Dudley and
Ward) had been a close friend of the Princess and had never
been estranged from her; he was also, in general, a good friend
and a great admirer of Brougham. And on 5 November 1815
he wrote: 'From what I heard in Italy . . . I imagine that
"Injured Innocence" which made such a run two years ago
would be hissed off the stage.'[1]

Ward was quite right about 'Injured Innocence', so far as
the upper classes were concerned. But he was wrong if he had
any thought of relating his remark to the middle and lower
classes. They heard little directly about the Princess's conduct
on the Continent, and Brougham had impressed 'Injured Innocence' so strongly on their minds that, on the whole, they
remained devoted to it. And for those classes he was to stage a
great popular revival of it in 1820.

Earlier that year in July 1815, Brougham had lost his partner
in the championing of the Princess of Wales. At the time of
Whitbread's suicide while of unsound mind, Brougham was very
ill himself. We can accept the sincerity of his eulogies of Whitbread and of his statement to Lord Grey that Whitbread's death
threw him back more than he could describe.[2] In personal
matters Brougham's emotions were always quick and intense.

The reports he received from the Continent did not help
Brougham's health. Common gossip about the Princess of Wales
he did not credit readily, but he had informants who were more
reliable. An indirect source of information was Lady Charlotte
Campbell, lady-in-waiting, who was shocked and frightened by
the Princess's conduct. 'I live in fear every moment of having
the horrid stories confirmed before my eyes.'[3] She wrote a letter
to Lady Charlotte Lindsay (who had left the Princess in March)
in which much more definite statements must have been made.

[1] *Letters to Ivy*, p. 292.
[2] *Memoirs*, ii. 287, 10 July 1815.
[3] Lady Charlotte Bury, *Diary illustrative of the Times of George IV*, 2 vols. (1838–9),
ii. 209.

For Lady Charlotte Lindsay, then in London, immediately wrote to Brougham a letter dated 4 August 1815:

I enclose a letter just received from Lady C.C. Nothing can be worse than the state of things described in it, but yet I do not see what can be done more than we have done. . . . Writing explicitly would be dreadfully dangerous and probably quite inefficacious for if the person alluded to is still fond of her birds all will continue as it is, and if she is beginning to tire of them, she will make the advice her excuse for dismissing the aviary in some sullen and offensive manner that will only hasten the ruin. . . . However I submit this to your better judgment. Perhaps a strong letter advising extreme caution of conduct from a certainty of her being watched, and watchful particularly in regard to this domestic bird might be advisable. . . . I think that a letter from you will be more attended to than one from me.[1]

Brougham wrote a letter to the Princess which he did not sign, and which must have been copied in a hand different from his own. To Lady Charlotte Lindsay, who apparently possessed safer means of communication, he wrote:

. . . You may give her a hint of its being from me, . . . And you also may tell her I was afraid to write more explicitly for fear of accidents. . . . The Princess's salvation depends on her seeing the thing in its proper light, and moreover she must recollect that her pension would all go the moment any mischance befell her. . . . We must help her out of this worst of scrapes *coute qu'il coute*. Pray say all this in your own words and burn this. . . . I am somewhat better, though still far from well.[2]

On 5 December Brougham wrote a candid and confidential letter to Lord Grey:

. . . The accounts of the Princess of Wales are worse and worse. She embarked on the 17th of November for Palermo, courier and all. . . . On her daughter's account I hope that she may not be got rid of, and it may be said that bad treatment drove her to it originally. My opinion is that they will be afraid to touch her, at least until they have evidence of *English witnesses*, for no Italian would be believed; but the voyage may supply this defect in their case.[3]

In the year 1815 the Regent moved definitely toward a divorce and began to use his public servants on the Continent

---

[1] Brougham MSS.   [2] Ibid., 'Friday'.   [3] *Memoirs*, ii. 298.

with that in view. Baron Ompteda, his Hanoverian envoy to the Vatican, was employed to spy on the Princess of Wales and her 'baron'. Ompteda's activities appear to have begun in March of that year when he followed her from Naples to Rome, beginning to establish himself as her friend.

Ompteda was operating in what was then Austrian territory and Lord Castlereagh, as Foreign Secretary, brought in his brother, Lord Stewart, British Ambassador at Vienna, to aid Ompteda. Castlereagh informed Lord Stewart that there were two objects: (1) to obtain evidence for a divorce, and (2) failing that a body of evidence that would justify the Prince Regent in refusing to receive his wife in England.[1]

In the summer of 1816 Caroline, Princess of Wales, made a pilgrimage to Jerusalem, where in July she set up an Order of St. Caroline with Bergami as Grand Master of the Order! The diplomas of the Order of St. Caroline, which the Princess granted to several of those who had accompanied her to Jerusalem, described Bergami's new honours in the following terms: 'The Colonel Bartholomew Bergami, Baron of Francina, Knight of Malta, and of the Holy Sepulchre of Jerusalem, equerry of her Royal Highness, shall be Grand Master of this Order, and his children, males as well as females, shall succeed him, and shall have the honour to wear this same order from generation to generation forever.'[2]

On 2 May 1816 the Princess Charlotte had been married to Prince Leopold. On 6 November 1817 she died in childbirth. The grief of the nation was unprecedented in that generation. The British Government did not send any word to her mother, a cruelty which the British people did not forget. Brougham, who had distrusted the young Princess at first, had acquired a real affection for her. And in that bleak November all his dreams of supreme political opportunity in the reign of Queen Charlotte I passed into the outer darkness. His hopes of saving the older Princess from disgrace were imprisoned in fog. There was no foretelling the supreme drama of three years later, in which he was to share with her the centre of the stage.

[1] Papers previously in H.O. 126. 3 and now in the Windsor Archives. The letter is given in Lewis Melville, *An Injured Queen* (1912), ii. 383–5, with some mistakes and with Castlereagh's strongest words in regard to the Princess carefully omitted.
[2] *Trial of Queen Caroline*, ed. J. Nightingale, 3 vols. (1821), iii. 130.

CHAPTER IX

The Cause of the Slaves, 1807–20

IN striking contrast to Brougham's efforts as an ambitious politician to whip up sentiment in support of such a woman as Caroline of Brunswick was his unselfish devotion in those same years to the Negroes of the West Indies and to the education of the poor in Great Britain. The enslaved Negroes were neglected by the British public partly because of the war and the sufferings of thousands in Britain itself, but largely because of the apathy that usually descends like a cloud after the success of a great reforming movement. The British slave trade had been 'abolished', an abolition act had been placed on the statute books and the conscience of the nation in relation to the sufferings of the Negroes folded its hands and slept.

The abolitionists had all assumed that since after the slave trade was abolished the planters would have to depend on natural increase for keeping up their supply of labour, better treatment of the slaves would inevitably ensue and the evils connected with slavery would gradually disappear. It is true that in a vague way they envisaged ultimate emancipation as a far-off divine event, but none of them dreamed of it as a possibility in his lifetime. They were called 'abolitionists' because they had abolished the *slave trade*. They were not 'emancipationists' as yet. That was to cause much confusion in later years, one result of which was that Wilberforce came to be called the Great Emancipator. He was the great abolitionist in the sense in which that term was employed in this period.

In 1807 the abolitionists founded the African Institution. As the name implies, the primary object was to work for the civilizing of Africa and the Africans. As a secondary aim, the African Institution undertook to watch for evasions of the Abolition Act and to work for the suppression of the slave trade conducted by other nations. This organization made no attempt at popular appeal. Its annual meetings were poorly attended. In a short time financial difficulties were encountered which could easily have been averted if there had been anything approaching zeal in the peers whose names lent prestige to its list of Vice-Presidents.[1] A few of those peers, however, displayed an active interest, notably the Duke of Gloucester, Lord Grenville, Lord Grey, and Lord Lansdowne.

The real importance of the African Institution was that it held together the 'abolitionist' leaders. Sir George Stephen, son of one of the greatest of those leaders, stated that 'for working purposes' the Committee of the Institution 'might be reduced to fifteen names', of which ten were those of members of the House of Commons. Four of them were members of the 'Clapham Sect', that remarkable group of neighbours at Clapham, whose religious zeal filled the sails of so many movements of that time.[2]

It is easy to select the four great leaders—Wilberforce, Macaulay, Brougham, and Stephen. In every recorded conference of the later days of the movement for abolition, Wilberforce had called in Macaulay, Stephen, and Brougham. These four, together with Buxton who replaced Wilberforce when ill health prevented the latter from playing an active part, became the great leaders in the later movement for the emancipation of the slaves.

The life of Wilberforce written by his sons implies, out of an excess of filial piety, that Wilberforce formulated all the policies of this period himself and called the others into conference to obtain their consent. From other sources it is clear enough that the policies emanated from the conferences which Wilberforce arranged. The extracts from Wilberforce's diary are the most valuable part of the biography. It may be assumed that the names given in connexion with the conferences included in the diary extracts give a fair indication of the attendance at all conferences held. In the years 1810 to 1818 twelve conferences are noted in the diary extracts. Stephen attended 9 of these, Brougham 9, Zachary Macaulay 8, William Smith 5, Lord Lansdowne 5, and others in lesser number. Of the three where Brougham's name does not appear, two belong to the year 1815

[1] See Sir George Stephen, *Anti-Slavery Recollections* (1854), pp. 57, 75–76, on the weakness of the African Institution. See also Birtwhistle, *The Development of Abolitionism, 1807–1823*, a thesis for the M.A. degree in the University of London, still in typescript, a valuable study of the period covered in this chapter.

[2] For the Clapham Sect see E. M. Howse, *Saints in Politics* (1952).

during which Brougham suffered the first severe illness of his life and for many months was not able to get to London. Probably similar circumstances account for the few absences of Stephen and Macaulay, and one concludes that those three were always summoned.

Zachary Macaulay was one of the great men of history whose memory has been eclipsed by that of a famous son. At the age of sixteen, in 1784, he was sent by a Scottish business firm to a Jamaican plantation to be 'book-keeper' (assistant to the overseer). He went out without any prejudice against slavery. His father, a Presbyterian minister, was satisfied that it was not for man to condemn the institution of slavery which God had sanctioned in Scripture.[1] That was the general Christian attitude of the time. But Zachary Macaulay saw for himself: 'I was exposed not only to the sight, but also to the practice of severities over others, the very recollection of which makes my blood run cold. . . , My mind was feelingly alive to the miseries of the poor slaves.'[2] He had five years of it. Before he returned to England his sister had married Thomas Babington who was a friend of Wilberforce and a member of the small anti-slave-trade group in Parliament. Babington's religious influence on Macaulay was very marked and carried him into the strong tide of Evangelical Anglicanism.

Young Macaulay was sent to Sierra Leone to help bring hope out of peril for that refuge for free Negroes and foothold for the civilizing of Africa. He became Governor of Sierra Leone at the age of twenty-six and his five years' governorship was as heroic as it was successful. After the drive against the slave trade was revived in 1804, Macaulay was taken by Wilberforce into every conference along with Brougham and Stephen. He was secretary of the African Institution for some years, and editor of the *Anti-Slavery Reporter* during nearly the whole of the movement for emancipation, of which he was the great organizer.

He was described as a 'stern silent man with quick step and keen grey eyes'.[3] The silence prompted the statement that he was 'the silent father of the greatest talker that the world has

---

[1] Sir George Otto Trevelyan, *Life and Letters of Lord Macaulay*, 2 vols., 1908 ed., i. 22.

[2] Charles Booth, *Zachary Macaulay* (1934), p. 9.

[3] J. S. Colquhoun, *William Wilberforce*, 2nd ed. (1867).

ever known'.[1] His religion was correspondingly undemonstrative. His grandson wrote: 'He was not one who dealt in personal experiences; and few even among his friends knew how entirely his outward behaviour was the express image of his religious belief'.[2] That religion was essentially practical. There was no thought of waiting on the Almighty with folded hands. No opportunity was to be missed, no detail overlooked, no hour to be wasted. Behind all that was an abiding sensitivity to the divine presence and the divine will.

There were times when the spirit of Wilberforce was willing but the flesh was weak, and Brougham with his other interests and commitments could not approach Macaulay's concentration. Macaulay supplied the cause with facts, accurate and irrefutable. Nothing escaped him. He devoured blue books, carried on a voluminous correspondence, studied every slave law, exposed every unsatisfactory provision, spotted every injustice. He could analyse and abridge with amazing rapidity. And no fact once captured ever escaped him. His trick memory retained the very words of what he had read and every nuance of meaning. His colleagues regarded him as a walking encyclopaedia, and in their need followed the advice of Wilberforce: 'Let us look it up in Macaulay.' He could assail his readers effectively with facts, although his literary style was as graceless as his person. He supplied the evidence which Stephen moulded into argument and which Wilberforce and Brougham transmuted into feeling. They were dependent on this intellectual and moral prodigy who rose to work at four o'clock every morning.

As Zachary Macaulay was the mightiest worker among those who befriended and ultimately freed the slaves, he was also the most dauntless. It was his spirit, much more than that of Wilberforce, that sustained the little group of leaders, and it continued to do so after Wilberforce was no longer active. Among Macaulay's heartening messages was one written to Buxton in 1831: 'Defeat I regard not. Let us do our duty and leave the issue to Him. . . . You dread failure. I have no such dread.'[3]

James Stephen was the ablest pamphleteer of the anti-slavery

---

[1] F. W. Cornish, *The English Church in the Nineteenth Century*, quoted in Howse, p. 21.

[2] Sir George Otto Trevelyan, i. 26.   [3] Booth, p. 63.

group. The movement produced a flood of pamphlets but none were as effective or played as important a role as those written by Stephen. His *Slavery Delineated* has been called the textbook of the cause. Stephen was ten years older than Zachary Macaulay and twenty years older than Brougham. When a young man of twenty-five on his way to St. Kitts to practise law in that West Indian island, he stopped off at Bridgetown in Barbados. There he got his first glimpse of the West Indies and West Indian justice. Two Negro slaves were most unjustly convicted and executed. James Stephens wrote in 1830: 'If I have contributed in any degree to the abolition of the slave trade, or shall ever have the happiness to promote the deliverance of its much injured victims in our colonies, the blood that was cruelly shed at Bridgetown, forty-seven years ago, was not shed in vain.'[1]

After a legal practice of ten years' duration at St. Kitts in which he learned much about the slave trade as well as about slavery, he returned to England, married Wilberforce's sister, and enjoyed for some years the largest practice in the Court of Prize Appeal. In Parliament he was a rather indifferent speaker on the Tory side. Like Brougham, Stephen hit hard. He could be as ruthless in writing as Brougham was in speech. Both left it to their opponents to look after themselves. When he was excited, his eyes gleamed like stars. On one occasion the quiet and balanced Zachary Macaulay turned to George Stephen and said: 'In anger your father is terrific.'[2]

Among the immortals Wilberforce, of course, occupies a niche all his own as a saint of spiritual achievement and heroic devotion. He had other qualities too, which are not necessarily a part of saintliness. Mme de Staël said that he was the best conversationalist and the wittiest man that she had met in England. His step-nephew, Sir James Stephen, stated that his blending of seriousness with 'the most contagious mirth' 'threw over his conversation a spell which no prejudice, dullness or ill-humour could resist'. 'His presence was as fatal to dullness as to immorality. His mirth was as irresistible as the first laughter of childhood.'[3] And Colquhoun described him as: 'Talking, jesting,

[1] James Stephen, *Slavery of the British West India Colonies Delineated*, 2 vols. (1824–30), ii. 27–29.
[2] Sir George Stephen, pp. 32–33.
[3] Article on Wilberforce in *Edinburgh Review*, Apr. 1838, written by Sir James Stephen.

joyous . . . with that silver voice of his, musical as a lark and lively as a boy.'[1]

According to Sir George Stephen, Wilberforce was indolent, 'destitute of system and desultory in his habits', indecisive, lacking in confidence. He had 'too much deferential regard for rank and power'.[2] Sir James Stephen, less severe than his brother, made the following comment on Wilberforce's leadership:

He was indeed associated with those whose aid would have assured the triumph of energies incomparably inferior to his. . . . He was aided by the genius and philanthropy of Henry Brougham, and by the affection and self-denial and unexampled energy of his brother-in-law, Mr. Stephen, and of Mr. Zachary Macaulay. It may further be admitted that systematic and very continuous labour were not consonant with his intellectual character or with the habits of his life. . . . But it required a mind as versatile and active, and powers as varied as were those of Mr. Wilberforce to harmonize all minds, to quicken the zeal of some, and to repress the intemperance of others, to negotiate with statesmen of all political parties.[3]

Brougham's habitual sharpness of tone almost entirely disappeared in his account of Wilberforce in *Statesmen in the Time of George III.*

He was naturally [he wrote] a person of great quickness and even subtilty of mind, with a lively imagination, approaching to playfulness of fancy; and hence he had wit in an unmeasured abundance and in all its varieties. . . . His eloquence was of a very high order. It was persuasive and pathetic in an eminent degree. But it was occasionally bold and impassioned, animated with the inspiration which deep feeling alone can breathe into spoken thought, chastened by a pure taste, varied by extensive information, enriched by classical allusion, sometimes elevated by the more sublime topics of Holy Writ, the thoughts and the spirit 'that touched Isaiah's hallowed lips with fire'. . . .

When a well-known popular member thought fit to designate him repeatedly, and very irregularly as the '*honourable and religious* gentleman', not because he was ashamed of the Cross he gloried in, but because he felt indignant at any one in the British senate deeming piety a matter of reproach, he poured out a strain of sarcasm which none who heard it can ever forget. A common friend of the parties having remarked to Sir Samuel Romilly, beside whom he sat, that

[1] Colquhoun, p. 29.   [2] Sir George Stephen, pp. 79–80.
[3] *Edinburgh Review*, Apr. 1838.

this greatly outmatched Pitt himself, . . . 'Yes' said he, 'it is the most striking thing I almost ever heard; but I look upon it as a more singular proof of Wilberforce's virtue than of his genius, for who but he ever was possessed of such a formidable weapon, and never used it.'[1]

The most fruitful policies of the period of this chapter were the enforcement of the abolition by making the slave trade a felony, the registration of slaves, and the massing of petitions against the foreign slave trade; the first was suggested by Brougham, the second by Stephen, the third probably by Romilly and certainly opposed by Wilberforce. From 1807 on to 1833 it is not one great leader that should challenge our attention but a great team. As they advanced into the movement for emancipation after 1822, Buxton, for all his devotion and astuteness, was no adequate replacement for the stricken Wilberforce, but that fact was compensated by the emergence of a number of secondary leaders, including Lushington and William Smith, who made the team stronger than ever.

Brougham's friendship with each of these men ran strong and deep. The friendship between Zachary Macaulay and Brougham was so precious that even Zachary's famous son, whose inhibitions on censoriousness were as feeble as Brougham's, and who wrote the most bitter things about Brougham in his private letters, said that he refrained from attacking him openly because of his father's friendship.[2]

With Stephen it was different. In 1808 and 1812 they were engaged in the bitter struggle over the Orders in Council, Brougham as the leader of the attack, Stephen as the principal author of the Orders and their most spirited defender. The cause of the slaves was not injured directly but personal friendship was affected for the time being. Brougham referred later to a quarrel with Stephen at this time which lasted for two years.[3] Yet just before the Liverpool election of 1812, at a time when he was undoubtedly smarting from his defeat by Brougham on the Orders in Council, Stephen, himself a Tory member of Parliament, wrote to John Gladstone a 'warm letter' backing Brougham for one of the Liverpool seats. That was without Brougham's

[1] *Works*, iii. 343-5.
[2] *Napier Correspondence*, p. 263, T. B. Macaulay to Napier, 20 June 1838.
[3] Add. MSS. 34619, f. 372 seq. (Napier MSS.), Brougham to Napier, 8 Sept. 1838.

knowledge, but he learned about it apparently a few days later.[1] After 1812 the old friendship was renewed.

When Brougham came into office in 1830 he made no secret of the fact that in the distribution of patronage he would not pay very much attention to party. He was equally candid in his resolution to do everything he could for his anti-slavery friends. He gave his first available living to a son of Zachary Macaulay, obtained for another son a good position in Africa, and secured a commissionership for Zachary himself.[2] He gave a living to a son of Wilberforce and another to a son-in-law.[3] An appointment for a son of Clarkson was solicited from a colleague. Three years earlier, during the Canning coalition government, Brougham used his influence with Lyndhurst to obtain a position as a Commissioner of Bankruptcy for Thomas Babington Macaulay.

The others in this group were knit together by a common religious outlook; Brougham was a warm-hearted and generous humanitarian rather than a fervently religious man. Yet his humanitarianism was a spiritual force that possessed a tremendous drive. He always appreciated religion as a social dynamic and appreciated it most when it was eminently reasonable in character as had been the religion of his Scottish Presbyterian forebears and his great-uncle Robertson. The religion of the 'Clapham Sect' was always a social dynamic eminently reasonable, a practical laymen's religion, tolerant and co-operative, and precisely the type of religion with which Brougham could most deeply sympathize. They were Evangelical Anglicans, the Evangelical tone coming from Whitefield rather than from Wesley. Whitefield's influence had been strong on Milner, Simeon, Venn, and Newton and it should be borne in mind that it *was exercised entirely within the bounds of the Church of England.* Wilberforce was 'converted' under the influence of Milner and Newton, Simeon's influence on the 'Clapham Sect' was strong, and Venn's son was the rector of Clapham. The members of the Clapham group were, like Whitefield, Calvinistic Evangelicals and they were entirely free from the hyper-emotional vagaries of the Methodists, who, in fact, contributed nothing to the leadership of the anti-slavery movement.

[1] Creevey MSS., Brougham to Creevey [7 Sept. 1812].
[2] *Napier Correspondence*, p. 99, T. B. Macaulay to Napier.
[3] Add. MSS. 34619, f. 372 (Napier MSS.), Brougham to Napier.

When Sydney Smith had launched his vicious attack on the Methodists in the *Edinburgh Review* of January 1808, Brougham had been indignant at Sydney's lumping Methodists and Evangelical Anglicans together. He had held up to ridicule, Brougham said, 'views which such men as Wilberforce and Henry Thornton, Babington, Stephen, and Macaulay were just as incapable of falling into as Sydney Smith himself'. 'Of all the offences' of Sydney Smith, this attack on the Evangelical Anglicans 'was the worst'.[1]

To these friends of the Negro slaves there was opposed a powerful and highly developed organization. The assemblies of the West Indian colonies displayed a united front and employed active and able agents in Great Britain. The more immediate opposition was centred in London where several bodies were headed by a West Indian Committee which directed the warfare in the interests of 1,800 plantation owners, 1,200 of whom were in 1807 resident in England, and the British merchants active in trade with the West Indies. Many of the slave-owners were peers of the realm and the powerful economic interests infiltrated the most influential families. We realize today that one of the glories of the Church of England was the fact that all of the greatest anti-slavery leaders were laymen within its ranks, but, as so often happens, officialdom was the enemy of spiritual power and many of the official leaders of the Church were active in prejudicing public opinion against Brougham and his Evangelical anti-slavery colleagues.

This organized interest carried on a constant propaganda and always had at its disposal a group of able pamphleteers. It has been estimated that it controlled from sixty to seventy pocket-boroughs.[2] That would mean over 120 members of the House of Commons. The estimate may be too high. Lushington said in 1825 that fifty-six members of the House of Commons were personally interested in slavery,[3] but he apparently meant direct interest and did not include indirect interest of members who were bound to support the political owners of their boroughs, the borough-patrons. Many borough-patrons were slave-owners

---

[1] *Memoirs*, i. 262; Add. MSS. 34617, f. 54 v. (Napier MSS.), Brougham to Napier, 9 Mar. 1835.

[2] Booth, p. 81.

[3] *Anti-Slavery Reporter*, i. 7, cited by W. L. Mathieson, *British Slavery and its Abolition* (1926), p. 118.

in any case, but the West Indian Committee was active in buying up boroughs.[1] Against this parliamentary army the leaders of the cause of the slaves could, during the movement for emancipation, count on the votes of thirty to forty members of the House of Commons, Whigs and Tories, irrespective of party ties.[2] But the number was much smaller during this earlier period from 1807 to 1822. The leadership in debate in the Commons was carried after 1816 by Wilberforce and Brougham, and after 1823 by Brougham and Buxton, with able supporters as well as able opponents.

The leaders, of course, were confronted by more than vested interests and political power. The talk about Wilberforce and his Saints being canting hypocrites, careless liars, and hopeless fanatics was readily accepted by men who had no personal interests in the matter and less knowledge. It was echoed by a number who fancied themselves as smart writers, and by a few who could really write. Since Brougham had so little to say about religion, it would not do to call him a canting hypocrite. He had to be represented as a self-seeking politician capitalizing on the supposed wrongs of the Negroes. His political ambition was apparent enough and at times he was not scrupulous in its pursuit, but so far as slavery was concerned it was overcome by the noblest impulses. He had nothing to gain by incurring the opposition of such powerful parliamentary forces. His advancement in his own party could only be impeded by his zeal in this cause. Lord Grenville, Lord Grey, and Lord Lansdowne were sincere friends of the slaves, but the Whig party as a whole 'cared for none of these things'. The magnates on the right wing distrusted Brougham because he stood too far to the left, yet beyond him, farther to the left still, were Cobbett with his bitter pen, Burdett with his sneers in the Commons at Wilberforce's religion, and Hobhouse bored by Wilberforce's 'sermonizing about slavery'. If Brougham said little about slavery in his letters to Creevey and Place the explanation is easy; they were not interested. In the mass of Creevey manuscripts there are hardly ten lines on the subject and almost the sole reference by Creevey himself serves only to make Saints and missionaries the

[1] For the purchase of boroughs see L. J. Ragatz, *Fall of the Planter Class in the British Caribbean* (1928), p. 52.
[2] Sir George Stephen, p. 115.

butt of his sardonic humour. We have already seen that Brougham's defeat at Liverpool with its consequent four years' absence from Parliament was caused mainly by his anti-slave-trade activities and that the slavery interest maligned him unscrupulously for decades.

The African Institution accomplished very little in its early years, but its Board of Directors, to which Brougham belonged, became convinced that the abolition of the slave trade was not being enforced, that the law was being openly and flagrantly violated. It set itself to collect evidence of this and it was Brougham, no doubt, who instigated an article in the *Edinburgh Review* for April 1809 in which an appeal was made asking for further information. Brougham had decided that the only way to enforce the abolition was to have slave trading made a felony. In his great speech of 14 June 1810 he gave notice of his intention to bring in a bill to that effect in the following session. He first discussed the question of the foreign slave trade and suggested arrangements for mutual right of search with other nations. Thus Brougham launched himself on a subject—the influence of the British government in securing a complete world abolition of the trade—which was to engage his interest and zeal into old age.

The real purpose of the speech, however, was to urge the enforcement of the British abolition. Brougham dealt with the evasions of the law. Vessels were fitted out in British ports, ostensibly for legitimate trade, with all the 'properties' of the slave trade carefully concealed. 'I hold in my hand the record of a court of justice, which throws so much light on the subject, that I moved on a former night to have it laid on the table.' On this ship had been found 'ninety-three pairs of handcuffs, a hundred and ninety-seven iron shackles for the feet, thirteen hundred and three quarters weight of iron chains; one box of "religious implements" and "that the bodily as well as the spiritual health of this human cargo might not be neglected, the slave merchants out of their rare humanity . . . allowed, for the medical wants of eight hundred negroes of all ages, crammed into a loathsome cage, and carried through new and perilous climates during a voyage of weeks or even months—one little medicine chest, value £5"'.[1] Six other vessels similarly fitted out had been recently discovered in one British port.

[1] Sir George Stephen, pp. 32–33.

He calculated that the net profits of a single illegal slave voyage carrying 800 Negroes amounted to £60,000. That enabled the dealers to underwrite their own insurance against detection and fine.

Is this to be stopped by a pecuniary penalty? . . . If an inhuman being of this class fits out ten or twelve such ships and escapes with three or four, his vile profits are enormous; but it should be recollected that all his vessels, those which escape as well as those which are taken, spread devastation over the African continent; and even a single cargo is the utter ruin of whole villages. . . . While you levy your pence, the wholesale dealers in blood and torture pocket their pounds and laugh at your twopenny penalty.

He gave notice that he would bring in a bill early in the next session making slave trading a felony.[1]

In regard to Brougham's Slave Trade Felony Act of 1811, Sir George Stephen wrote in his *Anti-Slavery Recollections*:

He [Brougham] was strongly supported by all the Saints, and by many who were by no means saints, in carrying through Parliament, the second great measure in the cause—the Slave Trade Felony Bill. It was passed on the 14th of May 1811. I believe that the bill was partly, if not substantially, drawn by Mr. Stephen [Sir George's father]; all the merit of suggesting and carrying it belongs to Brougham. . . . Such was the terror that it excited . . . that there were very few prosecutions under it.[2]

Brougham's Felony Act was passed on 14 May 1811 and sounded 'the death-knell' of the British slave trade. The act made all buying or selling of slaves or carrying them with a view to sale on the part of any British subject anywhere or of any one in British territory, a felony punishable by transportation up to ten years or imprisonment with hard labour up to five years. The crime included the fitting out of a vessel for such trade or the hiring of it for that purpose, or sailing in it as master, mate, supercargo or surgeon, being aware of that purpose.[3]

During what may be regarded as the last months of the British slave trade, just before the Felony Act went into effect, a British ship, ostensibly carrying on a legitimate trade, was stopped and searched thoroughly. A false floor was discovered

---

[1] *Speeches*, ii. 19 seq.   [2] Sir George Stephen, pp. 9–10.
[3] Statutes of the Realm, 51 Geo. III, c. 23.

under which were 126 Negroes of both sexes 'crammed into a space in which they could barely exist', and in another ship slaves were discovered in a similar position concealed by an overlaid legitimate cargo.[1] That is the last of such stories so far as British ships were concerned. As a result of the first trial under the Felony Act, an assistant ship's surgeon who had become a factor was convicted of slave trading and sentenced to seven years' transportation; a Negro who had rendered him assistance was given three years' imprisonment with hard labour.[1] A few months later a British warship raided a trading-post on the African coast and the two proprietors were convicted of slave trading and each was sentenced to fourteen years' transportation.[2] After that there were very few prosecutions because there were no traders to prosecute.

If leglislation like Brougham's had been passed in other countries, an incalculable amount of human suffering would have been prevented in the next half century. The Government of the United States was the only one to take similar action. In 1824 it made slave-trading piracy punishable by death. But the American legislation was not enforced until Lincoln's time. Brougham was eighty-four when he heard of the first hanging of an American slave trader.

In those years the cause of the Negro slave was supported by articles in about half of the numbers of the *Edinburgh Review*, which had a circulation far surpassing that of the annual reports of the African Institution. Those reports were themselves all reviewed in the *Edinburgh* which thus greatly multiplied their publicity. Nearly all the articles were written by Brougham.

Six months after the passing of the Felony Act, Brougham opened up another aspect of West Indian slavery in an article in the *Edinburgh Review* for November 1811, which dealt mainly with the official account of the Hodge case. The Huggins and Hodge cases were usually discussed together and they were occasionally thrown together in this article. Huggins was a West Indian planter who on 23 January 1810, in the market-place of Charlestown in the island of Nevis, with his two sons and two expert whippers, had a group of twenty of his slaves flogged for running away after being ordered to perform a task the imposition of which was forbidden by law. The ten men received from

[1] *Edinburgh Review*, Feb. 1813.   [2] *The Times*, 30 Nov. 1813.

47 to 365 lashes each and the ten women from 49 to 251 each. Several were permanently incapacitated and one of the women died. The law in Nevis restricted the number of lashes to 40. Several magistrates and several clergymen were among those who watched the Huggins flogging. Apparently no one protested and certainly no attempt was made to stop the proceeding. Although Huggins had had a reputation for brutal cruelty for years no charge had been laid against him. But cognizance had to be taken of this public scene. Huggins was placed on trial, although the grand jury overlooked the fact that one woman had been flogged to death. He was duly acquitted of any violation of law by a jury, one member of which was his overseer and another the overseer of an estate owned by his son-in-law.

In this article in the *Edinburgh Review* Brougham made brief references to the Huggins case which had already been described in the 1811 report of the African Institution.[1] He discussed the Hodge case at length in reviewing the strenographic official record of the trial of Hodge on 25 and 29 April of this year 1811 in the island of Tortola. Hodge was a wealthy planter and a member of the Council of the Virgin Islands. Brougham afforded his readers an abridgement of this record, promising to spare their feelings by omitting some of the worst of it. We can give only a much briefer summary.

Hodge had on separate occasions during a period of five years flogged eight of his slaves to death—that is, they died as a result of repeated floggings, several of them lasting an hour without a break. In addition to those cases, two women died as a result of continual floggings and having boiling water poured down their throats, and two other slaves died after being whipped, almost starved, and burned in the mouth with a hot iron. A child had had its skin taken off by being immersed in a copper of boiling liquid. Several children had been strung up by their heels with their heads in tubs of water and kept there until almost stifled, taken out and allowed to recover their breath, and then had the treatment repeated several times. So much for the sworn evidence in detail. One of Hodge's managers testified that he was satisfied that Hodge 'lost sixty negroes at least by the severity of his punishments'.

In later ill-advised pamphlets the Huggins and Hodge cases

[1] *Fifth Report of the African Institution.* See also Ragatz, pp. 399–400.

were cited as typical of the cruelty of the planters toward their slaves. To pretend that the existence of these two maniacal sadists indicated universal cruelty was valueless and only injured the cause. Brougham's contention was that these cases illustrated the manner in which *law* was administered under West Indian slavery and the hopeless situation of the slaves unless the British government intervened to protect them. He had pointed to the acquittal of Huggins. In regard to Hodge he wrote:

In the small island and confined society of Tortola, every particular of his conduct was well known [for five years]. And yet . . . no one shunned his society, not a thought was ever harboured of turning him out of the Council, in which he held his rank till the day of his arrest. Still less did any one entertain the romantic idea of bringing him to trial for cruelty to black negroes. Laws, it is true, existed . . . but like many obsolete statutes in this country, they were never thought of.

But Hodge was a deadly duellist, and a judge who had been challenged or threatened by him felt that he had to place him on trial with a view to conviction, to save himself. For that reason the trial was thorough enough (for offences four and five years earlier). The evidence, of course, had to be that of white men because no evidence by Negroes or persons of colour against a proprietor could be accepted in a West Indian court. The jury after being out an hour brought in a verdict of Guilty, but on a majority vote made a *recommendation for mercy*! The governor rejected the recommendation and proclaimed martial law until after the date of execution.

Brougham continued in regard to the planter and overseer class and the colonial assemblies: 'They have pretended to meliorate the condition of their slaves, and the pretense has been constantly detected; they have passed laws for this purpose and they have been clearly convicted of passing them only to deceive the mother country.' On the face of them, there had been marked improvements in the legislative enactments of the colonial assemblies since the beginning of the agitation against the slave trade, but Brougham's statement that better laws were made to deceive the mother country was not just an instance of his tendency to exaggeration. It was fairly well borne out by what parliamentary committees there had been. Leaving the matter of legislative action on the part of the British Parliament for further consideration, Brougham suggested some things which the British government should do immediately, beginning with the more careful selection of governors and military commanders.

The persons so chosen should have no colonial property, and should not have power, directly or indirectly, to acquire any such interest. If possible, they should even have no colonial connections; and this qualification should be extended to every considerable officer on the West Indian establishments. . . . A similar degree of care should be shown in the choice of persons to fill judicial and other legal situations. . . . The strictest attention should, of course, be paid by government to investigate instantly every case of inattention or misconduct, and to make the most striking examples of persons behaving either negligently or blameably in their official capacities.

While Brougham did not suggest that the cruelty of Huggins and Hodge was typical of the conduct of planters and managers, he knew that a considerable amount of cruelty did exist and in alluding to it he brought his readers to a focal point in the whole slavery situation:

Nothing can eradicate from their minds (we speak of the bulk of the community) the idea that the negro is an inferior animal, that his sufferings should not affect the heart like those of a human being, that his comforts, his rights, his enjoyments, may be sported with, and yet no violence be done to notions of honour, nor any sting reach the conscience. . . . Negro slavery brings with it this excuse, at least, for those whom it corrupts, that it begins with the head before reaching the heart. . . . He who ill treats or permits the oppression of his slave, under the influence of those perverse notions of his being something between a man and a beast, can scarcely be so much blamed as he who, with his eyes open, torments a being whom he knows and feels to be his fellow.

And it was that very fact, Brougham insisted, that threw on those who thought differently and felt a human fellowship with the Negro the heaviest responsibility of interfering in his interest. Throughout this whole story, no man felt more deeply and no man urged as passionately and as eloquently that the attitude of the white man toward the black man must be the same as the attitude toward those of his own colour.

In an article in the *Edinburgh* for July 1812 he discussed the Spanish and Portuguese slave trade. The coast of Africa north of the equator, thanks to the war and the British Navy, was for the moment free from the slave trade, with, however, the important exception of the Portuguese island of Bissao near the mouth of the Rio Grande, which was easily reached from the coast by canoes. Brougham asked what the feeling would be if the French took possession of an island at the mouth of the Tagus and carried off Portuguese:

... so that those banks which used to swarm with Portuguese, became a perfect desert. Suppose the spoilers hurried them away in the most crowded vessels, where they were laid in chains on their backs and scourged ... every time they made a noise, till after eight weeks of such misery they ... only survived to suffer and labour more. ... These Africans are as much human beings, as much their fellow creatures as if ... they bore the features of European ugliness instead of the marks of African beauty, and inhabited the filth of Lisbon instead of the uncultivated richness of the Rio Grande.

In the course of this article there was more than a little exaggeration. We are reminded that Brougham in the full flood of condemnation seldom paused for 'buts' and 'althoughs'. We are also reminded that it was said later in the days of Palmerston's leadership against the foreign slave trade that neither Palmerston nor Brougham was quite accountable for his actions where the Negro was concerned.[1]

As the general election of 1812 approached, Wilberforce considered giving up his Yorkshire seat and seeking a less arduous constituency. Brougham wrote to him, 19 September, promising to use his influence with the Yorkshire Whigs to remove any serious opposition to Wilberforce's Tory candidature. In Wilberforce's letter of thanks there are expressions which illustrate their personal relationship:

From our earliest acquaintance you have accustomed me to expect from you all that is kind and friendly. ... But the die is cast. [He gave the reasons for his decision.] I have not, indeed I never had, my dear Brougham, without a compliment, your strength either of body or mind; and now, at fifty-three I really begin to be conscious that I am growing older. ... [In referring to Brougham's activity in writing *Edinburgh Review* articles in the cause.] I know you never plead *alibis* ... or conceive it is any reason you may not do a twentieth thing that you have already nineteen others on your hands.[2]

[1] Herbert C. Bell, *Lord Palmerston*, 2 vols. (1936), i. 235.
[2] *Memoirs*, ii. 43–47, 23 Sept. 1812.

A year later, in the autumn of 1813, Europe and Great Britain were looking forward hopefully to the blessings of peace and in the early months of 1814 peace was established. This emerging into sunshine meant to Africa a plunging into darkness. What brought joy to the white man meant untold suffering to the black man. During the war the British Navy was in a position to control all trade, the trade of neutrals as well as enemy trade, and the international slave trade was greatly reduced, large stretches of the African coast being entirely freed from it. With the coming of peace that control ceased. By that time most of the European nations had formally abolished the trade. But new economic pressures—the financial gains promised by a reborn French slave trade, plans for further slave-trade development of Spanish and Portuguese colonies—challenged the spiritual warfare of those whose only interest was that of the call of a common humanity. With the coming of peace, the international slave trade threatened to descend upon Africa with renewed force, new wars were waged to make captives who could be sold by the slave-traders, black children kidnapped not individually but by the score, families torn apart.[1]

When Brougham heard that the treaty with France provided for the maintenance of the French slave trade for a period of five years and afforded France all her old slave-trade depots on the African coasts, he wrote to Wilberforce on 7 June (1814) suggesting pressure on the allied sovereigns who had just arrived in England:

You may easily believe that I have thought of nothing but the treaty for two days past, and have each moment found out new cause of vexation and indignation. . . . A strong expression of the sense of parliament on this unexampled atrocity is the best means, and while the allies are here—if possible while they are present. Public meetings and addresses are another. I have set the City men upon inserting a great deal to this effect in their addresses [to the allied sovereigns], and hope it may go round. Lord Grenville should do so at Oxford: The Duke of Gloucester at Cambridge, if they go there.[2]

---

[1] For the sufferings inflicted by the slave trade see the references to Coupland in p. 31 ante; C. M. MacInnes, *England and Slavery* (1934), pp. 54–86; E. B. F. D'Auvergne, *Human Livestock* (1933), pp. 50 seq.

[2] *Correspondence of Wilberforce*, ii. 287–8; 'Tuesday', 7 June is the only possible date.

The 'sense of parliament', that is of the abolitionists in Parliament, was not expressed as 'strongly' as it might have been. There was plenty of disappointment expressed—by Wilberforce with his customary eloquence—but little direct condemnation of the Government. Wilberforce was afraid of antagonizing the Government and also feared that an attack would stimulate the Whigs and make the matter a party issue. He consulted Opposition leaders and obtained their consent to that line of policy.[1] But some were impatient with it, and in the *Edinburgh Review* for November someone wrote an article criticizing it in the most scathing terms. Stephen and apparently others believed that Brougham (who, of course, was out of Parliament) wrote it, and that occasioned another tiff between Stephen and Brougham. It is altogether likely that Brougham did write the article. The author was prepared to criticize his friends publicly, was an abolitionist himself, and was not at the time a member of the House of Commons. He was also courageous and extremely rude. Brougham told Stephen that he had no right to ask him if he had written the article, 'but if he desired to know my opinion respecting his own or his friends' conduct, I should give it to him in any shape he pleased and with the frankness which he had always experienced from me in our various conflicts'.[2] It was a year before Stephen wrote to Brougham suggesting that they 'cancel the recollection of the subject of our last correspondence. ... I wish to regain what I have lost by it, and that not only for my own gratification but for the sake of the interests of that great and sacred cause in which we are fellow labourers.'[3]

The sons of Wilberforce were to give the impression in their life of their father that he initiated the appeal to the public, with its response in a flood of petitions to Parliament, in regard to the foreign slave trade in 1814.[4] The evidence of Romilly's diary which, in view of Romilly's character, cannot be questioned, disproves this. Romilly urged 'a demonstration of public opinion on the subject of the article in the treaty respecting the slave trade'. At a meeting of the directors of the African Institution on 13 June he proposed a general meeting 'of all the friends of the abolition' to consider petitioning the Regent or Parliament.

---

[1] *Life of Wilberforce*, iv. 191–3.
[2] Creevey MSS., Brougham to Creevey [early in 1815].
[3] Brougham MSS., 26 Dec. 1815.   [4] *Life of Wilberforce*, iv. 197.

Wilberforce, 'who is always afraid of giving offence to ministers', opposed the proposal, saying that the resolutions might be too violent and that very few persons would attend such a meeting on account of the furore over the visit of the allied sovereigns. He was overruled by a large majority. The public meeting on 17 June was extremely crowded, and it was decided to have similar meetings held in all parts of the country from which petitions would be sent to Parliament. The mass-petition procedure may well have been suggested by Brougham's success with that method over the Orders in Council.

An article entitled 'Revival of the Slave Trade' appeared in the 'April', 1814, number of the *Edinburgh Review* which was not out until nearly the end of June, after the movement for petitions had begun. It was almost certainly written by Brougham. Some parts of it were almost verbal repetitions of statements made in articles known to have been written by him. It contained a caustic and sarcastic attack on the treaty quite in Brougham's style and referred to the public meeting of 17 June.

There may be a new treaty at the congress which is about to assemble [the Congress of Vienna]; and the detestable stipulation of five years of crime may be abandoned. The treaty of Utrecht obtained for England an increased slave trade as the reward of her sacrifices and her victories. . . . The peace of 1814 has rewarded the sufferings and crowned the triumph of the Allies by reviving the slave trade seven years after we had abolished it and three after we had declared it a felony. Let the people but speak out their sense of this last disgrace to their name, and no other minister will ever dare carry on a slave-trading negotiation.

Within a few weeks Parliament was deluged by 806 petitions signed by over 750,000 persons. Considering the population of England at that time it was a tremendous expression of national feeling. The Government immediately recognized that it had to respond to this demand that every possible effort against the international slave trade should be made at the Congress. Castlereagh wrote to his ambassador in Spain: 'The nation is bent upon this object. I believe that there is hardly a village that has not met and petitioned upon it; both Houses of Parliament are pledged to press it; and the ministers must make it the basis of their policy.'[1] At Vienna Castlereagh became a giant

[1] Castlereagh's *Correspondence*, x. 73, 1 Aug. 1814.

abolitionist. Wilberforce's fellow leaders came to agree fully with his conclusion that Castlereagh did everything that could have been done. But that was a mild statement with which to describe his heroic efforts in the face of the greatest difficulties.

His negotiations effected an agreement with Portugal, and one with Spain in the same year limiting its slave trade to south of the equator, in return for Great Britain waiving the repayment of a loan and handing over £300,000 in cash 'in satisfaction of some doubtful claims'. He prepared the way for the 1817 treaty with Spain. He persuaded all the European nations to put on paper a joint statement declaring that the universal abolition of the slave trade was 'a measure . . . conformable to the spirit of the times', which they would seek to effect 'with all the zeal and perseverance which is due to so great and noble a cause'.[1] Its sincerity was hardly substantiated by the conduct of the powers most concerned with the slave trade, but it was something to get it on paper as a statement that could always be appealed to in the future and as a basis for abolitionist activities that were ultimately successful. It was very difficult to deal with France, but when Napoleon escaped from Elba, influenced by the British mass petitions, he immediately made a play for British goodwill by abolishing the French slave trade. After the restoration the French Government felt it wise not to abrogate that action, though so far as France was concerned abolition was one thing and its enforcement something very different.

George Stephen, who as a young man knew a great deal of what was going on behind the scenes at this time, said that while Castlereagh and Wellington were 'justly entitled to the honour of carrying with a high hand the demands of unrepresented Africa, the stimulus which they found irresistible was in the hands of Brougham, Wilberforce and other drivers'.[2]

When Brougham returned to Parliament in 1816 he took up the matter of the slave trade in his first speech, and that on the first day of the session. He expressed the hope that they would shortly hear that the Government had induced Spain and

[1] For Castlereagh's efforts see, of course, Sir Charles Webster's great work on *The Foreign Policy of Castlereagh, 1812–15* (1931), pp. 413–24, *1815–22* (1925), pp. 454–66.
[2] Sir George Stephen, p. 48.

Portugal to agree to relinquish the slave trade.[1] On 9 July 1817 Wilberforce moved in the House of Commons a resolution of 'solicitude for the universal and final abolition of the African slave trade'. Brougham supported Wilberforce and said in the course of his speech: 'If the effectual abolition of all these enormous evils was contemplated, there appeared to be but one method of accomplishing the object, the adoption of some arrangement . . . which would establish a *mutual right of search*. This was the only way of guarding against the evasion.'[2]

In September of that year a treaty was signed with Spain by which Spain agreed to abolish immediately her slave trade north of the equator and to abolish it completely in 1820. To obtain that Great Britain gave the Spanish Government £400,000. The treaty provided for a limited mutual right of search, the navy of each country being empowered to stop and search ships suspected of carrying slaves and to convey them to points where 'mixed courts', with British and Spanish judges, were established. Castlereagh had not needed Brougham's prompting to insist on the mutual right of search, but Brougham had urged it as the only means of enforcing foreign abolition as early as 1810, four years before Castlereagh became active in suppressing the slave trade. Apparently Brougham was the first to propose it and he urged it constantly.

The Spanish treaty was presented to Parliament in the following January (1818). Several weeks later Brougham spoke of that treaty negotiated by Castlereagh with the highest praise, and in reply to criticism that the sum paid was too large, said that the mutual right of search alone was worth the £400,000, to say nothing of the rest of the treaty.[3] Castlereagh referred his ambassador in Holland to this statement when the latter suggested some presents for the King and others in relation to a treaty with Holland (signed 4 May 1818) establishing mutual right of search in certain areas for further suppression of the slave trade. 'When Brougham has declared that this concession [mutual right of search] was cheaply purchased from Spain by £400,000, you are not likely to be quarreled with for a single £1,000 snuff box.'[4] Portugal also agreed to a limited mutual right of search.

[1] *Hansard*, xxxii. 38, 1 Feb. 1816.   [2] *Hansard*, xxxvi. 1321–34.
[3] *Hansard*, xxxvii. 1174, 18 Mar. 1818.
[4] Sir Charles Webster, *Foreign Policy of Castlereagh, 1815–1822* (1931), p. 461 n.

The United States, however, had no naval strength sufficient for their own abolition and any slave trader could protect himself by flying an American flag. The American attitude at this time is understandable. Right of search had been involved in the two principal causes of the war of 1812.[1] But that no exception to a doctrinaire position on 'the freedom of seas' was made for such a humanitarian imperative, decade after decade, is one of the tragedies of history.

During these years the leaders were concerned with a project for the registration of slaves in the West Indies. This plan had a strange and significant history. Its original object was to check the alleged illegal importation of slaves into the British West Indies. That is, it began with the *slave trade*. Even after 1811 it was believed, though erroneously, that there was a considerable amount of importation. In the bitter controversy on the matter with the West Indian interest, the abolitionists came more and more to emphasize the value of registration in ameliorating the *conditions of slavery* in the West Indies. The condition of the West Indian Negroes became a major interest, and then, in the next decade (that of the twenties), the leaders came to the conclusion that *emancipation* was the only adequate solution, not emancipation as a far-off event, but emancipation as a practical objective to be worked for with all their energies in their own time. The registration project was an important link between 'abolition' and 'emancipation'.

The Government was persuaded to introduce registration of slaves in the Crown colony of Trinidad and to extend it later to the Crown colonies of St. Lucia and Mauritius. Their Trinidad Order in Council to that effect was issued in March 1812. Two months before that Stephen, Wilberforce, Brougham, and Romilly met at Stephen's house and decided that Wilberforce should introduce that year a bill to establish registration in all of the West Indian colonies. The Government persuaded them to postpone the measure until more time was afforded to the Trinidad experiment. In 1814 it was again postponed because full attention had to be given to the treaties. In February 1815 the leaders agreed that the Registration Bill should be introduced immediately. Then came a clash with the Government. It is

---

[1] For a complete discussion see Hugh G. Soulsby, *The Right of Search in Anglo-American Relations, 1814–1862* (1933).

clear enough that the Government disapproved of legislating in
this matter for colonies that had their own legislative assemblies.
The West Indians asserted that 'the Colonial Legislatives enjoy
the right of internal legislation to the exclusion of any right of
the British Parliament'.[1] Where something was to be accomplished for the whole of the West Indies which could not be
effectively handled by acts of separate legislatures, the Government was not averse to parliamentary legislation. But ministers
believed that registration was a matter that might well be left
to the separate legislatures. They wished to avoid constitutional
controversies with the West Indians, and they were not in any
case convinced at this time of the necessity for registration. On
1 March they told Wilberforce that 'they could not support a
registry bill for a want of proof of actual smuggling of slaves'.[2]
On this point they were probably right: it is now generally
agreed that there was very little evidence of smuggling after
1811.[3]

Stephen, impetuous and heroically devoted to the cause,
resigned his seat in Parliament when the Government refused
to support his measure. A Tory member, he declared that he
could no longer support the Government. He turned to the
writing of pamphlets and became the great pamphleteer of the
Negroes' cause. In that he could serve much more effectively
than in Parliament, where he was a poor speaker; parliamentary
debate would always be conducted with supreme ability by
Wilberforce and Brougham, who was back in the House within
a year of Stephen's resignation.

A consultation was held on 3 June (1815) and Romilly entered
the following in his diary for that day: 'Wilberforce, who is unwilling ever to act against the wishes of Government, has doubted
whether it will not be advisable farther to postpone doing anything, in the hope that next year the Ministers may see the
matter in a more favourable point of view. Everyone else present
. . . thought that the measure ought not to be delayed any
longer.'[4] Wilberforce gave way and consented to introduce the

---

[1] G. W. Jordan, *An Examination of the Slave Registration Bill* (1816), p. 62. See
Jordan, pp 143 seq., and contemporary newspapers for the Barbados Assembly
resolutions to that effect, 17 Jan. 1816.   [2] *Life of Wilberforce*, iv. 224 (Diary).
[3] W. L. Burn, *Emancipation and Apprenticeship in the British West Indies* (1937),
p. 77 n.; Mathieson, p. 27; W. J. Gardner, *History of Jamaica* (1873), p. 253.
[4] Romilly, *Memoirs*, ii. 368-9.

bill, which he did on 5 July, too late in the session to be able to proceed with it that year. Brougham, too ill to stir from his home, was not present at that consultation.

In the months that followed a bitter controversy was waged between the abolitionists and the West Indian interest, with a spate of pamphlets on each side. The abolitionists came to realize more fully the value of a registry bill in ameliorating the lot of the slaves: it would provide for the recording of many details on each estate—the number of deaths, causes of deaths, physical condition of each slave—which was bound to lessen ill treatment. Brougham said later that no one but Stephen had ever supposed that there was any smuggling of slaves into the West Indies after 1811 but that the registration was very valuable for other reasons. That was a characteristic exaggeration. Wilberforce and others had mistakenly believed that there was considerable smuggling. But Brougham was fundamentally right. Before a year had passed, the abolitionists were successful. In May 1816 Lord Bathurst, Secretary for War and the Colonies, informed Wilberforce that 'he had told the West Indians frankly, he would next year pass a Registry Bill, if their colonial assemblies would not do it'.[1] Because of that threat each of the colonies passed its own registration bill.

In the meantime a slave insurrection broke out in Barbados. It was not caused by exceptional ill treatment; slaves were treated better in Barbados than in other West Indian colonies. The slaves had heard of the bitter opposition of the planters to the Registry Bill: the legislative assembly had declared that it was unconstitutional. Rumours spread among the slaves that they were to be emancipated by the British government, that they were to be registered for that purpose, and that their owners were refusing to obey and insisting on holding them in bondage. Much property was destroyed in the insurrection but only one white man lost his life. Martial law was declared, the rising quickly suppressed, and many of those who had taken part in it were hanged on the plantations to which they belonged in sight of the other slaves. The planters, overseers, and the West Indian interest generally were quick to blame the abolitionists and their registration project for the insurrection.

The Barbados insurrection was discussed in the House of

[1] *Life of Wilberforce*, iv. 292. Diary, 17 May 1816.

Commons on 19 July. Wilberforce said that it had been stated that the advocacy of emancipation by him and his friends had been a cause of the insurrection. He insisted that for twenty-seven years they had repeatedly asserted that they were not advocating emancipation, and that the slaves of Barbados had picked up the idea of emancipation from the talk of planters and overseers who were so fond of misrepresenting the slaves' friends in England. Of those who spoke after Wilberforce two members who represented the West Indian interest insisted that the slaves believed that Wilberforce had won their freedom and their masters had withheld it from them. One went so far as to blame future insurrections on Wilberforce and another spoke of the remorse that Wilberforce would feel when he came to himself. In fact he almost shed tears of compassion over him. The Methodist missionaries were also accused of making inflammatory statements and in part blamed for the revolt.

Brougham spoke in reply. He and his friends had never directly advocated emancipation. He warmly defended the Methodist missionaries and said (according to *Hansard*): 'If the exertions for religious instruction were confined to the Established Church, the light of the gospel could never reach these poor people.' He asked how the revolting slaves had caught the idea of emancipation. 'He held in his hands three Jamaica gazettes in which it was openly avowed that registration was only a cloak for emancipation.' Registration could not be safely left to the West Indian assemblies, who had too frequently placed their own constructions on what they were asked to do. He freely admitted that slave-owning members of that House could not be directly blamed for the maltreatment of the slaves. They were fulfilling their duties creditably but they belonged to the large class of absentee planters. 'The care of those estates must necessarily be committed to others, and he did not hesitate to say that the lower order of whites in the [West Indian] colonies were the grossest and basest rabble that ever disgraced the name of human population.'[1]

The West Indian registry acts were defective and their enforcement more so, yet much of what had been hoped for was effected. Parliamentary legislation in 1819 provided for a central register in London, a feature of Stephen's original plan, and

[1] *Hansard*, xxxiv. 1151–1218.

invalidated the inclusion of unregistered slaves in all United Kingdom sales of West Indian estates and all mortgages placed on them. The fierce registration controversy necessitated a closer study of conditions among the slaves and increased public knowledge of those conditions. The registration supplied valuable statistics that were used effectively in the later movement for emancipation.[1] George Stephen said of the registration project that no one 'except Mr. Wilberforce, Mr. Stephen, Mr. Brougham and Mr. Macaulay rightly appreciated its ultimate importance'.[2] The sons of Wilberforce said that 'for the first time in 1818 the word *emancipation* occurred amongst his secret counsels'. But their own account of that shows clearly that he did not use the word in its later and common meaning.[3]

Among the conferences held in 1818 was one at Stephen's house, attended by Stephen, Wilberforce, Brougham, Macaulay, Romilly, and three others, in which they discussed, according to Romilly, 'in what way the unhappy conditions of the negroes in the West Indies can be most advantageously brought before Parliament, with a view to some legislative measures being adopted for their relief'.[4] Actually no legislation was introduced, but papers were called for in Parliament and Romilly made some remarkably effective speeches revealing very bad conditions in some of the West Indian islands.

In the following year (1819) public feeling was anything but encouraging. When Wilberforce sought the support of the Methodists he found that they were 'for leaving to their masters all improvements in the condition of the slaves'. No efforts were made in 1820 because no one in the country had ears for anything but the Queen's Trial. A submerged logic was leading the leaders towards the conclusion that the only cure for the slave system was the ending of it,[5] but none of them in 1820 had the faintest suspicion that they were on the eve of launching a movement for the emancipation of the slaves.

[1] Sir George Stephen, pp. 18–19.
[2] Ibid., p. 25.
[3] *Life of Wilberforce*, iv. 366.
[4] Romilly's, *Memoirs*, ii. 483, 30 Jan.
[5] The latter part of Birtwhistle's thesis is very good on the development in the minds of the leaders and the significance of this period generally.

CHAPTER X

Political and Personal, 1812–15

WITH Brougham out of Parliament in 1812 after his defeat at Liverpool, the Whigs, with the exception of Lord Grey and the Duke of Bedford, made no effort to find a seat for him, as they did for the other leading Whigs who had been defeated. He proceeded to champion the Princess of Wales against the Prince Regent, without Whig support (except for Whitbread and the small left-wing group called the Mountain) but he had no intention of destroying what bridges remained to him as far as the Whig party was concerned.

The political coldness of the Whig grandees toward Brougham can be readily understood. Socially they liked him, politically they deplored him. He was too liberal for them and, from their point of view, too unreliable. Many of them felt, as Wellesley (not a Whig but always a possible ally) said, that Brougham was 'a rash and decided Jacobin'.[1] And he had already shown a tendency not to run well in party harness. Like Canning with the Tories he was too proud and too independent and this was the more to be resented in a new member whose meteoric rise to a leading position in Parliament had inevitably produced some jealousy, and who had not been born to the purple in a party whose leadership was so solidly aristocratic.

It has been said that Brougham was not an orthodox Whig. This is quite true. He was no more an orthodox Whig than Palmerston was later, or than Disraeli was an orthodox Conservative. And all these, of course, are only illustrations of the obvious fact that the greatest leaders have not been orthodox anything, no matter how they may have pretended to orthodoxy at times.

Nothing in England today can afford us any idea of the pride of the Whig aristocracy. They were the rightful rulers of England. It was not a matter of divine right. There was no need for that, for this conviction was something much stronger than their

[1] Hist. MSS. Commission, *Dropmore Papers*, x. 319.

religion. It had, in fact, a more convincing moral quality than formal doctrines of divine-right kingship had ever had. The Whig noblemen had always hated despotism. Sons believed that they were succeeding their fathers as the custodians of the liberty of the people. As for the people becoming the custodians of their own liberty, that, of course, was something else. The annual Fox Dinner and the ghosts at Holland House might suggest at times some vague concept of the sovereignty of the people, but it seldom emerged from the shadows. Faith in a benevolent ruling class was bred in the bone.

And, indeed, if aristocracy were ever justified, it was that British aristocracy. While they enjoyed their comforts and their luxuries, their hunting and the open country, many of them understood something of intellectual pleasure and were patrons of an art that enriched their lives. Political conflict and intrigue provided them with a game, which to them was the greatest of all games. The art of government, though to us it may seem narrowly conceived, was a serious matter that involved a call to public service. It was also a matter of pride to the Whig leaders that while Tory leadership had been so open to middle-class invasion, theirs had been rigidly, if not universally, exclusive, and to their minds the Tories could boast of no such noble traditions.

It was quite impossible for Brougham to assume such an attitude to politics. Whig politics were group politics quite as much as party politics, and Brougham had no natural affinity with any of the groups. As Charles Lamb said, 'These Whigs are all cousins', and Brougham was nobody's cousin. He was not born into the faith and nothing in his experience led him to reach after it. In his mind and heart he had little use for aristocratic government. Popular sovereignty would have to wait for the realization of his dream of universal education; but in 1812 he was already fully convinced that, in changing social conditions, the whole structure of government must be broadened, and he was already proclaiming what was to be a constant factor in his political career, that the voting power should include all who paid direct taxes.

Brougham owed little to either the Whig tradition in general or the Foxite tradition in particular. As a young man he had not been a great admirer of Fox's politics. As a close student of

oratory he was drawn to Fox the orator as he was later drawn
to Gladstone, and Gladstone to Brougham for the same reason.
And Brougham would have been the last man to escape the
attraction of the generosity of Fox's heart, in which he believed
his greatness mainly rested. But, although he could sometimes
talk about himself as a disciple of Fox when he was railing at
timid Foxites who lacked Fox's courage, there was never a
feeling of being in an apostolic succession. Brougham's liberalism
had its roots in his ardent humanitarianism, in the revolt of his
youth against the tyranny of exclusion in Scotland, in the hatred
of oligarchy that was then burned into his soul, and in his own
sympathy with the French Revolution.

As we look back at 1812 it is easy enough to see that the most
important question of home politics *should have been* that of
Parliamentary Reform, the reform of Parliament itself or more
specifically the election of members to the House of Commons.
Yet although the Whigs had a tradition of Parliamentary Reform behind them, by 1812 it had worn so thin as to be almost
negligible. Two years earlier Lord Grey had declared that, while
the best interests of the country depended upon Parliamentary
Reform, nothing should be done to hurry it on until it was
'taken up by the people of England seriously and affectionately'.
Holland House was a great inspirer of liberalism, but in regard
to Parliamentary Reform it was apathetic. Horner, a liberal
advocate on many questions, believed that some aspects of
Parliamentary Reform were desirable and he 'sometimes thought'
that others might be salutary, but in 1816 the only thing he was
sure of was 'the folly of connecting the present sufferings of the
people with anything in the state of the representation'.[1] Horner's
position was very similar to that of the Grenville group, who
might have looked on Parliamentary Reform with some favour
under different circumstances but who never really swerved from
the position which Lord Grenville had expressed in a letter to
his brother in 1809. 'The thing itself' might at some other time
be desirable but in those days anything in the way of 'innovation' was so dangerous that 'it must be resisted and everything
leading to it must be as far as possible checked and discounten-
anced'.[2]

---

[1] Francis Horner, ii. 414–15.
[2] Add. MSS. 41, 853, Grenville MSS., ff. 8–9, 27 Mar. 1809.

To all of this Brougham was decidedly opposed, but in his conviction that something should be done he could look for a fellow feeling nowhere in the Whig party except in that small left wing known as the Mountain. The Radicals, of course, were farther to the left than the Mountain, but the Radicals were not Whigs and they strongly disliked the Whigs. They could advocate all the varieties of Parliamentary Reform in different degrees at different times, and most of the time most of them were impossible extremists. It has been said that Brougham was a moderate Parliamentary Reformer, but that frequently repeated statement requires modification as well as clarification. There was nothing moderate about the advocacy of extending the electoral franchise to all who paid direct taxes, a position from which Brougham never swerved. This was very close to the borough franchise which was to be established by the Second Reform Bill, and Brougham had begun to advocate it when Britain was still a long way from the First Reform Bill. Nor was there anything moderate about his advocacy of triennial parliaments. He saw clearly enough how fantastic was the proposal for annual parliaments, with a general election every year, that idea so dear to Bentham, Francis Place, Major Cartwright, and most of the Radicals. And Brougham believed that in the existing state of education, universal suffrage, equally dear to them, was not feasible. In all of this he was remarkably consistent. Up to the eve of the Great Reform Bill he believed that only gradual legislation was possible. Every reasonable measure of Parliamentary Reform should be advocated and kept before the public, but Parliament would be able to proceed only a step at a time.

As in his other causes he employed the sounding board of the *Edinburgh Review*. In an article on the Influence of the Crown in April 1810 he had stated that any attempt to substitute for the present unsatisfactory constitution of the House of Commons a completely new system of representation was impracticable and would only make enemies to a good cause of many who might be its friends. What was necessary was to see the evils clearly and to correct them 'one after another'. Of those that should be envisaged a few only would be mentioned in that article. There were too many placemen in the House of Commons; no one holding an office under the Crown should be permitted to sit in that house except the heads of departments,

and 'perhaps one other member' of each department 'to facilitate
business'. There should be a thorough reform of the representation of Scotland 'where there was no popular representation at
all'. There should be general enfranchisement of copyholders in
the counties. There should be a 'gradual extinction of the worst
borough franchises' with compensation to the borough patrons,
the seats so abolished to be transferred to such unrepresented
large towns as Manchester, Birmingham, Leeds, and to the
representation of some of the larger counties. The substitution of
triennial for septennial parliaments was also suggested.

An article entitled 'Parliamentary Reform' in the February
1811 *Edinburgh Review* was undoubtedly written jointly by Jeffrey
and Brougham. Both later published the article in their Contributions, but careful comparisons reveal the fact that, for the
most part, they published different parts of the article. Jeffrey
apparently discussed fundamental principles and Brougham
detailed suggestions of reform.

In 1811 Brougham circulated a statement entitled *Principles of
Parliamentary Reform*. It was nearly forty pages in length.[3] It
repeats much of what Brougham had written in the February
number. The right of electing members should be taken away
from 'all places so small and insignificant as to have become, in
a great measure, the property of an individual'. A greater evil
lay in the boroughs which were held by 'jobbers' and are
'regularly disposed of by them at every election for a price paid
down, either through the mediation of the ministry, or without
any such mediation'. (These statements and much of the 'plan'
were verbal repetition of part, obviously Brougham's part, of the
article of the previous February.)

Another way, Brougham said, in which money was under-
mining the constitution of the House of Commons and making
impossible any true representation of the people was the power
of money in what were supposed to be popular constituencies
with relatively open elections. The tremendous expenses incurred
in such elections, 'more than all other causes put together, gives
money an undue influence, and prevents the people on the one
hand from exercising their free choice, and deserving candidates
on the other from presenting themselves with a fair chance of

---

[1] *Works*, viii. 347–84, where it is dated '1811 and 1812'. Sydney Smith in June
1811 spoke of it as being circulated. (*Letters of Sydney Smith*, i. 210.)

success'. One of the greatest items of expense was the bringing in of the non-resident voters, principally from London. The methods of the agents of the long purse in buying up votes in London were vividly described. An effective remedy for this situation would be to deprive non-resident members of the right to vote. Usually the candidates had to meet election expenses or a considerable proportion of them, and only very wealthy men need apply.

While 'a good and able man' who was not wealthy had the greatest difficulty getting into Parliament, a man 'of mere money and no other earthly qualification has a chance next to a certainty of getting into parliament if he chooses to spend so much as the *speculation* requires'. If the cost of elections were adequately reduced, then triennial parliaments would be desirable, with which reform the people would to a considerable extent come into their own and would gain strength and consequence. 'By the extension of the elective franchise, many of those who are most hostile to the existing system, because under it they are excluded from all share of power or political importance, will have a part assigned to them, both more safe and more active than murmuring or meditating vengeance against such a scheme of exclusion.' Such was Brougham's personal manifesto of Parliamentary Reform. Much of this statement was repeated in an article which he wrote for the July 1812 number of the *Edinburgh Review*. He urged that in popular constituencies the example of Westminster should be followed and committees should raise funds to support good candidates who were not wealthy.

By 1811 Brougham had been brought into personal touch with Bentham through James Mill, and on 6 July 1812 Bentham wrote to Mulford:

The member by whom this letter is franked is the famous Mr. *Brougham*—pronounced *Broom*—who, by getting the Orders in Council revoked, and peace and trade with America thereby restored, has just filled the whole country with joy, gladness, and returning plenty. He has been dining with me to-day and has but just gone. This little dinner of mine he has been intriguing for any time these five or six months; and what with one plague and another, never till this day could I find it in my heart to give him one. I mean this year; for the last we were already intimate. He is already one of the first men in the House of Commons, and seems in a fair way of being very soon universally acknowledged to be the very first; . . . many, indeed, say he is so now.[1]

From this time on Brougham was one of the small circle that was allowed to encroach upon Bentham's solitude. Three or four from this circle frequently dined with Bentham. They must often have been those whom Rush, the American ambassador, found there one evening in 1818: 'The company was small but choice. Mr. Brougham; Sir Samuel Romilly; Mr. Mill . . . M. Dumont.'[2] Admittance to the Hermitage was a rare privilege. When Mme de Staël arrived in England and said enthusiastically to Dumont: 'Tell Bentham I shall see nobody till I have seen him', Bentham's comment was: 'I am sorry for it, but then she will never see anybody.' For years Brougham was to keep his place in that favoured group. No record has survived of what Brougham thought of Bentham's abstemiousness in regard to wine, his many cats, the pet mice that scampered about his study (the cats and the mice suggesting problems, as Leslie Stephen said, concerning 'the greatest happiness of the greatest number') or the habit of expelling all guests before the strokes of midnight.[3]

Membership of the group did not make Brougham a Benthamite, however, except in one notable respect—law reform. Unlike the true believers, Brougham did not say much about the Benthamite philosophy. It is one of the few subjects that is hardly ever mentioned in his letters, in his speeches, or later in his books. It is difficult to think of Brougham as being enamoured of Bentham's elaborate and complicated calculus of pains and pleasures, or of his discussions of the natural and artificial identity of interests, or of any idea of morality being converted into a science.

In the years after 1812, and particularly after peace was fully restored in 1815, serious-minded men in public life turned their attention more and more to the political and institutional changes made necessary by the tremendous upheavals of the Industrial Revolution. In addition to the true believers for whom

[1] *The Works of Jeremy Bentham*, 11 vols. (1843), x. 471–2; A. Bain, *James Mill* (1882), p. 122 n.
[2] Richard Rush, *Residence at the Court of London* (1872), p. 286.
[3] Leslie Stephen, *The English Utilitarians*, 3 vols. (1912), i. 231–2.

Benthamism was a potent social and political dynamic, there were others to whom the catchwords of Benthamism made a ready appeal. Everything in the great industrial changes suggested 'utilitarianism'. After the inauguration of the Age of Reform in the early twenties, 'the greatest happiness of the greatest number' and 'utility' were good mottoes for the banners under which men marched. We are not to suppose that the active leaders in political life who seemed to be influenced by Benthamism read a great deal of what Bentham wrote. Brougham, however, did. He was an omnivorous reader, and he was one of the few among whom Bentham circulated some of his books years before he published them. With his remarkably good mind Brougham could follow and criticize the complexities of Bentham's thought. Of his reactions we hear very little, but we get a strong impression of scepticism. There is probably some significance in the fact that when Brougham, in a later period, wrote two volumes on the *Philosophers of the Reign of George III*, he did not include Bentham in his list. In his essay on Hume, from whom Bentham picked up the concept of utility, Brougham said that Hume spoke of the importance of utility, 'but rather as one leading motive than the sole source of either our actions or our judgments upon them'.[1] In one of his sketches, Brougham condemned a prominent aspect of the Benthamite philosophy, in reprobating as 'a very vulgar fallacy' 'the doctrine that all the motives of human conduct are directly resolvable into self-interest'. He spoke of 'the theory of utility' as being 'defective'.[2] And the following appears in his essay on Adam Smith:

How well he painted the man of system, and how many features of this portrait have we recognized in Mr. Bentham and others in our day.... He [Bentham] seems to imagine that he can arrange the different members of a great society with as much ease as the hand arranges the different pieces upon a chess-board. He does not consider that ... in the great chess-board of human society, every single piece has a principle of action of its own.[3]

Of course it would be a mistake to think of Brougham as a philosopher himself. He was never much of a theorist. In the first half of his life he was always too busy trying to get things done, and when he essayed political theory in his later days, in spite of occasional acute criticism which could always be

[1] *Works*, ii. 177.   [2] Ibid. i. 167, 198.   [3] Ibid. i. 203.

expected from him, he displayed little or no originality in the formulation of theory. He did not in fact care for systems. For him, humanity and justice, and, we may add, practical Christianity, spoke with imperatives independent of any system. It was only in the field of law reform that he was even a Benthamite, and in that sphere he was to be Bentham's representative in action. Their close association after 1812 was of the greatest historical importance; as Brougham said, law reform was 'the most important of all the branches of reform, the leading and ruling department of human improvement'.

Quite as important as this contact with Bentham was Brougham's friendship with James Mill, Bentham's brilliant expositor, the great systematizer of the Utilitarian faith, the founder of the Benthamite 'school', and, in every practical aspect of leadership, the leader of the Benthamites. Mill's biographer said that Mill was Brougham's 'greatest friend'.[1] Brougham had so many close friends that it is hard to say how true this is, but certainly a warm friendship between Brougham and Mill began early and remained unruffled until the latter's death. Mill, five years older, had begun attendance at the University of Edinburgh at the same time as Brougham. They may not have met there, but the fact that they had been fellow students in a university of which they were proud created an inevitable bond. Mill brought his great gifts from Scotland to London a few years before Brougham brought his. They became acquainted shortly after Brougham's arrival in London and thirty years later, at the end of Mill's life, their friendship was as strong as ever. As Bain said in his life of Mill: 'In the midst of much obloquy cast upon Brougham's character during those years, the favourable estimate of Mill can always be adduced as a counter-testimony in his behalf.'[2] In December 1833 Mill wrote to Brougham: 'I hope you consider one duty, the care of your health. I know not when the time was in the history of our species that more depended on the health of one man than depends at this moment on yours. The progress of mankind would lose a century by the loss of you.'[3] That James Mill, his temperament being what it was, should have said that of anyone, and particularly that he should have said it *to* anyone, would be incredible if it were not there on the written page.

[1] Bain, p. 459.   [2] Ibid., p. 76.   [3] Ibid., p. 371.

This whole friendship was a strange one—between James Mill, thinking machine, and Henry Brougham 'virtuoso of the emotions' (as the younger James Stephen described him). Mill despised any show of feeling and regarded emotion as a beggarly kitchen-maid at a court where reason was king. His son, John Stuart Mill, wrote of him: 'For passionate emotions . . . he professed the greatest contempt. "The intense" was with him a bye-word of scornful disapprobation. . . . I believe him to have had much more feeling than he actually showed. . . . He resembled most Englishmen in being ashamed of the signs of feeling, and by the absence of demonstration starving the feelings themselves.'[1] Brougham was constantly displaying 'passionate emotion' both in public and in private and he was never anything at any time if not 'intense'. He felt no shame in exposing his feelings to the world and he counted on rousing strong feeling in others. If life were really lived according to the rules made by the Benthams and the James Mills of this world, Brougham should have disgusted Mill. Yet with one exception, Mill never on any occasion expressed, apart from a criticism of Brougham's logic which went tripping too lightly at times, disapproval of Brougham. And Mill could say coldly cutting things (nothing 'intense' of course) about those who crossed his path of rectitude. The one occasion on which he took Brougham to task was for defending Christianity in a speech in Parliament, and Mill intimated strongly enough that he should have known better.[2] It may be noted in passing that Brougham was not in agreement with any of his friends on religion, although he never called attention to that fact. He did not share, though he sympathized with, the religion of William Allen the Quaker or that of Wilberforce and his colleagues, and he strongly disapproved, on the other hand, of the anti-Christian attitude of such close friends as Robert Owen and James Mill.

John Stuart Mill said: 'He [James Mill] was the good genius by the side of Brougham in most of what he did for the public, either on education, law reform, or any other subject.'[3] If this means that Mill exerted a steadying influence on Brougham's unstable temperament, it is true enough. But the context suggests that it was Mill who inspired Brougham in these activities.

[1] J. S. Mill, *Autobiography* (Harvard Classics), pp. 37–38.
[2] Bain, p. 76.   [3] J. S. Mill, p. 62.

That requires serious qualification. In practical efforts concerning popular education Brougham was always the leader.
He brought Mill into the Royal Lancasterian Institution
which became the British and Foreign School Society, into the
infant school movement and the Society for the Diffusion of
Useful Knowledge. In the movements against the slave trade
and slavery Brougham was at the centre and Mill on the circumference. In the founding of the University of London, Brougham
led and Mill followed. In the movement for Parliamentary
Reform there was strong mutual influence; although they differed
on details, both favoured step-by-step reform.

In spite of the sharp contrast of temperament, it is not difficult
to recognize bases for friendship. They were associated in a
number of enterprises and devoted to the public welfare. Their
ultimate aims for social improvement were not dissimilar. And
they both appreciated the growing importance of the middle
class. Both were men of wide interests and wide reading. Mill's
intellectual and literary range was one of the marvels of the age;
the scope of Brougham's practical and effectual activities was
greater than that of any one else in the period and possibly in
the century. Both were men of remarkable intellectual alertness.
If Mill's mind had greater depth, Brougham's was superlatively
keen. Both were marvellously industrious and both were good
conversationalists. Mill could be very entertaining if the atmo-
sphere was right, which it always would be when he was with
Brougham, and Brougham could be entertaining under almost
any circumstances.

Before the year 1812 was over Brougham had given up hope
of a pocket-borough seat being offered to him. Partly to keep
the road open with Lord Grey and partly because he was such
an incurable politician and so keenly interested in reform, he
wrote in 1813 and 1814 a number of good Whig letters to Grey,
in one suggesting that the party should push strongly for Catholic
emancipation, tithe reform, reduction of 'the expenses of law
proceedings', and amendment of the poor laws,[1] and in another
protesting against the exclusion of the members of the Mountain
from the annual Fox dinner.[2]

In October 1811 Sydney Smith had heard from Brougham's

[1] *Memoirs*, ii. 88 seq., 6 Nov. 1813.
[2] Also Brougham MSS., Brougham to Creevey, 7 Feb. 1814.

enemies that he had been 'getting business very rapidly on the Northern Circuit'.[1] A year later Horner said that Brougham's rise had been more rapid than that of any lawyer since Erskine.[2] Yet in 1813 he had very few briefs on the Northern Circuit.[3] In September 1814 Brougham wrote to Grey that he had lost almost all of his practice in Lancashire on account of the Liverpool election in 1812.[4] This explanation hardly seems adequate to the sharpness of the decline.

The frequent statements in Brougham's letters at this time that he was not anxious to get into Parliament again and did not greatly care whether he was in or out cannot be taken seriously. But he would not go begging to the Whig borough-owners. For some time he had had his eye on Westminster, the one large constituency in which conditions approximated to those of modern democracy. He wrote an article for the *Edinburgh* of November 1812, the month after his defeat at Liverpool, on the Rights and Duties of the People. In it he urged that Parliamentary Reform must go farther than the matter of how members should be elected. The people themselves must discuss public questions and bring pressure to bear on Parliament. The best way to do that was to hold public meetings, as did the people of Westminster, 'who have always given the tone through the rest of the country'. The article closed with: 'We must again turn to the free and enlightened people of Westminster; and bid both the supporters of the Constitution, and the wellwishers to the popular cause to look to them at once for example and for comfort.' From those last months of 1812 Brougham was, in his own mind, as well as in the thoughts of others, a candidate for Westminster. The sitting members were Lord Cochrane and Sir Francis Burdett. Early in 1814 Lord Cochrane, naval hero and blatant Radical, was involved in a sensational stock-exchange scandal. If he were convicted he would be expelled by the House and there would be a by-election in Westminster.

The report of the Stock Exchange Committee of Inquiry on 7 March strengthened the public conviction that Lord Cochrane was guilty. Brougham was being brought forward as a candidate by some of the Westminster Radicals encouraged by Mill, and

---

[1] *Letters of Sydney Smith*, i. 215.   [2] Aspinall, p. 35.
[3] Hardcastle, i. 293, Campbell to his father, 13 Apr. 1813.
[4] *Memoirs*, ii. 107.

Richard Brinsley Sheridan by a group of Whigs. No one could predict at that early date how Brougham and Sheridan would divide Whig support. Neither was *persona grata* with the party. The Tories would prefer supporting Sheridan to attempting to run a government candidate in Westminster.

Three days after the Stock Exchange Committee had issued its report, Byron wrote of Sheridan and Brougham: 'Sherry means to stand for Westminster, as Cochrane must vacate. Brougham is a candidate. I fear for poor dear Sherry. Both have talents of the highest order, but the younger has *yet* a character. We shall see, if he lives to Sherry's age, how he will pass over the red-hot ploughshares of public life.'[1]

By the end of May, Francis Place, tailor of Charing Cross, Benthamite Radical, great-hearted lover of humanity and the English working man, shrewd election manager, an impulsive and cantankerous man and very fond of getting his own way, had begun to lay down the law with regard to the political faith of any Radical candidate. He wrote to Brooks, the chairman of the Westminster Radical committee:

One thing is absolutely necessary . . . and that is to take from the person proposed a *declaration in writing* that he will on all occasions endeavour to procure a reform in the representation of the people as follows,—1. That every person subject to direct taxation have the right of voting for a member of the House of Commons. 2. That the election of members be annual.[2]

On 9 June all of the alleged conspirators were convicted, including Lord Cochrane. On the 10th Major Cartwright, the tireless veteran advocate of extreme measures of Parliamentary Reform, announced his candidature.[3] On the 16th at a Radical meeting at the Crown and Anchor tavern Brougham and Cartwright were both proposed, and doubts were expressed about Brougham's views on Parliamentary Reform. On or before that day Brougham informed Place through Wakefield that he would make the pledge indicated, with the addition now demanded of 'representation fairly distributed within the country'. Mill assured Place on the 19th that Brougham would make the required declaration. He pretended to do so in a poorly reported speech

[1] Aspinall, p. 31, quoting from T. Moore, *Letters and Journals of Byron*, 2 vols. (1830), ii. 10.
[2] Add. MSS. 27850, ff. 275 seq. Also in Add. MSS. 27840, ff. 220 seq.
[3] Ibid., f. 282 v.

at the Livery of London Parliamentary Reform dinner on the
23rd. Place insisted that he put his speech into writing and saw
that it was printed. He was satisfied that Brougham had made
the pledges.[1]

Two of the three pledges were easy enough for Brougham.
Throughout the whole period Brougham consistently advocated
the extension of the parliamentary franchise to all who paid
direct taxes (and in doing so placed himself far ahead of nearly
all of his Whig associates). He was quite as consistent in advocacy
of a fairer distribution of parliamentary representation. The
other point was annual parliaments, with a general election
every year. This was a pet mania with Francis Place, Jeremy
Bentham, and Major Cartwright. There is no record of any of
them ever being cured of it. Men called Brougham 'mad' at
times, but he was too sane for that. He never had anything but
contempt for the idea. Yet he made a statement which gave the
impression that he favoured annual parliaments. He sought to
win Radical support and a seat in Parliament on false pretences.

In the meantime Lord Cochrane had been sentenced on the
21st to a fine, to imprisonment, and to be placed in pillory in
front of the Exchange at some time during his term of imprisonment. Two weeks before, the trial itself had shaken men's belief
in Cochrane's guilt. Now the pillory sentence greatly strengthened
the reaction in his favour.

Brougham was confident that he had most of the Whigs. He
was assured of the support of the Mountain group, Lord Grey,
the Russells and the Cavendishes. 'To be sure the idea of Whigs
supporting a C[arlton] House candidate merely because he is a
rat from themselves is good.'[2] But he was worried about the
Radicals. He never supposed for a moment that Cartwright
could be elected, but he feared that he would divert enough
Radical votes to make Sheridan dangerous.

On 5 July the tide of sympathy toward Cochrane reached a
height that could not be ignored. There was a debate in the
House of Commons on the proposal to expel him. Cochrane
himself, though in custody, was permitted to appear and speak.
Opposition speakers, including their leader, Lord Ponsonby, expressed grave doubts about Cochrane's guilt. That and Coch-

[1] Add. MSS. 27840, ff. 225 seq., 27850, ff. 278 seq.
[2] Creevey MSS.

rane's own speech served as a challenge to the electors of Westminster, who shared those doubts, to stand by their member and re-elect him after expulsion, which they proceeded to do after all other candidates had withdrawn in the face of that feeling.

It was a disappointing summer for Brougham. A month after Cochrane's election the Princess of Wales left for the Continent. In the autumn, however, he got a great deal of satisfaction out of delivering a lecture to Lord Chief Justice Ellenborough, a lecture from counsel to the bench. For superlative invective Lord Ellenborough was as unrivalled in the House of Lords as Brougham was in the Commons, and he could not suppress his gift of sarcasm in court nor refrain from bullying counsel. Some of the sarcasm was merited. He was extremely patient in hearing counsel out. On one occasion in the middle of an excessively long and tedious speech, the counsel paused and asked: 'Is it the pleasure of the Court that I should proceed with my statement?' Lord Ellenborough replied: 'Pleasure, Mr. ——, has been out of the question for a long time, but you may proceed.'[1] Brougham did not mind the sarcasm, but he objected to bullying. Since the newspapers did not care to give full accounts of Brougham's bearding of Ellenborough on 14 November (1814) we are thrown back on Brougham's own accounts. Writing to Lord Grey:

I am sure that you will rejoice when I tell you that I have this morning, in the Court of K[ing's] Bench, given Ellenborough such a drubbing as he will not soon recover. . . . I was counsel for a man who had published a blasphemous book, and Lord Ellenborough made a clumsy attempt at mixing me up with the man and his opinions. I instantly fired into him, told him that no man should dare utter such things without instant and utter contradiction, and that I told him in the face of the court and the world that the insinuation was false (or utterly groundless, I forget the word). He was as meek as a lamb, and said that he had used no insinuation, and tried to explain it away. But I would not allow him; and again I gave him the flat contradiction as loud as I could roar it out, appealing to the court and the bar, and saying that I should defend my character and my profession as long as I could utter. He knocked under, and I enjoyed the satisfaction of having the united voice of the bar loudly with me.[2]

[1] Thomas Moore, ii. 312.
[2] *Memoirs*, ii. 268–9, 14 Nov. 1814. Two corrections made in this letter have been indicated by A. Aspinall in *E.H.R.*, lix. 107.

To Shepherd, Brougham said, six weeks after the event, that it had had a salutary effect on Lord Ellenborough and on the Bar 'who will never again suffer the tyranny they had so long submitted to'.[1]

In February 1815 Brougham thought he was going to die. On 1 March he suddenly left the Circuit, believing that he had a serious heart attack. He remained at Brougham Hall and gave up everything for several months. On 31 May Bennet wrote to Creevey who was in Brussels that Brougham's doctor, Baillie (an eminent physician), said that he 'has no bodily disease'. He is 'hypochondriac to an inconceivable degree. . . . You, who know what he has to fear, may imagine how anxious I am.'[2] What Bennet feared is clear enough. There was insanity in Brougham's family. Dr. Baillie could not convince him that there was nothing wrong with his heart. For many years Brougham clung to his belief in his heart trouble and 'its sudden natural termination'. Thirty-six years later he told Croker that he had hardly ever gone to bed 'without settling whatever I deemed a pressing matter'. That was unpleasant at first but he got accustomed to it. The effect of that on his life, he said, might have been more salutary, 'but at least it has maintained in my contemplation and thoughts Godward a certain influence'.[3]

Brougham's account of this illness in his inaccurate Memoirs does not square with these letters in all respects, but we can at least believe the following: 'I took much interest in the working of bees more especially as regards the mathematical perfection of the structure of their cells . . . and satisfying every condition of a difficult geometrical problem. . . . This did as much to cure me as the healthy air of Westmorland.'[4]

His recovery was probably aided by a letter from Lord Grey written 9 July, stating that one of Lord Darlington's borough seats had fallen vacant, that he had asked for it for Brougham and that Lord Darlington appeared to be favourable. The matter was arranged in a few days. One may guess that Lord Darlington was more willing than other borough-owners to bring Brougham into Parliament, for after having been on very friendly terms

---

[1] Brougham MSS., 12 Dec. 1814.
[2] Creevey MSS.
[3] Croker MSS., 4 Jan., 1 Dec. 1851.
[4] *Memoirs*, ii. 290–1.

with the Regent, he had now broken with him. As one of the two members for Winchelsea, Brougham would have seventeen constituents. Disappointed because he did not feel strong enough to write anything for the June number of the *Edinburgh*, Brougham probably wrote five articles for the October number. After returning, in mid-September, from a health trip to the coast he began preparing for the next session of Parliament and planning his campaign for the repeal of the income-tax.

CHAPTER XI

Political and Personal, 1816–19

BEFORE the meeting of Parliament in February 1816, Brougham wrote to Grey and to Creevey outlining his idea of Opposition policy. They should concentrate on retrenchment and the reduction of taxes, and in foreign policy act as a corps of observation, seizing opportunity as it arose. He hoped that Tierney and Abercromby would 'see the folly of their temporizing plans' and come to life, as they had during part of the last session. 'But . . . I am quite determined (tho' ready to meet them half way for peace and union sake) that the game of the country and the people shall be played in good earnest—if not with their help, without it—by God's blessing.'[1]

He spoke as if he were to be the leader of a party. Lord Grey indicated clearly enough that he welcomed Brougham into the top rank of the Whig leaders. But Brougham's determination was that he should be *the* leader of the Whigs in the House of Commons, even though there was no question of the *official* leadership as yet. Ponsonby's tenure of that position suited Brougham. Ponsonby had been selected largely because the leading Whigs disagreed about many things and he did not have strong enough convictions on anything to do much disagreeing. He was weak, desultory, amiable, inoffensive, and inefficient as a leader, although he could occasionally make a good speech. He would do very well as a figure-head until Brougham got a good grip on the reins of power. Brougham and Baring were very busy, before Parliament assembled, laying the foundation for petitions for the complete repeal of the income-tax, a massing of petitions such as had been successful against the Orders in Council.

An item in Brougham's preparation for the opening of Parliament was the healing of his personal breach with Lady Holland. He was very fond of Lord Holland, for whom he had the greatest admiration, and with whom he agreed on most matters. It would

[1] *Creevey Papers*, i. 247–8, 14 Jan. 1816.

not do, when he was back in Parliament aspiring to lead the Whigs in the Commons, for him to be still an exile from Holland House. So he made his peace with Lady Holland with that remarkable facility he had, as though nothing had ever happened. And Lady Holland and he were on terms of cordial friendship for the rest of her life.

So he was ready for the opening of Parliament and the role of leadership which he had cast for himself. Before the session was over he had spoken 147 times, nearly twice as often as Ponsonby. He was on his feet to take advantage of every opening. He made over fifty substantial speeches.

> A meagre form, with face so wondrous thin
> That it resembles Milton's Death and Sin,
> Long arms that saw the air like windmill sails,
> And tongue whose force and fury never fails.

Brougham was at his most fiery and compelling during this session. It was not only his tongue which had force and fury, but also his eye, and some said his nose. Bagehot once remarked that 'if he were a horse, nobody would buy him; with that eye no one could answer for his temper'.[1] The nose was the most prominent feature of his rather ugly but mobile countenance. When fully aroused his whole face was eloquent, including the remarkable nose which he seemed able to move at will. He was also distinguished by his black and white plaid trousers, which he wore on every possible occasion. It was said that he had seen this cloth and liked it, and had ordered far more than he realized. Feeling honour bound to complete the purchase he had bought enough of the cloth to last him for the rest of his life.

On the first day of the session, as soon as the address and the amendment were duly moved and seconded, he was on his feet with an onslaught on the whole policy of the Government. Bennet wrote next day to Creevey that Brougham's 'excellent speech . . . shook Castlereagh and frightened the other side more than they had been for years'.[2] As the session proceeded, Tierney became infected with the new energy, spoke more frequently than he had for some time, and displayed the ability that in his case waited only on courage. On the 12th Brougham made an

---

[1] Walter Bagehot, *Biographical Studies* (1881), 1907 ed., p. 69.
[2] Creevey MSS.

all-out attack on the financial policy of the Government. Without consulting Ponsonby or any of his colleagues, he gave notice of a motion for the 15th on the affairs of Spain, when he flayed the tyranny of Ferdinand and pleaded for the protection of his victims. Castlereagh's reply was enlightening and apparently convincing, but Brougham had focused public opinion on Spain and extracted information that would not otherwise have been available.[1] On 11 March he made an able speech on the army estimates.[2]

The real fun had begun on 13 February. The petitions calling for the repeal of the income-tax carefully organized by Brougham and Baring began to pour in to the House and poured more rapidly from day to day. They came from everywhere. Some later experts on taxation have stated in their books that there was no general feeling and that these petitions simply represented a clever political party move. But the evidence of the general feeling is too overwhelming to require any detailed citation. One meets it in every quarter. It was not created by Brougham, Baring, and their associates. They mobilized it. The income-tax had been unpopular enough during the war, but the people were patient because it seemed to be a war necessity. They had looked forward to its ending with the ending of the war. They were shocked when they discovered that the Government meant to retain it. And their impatience was not appeased by the proposed reduction of the tax from 10 per cent. to 5 per cent., nor by the fact that the legislation covered retention for only two years, as there was no guarantee that it would not be renewed at the end of that time.

There has been a tendency on the part of later and of recent writers to regard this movement against the income-tax as a mistake, and to agree with what Castlereagh meant when, with one of his strange twists of language, he spoke of 'the people's impatience of the relaxation of taxation'. Much of that has been associated with a reading back of later ideas formed in later circumstances. It is important to understand why people felt as they did. The prevailing distress was the primary factor. The first hopes of peace two years earlier had occasioned a feverish drive to supply the European markets which were reopened

---

[1] *Hansard*, xxxii. 350 seq., 362 seq., 391 seq., 578 seq.; *Letters of Harriet Countess Granville*, ed. F. Leveson-Gower, 2 vols. (1894), i. 85.   [2] *Speeches*, i. 607 seq.

with the first peace in 1814. But the demands of the European
market had been pitifully below expectations, and the bubble
had burst in heavy losses and mass unemployment. The losses
and unemployment diminished the home market and increased
losses ensued. They were accentuated by the cessation of war
industries and particularly by a marked decline in the iron
industry. The situation was at its worst later in the year 1816,
but at the beginning of the year the prospect was not favourable,
and there was even greater distress in agriculture. In the later
war years, to meet the apparent opportunities of an expanding
market, new and inferior land had been brought under cultivation, much of it on borrowed money. Then came three remarkably good harvests in 1813, 1814, and 1815 and the price of
wheat fell from over 100 shillings a quarter to 52s. 6d. in January
1816. At that price many tenant farmers could not pay their
rent, the inferior land proved to be a losing speculation, loans
could not be repaid, and many country banks failed. In such a
situation it was natural, however illogical, to blame the Government and expect it to cure the situation. Easing the pressure of
taxation was the readiest suggestion and the income-tax was the
most unpopular of taxes.

Why was this first income-tax the most unpopular of taxes
and why were people so eager to get rid of it? In the first place,
it was 'inquisitorial'. The officials were pledged to secrecy, but
apart from the distrust of such pledges, the Englishman's traditional concept of individual liberty was outraged by the thought
of having to reveal the secrets of his business to anyone. That
feeling persisted for a long time. Later in the century, at every
discussion of change in the income-tax, it was considered necessary to explain that the inquisitorial feature was being further
safeguarded. Now, at the beginning of 1816, the feeling was
particularly strong. Brougham was eloquent about the sacred
right of the individual to cherish the privacy of his financial
affairs, just as he called his soul his own. Baring had said the
year before, sincerely no doubt, that 'he would much rather be
summoned before the bench of bishops to be questioned about
his belief in the doctrinal points of religion than appear before
the commisioners under the property tax [income-tax]'. William
Smith stated in Parliament that, in spite of the pledge of secrecy,
many merchants with shaky businesses on their hands, sur-

rounded by business failures, preferred even to pay surcharges
than to reveal to the commissioners the true state of their affairs.[1]
Brougham scoffed at the pledge of secrecy. On two occasions (7
March and 11 March) he presented to the House evidence that
income-tax returns had in some instances been sold for old paper.
In one case a cheese-dealer had wrapped his cheese with them
and each customer, with each new purchase of cheese, might
learn all about the financial affairs of one more member of his
community.[2]

The incomes of tenant farmers were assessed at a sum bearing
a fixed proportion to the rent. But in the situation which we
have noted above, many of them could barely pay their rent,
and had no profit for 1815–16. Brougham had emphasized this
in his *Edinburgh Review* article intended to prepare the way for
the session of 1816. He could be counted on not to miss in his
parliamentary speeches the many instances of the payment of
income-tax where no income existed. He conceded that an
income-tax was the fairest form of taxation, if it could be fairly
administered, but he insisted that in the income-tax which he
was arguing against there were gross inequalities and injustices.

Speaking on 5 March, Brougham said that the income-tax
was too easy a means of gratifying the Government's 'passion
for expense'. 'It was an engine that should not be left at the
disposal of extravagant ministers or extravagant princes.'[3] Mill
had made this point in arguing with Place the previous September.[4] Four days after that speech of Brougham's, the economist
Ricardo wrote to Trower: 'I hope you will bring up a petition
with you against the property tax [income-tax]. . . . The
machinery of it is too easily worked to allow it to be at the
disposal of our extravagant ministers during a period of peace.'[5]

Brougham presented a number of the petitions himself, frequently making substantial speeches. For two weeks after the
avalanche of petitions began the Opposition had it all their own
way. Government supporters said nothing while Opposition
members fought with one another for the floor. Brougham said
that the Government supporters were 'stricken with dumbness'.
There was talk of an unusual amount of illness among the

---

[1] *Hansard*, xxxiii. 442.   [2] Ibid. xxxiii. 26, 126 seq.
[3] *Hansard*, xxxii. 1140.   [4] Add. MSS. 35152, f. 163.
[5] Works of Ricardo, vii. 274.

cabinet members. Brougham, in merciful mood, suggested that the members of the Government who were not ill should 'comfort their ailing brethren by telling them about the petitions'.[1]

Realizing that the one-sided situation in Parliament was making a bad impression, the Government began to debate the petitions, which were almost all against the tax. The Opposition speakers were still the keener. On one occasion all of the members on one Opposition bench rose and said 'Mr. Speaker' at the same time.[2] Some days Brougham spoke two to four times.

By the evening of 18 March when the vote was to be taken, Parliament had heard more than enough of speeches on the subject. But all the approaches to the House were thronged with people anxious to hear the result, hoping against despair. What hope they had was not shared by the Whig Opposition, where the most optimistic believed that the Government would have a majority of five or six.[3] The ministers knew that the pressure from the constituencies and the speeches in Parliament had been effective. They expected a greatly reduced majority. They had won every division that session by well over fifty and some by over a hundred. Two weeks earlier they had estimated that they would have a majority of twenty; on the morning of the 18th they hoped for forty.[4]

When Wilberforce rose to his feet it was after midnight. It had probably been arranged that Tory Wilberforce, who was making one of his independent stands, should be the last but one to speak against the tax and Brougham should close the debate for the Opposition. They had, no doubt, prepared their speeches carefully. The latter part of Wilberforce's was not given in *Hansard* because there was too much noise in the House for the reporter to hear it. Brougham had barely got started when his best shouting voice was checked by the noise and cries of 'Question'. He sat down and the members filed into the lobbies for the division. Then came the period of anxious waiting, then the report of the tellers: for the motion to continue the income-tax, 201; against, 238. The amazed Whig members and the packed gallery broke loose. In less time than it takes to tell it the up-

---

[1] *Hansard*, xxxii. 944–7, 1050.
[2] *Memoirs*, ii. 306.
[3] Romilly, *Memoirs*, ii. 412.
[4] Gore, p. 100, Sefton to Creevey; *Letters of George IV*, ii. 160, Castlereagh to the Prince Regent.

roarious cheering had been taken up by the farthest reaches of the dense crowd outside. So passed Britain's first peace-time income-tax, unwept, unhonoured, but not altogether unsung. Many, like Lord Sefton, were 'drunk with joy' and not a few were drunk with something else before the dawn broke. Brougham was unanimously given the main credit for the victory. A famous snuff was called 'Hardham's 37' and the majority against the income-tax was dubbed 'Brougham's 37'. A cartoon of the day showed Brougham offering the Regent a pinch of it.

Brougham was frequently at his worst in the hour of victory. Next morning, according to Place, Brougham talked wildly in Place's shop about *his* readiness to form a government and bring in a sweeping measure of Parliamentary Reform. Two evenings later he made one of the worst mistakes of his life and did much to spoil the situation for the Whigs, when he made a personal, unjust, and altogether outrageous attack on the Prince Regent. It occurred in the second of two long speeches on 20 March.[1] He protested against the raising of the salaries of the Secretaries of the Admiralty. The senior secretary was Croker. Brougham said that this was 'a most profligate and scandalous waste of public money'. So far all was well. Brougham and Croker were expected to attack one another at every given opportunity, and the only thing that could have shocked anyone would have been for either to have at all spared the other. But when, in the midst of a tirade against the Government's extravagance, Brougham brought a scathing indictment against the extravagance of the Prince Regent, his lack of concern for the suffering of the people and his general way of life, that was quite a different matter.

Sir Samuel Romilly, though a close friend of Brougham, wrote in his diary:

Brougham . . . made a violent attack upon the Regent . . . in terms which would not have been too strong to have described the latter days of Tiberius. . . . Brougham's speech was very injudicious as well as very unjust; for, with all the Prince's faults, and they are great enough, it is absurd to speak of him as if he were one of the most sensual and unfeeling tyrants that ever disgraced a throne.[2]

'Squire' Western, aggressive Whig, solid country gentleman,

---

[1] *Hansard*, xxxiii. 462 seq., 489 seq.
[2] Romilly, *Memoirs*, i. 412–13.

expressed himself more vividly in a letter which he wrote that night:

He [Brougham] has uttered a speech which, for power of *speaking*, surpassed anything you ever heard, and by which he has damned himself past redemption. . . . Where the devil a fellow could get such lungs and such a flow of jaw . . . surpasses my imagination. I was sitting in the gallery . . . and he made my head spin in such a style I thought I should tumble over. When I recovered, I began to think this will *never* do, impossible, I will go down and see what other lads think of it. . . . I soon found that everybody was struck in the same way and even more. Now, when I say he has damaged himself past redemption, I mean as a man aspiring to be Leader. . . . Ministers would have been beaten to-night, I do believe, again. Brougham has put them up 20 per cent.[1]

Some Tories, who would have voted with the Whigs again, were so disgusted that they voted with the Government. Other Tories, who felt that they could not vote with the Government on this salary question, made Brougham's speech an excuse for leaving the House. When the division came, the Government carried an amendment shelving the question of the secretaries' salaries by a majority of twenty-nine. The belief that if it had not been for Brougham's attack on the Regent the Government would have probably suffered a second defeat within three days was practically unanimous on both sides of the House. The more intelligent Whigs did not accuse Brougham of keeping them out of power, for they did not think there had been much chance of their coming into it, but the underlings with keener eyes on the loaves and the fishes blamed him bitterly for keeping them out. All felt that he had displayed a lack of judgement. The party could never again trust him; they would never think of giving him the responsibility of their *official* leadership in the House of Commons.

Romilly was a man of exemplary honour, a devoted reformer, and a good friend of Brougham. His judgement as recorded, not publicly but in his diary, on the night of Brougham's attack on the Prince Regent strikes one as being eminently just:

Brougham is a man of the most splendid talents and the most

---

[1] *Creevey Papers*, i. 249–50. The letter speaks of 'the glorious victory' over the income-tax (18 Mar.) and to a possible second defeat of the ministry on the night it was written. The only possible date is 20 Mar.

extensive acquirements. It would be difficult to overrate the services which he has rendered to the slaves in the West Indies, or that of the friends to the extension of knowledge and education among the poor. . . . How much more is it to be lamented that his want of judgment and of prudence should prevent his great talents and such good intentions from being as great a blessing to mankind as they ought to be.[1]

It should, however, be said once for all that while everyone said that Brougham lacked judgement, on most matters his judgement was remarkably good. What troubled men was that there was no predicting when his judgement would appear to be very bad indeed, carried away by impulse.

Brougham wrote to Leigh Hunt that in attacking the Regent he was speaking to an audience outside the House.[2] And it is difficult to dissociate such an attack on the Regent intended for the public from the talk of his seeking a divorce and Brougham's fear in 1816 of such a divorce imperilling the Princess Charlotte's succession to the throne.

A joint letter from the Prime Minister, the Foreign Secretary who was Government leader in the House of Commons, and the Chancellor of the Exchequer was addressed to the Prince Regent on 15 March, three days before the vote on the income-tax, urging the most rigid economy. It should be noted that the policy of retrenchment and economy enunciated in that letter was the policy which, with all the ardour of his temperament and his supreme gifts as a parliamentary speaker, Brougham had been urging for a month and a half. Before the date of the letter very little had been done about it; after that, a good deal was done.

Castlereagh wrote to the Prince Regent on the night of the 20th and Liverpool wrote to him on the 21st. The Prime Minister said: 'The Government hangs by a thread.'[3] He wrote again to the Regent on the 23rd: 'We are exposed to the most acrimonious, systematic and persevering Opposition that I ever recollect to have seen in Parliament.'[4] This had been Brougham's work. In the face of it, the Government surrendered on certain pressing matters. Western and Brougham had attacked the malt-

[1] Romilly, *Memoirs*, ii. 413.
[2] Add. MSS. 38108, f. 161. The letter is given in full in Aspinall, pp. 62–63.
[3] *Letters of George IV*, ii. 61; C. D. Yonge, *Life and Administration of 2nd Earl of Liverpool*, 3 vols. (1868), ii. 270–1.   [4] *Letters of George IV*, ii. 162 n.

tax. The Government gave up the malt-tax. And it also announced that the salaries of the Secretaries of the Admiralty, Croker and Barrow, would not, after all, be increased. When Brougham had last been in Parliament in 1812, the Government had surrendered to him on the Orders in Council. Brougham might, as Western said, have 'damned himself beyond redemption' as far as the official leadership of the party was concerned, but the Whigs had at last found the man who *could* lead when leadership was most necessary, and who could get things done.

On 27 March Brougham made a long speech on the navy estimates. He complained of extravagance generally and of offices that were practically sinecures. He discussed superannuation. 'The committee would be surprised to learn that one of these superannuated gentlemen was twenty-five and another twenty-two years of age.' 'A third person on the same list was said to have been thirty-five years in the service; but as he was no more than forty-four years old, it could only be on the ideas of prematurity prevailing in the Admiralty that he could have been deemed fit for public service at the age of nine.'[1]

On 9 April he made a great speech on the agricultural distress.[2] It was simply an analysis of the causes, accompanied by his own suggestions for a remedy. Among the remedies suggested were a further easing of taxation; the revenue to be compensated by an emergency invasion of the Sinking Fund; drastic revision of the poor laws; the repeal of prohibitive laws regarding the export of wool; and the more aggressive development of new lines of general trade, particularly trade with South America. One part of this speech which was somewhat incidental has an interest of its own. It has been said that Brougham showed inconsistency in favouring the Corn Law of 1815 at this time (1816) and opposing it later. What he said was: 'I conceive the measure to be politic, at least as a palliative, or as affording the means of carrying the country through difficulties, the greatest pressure of which we may hope will only prove temporary. . . . If it enables us to get over existing evils, arising in great part from a transition to a new state of things, it does a great permanent good.' There is nothing inconsistent between that and his oppos-

---

[1] *Hansard*, xxxiii. 631 seq.; *The Times*, 28 Mar. 1816.
[2] *Speeches*, i. 503 seq.

ing its continuance at a later date. This is only one instance of the tendency of all later writers to exaggerate Brougham's supposed inconsistency. There is very little of it in his public utterances, though there is some in his private letters where he was to a greater extent at the mercy of his impulses.

On 8 May Brougham introduced his Bill 'for securing and extending the liberty of the press'. He pointed out grave injustices in the law of libel, both in his speech in the House[1] and in an article in the September *Edinburgh Review*, which he wrote with the reintroduction of the Bill in the next session in mind. As the law stood, no evidence for the truth of the statement alleged to be libellous could be presented in a case of criminal libel, though it was permitted in a civil case. Brougham insisted that this placed the press in an embarrassing position, living in constant fear of prosecution instituted by the Government and unable to place in evidence proof of truth of its statements. A juror would find himself in a much better position to determine guilt or innocence if he were permitted to give consideration to the truth or falsehood of the statement. Brougham's Bill also proposed to do away with the special privileges enjoyed by the Attorney-General in his *ex-officio* informations in regard to libel. Such informations were not submitted to a grand jury, and at the trial of the case a special jury might be selected, usually from civil servants and magistrates. Brougham's Bill provided for the abolition of special juries in libel trials, except in cases where both parties desired one.

The *ex-officio* information further intimidated the publisher of newspapers by postponing action indefinitely in many cases after the information had been filed. Of the forty-two informations for criminal libel filed by Attorney-General Gibbs between 1807 and 1810, only sixteen were brought to trial. Gibbs apparently believed that the sword of Damocles could protect the Government against free discussion in the press better even than prison terms after convictions by special juries.

The measure proposed by Brougham also permitted a defendant to submit evidence to the effect that the alleged libel was published without his consent or knowledge. Such evidence would not be decisive, but would be weighed along with other evidence.

[1] *Hansard*, xxxiv. 377 seq.

When Brougham reintroduced his Bill next session it was clear enough that its support would be weak, and it was dropped. But Brougham was always a blazer of trails. Another Bill of his to provide for evidence of the truth of statements in criminal libel cases was submitted unsuccessfully in 1830. Lord Campbell's libel act in 1843, which was strongly supported by Brougham, effected this in cases instituted by individuals; both Campbell and Brougham were disappointed in failing to have the principle extended to Government prosecutions.[1] Lord Campbell's act also afforded the protection to publication without consent or knowledge, which Brougham had sought to effect. A successful Whig amendment to one of the Six Acts of 1819 required the Attorney-General to bring a case to trial within a year of his filing information.[2] The employment of special juries in libel cases was abolished in 1825. All of this, of course, meant the removal of obstacles to the freedom of the press, for which Brougham was always enthusiastic.

On 2 July the session was over and Brougham was exhausted and ill. Probably on medical advice he made what for him was the hard decision of taking a holiday for the remainder of the year. In mid-July Lady Shelley and her party met him in Switzerland. As usual he had a fund of amusing anecdotes. Lady Shelley wrote in her diary:

Mr. Brougham throughout this expedition has made himself very agreeable . . . and we told him that we had saved him from committing suicide. He hates travelling, abhors Switzerland and the Swiss generally, scoffs at fine views. . . . He wishes himself back in England and yet has no intention of going there. . . . It is evident that great talents are of no use without a little sunshine of the mind.[3]

The trouble was that Brougham could find no 'sunshine of the mind' in trying to take a holiday. His happiness depended on constant activity. He had rested in the previous year because he had been afraid he was going to die; now that he was not going to die, he did not know how to rest. On 15 August he wrote from 'Geneva (uninhabitable)': 'I have been here for some time. . . . It is a country to be in for two hours, or two hours and a half, if the weather is fine and no longer. Ennui

---

[1] Campbell, viii. 150–3.
[2] *Hansard*, xli. 1480. See Aspinall, *Politics and the Press*, p. 42.
[3] *Diary of Frances Lady Shelley* (1912–13), pp. 227–8.

comes on the third hour, and suicide attacks you before night. There is *no resource whatever* for passing the time, except looking at lakes and hills, which is over immediately.'[1] There we have it. For Brougham everything had to be changing and changing for the better. The lakes and the mountains were always there. They belonged to eternity. Anybody might have eternity and welcome to it. What Brougham was interested in was time. The lakes and the mountains were peaceful. He loved to talk about peace— between nations. But peace for himself was the last thing he wanted.

Before the month was over he was at work again. He wrote an anonymous pamphlet on the rumours that the Prince was seeking a divorce. (The Princess Charlotte was still living, and there was his old fear of a divorce imperilling her succession to the throne.) He wrote two articles for the *Edinburgh*. He discovered something good in Switzerland; there was material for the study of education in the experiments of Pestalozzi and Fellenberg. And he began collecting information for an attack on Castlereagh's foreign policy next session. In mid-September Lord Lansdowne met him in Milan 'in good spirits and health'.[2] In the session of 1817, though suffering from quinsey, Brougham was on his feet more frequently than the Government leader in the Commons (98 times to Castlereagh's 85) and much more frequently than any other member. On thirty-two occasions he made long, substantial, well-informed speeches.

At the opening of the parliamentary session of 1817 there was serious unemployment throughout the country, particularly in the manufacturing districts. There had been some outbursts of impatience among the workers, some rioting, but on the whole the traditional British respect for law and order survived. Parliament, however, set up secret committees of both Houses to inquire into the danger of revolution. They reported that there was a widespread movement, with close links between many districts, aiming at a general insurrection. Much of the evidence laid before the committees was that of frightened magistrates who were the victims of their own exaggeration (as Brougham said, 'it was the nature of alarm to be infectious') and, worse

---

[1] *Creevey Papers*, i. 258, Brougham to Creevey.
[2] Add. MSS. 34456, ff. 172 seq. (Auckland MSS.), Lansdowne to Auckland, 16 Sept. 1816.

still, some of the evidence was provided by government spies who were anxious to increase a demand for their own services. Many believed that they were threatened with a revolution, and the ministers planned drastic action, not because they themselves were caught in a panic, but because something approaching panic was spreading in the squirarchy on whom, along with the clergy, Tory governments depended for political support. On the basis of the committee reports the Government introduced two bills, one suspending habeas corpus (the only suspension of habeas corpus in time of peace in the nineteenth or twentieth century) and the other giving magistrates an extraordinary control of public meetings, including meetings of literary societies.

Since 1815 there had developed a strong movement for Parliamentary Reform. In this year (1817) it moved in on Parliament in the form of a number of petitions, all of which asked for universal (manhood) suffrage and annual parliaments. They represented an extreme programme of Parliamentary Reform, which it was impossible for Brougham to support.

In the previous September Place had told Bennet that Brougham would not be a satisfactory member for Westminster,[1] although a year earlier he had expressed to Mill a decided preference for Brougham over Cochrane. Why did Place turn against Brougham? According to his own statement,[2] because Brougham had supported the incarceration of Napoleon at St. Helena, which Place said was illegal; because Brougham had urged a special grant to the Princess Charlotte in view of her marriage; and because Brougham had left the platform of a Westminster meeting with a group of Whigs when 'Orator' Hunt was launching a violent attack on all Whigs. As for the grant to the Princess Charlotte, Place said that if Brougham was looking toward the Court, he could not expect support from the people. A year earlier he had written of Brougham: 'In political affairs I always fear for those who are not in all things republicans from principle.'[3] Place exhausted an extensive vocabulary in abusing the Whigs on all occasions. His policy was that of obtaining support from members of the Whig Mountain, if possible, but for the rest making as much trouble for both parties as the Radicals could make. He had no use for Brougham's

[1] Add. MSS. 35153, ff. 6 seq.   [2] Ibid. 27809, ff. 30-31.   [3] Ibid., f. 26.

hope of a Whig–Radical alliance, in spite of the fact that Parliamentary Reform would have to come from a parliamentary party or combination of parties.

Now, at the opening of the 1817 session, Place was bitter against Brougham for refusing to support the extreme Parliamentary Reform petitions, which asked for universal suffrage and annual parliaments. The Place manuscripts record Place's statements to the effect that Brougham abused the Radicals outrageously and that it was because of a personal attack by Brougham on Cochrane that he, Place, supplied Cochrane with a copy of Brougham's 1814 speech when he was a candidate for Westminster.[1] Neither *Hansard* nor the press bear out these statements. On 31 January Brougham, after stating his interest in Parliamentary Reform and his opposition to universal suffrage and annual parliaments, said:

He gave them [the petitioners] credit for the best intentions, and he could find apologies for all their errors. . . . They were goaded on by distress. . . . What he objected to was well-educated men urging the un-instructed and the illiterate to demand universal suffrage as their birthright, to declare it the ancient imprescriptible right of Englishmen and told that . . . it was for this right that their ancestors fought and bled.[2]

There is no record of any attack on Cochrane by Brougham, as Place supposed or pretended to suppose, but on 14 February Cochrane attacked Brougham for saying that the petitioners had been misled. Place then gave Cochrane the copy of Brougham's 1814 Westminster speech and Cochrane read parts of it to the House on 17 February.[3] The one bad part of that 1814 speech was Brougham's dishonest attempt to mislead his hearers into thinking of him as an advocate of annual parliaments, a proposal which Brougham on every other occasion denounced as being absurd.

Although Brougham's hopes for a Whig–Radical alliance were wrecked by the Radicals, he was optimistic in visualizing some sort of effective unity at last in the Whig party in the Commons. On 6 February he had written to Lord Lansdowne, who was on the Continent, that within the party 'mountains are becoming valleys'. 'I even hope to throw out their [the ministers'] gagging

[1] Ibid. 35153, ff. 6 seq.
[2] *Hansard*, xxxv. 162.   [3] Ibid. 370 seq.

bills.'[1] He had more to say about the parliamentary reports and the repressive legislation after the session was over in an article on 'The Present State of Public Affairs' in the August number of the *Edinburgh*, contending that much in the reports had been disproved and that there had been remarkably little rioting considering the prevalance of distress.

On 24 February and 14 March [1812] Brougham spoke against the Seditious Meetings Bill. He attacked as unreliable the reports on which it was based. If there was so much sedition, disturbance, and revolutionary plotting, was it not strange that the Government had not made more use of the existing law before it proposed despotic legislation? 'When has it ceased to be a crime to publish or to utter sedition?'[2] Brougham objected strongly to legislation that empowered a magistrate to dissolve a meeting whenever, *in the magistrate's opinion*, words were spoken which held the government of the country in contempt. 'Was it then meant that no meeting shall henceforth be holden to petition against existing defects in government? Better say at once there shall be no more petition for reform.' He denied that they were living in the midst of plots, conspiracies, and rebellion. He ascribed to the recent advances in popular education the remarkable calmness and sense of order displayed by the people. 'Nor could he in any other way explain the marvellous patience which they displayed in bearing such unparalleled distress and burthens hardly to be endured, . . . yet how did parliament reward them? . . . The House, instead of inquiring into the causes of their sufferings . . . passed a bill to gag them with.'[3] The general Whig opposition to the Seditious Meetings Bill was weak, and its third reading was passed by a vote of 179 to 44.

In speaking against the Habeas Corpus Suspension Bill on 23 June, Brougham again questioned the report on which the measure was based. He believed that Sidmouth, the Home Secretary, had been deceived by men like Oliver, the spy. Brougham poured out his supreme contempt. They should trust to the operation of law: 'The constitution of England was not made merely for fair weather.'[4]

On 13 March he made a great speech on Manufacturing

[1] Lansdowne MSS. Parts are given in Aspinall, pp. 74–75.
[2] *Hansard*, xxxv. 622 seq.   [3] Ibid. 1121 seq.
[4] Ibid. xxxvi. 1133 seq.

Distress[1] in which he described the sufferings of the industrial workers as feelingly and eloquently as he had when opposing the Orders in Council in 1812; he said that the situation was very much worse than it had been then. This was also one of the first parliamentary speeches on behalf of free trade. 'The period now arrived when . . . it becomes absolutely necessary to enter upon a careful but fearless revision of our whole commercial system. . . . The old mercantile system has long been exploded.' In this speech also Brougham referred to the Corn Law of 1815 and made it quite clear that he did not favour it as permanent policy. 'We approved of it for special reasons many of them temporary in their nature.' The removal of 'the numberless trammels' which had been devised for trade in general 'might very well alter our whole opinion upon the Corn Bill'.

When he came out with this clear-cut advocacy of free trade, Brougham spoke for himself rather than for his party. In the next twenty-eight years the steps toward free trade were to be taken by the Tories. Now in 1817 Brougham's motion to take the matter under consideration would probably have received government support if it had not been that half of his speech was a vigorous and rather unfair attack on the Government's foreign policy, his resolutions being so worded that they embodied a condemnation of the Government. Robinson, who within a few years was to move definitely, if cautiously, toward free trade, was already Vice-President of the Board of Trade, and in replying to Brougham on behalf of the Government he said that he agreed with much of what he had said. The statements 'respecting the prohibitory system adopted toward other countries had his entire concurrence'. But the honourable and learned gentleman had spoken without appreciation of the great difficulties that lay in the path of any attempts to change the situation. Castlereagh agreed with Robinson and defended his foreign policy vigorously against Brougham's attacks, 'however willing he would have been to have entered into the discussion of the commercial question, had it not been rendered subservient to a political one'.[2]

The attitude of the ministers and of the Tory party toward reform is not to be dismissed as being that of Eldon and some of his colleagues. The forward-looking view was there; and when

[1] *Speeches*, i. 549 seq.   [2] *Hansard*, xxxv. 1044 seq.

it manifested itself in more definite action after 1820 it was because the country had settled down and the worst of the unrest was over, and partly because the circumstances of the Queen's Trial helped the liberal forces in both parties. To make the death of Castlereagh in 1822 a watershed in British history is as untrue to the facts as it is unfair to Castlereagh, the victim of the savage ignorance of persons like Shelley and Byron.

The Government's record in this session of 1817 indicates this clearly enough. There was more than the cautiously expressed economic liberalism of Robinson and Castlereagh. Brougham might continue to be a voice crying for retrenchment, but he had lost his wilderness. Liverpool spoke of retrenchment in the session of 1817 much as Brougham had done in 1816. And the Government made substantial, if not drastic, reductions in public expenditure in various departments. There was a quite remarkable reduction of the shameful sinecures which had been vigorously attacked by Brougham, Brand, and the more liberal Whigs. The first factory bill (the elder Peel's) was supported by the Government and it was passed in the following year. The appointment of a committee on the poor laws indicated an awareness of their unsatisfactory nature and some interest in their reform in spite of the difficulties that invested the question at such a time. There was little or no appreciation of this in Brougham's State of the Nation speech and resolutions at the end of the session. He was not conceding anything to the enemy. Neither the speech nor the resolutions are worth describing here. Both were poorly conceived and bundled together a number of matters without consultation with the other Whig leaders in the House. Replying to Brougham, Castlereagh repeated his statement of belief in freer trade on principle, but 'a more enlarged policy must be progressive and mutual and could not be adopted *per saltem* as the honourable and learned gentleman appeared to think'.[1]

Canning twitted Brougham on his failure to mention what had been done this session in retrenchment, the abolishing of sinecures and the discussion of the poor laws, matters on which Brougham had been very insistent. Some future historian, he said, would record that 'session after session' abolition of sinecures had been 'attempted in vain', but at length 'in the year 1817

[1] *Hansard*, xxxvi. 1396 seq.

they had been abolished; and that in that year there lived a sagacious seer, who, taking it upon himself to characterize parliaments and to purvey for history had failed to mention that fact'.[1]

In the Whig party Brougham was regarded as too liberal in his outlook and as acting with too much ardour on the belief that the principal business of an Opposition was to oppose. Some of this and Brougham's feelings about it are reflected in a letter of his to Lord Lansdowne:

> Our own friends . . . shrink from, disapprove, shake their heads at the constant galling opposition which alone does the business, which for example destroyed the Orders in Council and the Income Tax. . . . It is thought that certain individuals stop the way. . . . I am one. I believe Romilly is another. . . . I know that in a short time they will see their mistake and then we shall all go on perfectly well together. . . . I think I can venture to say that you will find Romilly of the same sentiments. I do not think we have ever differed on any matter of the least importance.[2]

In his reply, Lansdowne suggested, with all kindness, that Brougham had acted too much on his own without consulting the party. Thus far Brougham published the letter in his Memoirs. It is strange that he left the following unpublished. Lansdowne continued:

> There is now more than ever a mass of political opinion, in and out of Parliament, if not quite independent of party feeling, at least much more so than on either side of the Speaker's chair, which must be considered not for the sake of power in the vulgar sense, but of any power to do good by public men like yourself and which, if you expect to direct in some instances, you must submit to in others. . . . If anything so improbable was to occur as my being advised with a taking any part in an administration, one of my first endeavours, both on private and public considerations, would be to secure for it and for the public . . . the assistance of those talents which you possess perhaps in a greater degree than any man now living for the public service.[3]

In his reply Brougham said that they must appeal to 'the well-informed and weighty parts of the community'. Previously party politics had been a matter of great leaders and great

[1] Ibid. 1423 seq.
[2] Lansdowne MSS., 21 July 1817. The letter is given more fully in Aspinall, pp. 80–82.　　　　　[3] Brougham MSS., 28 July 1817.

aristocratic families. 'Now, it is plain that those powers cannot settle the state by their agreements or differences. All this is as nothing *against* the principle of party, but it is a modification and improvement of that corner stone of free government.'[1] This correspondence between Lansdowne and Brougham is the more important because for some years Lansdowne was to be the effectual Whig leader in the Lords as Brougham was in the Commons.

As we have seen, the year 1818 was a very busy one for Brougham with his education committee. Over the whole session Brougham was on his feet oftener than Castlereagh, the Government leader, and twice as often as Tierney, though it must be admitted that the 1818 debates were not of great importance. On 2 June Burdett, who, after advocating household suffrage, was back again on the hopeless road of annual parliaments and universal suffrage, presented resolutions favouring these as well as other aspects of Parliamentary Reform, including equal electoral districts. The resolutions were prepared in whole or in part by Bentham. In opposing the resolutions so far as they advocated annual parliaments and universal suffrage, Brougham further offended Francis Place, whose acrid humour was poured out in a fresh stream of misrepresentation. To judge from the Place manuscripts one would suppose that Brougham had attacked the Burdett resolutions with an extraordinary degree of violence. *Hansard* presents a different picture, one of friendly and reasoned disagreement.[2] 'Far be it for him to view with levity, or to treat with ridicule, opinions which were conscientiously held by a great body of people in this country . . . and he claimed from them the same degree of charity which he was willing to extend to them.' This was rather an unusual line for Brougham to take. He habitually gave no quarter and expected to receive none. He might claim charity on this occasion; he did not receive it. Burdett, in his reply, attacked Brougham bitterly. Francis Place applied to Brougham Dryden's lines:

> This Trimmer is for holding all things even
> Just like to him that hung twixt Hell and Heaven.
> Damned neuter! in this middle way of steering
> He's neither fish, nor flesh, nor good red herring.[3]

---

[1] Lansdowne MSS. Quoted more fully in Aspinall, pp. 82–83.
[2] *Hansard*, xxxviii. 1151 seq.   [3] Add. MSS., 36627, f. 47 v.

He was at the same time being denounced as a dangerous revolutionary by such intelligent men in his own county of Westmorland as Wordsworth and Southey. When one considers the
change that would have been effected in the government of
Britain by the measure of Parliamentary Reform favoured by
Brougham, one is bound to conclude that there was some justification for the charge of his being a revolutionary; for that of
being a trimmer there was none at all. Yet the latter found
credulous enough acceptance. When Trower wrote to Ricardo
praising Brougham's speech on the Burdett resolutions and
stating that 'his talents will obtain for him' the honour of leading
the Opposition 'which he would never procure from the consent
of the party', Ricardo replied:

Brougham is a very clever man, but will never rank high as a
politician, for there is no steadiness in his opinions and he appears to
me to sacrifice too much for his immediate objects. Sometimes he
wishes to conciliate the Whigs, and then the violent reformers receive
no mercy at his hands; at other times one would conclude that he
went so far in the cause of reform as even Burdett himself. A man
who wishes to obtain a lasting name should not be a vacillating
statesman, too eager for immediate applause.[1]

Ricardo did not know Brougham well, and he did not follow
very closely the proceedings of Parliament. He was repeating in
a gentler form the talk of Place and his Radical friends. But, of
course, coming from Ricardo, this statement is interesting. It
was given in an early publication of Ricardo's letters and played
its part in forming the general judgement on Brougham.
Brougham may have, at times, made sacrifices for immediate
objects, as most men do, but it cannot be said that he did so in
relation to such important matters as the anti-slavery movement, popular education, and the democratizing of the Whig
party; and Ricardo's statement is quite untrue in relation to the
matter under discussion, Parliamentary Reform. The reference
to Burdett is quite absurd; it was Burdett who was inconsistent,
not Brougham.

During this session of 1818, much of Brougham's thought and
not a little of his activity were captured by an election contest in

[1] Works of Ricardo, vii. 27.

Westmorland, his own county. The thought of an election in Westmorland in 1818 was like the suggestion of a miracle. There had not been a contested election in Westmorland for over forty years. The great family was the Lowthers. The head of the family was Lord Lonsdale, who was one of the great borough owners. In addition to his array of pocket boroughs, he named at every general election two members of Parliament for the county of Westmorland, usually members of his own family. In December 1817 Brougham decided (no one but he would have thought of it) to attempt to break the power of the Lowthers in Westmorland by having himself nominated as a candidate against the two sitting members, Colonel Lowther and Lord Lowther. Meetings were held in London attended by resident and non-resident freeholders of Westmorland. The pretence was that they organized for the 'independence of Westmorland' and selected Brougham as a candidate. There can be no doubt that Brougham originated the movement.

He had assumed that if he were defeated in Westmorland in the approaching general election, he would continue to sit in Parliament for Lord Darlington's borough of Winchelsea. But he received a jolt from a letter from Lord Darlington who pointed out that there was a family connexion between him and the Lowthers. 'I feel so strongly the impropriety of countenancing in any way so direct an attack upon what has been so long considered an honorable and certain appendage (however I may disagree in that idea) to that family' that if Brougham stood for Westmorland, he could not sit in the new parliament for Lord Darlington's borough of Winchelsea.[1] After some hesitation, Brougham decided to respond to the Westmorland invitation which he had initiated.

This, of course, was more than a wild adventure suited to Brougham's temperament. It was a dramatic play in his movement for Parliamentary Reform. Although it lay outside the orbit of general Parliamentary Reform proposals and was not considered corrupt, so long as county members were returned by the mere fiat of the great family of the county, the House of Commons could not be representative of the people of the nation. In the counties, every forty-shilling freeholder had the vote. Brougham was giving the freeholders of Westmorland

[1] Brougham MSS., 15 Jan. 1818.

the first opportunity to vote for a representative in Parliament in forty-four years. The Whig borough-owners were concerned at the nature of the attack, and the great Whig families who dominated their own counties were bound to resent it.

Brougham wrote to Creevey: 'The regular Coles are astonished at this rebellion against legitimate authority. Lord H[olland] won't touch the subject, no more will young C. [Abercromby], nor Eden, nor Macdonald, etc.; and Lord Derby, being applied to by Thanet, declined interfering, as did the Duke of Devonshire and Lord G[rey], each on his own ground.'[1] In spite of the public attitude of the Whigs, one seems to catch a glimmer of favourable interest in a letter from Tierney to Grey, in which he says that Brougham seemed to be quite confident of victory in Westmorland, and although the subject was banned at Holland House, apparently by Lady Holland, Lord Holland and John Allen smuggled Brougham, from time to time, into a small room when they wished to know about progress in the Westmorland campaign.[2] Brougham was nominally a Whig candidate, but he received no active support from members of the party except from Lord Thanet locally and from Lambton (later Lord Durham) who went to Westmorland to help him. Yet this bold stroke caught the public eye, and this Westmorland election received twice as much attention in the London newspapers as any election in the country outside the London constituencies.

Wordsworth was very active. He had applied to Lord Lonsdale for a position which would not involve much in the way of work, but would ensure him a livelihood.[3] Lord Lonsdale had used his influence to have Wordsworth appointed Distributor of Stamps for Westmorland. There can be no doubt, however, that Wordsworth would have supported the Lowthers against Brougham in any case. To him the great enemy was democracy. He was sincere enough when he wrote to Lord Lonsdale that nothing could check democracy but 'the existence of large estates continued from generation to generation in particular families, and

---

[1] Creevey MSS. Given in *Creevey Papers*, p. 120, where it is printed at the bottom of a letter to which it does not belong. This is part of the letter given in *Creevey Papers*, i. 254, where it is wrongly dated.

[2] Howick MSS., Tierney to Grey, 3 Feb. 1818; Brougham MSS., Brougham to Lambton [Feb. 1818].

[3] *Letters of William and Dorothy Wordsworth: the Middle Years*, 2 vols. (1937), ii. 485, 554.

parliamentary power in proportion'.[1] Wordsworth regarded Brougham as a revolutionary, or at least as one whose ideas had to be checked if a revolution were to be avoided. He wrote a pamphlet in support of the Lowthers as well as several newspaper articles; he tried to manipulate the control of local newspapers and he presented to Lord Lonsdale a plan by which he [Words-worth] was to be enabled to buy an estate and divide it up into twelve [estates], thereby creating eleven extra votes. No part of Wordsworth's 'Addresses to the Freeholders of Westmor-land' is worthy of quotation here. They constitute a dull eulogy of stability badly expressed.

The Anglican clergy could, of course, be counted on to support the Tory candidate. Brougham said in one of his speeches:

I am a Church of England man, and I view its institutions with a most affectionate regard, but I trust those institutions do not require me to venerate the priest who spends six days among publicans, plying the peasantry with liquor by day and by night, and rests on the seventh to preach against drunkenness. . . . They [the clergy] have represented me as a Dissenter and as a Roman Catholic. Both stories could not be true; so they were circulated in different quar-ters. . . . Think you that these men trouble themselves at all about my religious principles? . . . They would never enquire whether I belonged to the Church or no, if I had but the patronage of churches. . . . We have not, indeed, quite the same God. It is Mammon whom they serve. . . . In the bosom of the Established Church, I have lived and shall die; but it becomes me not to judge other men, and I am an advocate for unbounded toleration.[2]

Some of the free Lowther beer went astray. When the Lowther candidates were making their grand entry into Kendal, some canal workers, Scottish and Irish, who had come into the county to do a job, partook too freely of the Lowther beer and were fairly drunk. They had entered into the spirit of the Brougham campaign and, on this occasion, joined the Brougham supporters in attacking the Lowther procession. The gentlemen in the Lowther procession were plastered with mud, some of them were slightly injured, several of their carriages were smashed, and, according to Brougham's informant, the 'two cubs them-selves [the Lowther candidates] sought refuge in flight'. All the

---

[1] *Letters of William and Dorothy Wordsworth*, ii. 804.
[2] *The Times*, 8 Apr. 1818, from the *Carlisle Journal*.

time the canal workers kept shouting 'Lowther ale and Brougham forever'.[1] After that the Lowthers had troops brought in to keep order.

On 23 March Brougham made his entry into Kendal. Dorothy Wordsworth had not been able to resist her curiosity and had come in to see the man and the show. She liked the show. 'When he drew up towards the door, with music, banners, horsemen, and the immense multitude on foot, all joining in one huzza, fearless of the driving [snow] storm, the spectacle was grand. To my feelings, it would have been sublime if the cause had been a good one.' She did not think much of Brougham's speech. 'If such be House of Commons oratory, commend me to a mountebank doctor.'[2] That was probably what Brougham was to Dorothy Wordsworth, a mountebank doctor, deceiving the people with quack nostrums for the ills of the body politic.

Brougham employed the word 'romantic' to express his feelings evoked by the open-air meetings in the Lake District by night and by day, always accompanied by music, banners, and gunfire. His speeches were from half to three-quarters of an hour in length, and he gave from five to seven of them a day, his carriage drawn from place to place by relays of men, a certain number supplied by each township, more expeditiously than it could be done by horses.[3] Lambton joined Brougham, who worked him so hard that he had to get up early in the morning to write his letters to his wife. After it was over, Lambton, writing to Sir Robert Wilson, gave a picture of Brougham in the heat of the conflict. 'He worked like a horse. He was at once candidate, counsel, agent, canvasser, and orator, and changing his characters every hour, and always cheerful and active. Really his energy of mind is beyond anything I could ever have conceived.'[4]

The voting began on 30 June. There was only one polling place for the county, at Appleby. About 500 Brougham voters (a majority of those who voted for him) walked, that is, marched, the twenty-six miles from Kendal to Appleby. Most of them were voting for the first time. Brougham had arranged to look

[1] Brougham MSS., Brougham to Lambton [Feb. 1818]. *The Times*, 26 June 1818, referring back to Feb. 11.   [2] *Letters*, ii. 809.
[3] Brougham MSS., Brougham to Lambton, 'Wednesday night' [25 Mar. 1818].
[4] Add. MSS. 30108, ff. 17, 18, quoted in C. W. New, *Lord Durham* (1929), pp. 19–20.

after his voters in houses, barns, and tents.[1] In the London betting, Brougham was the favourite. Among the Tories there was the greatest apprehension. When he heard that Brougham led on the first day's poll, Croker wrote to Lord Lowther: 'We are all in the greatest anxiety . . . people are frightened . . . from the bottom of my heart I wish you success.'[2] Each voter might, of course, cast two votes. The final count was: Lord Lowther 1,211, Colonel Lowther 1,157, Brougham 889.

Before he left the hustings on the final day, Brougham announced his intention of forming an association to work for 'the independence of Westmorland'. He intended to be a candidate for the county in the next general election. To commemorate the battle, he had a medal struck and presented one to every freeholder who had voted for him. He promised to each of these men that if he needed assistance in any way in any part of the world, he would do everything he could to help him.[3] Among the interesting claims on this promise was a letter which Brougham received in December 1831 when he was a member of Lord Grey's Cabinet, from William Lyon Mackenzie, who was later to be the leader of the Upper Canada Rebellion of 1837. Mackenzie said that Mr. Stephen Washington, a prosperous farmer in the township of Scarborough, had been one of Brougham's 'grey coats of Westmorland', that he was the proud possessor of the Brougham medal of 1818, and that he remembered gratefully Brougham's promise. Mr. Washington now respectfully requested Brougham to lay before His Majesty and to support the enclosed petition from the people of Scarborough 'so that . . . a Lieutenant Governor and an Executive Council may be given to Upper Canada, who will possess some sympathy with the people they govern, and aid them in their efforts to obtain good laws and free institutions'.[4]

During the election Brougham spoke angrily about the failure of the Whig party to support him,[5] but he was appeased somewhat when Lord Darlington relented and permitted him to continue to sit for Winchelsea. When Brougham and Lambton went to Lambton Castle afterwards they discussed, among

---

[1] *The Times*, 3 July 1818; Brougham MSS.; Lambton MSS.
[2] Croker MSS., Letter Book 7, 4 July 1818.
[3] Brougham MSS., *passim*; *The Times*, 7, 29 July 1818.
[4] Brougham MSS., 19 Dec. 1831.
[5] Letter to Lord Holland quoted in Aspinall, p. 89.

other things, the leadership of the Whig party in the House of Commons. Tierney was the almost unanimous choice, with Lambton and Creevey among the dissentients, but the more discerning realized, as several of them said, that whoever was selected Brougham would be the real leader.

In the meantime Brougham had probably written an article on the state of Parties in the June *Edinburgh*. 'The scrambles for power among a few great families are no longer to be dignified with the title of party differences. . . . Statesmen must mingle with their party discussions a perpetual appeal to the undeniable interests and strong feelings of a well informed and inquiring nation.' Political delusions were breaking up 'as the education of the poor advances'. The refusal of the Radicals to join forces with other Parliamentary Reformers was deplored. 'They chose to say Annual Parliaments; and therefore no man must whisper a word of Triennial. They said every male of twenty-one should vote; and therefore no honest man could presume to confine the franchise to . . . householders.'

In December 1818 Romilly died by his own hand while of unsound mind. Brougham said that Romilly and he had never disagreed on anything. Both were staunch liberals, too liberal to please the Whig party. Romilly had been the great pioneer of criminal-law reform, had pleaded the cause of the Negro slaves in words almost as eloquent as those of Wilberforce or Brougham, and had followed Brougham's lead in efforts for universal education. The friendship between them had been close. In the weeks following Romilly's death, Brougham said that he was fit company only for himself.[1] Lady Granville met Brougham at Mrs. Lamb's before the end of the month and said that he was 'looking like something just dug up'. His appearance was ascribed to the effect of Romilly's death.[2] Two months later, Brougham still looked ill. Sydney Smith wrote to Lady Grey: 'If he would stint himself to doing twice as much as two of the most active men in London, it would do very well.'[3]

In that month of January 1819 George Ticknor, the American, wrote in his journal his impressions of Brougham:

---

[1] Brougham MSS., Brougham to Mrs. Spalding, 5 Nov., and Brougham's letters to Grey.

[2] *Letters of Countess Granville*, i. 138.

[3] *Letters of Sydney Smith*, i. 315.

Brougham . . . is now about thirty-eight, tall, thin, and rather awkward, with a plain and not very expressive countenance, and simple or even slovenly manners. . . . In short, all that is exterior in him, and all that goes to make up the first impression, is unfavourable. The first thing that removes this impression is the heartiness and good will he shows you, whose motive cannot be mistaken, for such kindness can come only from the heart. . . . On common topics nobody is more commonplace. He does not feel them, but if the subject excites him, there is an air of originality in his remarks, which, if it convinces you of nothing else, convinces you that you are talking with an extraordinary man. He does not like to join in a general conversation, but prefers to talk apart with only two or three persons, and, tho' with great interest and zeal, in an undertone. If, however, he does launch into it, all the little trim gay pleasure boats must keep out of the way of his great black collier, as Gibbon said of Fox. He listens carefully and fairly, and with a kindness which would be provoking if it were not genuine, to all his adversary has to say, but when his turn comes to answer, it is with that rare, bold, bullion talent that either crushes himself or his opponent. . . . I suspect the impression that Brougham generally leaves is that of a good natured friend. At least that is the impression I have most frequently found, both in England and on the Continent.[1]

In the spring of 1819 Brougham was married to Mrs. Spalding, a widow with two children, at Coldstream across the Scottish border. Mrs. Spalding had been Mary Ann Eden, a niece of the first Lord Auckland. The second Lord Auckland was her cousin and was to be closely associated with Brougham, particularly on the first Council of London University and as a ministerial colleague (though they were in the Cabinet together for only a few weeks). The attitude of the Eden family toward Brougham was always one of warm friendship and admiration.[2] For nearly a year Brougham's friends had been speculating as to whether he would marry 'the widow'. In January 1819 Sydney Smith wrote to Lady Grey: 'Who Mrs. Spalding is, I hardly know. I have dined in company with her, she is a showy, long, well-dressed, red and white widow who made some impression on me by her beauty. What will happen I do not presume to conjecture.'[3] Whishaw, after the marriage, spoke of her as 'a handsome and dashing widow', but no one else ever suggested that she was 'dashing'.

[1] *Ticknor*, i. 266.
[2] Brougham MSS., *passim*.   [3] *Letters of Sydney Smith*, i. 309 [4 Jan. 1819].

Brougham's marriage had very little effect on his public career. His wife seldom appeared in society, and when she did she was the subject of unfavourable comment. She was probably lacking in the social graces, but those harsh judgements made no allowance for the fact that after the birth of her second child in 1821 (a first daughter died in infancy) she was a sick woman, in fact a semi-invalid. She was highly neurotic and Mrs. Hawes, who was enabled to use her diary, says that she was a hypochondriac even before she married Brougham.[1] She did not accompany Brougham on his visits to the great houses and was seldom with him at dinners and parties in London. Mrs. Hawes, on the authority of her journal, says that she was not invited.[2] Brougham loved to entertain his many friends at Brougham Hall; on those occasions there was frequently enthusiastic comment from those who visited him on his charming mother and his interesting daughter, Eleonor Louise, but little or no mention of his wife. She was, however, at Brougham Hall very little during the earlier years of their married life; she was usually in London or at some place where she went in search of health.

There is no evidence of her sharing Brougham's interest in his great causes or in his politics, though when the great successes and honours came she was duly appreciative and proud. There were ugly passages in their letters and a number of tender ones. With a very few quarrelsome exceptions, he was constantly solicitous of her comfort. When in the late thirties and forties there was talk of her madness, one comment was that Lady Brougham was no more mad than her husband. The existence or extent of Lord Brougham's madness will call for serious consideration later, as well as the certain fact that Lady Brougham was definitely insane by the forties. After her death, her daughter by her first marriage, Lady Malet, who wrote frequent and affectionate letters to her stepfather, said in effect: Poor woman! she suffered a great deal. She never created any debts; she was always very careful about financial matters. You had your quarrels, but she was always forgiving. She was as devoted to you as any woman could be.[3]

Returning to 1819, we are reminded that it was the year of

---

[1] Frances Hawes, *Henry Brougham* (1957), p. 176.
[2] Ibid., p. 89.
[3] Brougham MSS.

Peterloo. There has been a great deal of misrepresentation of the events of that year. But some things are clear enough. It was one of the greatest periods of suffering in English history. Influenced by Radical agitation, many people believed that the remedy lay in Parliamentary Reform and the repeal of the Corn Laws. A number of very large meetings were held to petition for these objects. 'Orator' Hunt was the most frequent speaker at the meetings. He was a wild man and a firebrand, and some of his political views were as absurd as they were dangerous. The popular agitation was aided and aroused by a flock of Radical publications which, though they played a part in quickening the political mind of the English people, were frowned upon by the more comfortable as seditious and anti-religious. At the meeting held in St. Peter's Fields, Manchester, on 16 August there were 60,000 persons, many of whom had marched in from the surrounding districts. The objects of the meeting were legal. The Manchester magistrates had given permission for it to be held, but they decided, some time before the meeting began, that they would arrest Hunt, who said nothing seditious in the short time he spoke. The Manchester magistrates added to that the folly of employing the Manchester Yeomanry to form the escort for the constables who made the arrest. If the regular troops who were at hand had been used for that purpose, there would have been no Peterloo. The Manchester Yeomanry was a local unit, sadly lacking in military training, made up largely of members of the employing class, and they evoked all the feeling which had been simmering for months between employers and employees, and which was the legacy of a strike in Manchester and the surrounding districts a year earlier. In a disordered situation, the regular troops were called upon to clear the field. They did not act with the cruelty and bad feeling of the Yeomanry and probably performed a difficult task as best they could. Many of the injuries were caused by sheer pressure and panic of the crowd, particularly because exit was blocked in one direction by the hustings. The casualties at Peterloo probably totalled eleven killed and several hundred injured. There has been, of course, a myth of Peterloo that enjoyed a long and vigorous life and is not yet quite dead. But what happened was bad enough.

The story of 'massacre' was carried on the wings of passion and exaggeration to every corner of the country. Seldom in English history has there been as angry a state of mind in the lower strata of society as there was through the remainder of 1819. It is difficult to say what might have happened if a safety valve had not been provided in the Queen's Trial in the following year. The popular indignation and hatred of the Government were greatly intensified by the fact that five days after the tragedy of Peterloo a letter was written by the Home Secretary, the arbitrary and blundering Sidmouth, and published, conveying the thanks of the Prince Regent to the commander of the Yeomanry and the Manchester magistrates. The magistrates were assured of 'the great satisfaction derived by His Royal Highness from their prompt, decisive and efficient measures for the preservation of the public tranquility'. This made Brougham very angry. In his anger he was only one of millions (though few possessed his gift for anger), but he and his fellow Whig leaders had to consider what they should do about it.

The leaders of the Whig party felt themselves caught between what they considered the danger of encouraging the extreme agitation of Radicals like Hunt, and the failure to express sympathy with the people in an hour of injustice. A week after Peterloo, Grey wrote to Brougham that 'nothing could be more unjustifiable than the conduct of the magistrates in employing the military as they did', and that if there were not something like general agreement in that feeling 'the consequences may prove most fatal to the freedom of the country'. He said that he would like to see the Whigs take a position by which the people might 'again' be brought to regard them as 'their natural leaders'. But he had not much hope of that and in any case, unless challenged by a very strong expression of popular feeling, the Whigs should reserve action until Parliament met.[1] Brougham in his reply wrote: 'The magistrates there [in Manchester] and all over Lancashire I have long known for the worst in England, the most bigotted, violent and active. . . . I am quite indignant at this Manchester business, but I fear, with you, that we can do nothing till Parl't meets.'[2]

As the days passed, however, Brougham became more and more impatient. He had to speak at a dinner at Kendal and was

---

[1] *Memoirs*, ii. 342–3, 25 Aug. 1819.
[2] Brougham MSS., 'Tuesday' [31 Aug. 1819].

strongly inclined to let himself go. Writing to Lambton he said:
'The case of the [Manchester] magistrates is desperate.... There
is no speaking with patience on it. I wish to God Parliament
were met. My tongue itches to be at them. I dare hardly venture
to go to a meeting at Kendal for fear of being carried away and
then carried off to Appleby Jail under the new law of commitment.'[1]

Radical meetings, very orderly, were held in the large towns
and cities. A certain number of country gentlemen also wished
to have county meetings held for the purpose of passing resolutions demanding an investigation of what had happened at
Manchester. In spite of what he wrote to Grey earlier about the
wisdom of the Whigs following rather than leading in regard
to county meetings, Brougham was very active in organizing a
county meeting for Westmorland, and wrote unsuccessfully to
the Duke of Devonshire urging him to support a meeting in
Cumberland.[2]

On 19 September Lord Holland wrote to Brougham: 'What
say you to public meetings, plans for which are much in agitation?' He gave a balanced estimate of reasons pro and con.[3] Five
days later in another letter to Brougham, Lord Holland said that
the consensus of opinion among 'our friends' was that all thought
of starting county meetings should be abandoned except in
Norfolk and Yorkshire where a lead had been taken by Milton
and Fitzwilliam, 'whom no one will suspect of courting popularity or promoting reform [Parliamentary Reform]'.[4]

Dissociation of the Whigs from Parliamentary Reform was,
however, the opposite of what Brougham wished for. And within
a few weeks he went all out for county meetings with, apparently,
considerable support in the Whig party. In mid-October he
wrote to Lord Grey: 'The Yorkshire [meeting] went off admirably, tho' there as elsewhere the merely agricultural districts
were lukewarm. But what could Brand mean in Herts, and
W. Whitman and that fumbling old ass Wilshire in Bedfordshire,
by refusing to promote meetings. However the business will be
done without them and I must say we are bound in fairness to

[1] Brougham MSS., n.d.
[2] Memoirs, ii. 345, 346; Brougham MSS., Brougham to Grey, 20 Sept. 1819;
Chatsworth MSS. [Sept. 1819].
[3] Brougham MSS.
[4] Ibid., 24 Sept. 1819.

allow that the Radicals have behaved well wherever they have been tried.' In the same letter he said frankly that advantage should be taken of this situation to prepare for a definite Whig move for a measure of Parliamentary Reform.[1]

There we have Brougham's sense of a call to popularize the Whig party and make it a strong instrument for Parliamentary Reform. In a letter written a week later to the Duke of Devonshire, he urged that the Whig party should show unity in protesting against arbitrary measures, increase in the army, and any attempt at severe restrictions on freedom of speech and writing.[2] At the same time Brougham wrote to Creevey that the freeholders of Cumberland would have taken more interest if there had been a resolution urging Parliamentary Reform. 'This feeling is not confined to Cumberland. I believe it prevails much everywhere, and that the aristocracy alone are deaf to it. . . . If the Whigs sail straight and listen to no crotchet or fears, they may regain the people, and do most essential service to the country; but they are full of crotchets, even the best of them . . . Holland House however is running straight.'[3]

Because of the part which he played in organizing the Yorkshire meeting, which simply petitioned for an investigation of Peterloo, Lord Fitzwilliam was dismissed by the Government from his position of Lord Lieutenant of the county. In this action, as well as in what he considered excessive military preparations, Brougham said that he recognized the hand of the Duke of Wellington; it was not, he said, like Lord Liverpool. As might be expected, Lambton was very active in organizing a meeting in Durham. Brougham wrote to Grey: 'Lambton has been doing great things in his county. His movement at Sunderland was most masterly and had all the success it deserved.'[4] The Westmorland and Cumberland meetings which Brougham organized went off well. In addition to those mentioned, county meetings were held in Northumberland, Cornwall, and Berkshire, initiated by Whigs.

In the early days of this correspondence there appeared in *The Times* a statement about Brougham's health that suggested

[1] Brougham MSS., 18 Oct. 1819.
[2] Chatsworth MSS., 26 Oct. 1819.
[3] Creevey MSS. (Oct. 1819).
[4] Brougham MSS., 18 Oct. 1819; New, p. 59.

to his friends a mental ailment. Their anxiety is understandable. That of Francis Place is striking. 'I grieve for Brougham. He had fine talents, good nature, and a strong desire to be useful, had he but possessed a sound judgment to guide him. . . . He was forgiving, liberal, and exceedingly industrious, but all these fine qualities have become useless if it is true that the greatest of all possible calamities has fallen upon him.'[1] When Place learned that Brougham was well again, he felt free to abuse him as he pleased.

When Parliament met late in November the Whig Opposition made a strong attempt to obtain an investigation of Peterloo, but the Government staunchly and successfully opposed it. Then came the famous Six Acts which have been almost universally abused and, in fact, abused altogether too much. Two of them, with some modifications, are still on the statute books. Nor was there anything in the Six Acts that invaded the freedom of the individual as much as the suspension of habeas corpus of two years earlier, which had passed its time limit and was not renewed. The first act prohibited meetings to train men in the use of arms. The second authorized justices of the peace in certain disturbed counties to search for arms, even in private houses, and to seize arms carried by individuals if they believed that the intention was dangerous to the public peace. The third removed methods by which accused persons could postpone their trials and (following an Opposition proposal) prevented the Attorney-General from postponing prosecutions. The act dealing with seditious meetings gave a more rigid definition to sedition, forbade any meeting, unless officially summoned, of more than fifty persons if called by a person who did not live in the parish where it was held. The notice of all meetings had to be given to a justice of the peace; they were to be attended only by residents of the county or town; and arms, flags, and military formations were barred. Two acts restricting the freedom of the press, however, were particularly objectionable. The whole of an issue containing a blasphemous or seditious statement might be seized, and banishment was made the penalty for a second offence. Pamphlets containing news or comments on the news, which sold for less than sixpence, were subjected to the newspaper stamp duty.

[1] Add. MSS. 35153, f. 72.

Perhaps the most surprising thing about the Six Acts was the extent to which the Government accepted changes suggested by the Opposition. One of these was the exception of indoor meetings from the restrictions. Lord Holland suggested that the prevention of delays by the accused should be accompanied by a similar prevention of delays by the Attorney-General in prosecutions. This had been an important feature of Brougham's unsuccessful libel bill of 1816. It was now adopted. It removed the sword of Damocles from over the heads of newspaper publishers, ended the Government intimidation against which Brougham had protested so strongly, and constituted a notable contribution to the freedom of the press.[1]

The general Whig opposition to the Six Acts was 'moderate'. Brougham, no doubt, agreed with the acts in part, but he spoke with his usual vigour in support of the right of Englishmen to possess and carry arms, and in opposition to the acts restricting the freedom of the press, which he blasted as despotic. The popular feelings of grievance, unrest, and anger which followed Peterloo and the Six Acts were lost in the following year in the all absorbing interest created by the Queen's Trial.

[1] See pp. 173–4.

CHAPTER XII

Schools For All, 1810–19

THOMAS ARNOLD of Rugby once wrote in a letter to Brougham: 'Upon the general subject of popular education you are the founder and leader of us all.'[1] Brougham's activity in the direction of universal education, 'schools for all', began in 1810, more than fifty years before Arnold wrote those words. At that time more than half the children of school age in England and Wales attended no school of any kind. Since the children of the upper and middle classes were all looked after in some fashion, the proportion of the children of the poor who were entirely out of school was very large.

But there were at that time a few people who, for a variety of motives, were beginning to cherish vague hopes of universal education, or the 'education of the poor'. Brougham was soon to be their leader, though his own motives were often very different from the motives of those whom he led. He sympathized with the Benthamites who believed that a broad increase in education would contribute to 'the greatest happiness of the greatest number'. He often emphasized the value of education in reducing crime, an argument resorted to by those who feared the increase of crime and a disturbance of the social equilibrium more than anything else, but his own conception of education was much broader than that. He respected religion as a social force, but it was not merely that children might learn to read the Bible that he believed in 'schools for all'. He felt the general influence of the French Revolution and, of course, he had read Rousseau, La Chalotais, and other French educational writers, not to mention Tom Paine. But he disapproved of much more in them than he approved. As for the Revolutionary slogan of education 'universal, compulsory, gratuitous and secular', he agreed only with the 'universal', and that quite independently of French influence. Except for the very poor, he did not believe that education should be free; the rich would have to help the

[1] Brougham MSS., 31 July 1861.

poor, but if the latter did not pay *something* for education they would be unappreciative and unresponsive. He would be willing to accept purely secular education if it appeared to be the only way to effect universality, but he would accept it as a last resort and not as an ideal; he believed as strongly as any cleric that there must be a religious element in any complete education.

The strongest influence behind Brougham's drive for 'schools or all' was that of the Scottish system of parish schools. It approached universality and he contrasted the education afforded in his native land with the lamentable situation in his adopted country. The traditional Scottish faith in education, which led Scottish parents to skimp themselves for the best possible education for their children, was bred deep within him. His leadership in every field of education in his time was a Scottish invasion of England. Of course, he only led the invasion. Many of his colleagues in the British and Foreign School Society, in the Mechanics' Institute movement, in the Society for the Diffusion of Useful Knowledge, in the launching of the University of London and its Council, had come from Scotland, and others had received some of their education there.

It should not be necessary to say much about the various types of schools in England in 1810. The facts are well known. Apart from religious instruction most of the Sunday Schools taught reading only. The dames' schools were incapable of doing much for the minds of the children and they did only a little for their habits. There were private day schools kept usually by men who had failed in other occupations or suffered physical disabilities. If one could do nothing else, one could always become a school-teacher. They imparted some knowledge, but as Lancaster said of them: 'The drunkenness of a school master is almost proverbial.' Most of them were very fond of flogging and relied on it for what little discipline they achieved. In charity schools supported by philanthropic contributions, many of which were established by the Society for Promoting Christian Knowledge, an Anglican organization, the teaching was somewhat better, but still very poor. There were some schools in factories and some parish schools. In the latter the local clergymen who had been interested enough to establish them were obviously conscientious and were better educated than the teachers in other schools. The grammar schools and public schools were by this time, in general, outside the orbit of popular education. Some of their endowments and early bequests had been intended for the education of the poor, but had been diverted to other ends, a fact which Brougham had much to say about later.

During the first decade of the nineteenth century schools appeared which were greatly superior to those which already existed for the education of the poor. These were the 'monitorial schools', frequently referred to as the schools of the Bell–Lancaster system. It has been universally stated that the Bell schools were maintained by Anglicans and the Lancasterian schools by Dissenters, but that distinction gives a false impression. The statement may be true so far as general interest and support were concerned, but most of the money that backed the central organization of the Lancasterian schools came from Anglicans, and while the front rank of Lancasterian leaders included William Allen, who, like Lancaster, was a Quaker, and Joseph Fox who was a Baptist, there were also Anglicans, notably the Duke of Bedford, the Duke of Kent, the Duke of Sussex, Brougham, Lord Lansdowne, and the Bishop of Norwich, to say nothing of the generous patronage of George III and the more generous support of the Prince Regent. When a society was organized, largely by Brougham, to take charge of the Lancasterian schools, the great majority of the members of its committee were members of the Church of England.

It is the Lancasterian schools, and Brougham's interest in them, that we are concerned with here.[1]

Joseph Lancaster when he was about eighteen opened a school for children of the poor in his neighbourhood[2] in a room lent him by his father. A few years later he moved to premises in the Borough Road, where he established a school under a sign which read: 'All that will may send their children and have them educated freely (the expense of writing books excepted), and those to whom the above offer may not prove acceptable may pay for them at a very moderate price.'[3] So many pupils came to him that he could not teach them all himself and he could not afford to employ an assistant. So he resorted to monitors. There was

[1] A. M. Gilbert, *The Work of Lord Brougham for education in England* (1922), a published University of Pennsylvania thesis, is a comprehensive factual guide to Brougham's educational activities.

[2] Joseph Lancaster, *Improvements in Education* (1805), pp. 3–5.

[3] Frank Smith, *A History of English Elementary Education, 1760–1802* (1931), p. 71.

nothing new about the use of monitors in schools. Lancaster adopted a system in which he taught each lesson to the monitors who in turn taught it each to his group. Thus one teacher could provide instruction to hundreds of pupils. There were monitors for order, for checking attendance, for supplies, for every item of school routine. And everything was conducted with military precision. In 1804 there were 500 pupils and the school, on certain visiting days, was one of the show places of London. What did ambassadors, peers, members of Parliament go to the Borough Road to see? The employment of monitors? Hardly. They knew about the employment of monitors in other English and European schools. The elaborate monitorial machinery set up by Lancaster, as a means of extending the education of the poor in the face of lack of funds and shortage of teachers, interested them, but that is far from being the whole story. They were interested because this was a *better school*. Francis Horner gave his impression of it to Dugald Stewart in a letter dated 6 April 1805. He said nothing about monitors. He approved of Lancaster's rewards and punishments, and the competition that stimulated learning. He continued:

Nothing can be more pleasing than, on going into this school, you discover nothing of the languor and sickly idleness which makes a common parish school so melancholy to see. I saw here the other day more than six hundred boys of the poorest parents in the suburbs, taught for nothing, all in rags but cheerfully engaged.[1]

James Pillans, who had been with Brougham and Horner at the Edinburgh High School, and in university days had been Brougham's companion at the theatre when Brougham broke up the show, became the Rector of the High School in 1810. He applied Lancaster's methods in his rector's class, and he reported to the organization that had taken over the Lancasterian schools that his school was much improved as a result. He especially emphasized the boys' greater interest in, and enjoyment of, their work. There can be no doubt that what Pillans said about the development in the monitors of the qualities of good judgement, prompt decision, impartiality, and command of temper was applicable to the monitors of the Lancasterian and Bell schools generally. Pillans became

[1] Lacaita-Shelburne MSS., in the Clements Library, University of Michigan.

a great Scottish educationist. Testifying before an educational committee of the House of Commons in 1834 he said that learning by rote was not an essential feature of monitorial schools, and that where it existed it was the fault of the teachers and not of the employment of monitors. In his later years Pillans continued to state that the employment of monitors failed only when teachers failed to understand their craft, and that it was, on the whole, successful up to the time when monitors were replaced by pupil-teachers or apprentice-teachers, and a great improvement was thus effected.[1]

Lancaster loved children and he understood them. He knew that children enjoy competition of every kind. There was plenty of competition between the boys for inexpensive prizes. There were competitions between classes of the same grade and the boys loved it. Their respective monitors rooted them on and victory was followed by a celebration.[2] Certainly there was much in this programme of education that went far beyond the 'monitorial' and the 'mechanical' with which terms historians of education generally have been inclined to dismiss Lancaster's efforts. There had been no training of teachers before Lancaster. Brougham fully recognized the inadequacies of the Borough Road training school and one of his most constant activities was the urging of the establishment of adequate teachers' colleges for the training of more and better teachers. Lancaster believed strongly that religion was essential to education. He emphasized the value of children of different denominations being brought together in one school. The statement that in the Lancasterian schools religious instruction was confined to the reading of the Bible is a mistaken one. While he had the pupils read the Bible in school and memorize selected passages, used the Bible for all reading lessons and strongly inculcated Bible-reading outside of school, he attempted to teach 'general Christianity' in a manner that would be offensive to none. The great hymns are non-denominational and he used hymns extensively, particularly Watts's *Hymns for Children*.

Lancaster obtained royal patronage, went out to the country to lecture on his system, and by 1807 there were forty-five

---

[1] James Pillans, *Contributions to the Cause of Education* (1856), see pp. 20–29, 242–4, 315–35 on the employment of monitors.

[2] J. Lancaster, *British System of Education* (1810), pp. 15, 57–65.

Lancasterian schools. Having no business sense he was in that year imprisoned for debt. Joseph Fox stepped in to save Lancaster and his cause. He discovered that Lancaster's debts amounted to £3,600 and cleared them off partly by gift and partly by pledge after selling a considerable amount of his own property.[1] Fox was aided in this by Corston, a close friend of Lancaster, who was more willing to take their money than to take their advice. Probably fearing interference with his plans he said: 'What God began, He alone shall finish.'[2] So, under God, he continued to pile up debts. Fox brought in William Allen and Lancaster was persuaded to permit a committee of six to take in hand the business side of his enterprise.

Joseph Fox was a 'surgeon-dentist' of Guy's Hospital, lectured on dentistry there, and had an extensive and fashionable private practice. He was irritable and arbitrary in temper, but his generosity and zeal were exemplary. Brougham always assigned to him the first place among those who befriended Lancaster. He was a Baptist[3] and his friendship with William Allen, who was a Quaker, was one of long standing. They were associated at Guy's Hospital where Allen lectured on chemistry. Allen was also head of a firm of manufacturing chemists. He possessed a genuinely humble spirit and a broad-minded co-operative friendliness with all who were serving humanity. Brougham spoke of him as 'a man in a million'. When Harriet Martineau wrote her history of the period forty years later, she spoke of William Allen, Thomas Clarkson, and Elizabeth Fry as supreme examples of the potency of the Christian spirit in social service, devoting their lives to the unfortunate and neglected, 'to seek and save that which was lost'.[4]

The committee of six failed to keep up with expenses and avoid new debts. In the autumn of 1810 they turned to Brougham as an 'old friend'. He was especially the friend of Allen with whom he had been closely associated for six years in the suppression of the slave trade. Brougham, apparently, suggested the formation of an organization or society to secure *public*

---

[1] William Allen, *Life, with selections from his Correspondence* (1847), i. 72.

[2] W. Corston, *Life of Lancaster* [1840], p. 41.

[3] G. Wallas's *Francis Place* (1898) makes the strange mistake of speaking of him as a Quaker and as being guided by the Inner Light, a Quaker doctrine.

[4] Harriet Martineau, *History of England during the Thirty Years' Peace*, 4 vols. (1877–8), iv, pp. 430–1.

support. A semi-public meeting was planned for those who would be willing to act on a large committee of such an organization and, since it was considered injudicious for the members of the existing committee of six to appeal for public help, it was Brougham who, with characteristic energy, went out to get the men, contacting them directly and indirectly. Brougham was in the chair at the semi-public meeting which was held at the Thatched House Tavern on 14 December 1810, and explained fully the purposes to be served. Those present undertook to serve as a committee, and at a public meeting held on 11 May 1811 the Royal Lancasterian Institution was established. This was the real founding of the British and Foreign School Society, for in 1814 there was no alteration except a change of name and a new set of regulations.[1]

More than half of the committee members were personal friends of Brougham, and a good majority were Anglicans. Brougham actively, and perhaps Allen by suggestion, brought in a number of the men who had been active on behalf of the slaves: Wilberforce, Clarkson, Lord Lansdowne, Horner, Romilly, Thornton, and William Smith were amongst them. There was a sprinkling of Quakers, including Joseph Fry and several members of the Gurney family. James Mill became one of the most active members of the committee. He wrote a pamphlet in support of the enterprise in 1812 entitled *Schools for All* (probably the origin of that slogan) and an *Edinburgh Review* article in 1813. Fox was to become the secretary of the new organization and Allen the treasurer.

Brougham, as so frequently when at a critical stage in his plans, wrote *Edinburgh Review* articles in support of the project. The first appeared in November 1810 before the committee was completed. It was entitled 'Education of the Poor'. Brougham urged 'the more general diffusion' of the Lancasterian system and discussed two obstacles to doing so. The first was the unfortunate controversy in regard to the priority and superiority

---

[1] See Brougham's public letter on Education to the Duke of Bedford. The refusal of the members of the committee of six to approach the men who were to launch the Institution was explained in the article entitled 'Education of the Poor' in the *Edinburgh Review*, Nov. 1811. Brougham, who wrote the article, did not mention himself by name but he said: 'A proposition that the rest of the community should unite in supporting the system, might, if proceeding from them, be liable to misconstruction. It was therefore necessary that others should exert themselves.'

of the work of Lancaster and Bell. Another obstacle was the idea that it was a bad thing to teach the poor, or to teach too many of them and to teach them too much. Even Dr. Bell, whom he greatly admired, had countenanced this idea. Brougham quoted the following from one of his books:

It is not proposed that the children of the poor be educated in an expensive [extensive?] manner, or even taught to write and cipher. Utopian schemes . . . for the diffusion of general knowledge, would soon . . . confuse that distinction of ranks and classes of society, on which the general welfare hinges. . . . There is a risk of elevating by an indiscriminate education, the minds of those doomed to the drudgery of daily labour above their condition, and thereby rendering them discontented and unhappy in their lot.

Brougham was always in revolt against ideas such as these. Why should not the children of the poor have their chance?

Is it contended that persons of a certain yearly income engross among them all the natural genius of the human race? We apprehend that the most devoted slave of aristocracy will scarcely maintain the affirmative of the latter question. If, then, among two millions of persons in the lower ranks, who now receive no education at all, there are a certain proportion of fine understandings, utterly buried and for ever lost to the world for want of cultivation, would it not be worth while . . . to give that matter a certain degree of attention? . . . Mr. Lancaster was a sectary, a respected and cherished member of that peaceful body of Christians, the Quakers, who alone never either persecuted, nor fought, nor intrigued, nor ruled; and who, having no establishment, nor indeed any order of priests, are not much in favour with such as delight to mingle with the pure clerical functions of Christian ministers the enjoyment of patronage, wealth and power. If then the first alarm was given by the idea of '*the poor being taught*' a louder note was soon sounded when it was found that 'the poor were to be *taught by a Quaker*'.

Brougham commended the cheapness of the Lancasterian system as a means of educating a larger number of the children of the poor. But the stress was not to be laid on the mere use of monitors, which was not distinctive. Brougham emphasized other advantages of the Lancasterian system, such as the method of teaching reading, the fact that every boy was always kept on the alert and the importance of the *teachers* (as against the monitors). In an obvious appeal for Anglican support of the

Lancasterian schools, Brougham called attention to the starting of one of them by a group led by the Dean of Westminster, and the recent preaching of a sermon in favour of the Lancasterian system by the Bishop of Norwich.

This is a very brief summary of Brougham's fifty pages in the *Edinburgh Review*. His second article entitled 'Education of the Poor' appeared in the *Edinburgh Review* for November 1811. He sketched Lancaster's work from the beginning. He proceeded to give figures of Lancaster's journeys drawn from the Report for 1810. In this travelling through the country Lancaster gave 'lectures' to awaken interest, raised money for both central and local purposes, and organized local committees to establish new schools. In the four years ending in 1810 he had established ninety-five new schools educating 25,500 pupils. Brougham believed that the total number of children who had at some time attended Lancasterian schools up to the close of 1810 was fully 100,000.

Brougham quoted a long passage from Lancaster's 1810 Report. In the course of it Lancaster mentioned a boy who had attended the Lancasterian school at Southwark. His father was dead and his mother so poor that he had nothing to eat in the daytime, until the other boys found him crying from hunger and shared lunch with him. Learning of this Lancaster took him into his home. His name was James George Penney. Four years later after teacher training Lancaster sent him into Shropshire where, living with an Anglican clergyman, he organized and taught a school for 250 children, who made such rapid progress that one man wrote to the clergyman asking him 'if such improvement could be made by anything short of witchcraft'. Before young Penney had left that part of the country he had organized schools for nearly a thousand children. He then became teacher of a school at Bath.

(We can trace this boy farther. For many years Penney organized and superintended the Baptist Lancasterian schools in and around Calcutta. Cox's *History of the Baptist Missionary Society* contains frequent references to him, in one of which it is stated that he was no slave of routine, but varied methods and introduced new 'pursuits' as well as new subjects. He had apparently caught some of Lancaster's spirit and inventiveness.)[1]

[1] Bain, p. 149; *14th Report of the British and Foreign School Society*, p. 27; F. Cox,

In this *Edinburgh Review* article, Brougham in four places paid tributes to the generous interest and support afforded by the Prince Regent to the Lancasterian schools. He said that he had excelled his father in this respect. The article contained a direct appeal for funds for the new organization. Brougham inserted a footnote stating that the publishers of the *Edinburgh Review* would be glad to receive and transmit contributions and giving the names and addresses of their London bankers.

The latter part of the article consisted of an attack on Dr. Marsh, Professor of Divinity at Cambridge, who had preached and published a sermon in St. Paul's on the subject. Brougham naturally resented Marsh's statements that Lancaster was inimical to the Church of England and that the Lancasterian schools, with *their* conception of religious instruction, constituted 'the most powerful engine that was ever devised against it, now at work for its destruction'. In conclusion he reasserted his respect for the Church of England, of which he was a member. 'Hence it is that we view with more than common indignation the men whom we have now been occupied in exposing to the public, because in them we see at once the enemies of the Poor and of the Church, of Education and of Religion.'

Before the article appeared in print there was established 'The National Society for promoting the Education of the Poor in the Principles of the Established Church'. Brougham never at any time attacked the National Society or its schools and he frequently spoke of them with the warmest praise. He had no sympathy with the cry raised against them that their aim was to put down Dissenters and undermine the Lancasterian schools, and that they owed their origin and their maintenance to Anglican bigotry. This may have been true of some, but those who took over the leadership of the National School Society and those who manned the schools were, without doubt, much more interested in the welfare of the children and in the education of the poor than they were in the war of the Church against Dissent.

It was inevitable, of course, that Anglicans tended for the most part to support the National Society and Dissenters to

History of the Baptist Missionary Society, 2 vols. (1842), i. 302, 315, 326-7, 404, 413, ii. 284. For Penney see also J. C. Marshman, *Carey, Marshman and Ward,* 2 vols. (1839), p. 134.

support the British and Foreign Society. Very early in its history a number of the National Society schools were thrown open to the children of Dissenters, exempted them from attendance at the hours when the tenets of the Church of England were taught, if their parents so desired, and established the rule that while all children in their schools should attend places of worship on Sunday, children of Dissenters might attend the Dissenting chapels. Brougham cordially welcomed this liberal practice in the rival organization and frequently emphasized it. In every article he wrote and in nearly all of his speeches on the education of the poor he spoke of the two societies as competing organizations working in the common cause of universal education, which should never be regarded as the enemies of one another.

In the meantime Lancaster, feeling that his work was being taken away from him by the new central organization, acted in a manner which was in clear violation of his agreement with it and ultimately set up his own fund, claiming that subscriptions made to the Lancasterian schools were made to him personally. He severed his connexion with the organization in April 1814 and in the following month his name was dropped from its title. What had originally been called the Royal Lancasterian Institution was now renamed the British and Foreign School Society. The new name was obviously suggested by that of the Bible Society. The 'Foreign' part of it was fully justified by the established of Lancasterian schools in several European countries as well as in the United States, in Africa, and in India. The annual meetings always made much of this extension of the society's influence. Most of the schools established in Europe were short-lived, but they had some influence on the development of education in the countries concerned. William Allen spent months of arduous labour travelling through Europe imparting and acquiring educational information. That remarkable Quaker interviewed statesmen, thou'd and thee'd the crowned heads, and among other activities prepared for the Czar Alexander I a book of selections from scripture which was employed in Russian schools, translated into French and Italian, and apparently displaced in the English schools the selections that had been used by Lancaster.[1] There was a widespread establishment of British and Foreign schools by missionaries in

[1] James Bonwick, *An Octogenarian's Reminiscences* (1902), pp. 41–42.

India. Brougham and his friends who were active in both the Society and the African Institution saw that boys from Africa were trained at the Borough Road School for teaching in British and Foreign schools on the African west coast.

At the annual dinner of the British and Foreign School Society in 1815 Brougham was seated at the left hand of the chairman, the Duke of Sussex (with the other royal duke, the Duke of Kent at the right). Although his speech followed months of illness, it lacked none of his characteristic vigour and eloquence.[1]

In the summer of 1815 it became known that Brougham was to be back in the House of Commons at the beginning of the next session and that he intended to bring the education of the poor to the attention of Parliament. The Whigs as a party had little or nothing to do with his return and showed no indication of having any interest in his educational plans so far as the party was concerned. But those who were closest to Bentham rejoiced. James Lindsay wrote to Mill in October 1815 with enthusiasm, but also with some concern for Brougham's health:

I am happy to hear that Brougham means to take up two subjects so greatly important as the Law of Libel and the Education of the Poor. To support a free press, and to give the whole mass of the people the capacity of profiting by it, is to prepare the triumph of truth and liberty. . . . God grant him health and vigour. The rest he will command from the energies of his mind.[2]

That the education of the people should be brought to the attention of Parliament was almost unprecedented. Brougham moved, on 21 May 1816, that a committee be appointed 'to inquire into the education of the lower orders in the metropolis' and to report to the House 'from time to time'. He hoped that on the basis of such an investigation a measure 'under parliamentary sanction and on parliamentary aid' might be tried first in London and later extended to other communities throughout the nation. He suggested also as a proper project for Parliament the establishment of a school for the training of teachers, without which the education of the poor would be badly hampered.[3]

Brougham's motion was carried and a committee was ap-

[1] *The Times*, 27 Nov. 1815.   [2] Bain, p. 149.
[3] *Hansard*, xxxiv. 633 seq.

pointed. He, an active Opposition leader, was permitted to select his own committee. The Government had suffered enough from Brougham. Immediately before his forced retirement from Parliament four years earlier, he had led the movement which had compelled the Government to repeal the Orders in Council, and within seven weeks of his reappearance in Parliament he had defeated it to the accompaniment of vociferous popular applause, by securing the abolition of the income-tax. The Government might well be pleased to give Brougham his head and see him consume his energy and his time on a project with which it had no concern and on which, since it was not a party issue, it could not again be defeated.

The meeting of the expenses of Brougham's committee was the first money spent on education by a British government since the establishment of 'parliamentary government' in the seventeenth century. It was a strong committee, all of whose members were active and able members of the House. The Radicals were well represented as well as Tories and Whigs. Five of the members of the committee were vice-presidents of the British and Foreign School Society (including Brougham himself), and the National School Society was fully represented by members of the House who were active in that organization. There were old friends of Brougham, including Romilly, Wilberforce, and Mackintosh. And there was a new friend, a young man who had entered the House in Brougham's absence, whose abilities Brougham had been quick to recognize, John George Lambton (later Lord Durham).[1] After its work was finished, Brougham said that the committee was unanimous throughout, that there was never a division during the three years of its existence, that those who attended regularly were a minority and that most of them were Tories.[2]

One reason for the survival of only the zealous was that Brougham drove them as he always drove men when he was in a commanding position. During the investigation of the Orders in Council he had insisted on unconscionable hours and refused to stay proceedings for the death of Perceval. Later, when he presided in the Court of Chancery, he drove court and counsel with unprecedented rigour for a year and a half until all the

[1] New, p. 11.
[2] Brougham's Letter to Romilly, Speeches, iii. 21.

arrears that had been crippling fortunes and sowing broadcast
impoverishment and private tragedy were wiped off the slate.
Now he insisted on the committee meeting for three hours every
day, including Saturday, for weeks on end.[1] They examined a
succession of witnesses who had been active in education and
in just over a month they had their first report ready, written by
Brougham himself. That he could give so much time to this, in
the midst of a parliamentary session in which he spoke 147
times—to say nothing of his other interests, including the
vagaries of the Princess of Wales, the cherishing of the Princess
Charlotte, and conferences on the welfare of the Negro slaves—
is only further proof of Brougham's consuming interest in the
education of the poor.

In speaking to this report on 20 June[2] Brougham said that
120,000 children in London were 'without the means of education'. Of those children, roaming the streets, between 2,000 and
4,000 were rented out by their parents to professional beggars
and 'out of this number were most of those juvenile depredators
who swelled the calendar of Newgate'. Brougham suggested that
in this matter the Government might well exercise 'forcible interference between parent and child'. All types of schools in
London had been investigated. The committee had included
Charterhouse, Christ Church, Westminster, and St. Paul's.

Brougham argued that if the amount spent on housing, feeding,
and clothing in schools were to be spent on education alone,
ten times as many children could be educated on 'the new plan',
that is, the Lancaster–Bell plan. From this time on, Brougham
frequently emphasized this contention, and he said later that
one of his greatest contributions to popular education was to
persuade the philanthropically minded to give their money to
the *educating* of the children of the poor rather than to supplying
them with free board, lodging, and clothing.[3] He added that
though any such rumours concerning London schools were
unfounded, many communications from different parts of the
country had been addressed to him as chairman of the Education Committee complaining of flagrant abuses in the adminis-

[1] Brougham MSS., Brougham to Shepherd, 16 Aug. 1825.
[2] *Hansard*, xxxiv. 1230 seq.; *The Times*, 21 June 1816.
[3] Brougham MSS., Brougham to Shepherd, 16 Aug. 1825. See also Brougham's
Practical Observations upon the Education of the People (1825); *Speeches*, iii. 149–50.

tration of charitable endowments made for the education of the poor.

His strongest political opponents were Castlereagh and Canning. In this instance Castlereagh complimented him on having devoted 'so much of his valuable time' to this important subject and indicated government co-operation with the further work of the committee; Canning promised his hearty support.

His arduous parliamentary session of 1816, following the serious illness of the previous year, exhausted Brougham and again his health was in danger. Within two weeks of the prorogation of Parliament he was off to the Continent for what should have been a complete rest. But that was always impossible for his restless spirit. On this health trip he was collecting material for an attack on Castlereagh next session.[1] And his interest in education drew him to the famous Swiss schools of Pestalozzi at Yverdon and of Fellenberg at Hofwyl. He was the second Englishman to visit them, Dr. Bell having beaten him by a few weeks and Robert Owen making that pilgrimage two years later.

Pestalozzi made less impression on Brougham than did Fellenberg. He seems to have regarded Pestalozzi as over-confident and too theoretical, Fellenberg's experiments appeared to him to be more practical. Any suggestion of Pestalozzi's influence on Brougham must be purely speculative. He may have learned from him the importance of studying the child, although it is more likely that he learned it, at about this time, from Robert Owen. Certainly Brougham was, after this, more interested in children, rather than simply in the idea that education for all was a good thing. His generous heart had already gone out to the neglected children of the poor, but looking at children from a man's point of view is, of course, something very different from trying to understand the nature of children. Brougham had already come to realize that there was too much learning by rote in the Lancasterian system (though there were better things also) and too little emphasis on understanding and thought. Within a few years, in the early 1820's, Pestalozzi's influence was strong in the Borough Road School, the mother school of Lancasterianism, and Brougham as a frequent visitor, encouraged it and praised it.[2] But it seems to have been a matter of backing a Pestalozzian master because of what he, Brougham, had

[1] Add. MSS. 35153, f. 1.   [2] Bonwick, *passim*.

learned from Fellenberg. For a man who was always catching at new ideas and playing them up vigorously to his large audience, he was singularly silent about Pestalozzi. He had much to say about Fellenberg, but apart from his evidence before his own committee in 1818, he waited until the work of the committee was finished.

In 1817 the Committee on the Education of the Poor was reappointed, but Brougham was ill through the greater part of the session and he could not carry his committee into anything approaching its vigorous activity of 1816 and 1818. He suggested that Parliament should give financial aid to the two great school societies (National, and British and Foreign) for the building of school houses.[1] He could get no further with this proposal until he came into office in Lord Grey's government when, in the face of some Cabinet opposition but with Althorp's support, he persuaded Grey to make the first government grant to education in 1833.[2]

In 1818 the range of the committee was extended to the whole of England and Wales, and also to Scotland. Brougham brought in a bill to appoint a commission to investigate all charities and generally to investigate the education of the poor. Speaking on 8 May[3] he said that in larger towns whose population exceeded 7,000 or 8,000, although the existing provision for education was inadequate, private philanthropy could be trusted to provide it if Parliament would meet the initial cost of establishing schools to the extent of making grants for school buildings and master's houses. In the smaller towns and in thinly populated country districts, although the committee had found that everywhere the poor desired the education of their children, they were doomed to disappointment because financial means were not forthcoming, and Brougham suggested that the Government should establish in these places, where necessary, parish schools such as existed in Scotland. Here he was looking forward to his own Bill of 1820, to be discussed in a later chapter. Brougham was also suggesting the policy of government schools 'filling in

[1] *Hansard*, xxxvi. 1303 seq.

[2] Clements MSS., University of Michigan. Letter of Brougham to Lord John Russell, 3 Aug. 1853, recalling this to Russell, who had been his Cabinet colleague in 1833. There were similar statements by Brougham elsewhere. He was generally given credit for the legislation at the time.

[3] *Hansard*, xxxviii. 585 seq.

the gaps' which was at last to be adopted in the great Forster Education Act of 1870. The committee, Brougham said, had issued a circular letter, containing queries, addressed to all the clergy of England and Wales respecting their parishes. Seven thousand had already reported. A study of the returns would indicate where need lay.

In the remainder of this speech Brougham addressed himself directly to his bill for the creation of a commission to investigate charity abuses. He gave examples. In one case a master received a salary but had done no teaching for some years; the funds were in hopeless confusion and the trustees were all dead. In another place the trustees were very much alive and had pocketed all the profits of the estate established as an endowment for the education of the poor.

Two weeks later Brougham described a number of other cases of abuse of educational charities.[1] In most of them there was no school. In one where there were two or three pupils, the endowment was sufficient to educate 1,500 'according to the Bell and Lancaster system'. In Worcestershire a school had been endowed by Edward VI. There were no pupils, but a schoolmaster and a second master each enjoyed a good salary with a house and garden. The rents of the estates attached to this non-existent school 'would educate three or four thousand scholars, probably all the poor of the city of Worcester'. In one case the trustees 'had paid 20 l. a year for the purposes of the trust and had been in the habit of pocketing the remainder'. In many educational endowments, the estate was parcelled out in long-term leases at ridiculously low figures to trustees, their friends and other parties to a deal.

The Government did not seek to impede in the House of Commons Brougham's Bill to appoint a commission to investigate all charities whether educational or not, except those associated with the two universities and a few of the great public schools, the commissioners being empowered to hear evidence on oath, to compel the appearance of all persons and the production of all documents, and to institute proceedings in the courts against offenders. But Lord Chancellor Eldon and government supporters in the Upper House were determined to cut it down in the Lords. No one knew whom such a broad and high-powered

[1] *Hansard*, xxxviii. 761 seq.

investigation might inculpate. Brougham's committee had already been busy for weeks hearing evidence three or four hours a day. It had called on Eton and Winchester to produce documents to determine questions relating to original provisions for education of the poor, and although Brougham's Bill excepted Eton and Winchester from investigation by the commission, he had refused to exempt Rugby and Harrow, and a proposed amendment to except Harrow had actually been voted down in the House of Commons. It was known by this time that a number of clergymen were implicated in the abuses. The *Quarterly Review* had seven-league boots and could step from this to 'the Church is in danger' and confident assertions that the whole honoured tradition of what was best in English education was being attacked by a mad Scot who was bent on becoming a dictator. The *Quarterly*'s article did not appear until the next number, but when Brougham's Bill reached the Lords at the end of May, dignitaries in both State and Church were panicky about their friends, and the old school tie had become a battle standard.

The House of Lords amended Brougham's Bill almost beyond recognition. The Commission to be appointed was limited to educational charities, the provision for general investigation of the education of the poor was omitted, Rugby and Harrow were added to the exempted schools, there was to be no investigation of charities for which there were special visitors (a very large proportion of the whole and, as Brougham contended, containing the worst cases of abuse), and the commissioners were deprived of the powers of requiring attendance of persons and the production of any document unless the whole of it related to a particular charity. The power to institute legal proceedings was also withdrawn from the Commission. In presenting another report from his committee on 3 June[1] Brougham took strong objection to the amendments which weakened his Charities Bill.

He also deprecated suggestions that there was ready recourse to the courts for the punishment of the frauds perpetrated on charitable endowments. Here a long quotation from *Hansard*'s account of this speech will serve as an illustration of Brougham's parliamentary style and provide a foretaste of his great speech

[1] *Hansard*, xxxviii. 1207 seq.

of 1828 which inaugurated an era of general reform of the courts:

He confessed that he himself had not much reliance on courts of law . . . with reference to expedition and cheapness. The committee had been inquiring into a charity that existed at Yeovil. It appeared from the testimony of three most respectable churchwardens, that of an income of 2000 l. a year bequeathed to a charitable purpose, not above 30 l. or 40 l. were rendered available to it. Questions and answers to the following effect passed between the committee and those individuals: Why did you not go into a court of law? We did. Did you go to the Court of Chancery? We instituted proceedings there eight years ago. How long did they continue? We are not out of court yet. The first witness examined: I have paid 1300 l. costs and have received 300 l. of them from the town. . . . Have you found the other expenses heavy? Oh, good God, I have a thousand times wished myself out of the world. It has entirely ruined me; it has destroyed an excellent business of which I was possessed. [Questions and answers to the other two were to the same effect.]

In another case of abuse of a charity, the case was 'actually called on', in the Court of Chancery, December 21st, a year and a half ago. But the court made up its mind that it would not make up its mind. On the 9th of April, for which it was fixed, the court with its usual promptitude determined that it would not determine. On the 13th of May it came on, and the court pronounced on one point, . . . but reserved judgment on the other points. To elucidate those points the court [Lord Chancellor Eldon, of course] took home the papers and no more was heard of the cause for many months. . . . It was postponed to the 20th of January, on which day it was not judged. Two days afterwards the same occurrence took place. It was then decided that it should not be decided until another day, on which other day it was again decided that it should not be decided till another day. . . . It was appointed *positively* for the 29th of February, there being but 28 days in that month. . . . On a subsequent day it was mentioned. This word 'mentioned' was a light and airy word in that House, but in the Court of Chancery it was attended with fees to the counsel, fees to the agents, . . . In short a 'mention' was not the most inexpensive and agreeable procedure that could befall a suitor. Some days after, the court acknowledged that it had mislaid the papers which, so many months before, it had taken home to peruse, and desired that a brief (attended with considerable expense) might be left with the court. On the 17th of March it was again called on, and at length it was—not decided, for decided it was not until the present moment,—but it was referred to the Master. That meant that it

was sent out of one expensive court into another expensive court.
. . . The Court of Chancery might be excellent for many purposes,
but to the suitors in it it was ruinous.

At this point Brougham paid a tribute to Lord Eldon that was
unquestionably sincere:

He unequivocally disavowed the intention of throwing the slightest
imputation on the integrity, or the talents, or on the unprecedented
learning of the noble lord at the head of the Court of Chancery. He
sincerely believed that from the days when English law and equity
were separated to the present time, there had never been an individual
in that situation more anxious to do justice to all parties. . . . He was
by far the man of the most wonderful legal learning that had for
ages appeared in any of our courts. . . . He must add that a more
kindly disposed judge to all professional men who practised in his
court never perhaps existed. But notwithstanding all these good
qualities on the part of the noble and learned lord, it was his [Mr.
Brougham's] duty to say that there was something in the Court of
Chancery that set at defiance all calculations of cost and time.

This was, of course, thirty-five years before *Bleak House* with
its account of the sufferings of the victims of the Court of
Chancery and Jarndyce versus Jarndyce. When *Bleak House* was
published in 1853 Lord Denman wrote a review of it, in which
he pointed out that Dickens's caricature was out of date. Years
earlier it would have been valuable, but during the quarter of a
century in which a group of law reformers had almost completely
abolished the Chancery evils which were now belatedly depicted,
he (Lord Denman) and the others (including Brougham, of
course) had never received any assistance from the pen of
Charles Dickens.[1]

In the discussion that followed, Canning assured Brougham
that he heartily agreed with him in principle, though not in
detail. He praised Brougham for his hard and valuable work on
this matter of abuse of charities and for his speeches 'which, if
the honourable and learned gentleman would receive a compliment from him, . . . came home to the feelings of every man
in that House'.[2] Brougham's bill was passed, mutilated as it
was by the Lords' amendments, and the first Charity Commission began its work. The Government, however, refused to

[1] Lord Denman, *Uncle Tom's Cabin, Bleak House* (1853).
[2] *Hansard*, xxxviii. 1228 seq., 1238 seq.

accept Brougham's offer to act as an honourary commissioner without pay.

Bitterly disappointed as Brougham was, he was determined to keep fighting and in October (1818) he published as a pamphlet an appeal to the public in the form of *A Letter to Sir Samuel Romilly M.P. upon the Abuse of Charities* (originally dated 20 August). He described cases of gross abuse of charities unconnected with education and of educational charities which had special visitors, in both of which classes the amendments of the Lords had shut off all inquiry. Several pages were devoted to Brougham's insistence that endowments originally made for the education of the poor were not being employed for that purpose. The boys admitted to Winchester on the foundation 'are, in fact, all children of persons in easy circumstances, many of opulent parents'. Leglislation should be applied to the disposal of funds, in accordance with what might be considered the desire of the original donors under changed conditions. Brougham recognized that the more successful endowed schools had to a considerable degree followed the natural course of historical development, but the children of the poor were entitled to a fair share. Where there was little or no education accruing from the endowments, ample provision should be made for the children of the poor to enable them to receive the sort of education which the poor needed and desired. There was no attack on the Government. Brougham reprobated any attempt to give a party complexion to this matter.

The most remarkable feature of the *Letter to Romilly* was its moderate tone. It confined itself to cold fact and argument, omitting anything approaching violent invective. This, no doubt, was why Sydney Smith called it 'very dull', although Brougham 'makes out a great case in general'.[1] Romilly, to whom the pamphlet was formally addressed, who as a member of Brougham's committee knew all about the matter and who was in full sympathy with him throughout, said when he read the *Letter* that no pamphlet had ever been published on a drier subject or one that was less likely to attract attention.[2] Sydney Smith and Romilly were both wrong. The reading public did not find it dull, and it ran into twelve editions in a few months.

---

[1] *Letters of Sydney Smith,* i. 302, To Lady Holland, 11 Oct. 1818.
[2] Introduction to the reprinting of the *Letter* in Brougham's *Speeches,* iii. 14.

It was stated later on Brougham's authority that nine-tenths of the cases of abuse that had been brought to the attention of his committee were those where trustees of endowments had rented the land to themselves or their friends at figures far below their rentable value or where as tradesmen they swindled the estates.[1] In one case a charity had been endowed for the support of a certain number of poor men and a resident warden who was to read to them and pray for them. But in 1818 the warden, a clergyman, did not reside, did no reading or praying for the poor, and in fact did nothing but draw profits from the estate, from which he doled out £4 a year to each of six poor men. In many of the educational trusts a schoolmaster, frequently a clergyman, enjoyed a salary and a free house for doing no teaching, and in some he was at the same time conducting a school of his own, teaching modern subjects for profit. Many of the educational endowments had been made for the children of the poor in earlier centuries when they were to be educated for the service of the church, and the teaching of Latin was essential to that object. But the children of the poor could no longer benefit from the endowments, for their parents wished them to learn the three R's, with or without other modern subjects. The reasonable thing would have been to use the endowments for the latter purpose. But when this was attempted in a grammar school at Leeds, Lord Eldon had handed down a judgement in 1805 which declared that a grammar school was a school for the teaching of Latin or of Latin and Greek, and that no school endowed as a grammar school could be used for any other purpose. Brougham's hope was that this difficulty would be overcome by legislation. His attempt to do so in 1820 was unsuccessful, and it was not until 1840 that Lord Eldon's judgement was largely overridden by legislation.

In December the *Quarterly Review*, which had not issued a number since April, stepped into Brougham with no holds barred. It purported to discuss every aspect of the questions raised, but in effect and intent it was a seventy-seven page attack on Brougham. While neither was the principal author both Canning and Croker probably wrote parts of the violent abuse. Croker was the chief political gladiator of the Tory *Quarterly* as was Brougham of the Whig *Edinburgh Review*. On his return to

---

[1] *Edinburgh Review*, Jan. 1820.

Parliament, Brougham had lost no time in attacking Croker's salary as Secretary to the Admiralty, and in the session that had just ended Croker had given Brougham the lie direct across the House. They were to be spirited antagonists for many years. (All of this, by the way, was to prove an excellent preparation, the two men being what they were, for a close friendship in their later years, when neither could bear to let much time go by without writing to the other, their cordial letters discussing a wide variety of topics.)[1] It was to be expected that in this article the full vocabulary of vituperation should be called upon, but it is surprising to find that Brougham, in seeking to shape the Commission, is charged with having aimed to make himself the *dictator* of the nation. It was equally absurd to say that educational endowments were ordinary ecclesiastical estates. Throughout the article the pretence was maintained that the Church had been endangered and the schools, of which Englishmen were so proud, had been viciously attacked by a presumptuous Scot. On a more reasonable basis there is much to be said for the article's criticism of Brougham's original provisions for the selection of the commissioners.

Whatever might be thought of the case which the *Quarterly* had sought to build against Brougham and in defence of the amendments effected by the House of Lords, within six months it came tumbling down like a child's house of blocks. For in the session of 1819, to the surprise of everyone, the Government introduced its own Charitable Foundations Bill, which repealed that of the previous year and, while maintaining the fence around the sacrosanct public schools and charities with special visitors, incorporated practically every other part of Brougham's original bill which the House of Lords had destroyed. This included Brougham's original extension of the scope of the commissioners to all kinds of charities. And that in spite of the fact that several ministers, including Eldon, had in the Lords branded those provisions as utterly unreasonable and perilously mischievous. Good intention, no doubt, played a part in this surrender to Brougham, but the wave of public feeling created by Brougham's *Letter to Romilly* was a large factor.

When Castlereagh introduced the new measure Brougham gladly seconded his motion. On 23 June Brougham objected,

---

[1] The letters are in the Clements Library MSS., University of Michigan.

quite hopelessly, to the exemption of charities which had special visitors. This gave Peel the opportunity for which he had been waiting with a carefully prepared speech. He vigorously attacked the conduct of Brougham's committee, which had now completed its work. Peel was member for Oxford where the feeling against Brougham was strong. And Peel's old school was Harrow. His attack caught Brougham completely by surprise. He had just come through an exhausting illness, most of the members of his committee were not in the House at the time, he was totally unprepared and he did not have with him a single note. But he replied to Peel on the spot. By pure chance a visitor in the gallery made a stenographic report of this speech, which was copied into *Hansard* and took up over thirty pages in Brougham's published speeches.[1] No adequate summary of its various points can be attempted here, but the following passages may afford some impression of it:

. . . If I do not now satisfy all who hear me, . . . that the Right Honourable gentleman is utterly wrong in all his charges—wrong from the beginning to the end of his laboured oration, . . . if I do not show him to be mistaken in his facts, out in his dates, at fault in his law, ignorant of all Parliamentary precedent and practice, grossly uninformed, perhaps misinformed, upon the whole question which in an evil hour he has undertaken to handle . . . I shall next advert to the charge of having packed the Committee with Whigs [Brougham then proceeded to give the party affiliation of members at every change of personnel, with dates.] . . . [Peel had sneered at the appointment of three London aldermen whom he supposed to be not highly educated, to inquire about schools.] It is strange that one who has received so liberal an education, that he seems to think nobody else knows anything, should be unable to explain this phenomenon. Did it never occur to him, that as the Committee was originally appointed to examine the state of education in the metropolis, so it was a matter of course . . . to name the members for London and Westminster? . . . But there were others on the Committee, in whose hands the cause of learning seems to me to have been almost as safe as in those of the Right Honourable gentleman himself, who will suffer no one else to touch a college or a school. What does he think of Sir Samuel Romilly, of Sir James Mackintosh, . . . of Mr. Wilberforce, of Mr. John Smythe, the member for Cambridge University? But he said, and repeatedly said, that he

[1] *Hansard*, xl. 1308 seq.; *Speeches*, iii. 181 seq.

preferred no charge. . . . He was the last man in the world to make
personal allusions. He accuse or attack any body! . . . And these
disclaimers were sown thickly among insinuations, and charges, and
personalities as thickly sown; . . . and the speech was wholly made up
of invective, save and except the parts devoted to those denials of
any design to inveigh. . . . The Right Honourable gentleman was
pleased with even unusual solemnity to attack—I ought perhaps
rather to say, reprimand—us for what he termed the disregarding
the obligations of the Winchester oath, compelling the Fellows to
produce the statutes which they had sworn to conceal, and then
publishing these arcana to the world. . . . The Winchester statutes
were never published at all—never—and purposely, because, on
account of the oath, it might be deemed objectionable to publish
them. . . . The Right Honourable gentleman was thinking of the
Eton statutes; but then there was no oath at all pleaded in the
Eton case. . . . It might be a caution to people before they begin
lecturing, to learn a little. . . . I do not impute all this wretched
blundering to the Right Honourable gentleman. . . . But he should
have been far above suffering any designing or bigoted persons from
getting possession of him. . . . I am beset and attacked . . . as if the
enemies of the cause supposed that a person giving up his days and
nights to such a work must needs have some bad purpose to serve.
But I shall leave it to time and the contempt of the community, to
cure men of such absurd prejudices, which I assure you give me no
sort of angry feeling, and only move my pity.

In the discussion that followed, several members of the Committee, including Wilberforce (a Tory, of course), said that every
statement made by Brougham, in the hour which he had
devoted to proving Peel to be entirely wrong, was true. We
can readily understand the remark made later by the second
Lord Ellenborough that when Brougham left the Commons for
the House of Lords, Peel became a better speaker because he
was freed from his fear of Brougham.[1] Brougham, doubtless,
never gave a thought to the fact that Peel was a very sensitive
man. By the unanimous verdict of his contemporaries Brougham
in all the ordinary relationships of private life and of society
was kind, amicable and, on occasion, remarkably considerate.
But when he was on the warpath nothing was to be wasted on
men's susceptibilities.

Sydney Smith was delighted at 'the beating' Brougham 'gave

[1] Ellenborough's manuscript diary in P.R.O., 19 Feb. 1831. G.D. 12/28.

to Peel'. About a month earlier Sydney had written to Lady Holland:

Have you read the Edinburgh Review? I see in it an article of endless length *concerning*, and probably *by*, Brougham. The Scotch, whatever other talents they may have, can never condense; they always begin a few days before the flood, and come *gradually* down to the reign of George the third, forgetful of nothing but the shortness of human life, and the volatility of human attention.[1]

The article referred to was not written by Brougham. It was the first of three articles in the *Edinburgh Review* of March 1819, July 1819, and January 1820 on charity abuses, the Committee and the Commission, written by others on the basis of material supplied by Brougham.[2] In the first of these it was asserted that much good was being effected apart from the direct action of the Commissioners. 'There is not a parish in the land, we veritably believe, where people are not now beginning to look into those abuses. . . . The culpable are reforming from fear of exposure and punishment; and the indolent and inattentive from shame.' Special visitors had begun to take their duties seriously, and in several cases the rents paid by the trustees to the trust were greatly increased. The article might have added that the minutes of evidence indicated that since the Committee's investigation had begun schools had been established in relation to endowments where no school had existed before and the revenues had been plundered.

The January 1820 article pointed to the fact that the Commission had already instituted several prosecutions, and had obtained convictions in the courts, and orders to make restitution. 'All over the country, trustees are alive and on the alert; new regulations are made; bad courses of management are abandoned; and restitution is anxiously, though silently, made to injured endowments, in order that everything may be right and straight to meet the expected inquiry.'

The history of successive Charity Commissions was to be long and complicated. Over the years many abuses were remedied but for the crushing of all of them the mills ground slowly. In 1831 when Brougham himself was Lord Chancellor the exception

---

[1] *Letters of Sydney Smith*, i. 336, 327.
[2] Brougham MSS., Brougham to Shepherd, 16 Aug. 1825.

of charities having special visitors was abolished, and thus many
of the worst cases were reached at last. In 1859 a permanent
Charity Commission was appointed with extensive powers of
administration. In relation to one of the later bills, Lord John
Russell, who was Prime Minister at the time, wrote to Brougham:
'I congratulate you on the fruit of the tree which you planted
thirty-seven years ago.'[1] Brougham, of course, *had* started it all
and he was to pay the price for it. Another influential group of
enemies was created, as implacable as the slave-traders and their
associates. It was not only the peculators and their friends, but
those in high places in Church and State who, though innocent
themselves, feared for those who were close to them. To open up
this whole matter had not been, in the early nineteenth century,
a gentlemanly thing to do. Brougham had had the hardihood to
rush in where gentlemen feared to tread. His humanitarianism
was to win for him other groups of enemies, and the biographer
in search of truth has to make his way as best he can through a
mass of malice carefully concealed, with its whispers, gibes, and
sneers, to say nothing of sheer untruths assiduously invented
and circulated.

Brougham and his committee did not allow their campaign
against abuses in charities intended for the poor to deflect them
from their investigation of existing provisions for popular education. The digest issued by the committee after it had completed
its work embodied details of the education provided by every
school in Great Britain, and well-organized general statistics
were presented in tabular form under Brougham's supervision.
Separate editions were prepared for each county to be circulated
in that county. These were the first educational statistics for
Great Britain that possessed any measure of approximation.
They were based on returns made to the Committee by the parish
clergy whose interest and ready assistance Brougham praised in
the highest terms in Parliament and in the reports. Some of the
clergy were not careful to check duplication and exaggeration;
there was sometimes confusion between enrolment and attendance, and the figures were too high. But when due and reasonable allowance is made for this, the statistics are enlightening.
And they were very valuable for those who were to carry on the
campaign for 'schools for all'.

[1] Brougham MSS., 4 Aug. 1853.

According to these figures there were, in round numbers, 12,000 parishes in England and in 3,500 of these there was no school of any kind. As Brougham said in Parliament in 1820, those parishes had no more means of education than were to be found among the Hottentots. In a letter written fifteen years later, Brougham said that the number of parishes in which there was no school had been reduced from 3,500 to 2,000 and that the number of schools had probably doubled since 1818.[1] In the whole of England in 1818, 165,433 children were being educated in endowed schools, 478,849 in unendowed day schools, and 452,817 in Sunday Schools (by far the greater number of whom were also in day schools). Of the day-school pupils 145,172 were in schools connected with the British and Foreign or National School Society; the older of these societies had been in existence only seven years when the returns were made, although, of course, there had been Lancasterian and Bell schools for several years before that. Brougham estimated that to the total of 644,282, there might be added 100,000 who were in Sunday Schools but not also in any other school (as an outside figure), 10,000 for incomplete returns, 50,000 for children of well-to-do parents who were being educated at home or at boarding schools that had been omitted from the tables, though not from the digest, to give a total of 804,282 children who were in some sort of school. But of these 53,624 were in dames' schools where very little was taught, and practically all of the children were under the ordinary school age. Deducting this number in dames' schools, that left a total of approximately 750,000 children in England attending school. This was between one-fourteenth and one-fifteenth of the *actual* population of England in 1818. (When Brougham said one-sixteenth of population, he meant the number in *day* schools, exclusive of dames' schools, and, of course, not including the 50,000 omitted from the tables. His population figures were those of the 1810 census.) Brougham estimated that the proportion to population of the children who should be in school was one-ninth, although in his speeches, where in any case he was not very exact, his implication was frequently one-tenth.

The figures for the various parts of Great Britain are striking and they served as a useful guide for the future. The proportion

---

[1] Add. MSS. 34616, ff. 156 seq., Brougham to Napier, 27 Sept. 1833.

of children in school to population in Wales was only one-twentieth. In Scotland it was between one-tenth and one-ninth, in the four northern counties of England one-tenth, in Essex, Norfolk, and Suffolk one in twenty-one, in Lancashire and in Middlesex one twenty-fourth. The highest percentage obtained by an English county was that of Westmorland, Brougham's own county.

In 1818, that great year of conflict over Brougham's proposals regarding charity abuses, he had gathered together a group of his friends, including Lord Lansdowne and James Mill, to start the first infant school in London and the second in Great Britain. Two years earlier Robert Owen had established an infant school for the children of his employees in his model factory at New Lanark. When Owen had been in London during the greater part of 1812 and 1813, the basis of a lifelong friendship had been laid between Brougham and Owen, two great humanitarians who, although they disagreed on many matters, had the utmost confidence in each other's benevolence. In a eulogy of Owen in the House of Commons, Brougham said that argue against Owen's theories as you might, 'he listened with the utmost mildness, his nature perfectly free from all gall; he had none of the feverish or irritable feeling which too generally belonged to projectors'.[1] Brougham frequently visited New Lanark and displayed an interest in Owen's experiments, particularly in the classes for children under seven. He caught from Owen that enthusiasm for infant schools and the insistence on the tremendous importance of the first six years of life that he was to express in so many of his speeches and writings on education.

In writing to Ricardo, 7 December 1818, James Mill had said that Brougham, 'strongly impressed with the importance of Owen's infant school', was 'very hot' about it. 'It is part of his schemes on the education subject, which seems to be engrossing his whole mind.'[2] A 'pattern school' or 'model school' was needed. Brougham undertook to form a managing group and to raise the money required. So the Brewer's Lane School was begun in 1819.

Owen said that the infant-school idea came into his mind

---

[1] *Hansard*, xli. 1191, quoted in R. H. Harvey, *Robert Owen* (1949), p. 58, and in F. Podmore, *Robert Owen*, 2 vols. (1906), ii. 637-8.
[2] Ricardo, *Works*, vii. 355-7.

because the parents in his factory knew nothing about training children; he desired to save the children from evil influences and to form their characters in this plastic and most important period of their lives. His general programme was one of satisfying their curiosity about natural objects, play, singing, dancing, and military movements accompanied by fife and drum. He needed as teacher a mild-mannered man who loved children and would be patient and kind with them, and he selected a weaver named James Buchanan, who possessed these qualifications and would do without question everything Owen asked him to do; Buchanan 'had been previously trained by his wife to perfect submission to her will'. Brougham and his associates asked if they might have Buchanan, and Owen generously consented. Of course they also got Mrs. Buchanan. Owen blamed her and Buchanan's hopelessness without Owen's guiding hand for the failure of the London school to approach his own in excellence. Owen was shocked to discover Mrs. Buchanan in the schoolroom with a whip. He believed that she was threatening the children with it.[1] But perhaps she was only looking for her husband.

A group of Quakers, including William Allen, established another infant school at Spitalfields and engaged Wilderspin, who had been a frequent visitor to Brougham's school, as instructor. Wilderspin became the great organizer of the infant-school movement, travelling around the country and establishing schools with something of the zeal that had been displayed by Lancaster in his enterprise. Wilderspin dedicated to Brougham his book *The Progress of Infant Education*. Owen's remarks in his autobiography, written at the age of eighty-eight, on the general inferiority of all infant schools except his own, may be taken with more than a grain of scepticism.[2] For all his good qualities, Robert Owen could never believe that anybody could do anything as well as he did it.

In the *Edinburgh Review* for December 1818 and for October 1819 Brougham introduced the British reading public to the work of Fellenberg which he had studied in Switzerland in 1816. Some of the contents of the articles had already been presented by Brougham in his evidence before his own Education Committee.

---

[1] *Life of Robert Owen*, written by himself, 2 vols. (1857-8), 1920 ed., pp. 196-210.
[2] Ibid., pp. 115, 192-9; Margaret Cole, *Robert Owen* (1953), pp. 87-88.

CHAPTER XIII

The Queen's Trial

IN a previous chapter we followed the relations of Brougham and the Princess of Wales as far as the death of the Princess Charlotte in November 1817. Some time before that, Leach, who was to become Vice-Chancellor in the following year, was asked to examine all the information so far received on the conduct of the Princess of Wales. Leach reported two days after the death of the Princess Charlotte. The Prime Minister assured him that if the Prince Regent wished to set up a commision of inquiry, the Government would pay the expenses.[1] So there was appointed the Milan Commission. Most of the evidence submitted to it was unsworn.

We have seen that Brougham's fears over the Princess's conduct had been growing as he acquired more precise knowledge than that afforded by general rumour. His apprehensions were fully confirmed by two letters which he received from his brother James in March 1819, shortly before the completion of the work of the Milan Commission. He had sent James to the Princess, who was living in Italy at the time, to help her straighten out her financial affairs. In the first of these letters James praised Bergami's ability to manage things. 'His picture is in every room.' By the time James wrote his second letter, all his remaining doubts had vanished. 'They are to all appearances man and wife, never was anything so obvious. . . . The whole thing is apparent to everyone.'[2]

In the second letter James Brougham gave his brother further information and advice:

She says she has no ambition to be Queen and never had . . . all she wants is to pass the remainder of her life quietly . . . All the work the P[rince] makes worries her. . . . Except Ly. C. Lindsay and yrself, there is not a person in England she ever wishes to see again . . . Why not make a good bargain for her as to money, and come to

[1] Leach's Memorandum. *Letters of George IV*, ii. 410.
[2] *Letters of George IV*, ii. 272 seq., 280 seq.

terms about a divorce or separation with ye P.? I do assure you she seriously wishes for this . . . she wished all this to be communicated to you by me . . . If we could get for her £50,000 down and 25,000 a year, it would be 4 times as much as she wd. expect . . . She has no other advisor, and feelings of pity for her, were there no other reason, wd. make you do it, when she, as it were, throws herself upon you.[1]

Brougham always placed the fullest reliance on his brother James. After this letter Brougham was convinced that the Princess could not be defended successfully, that she must be kept out of England, and that he must make the best possible bargain for her with the Government and the Prince. Those who critized his conduct at the time and afterwards knew nothing of the existence of the letter. It was entirely unknown until its publication by Professor Aspinall with the letters of George IV a relatively short time ago.

The Princess had more to say about a divorce in a letter to Lady Charlotte Lindsay written probably a few days later, on 20 March: 'Toute ce que je désir est, comme il est très evident que le Regent agit si malicieusement pour qu'il puisse a rémarier, que moi je porte une petition au Parlement pour être quitte au fin pour toujours de ce tyrann et ce celerat de mari.'[2]

The Princess urged Lady Charlotte to persuade Brougham to effect for her this deliverance. Brougham knew, of course, that for a divorce in our sense of the term (*a vinculo*) there would have to be evidence of adultery on one side or the other. But he hoped that a legal separation might be acceptable to the Princess. He approached the Prince Regent through Lord Hutchinson, a personal friend of the Prince, though not a member of the inner Carlton House circle, and a Whig in politics. On 14 June Brougham made a definite proposal. The following letter of Brougham to Lord Hutchinson, in which it was embodied, indicates how closely Brougham followed the instructions of the Princess as conveyed to him by his brother.

I am disposed to advise the Princess to accede to an arrangement grounded on some such basis as the following. That she shall agree to a formal separation to be ratified by Act of Parliament . . . that she shall renounce the right to be crowned . . . and shall henceforth

---

[1] *Letters of George IV*, ii. 280 seq.
[2] Brougham MSS.

take some other style and title, as that of Duchess of Cornwall, that she shall renounce the jointure to which she is entitled should she survive the Prince Regent, and that her annuity shall be granted for her life, instead of ceasing on the demise of the Crown. My firm belief is that although the Princess can have nothing to dread from the result of any proceedings, she will be more comfortable after such arrangement, since the Princess Charlotte's death has in all probability removed any desire of returning to England; I am quite sure that if it prevents the manifold evils of a public inquiry into the most delicate matters connected with the Royal Family, it will be highly beneficial to the country.[1]

The Cabinet was favourable to this proposal of settlement, but the Regent was hard set on obtaining a complete divorce. While Brougham believed that the case against the Princess would be overwhelming, the ministers, having received the report of the Milan Commission, felt that their case was not strong enough. A Cabinet minute stated that it would not be possible to advise the Prince Regent to proceed against the Princess unless, and until, there was further investigation.[2]

Brougham did not know, and never knew, about these misgivings on the part of the ministers. But it still seems strange, at first sight, that three days before he made his proposal on 14 June his brother James wrote to the Princess that she would probably have to stand trial in November.[3] In view of the whole of Brougham's conduct during the next year, this looks like the first move in strategy by which Brougham hoped to frighten the Princess with the threat of imminent proceedings against her, in order to make her favourable to a reasonable settlement. He would at the same time try to frighten the Government and the Prince with information that she was bent on coming to England, in order to induce them to agree to a reasonable settlement. Brougham thus attempted to keep both parties in balance and at the same time to keep the Princess out of England and avert public proceedings. This is confessedly speculation on our part, but all of Brougham's conduct fits into the pattern. It was not, of course, a line of policy which he could announce to the world or reveal to his closest friend.

On 5 August Brougham wrote to Lord Hutchinson that a letter from the Princess indicated that she intended to come to England. 'Her coming would be pregnant with every sort of mischief (not to mention the infernal personal annoyance of having such a devil to plague me for six months). I think it would expose things to the risk of clamour and violence which no one can hope to estimate, far less to direct, or, in case of necessity, disarm. . . . Therefore I am disposed to prevent her coming by every means in my power.'[1] Naturally the Princess was annoyed with Brougham who would not leave England so soon after Peterloo to go and see her, but Brougham assured her that he would go as soon as it was necessary, adding that he felt sure that there would 'be some proceedings, tho' they may be delayed till after Xmas'.[2]

On 29 January (1820) George III died. It was no longer the Prince Regent and the Princess of Wales; it was King George IV and Queen Caroline. Brougham was wakened at two o'clock in the morning, and the new king's brother, the Duke of Sussex, stood by his bedside to give him the news. At seven o'clock Brougham had the new Queen's courier, Sicard, ready to carry a letter to the Queen. She was to come to Brussels or Paris or Calais, where she was to demand a yacht to take her to England.[3] It is possible that Brougham, for once, intended her to come. He may have been swept away by the drama of the situation and felt willing to take a chance. But that is very unlikely. It is altogether probable that this was his game of having her frighten the Government by proposing to come to England and then stopping her on the way to open negotiations.

While the ministers feared an imminent arrival of the Queen, a Cabinet minute of 14 February reveals a staunch position on the part of the Government and a willingness to speak candidly to the King. It pointed out that in an ordinary divorce case there was a right of recrimination with countercharges backed by evidence. 'If Your Majesty and the Queen were in the situation of private individuals, it may be assumed as certain that a divorce could not possibly be obtained.' (A draft had said 'Under all circumstances Your Majesty could not possibly obtain a divorce'.) 'A Bill of Divorce could therefore in this case be

---

[1] Add. MSS. 40344, f. 17. [2] *Letters of George IV*, ii. 297.
[3] Brougham MSS.

proposed only on the paramount consideration of a great public interest.' The Cabinet could not apparently discover a great public interest, for it stated as their unanimous opinion that they could not recommend a Bill of Divorce. A 'qualified measure' was suggested, which, they said, would be similar to, but not identical with, the proposal made by Brougham in the previous summer. 'The annexation of the condition of her [the Queen's] continued residence abroad with a grant of a liberal provision is not in their judgment a condemnation.'[1]

During the next few days, rumour was rich in stories of the clash between King and Cabinet, of ministers resigning, and of the King contemplating new ministers. The one thing certain is that the King submitted to the advice of the ministers and gave up the divorce.[2] And on the 18th, four days after the Cabinet minute, the Prime Minister sent for Brougham. On the same day, the 18th, Brougham wrote to Lady Charlotte Lindsay: 'All now depends on her coming to Brussels or some near and handy spot. If she arrives plump on you at Paris make her either stay there or at Calais till I can come out to her. It would be *frightfully dangerous* for her to come here all at once.'[3] But the Queen remained in Italy. On 23 February Lady Charlotte Lindsay wrote to Brougham: 'I suppose if the Baron [Bergami] still retains his dominion over her, that she will accept a proposal, but if she should happen to be tired of him, perhaps by way of amusement, and to bully her *caro sposo*, she may demand a tryal.'[4]

On 21 February Tierney made a speech as the official leader of the Whig party in the House of Commons. He was all for a parliamentary investigation of the Queen's conduct. He would not grant to a person labouring under so heavy a cloud of suspicion any portion of the public money until that suspicion was removed. Brougham made an adroit speech in direct reply. He could always strike a pose with remarkable effect. His attitude now was to see no evil, speak no evil, hear no evil. If charges and evidence were placed before that House, every member would have to take an impartial attitude. As it was

[1] Add. MSS. (Liverpool MSS.) 38283, ff. 46 seq.
[2] The journal of Mrs. Arbuthnot places that as early as 15 Feb. Other sources place it later.
[3] Brougham MSS. [18 June 1820].
[4] Ibid., 23 Feb. 1820.

they owed the Queen respect and consideration. They should scorn to pay attention to vague rumour and to malicious and indefinite slander. As for himself he recognized no suspicions, he had never heard of the Milan Commission, and he could not allow his mind to receive any sinister impressions.[1] Brougham's speech went well with the House, and many believed that Tierney's was a crawling to the King for office. Certainly that was not the attitude of most of the Whig party, and least of all was it the attitude of Lord Grey.

In the course of his speech Brougham referred to the omission of the Queen's name from the amended liturgy of the Church of England as a 'trifle light as air'. George III had died on a Saturday, and on the next day, a Sunday, the mind of the new King was turned to sacred thoughts, and he was shocked by the blasphemy and outrage of this woman being prayed for along with him. That Sunday he made a collection of prayer books of various dates and reigns. Although he spent the whole evening with them, the prayer books brought no comfort to his soul. On Thursday, however, Croker arrived with what he called 'a religious point of view', which he expounded enthusiastically to the King's private secretary. 'If she is fit to be introduced to the Almighty, she is fit to be received by men, and if we are to *pray* for her in Church we may surely bow to her at Court. The praying for her will throw a sanctity round her which the good and pious people of this country will never afterwards bear to have withdrawn.'[2] There may have been some hard sense and sly expediency in that last sentence, but one fails to find religion anywhere, and particularly the Christian religion, in this uneasy vision of God waiting for certain persons to be socially introduced to Him. Croker's religious feeling found expression in a diary; if he could have foreseen the popular enthusiasm of four months hence, he would not have recognized even practical wisdom in the exclusion of the Queen from the liturgy. When the nation (by far the greater part of it) was in its angriest mood, nothing disgusted it so much as the thought of the liturgy presenting George IV in all his panoply of virtue before the Almighty in lonely grandeur, while the Queen was not even to be mentioned. Much of the later trouble would have been avoided if in

[1] *Hansard*, xli. 1623 seq.
[2] *The Croker Papers*, ed. L. J. Jennings, 3 vols. (1884), i. 159.

February, simply as a matter of form, Queen Caroline had been given the place that had been occupied by nearly all Queens Consort. According to Croker, only four or five of the Cabinet opposed the change and the matter was 'finally settled' on 12 February. But Greville, giving Lord Harrowby, a member of the Cabinet, as his authority, said on 14 February: 'The ministers wished to suffer it to be done [the admission of the Queen's name to the Liturgy], but he [the King] peremptorily refused, and said nothing should induce him to consent, whoever might ask him.'[1] It should be said to its credit that it was not the Church's doing. The Archbishop of Canterbury was strongly opposed to the exclusion and most of the clergy agreed with him. In the Dissenters' chapels, for the most part, there was no set form of prayer, and the ministers were authorized by their congregations to pray for the Queen on occasion. In the year that followed, those occasions were many, and in the chapels of the Dissenters the Queen was prayed for with a pleasure and vigour that were not purely religious.

In the month of March the attention of both the Government and Brougham were occupied in the general election occasioned by the King's death, and there was little or nothing in the way of negotiation between them. Brougham fought another gallant fight in Westmorland, which was largely a repetition of that of 1818. He was defeated by a very small margin.

The period from the end of March to the beginning of June is one of a great deal of talk of comings and goings that never occurred. The Queen in all her letters was determined to go to England and Brougham was telling his friends that she was certainly coming. In fact, some time in March he had said that to Tierney, who replied that he did not believe it and offered to bet Brougham a guinea that she would not be in England six months hence.[2] Brougham took up the bet; but, as we have already pointed out, it was his game to frighten the Government with stories of her coming, and a guinea was not much to lose if he could throw dust in his opponents' eyes. Meanwhile he was constantly telling the Queen that he must meet her and talk with her at some place before she came to England. That place was always within easy reach of England, and Brougham

---

[1] *Greville Memoirs*, i. 25.
[2] Howick MSS., Tierney to Grey, Mar. 1820.

apparently felt that there she would be in the best position to bargain. It seems clear to us that Brougham always intended to give the Queen a chance to make a better bargain than the best the Government would offer to her. When the right time came it would be essential that he should be able to come and go readily between the Queen and the Government, which was quite impossible from Italy or Geneva.

It became well known that Brougham was in close touch with the Government and with the King through Lord Hutchinson. As a result there were those, in this very uncharitable generation, who suspected that Brougham was prepared to betray the interests of the Queen. Those who expressed that suspicion were ignorant of facts related in this book, beginning with that letter from his brother James in June of the previous year. The Duke of Wellington said to Littleton in June (1820) that Brougham 'had betrayed everybody, King, Queen, ministers and Lord Hutchinson'. It was an angry outburst, entirely unsupported by facts.

Then there was the story that Brougham was willing to sell the Queen for a silk gown, that is appointment as King's Counsel. Croker, who hated Brougham at this time, not without cause, made this accusation, and Canning spoke as though he, too, suspected it. Appointment as King's Counsel in this period was a rare honour enjoyed by only a very few distinguished lawyers. Under Lord Eldon as Lord Chancellor such appointments were few and far between. This was partly because of his distaste for any alteration in things as they were and partly because of the unconscionably long time that he took with any matter that required decision. Jack Campbell (later Lord Campbell) had written to his father some years before: 'Lord Eldon is determined to make no more silk gowns till Bonaparte is dethroned, and when the news arrives he will take seven years to read the affidavits, to make up his mind whether the event has really happened.'[1] Brougham merited the honour on his record at the Bar. He had asked for it in 1817 and at the time of Romilly's death. To say that Brougham would have sold the Queen for a silk gown is nonsense. But Brougham felt, no doubt, that the circumstances might be exploited nevertheless.

The Queen had sent to Brougham and Denman patents of

[1] Hardcastle, i. 302.

appointment as her Attorney-General and Solicitor-General. When these were recognized and announced, they would be called within the Bar, in silk gowns, but that would last only as long as she employed them in those capacities. Brougham and the Government had a common interest in keeping the Queen's affair as quiet as possible while they were trying to arrive at a satisfactory settlement. Announcement of these appointments would stir up the public mind and possibly stir up Parliament. If the Lord Chancellor did the just and generous thing, Brougham and Denman would, at the beginning of the law term, be within the Bar, in silk gowns, in their own right and not in that of the Queen, and announcement of their appointments could be postponed indefinitely. The Prime Minister may have felt that Brougham was an impulsive man and that a generous attitude on Eldon's part might result in a more rapid and enthusiastic course toward their common goal. Canning and Liverpool both pleaded with Eldon, who was obdurate. Writing to the Lord Chancellor on 3 April, Lord Liverpool said that Brougham had fixed on the 27th of that month to meet the Queen at Aix-la-Chapelle or Lille and that he wished Lord Hutchinson to go with him.

The reputation of a large part of the Royal Family depends upon keeping this question out of hostile discussion in Parliament. The possibility of doing this must in a great degree rest with the Princess's [sic] advisors. I am satisfied that Brougham for his own interest will be sincere in this business if he does not consider himself as ill used, but I should really deplore the unfortunate determination of such a question upon a mere matter of etiquette.[1]

When it came to the opening of term Denman was insistent that they should announce their appointments. On 20 April the appointments were announced in open court. On the same day Lord Liverpool wrote an apologetic letter to Brougham in the course of which he said: 'No person has certainly any right to complain of your not [illegible] the just rights of the Queen in the professional relation in which you stand towards her'.[2] Just before this Lord Hutchinson wrote to Brougham: 'You must present your patents on Thursday. Nothing can be gained by delay because the only decision that the Chancellor will ever

---

[1] Add. MSS., Liverpool MSS. 38283, ff. 25–26. Quoted in Aspinall, p. 108.
[2] Brougham MSS., 20 Apr. 1820.

come to is not to decide.' He said that Brougham's enemies and
those who wished to misrepresent him to the Queen would be
aided by any further delay. It was not in the interest of anyone
who hoped for a settlement.[1]

The ministers had decided to make definite proposals to the
Queen. And so we have the memorandum of 15 April. The
Queen's annuity, which had lapsed on the death of George III,
was to be continued and to be increased to £50,000 a year; she
was to give up any claim for a jointure; she was not to come into
'any part of the British dominions'; and she was to take 'some
other name or title than that of Queen'; the rights and privileges
of a Queen Consort were not to be exercised by her except with
respect to the appointment of law officers, 'or to any proceedings
in courts of justice'. If the Queen violated this agreement after
having subscribed to it, she was to lose her annuity. If she agreed
to the proposals, Brougham was to obtain from her a signed
statement to that effect.[2] Brougham was not to inform the
Queen of this by letter but was to place the memorandum in
her hands; it was left for him to decide where and when. He
did not deliver it at once. He kept it for six weeks. He has been
blamed for doing so, and also, strange to say, for not letting the
Government know that he was keeping it. The Prime Minister,
of course, knew that all along, although he felt that Brougham
should have taken the memorandum to her at Geneva when
she asked him to meet her there. In fact everyone from that
time to this seems to have blamed Brougham for not going to
Geneva. The reasons which he gave were very thin and need
not be taken seriously. But Brougham had constantly urged on
the Princess that their meeting should take place not far from
Calais. We have already suggested Brougham's reasons for this.
The ministers counted on bargaining and expected it to begin
at Geneva; Brougham was determined that it should begin near
Calais. After having refused to go to Geneva Brougham expected
the Queen to name promptly a place and date of meeting near
Calais; and if she had done so the loss of time would not have
been great.

There was, however, an intervention from another quarter,
of which neither Brougham nor Liverpool had any knowledge

[1] Ibid., n.d.
[2] Add. MSS. 38565, ff. 93–94. Given in *Annual Register for 1820*, pp. 126–7.

or apprehension. Alderman Matthew Wood was a very popular Radical London politician. He had been twice elected Lord Mayor. Now he decided that he, Matthew Wood, would bring the Queen to London and to the cheers of the London crowds, as a heroine who in the face of concerted power and persecution was claiming her rights as Queen and defending her honour as a woman. There was probably some ignorant chivalry about this as well as much demagoguery. Wood knew nothing about the Queen. He may have felt as sure of her innocence as Brougham felt sure of her guilt. Brougham sadly underestimated Wood's ability and always regarded him as a fool. It was all very well for Brougham to entertain his aristocratic friends with stories of Alderman Wood, and to raise a laugh in the House of Commons by suggesting that the A.W. frequently employed meant Absolute Wisdom, but Matthew Wood was not ridiculed among London's wealthy merchants. Brougham did not know that Wood had been corresponding with the Queen as early as the middle of April and he did not associate him with the Queen until nearly the end of May. On 27 May he wrote to Lord Hutchinson: 'Wood the ass and alderman talks of going to see his son at Paris but I suspect he means to see the Queen also for he tried to get my approbation which I withheld'.[1] On the same day he asked Lady Charlotte Lindsay to write to the Queen immediately and warn her against Wood.[2] Wood had sent his son to meet the Queen at Geneva, where he had to encounter James Brougham who had been sent there by his brother. The Queen chose St. Omer as the place for meeting Brougham, and Brougham and Lord Hutchinson left London on 1 June. Wood was a few days ahead of them in meeting the Queen, and following up his letters and the work of his son could be counted on to paint for her glowing pictures of the great welcome she would receive from the London crowds and the invincible support which the nation would afford her against her oppressors.

Writing to Lord Liverpool on the day he left for St. Omer Brougham stated that he could not say what advice he would give the Queen until he had talked with her.[3] Lord Liverpool replied:

[1] Add. MSS. 40344, ff. 29 seq.
[2] Brougham MSS.
[3] Ibid., 1 June 1820.

. . . Mr. Brougham may rely upon Lord Liverpool doing full justice to Mr. Brougham's conduct in every part of the delicate transaction in which he has been engaged. Lord Liverpool has never doubted that it was Mr. Brougham's sincere wish to prevent the unpleasant consequences which must arise from the arrival of the Queen, and that he would be actuated by a due regard to these considerations as far as the professional relation in which he stood to the Queen would permit.[1]

The Prime Minister had always expected bargaining. In a later memorandum, reviewing some aspects of his relationship with Brougham, he wrote: 'Lord Liverpool did understand Mr. Brougham substantially to approve of the terms contained in the memorandum [of 15 April], but not thereby to be precluded from preparing modifications of them, if upon conversation with the Queen he should deem such modifications reasonable.'[2] It was also understood between Lord Liverpool and Brougham that the latter was to present the memorandum of 15 April to the Queen, and that Lord Hutchinson should carry no written instructions, except that he should be prepared to give the Queen the warning that if she came to England all negotiation and compromise must cease.[3]

Lord Hutchinson, apparently, misunderstood this arrangement. But that hardly mattered. Brougham and Hutchinson arrived at St. Omer on 3 June at three o'clock in the afternoon. They put up at different hotels and next day took to writing notes to one another. Lord Hutchinson saw the Queen for an hour on the evening of the 3rd and drank tea with her. Brougham had several long conversations with her on that day and the following morning. In spite of his carefully arranged agreement with Lord Liverpool, Brougham decided to reverse the roles and have Lord Hutchinson present to the Queen the memorandum of 15 April. With this in mind he had his brother William, who had accompanied them, place the memorandum in Lord Hutchinson's room. William told Lord Hutchinson what he was doing and where he was placing it, but the latter was busy writing and absent-mindedly failed to note what was being said. So Brougham believed that Hutchinson had the memorandum, and Hutchinson believed that it was in Brougham's pocket.

[1] *Memoirs*, ii. 415–16. [2] Brougham MSS., n.d.
[3] Ibid., Lord Liverpool's memorandum referred to in the text.

Brougham, who had always desired to get something better for
the Queen, something that she would be willing to accept, began
by advising her what to ask for. If the Government should grant
her those things (or a substantial part of them) it would be very
foolish of her to think of going to England, which would have
unfortunate results for all concerned. She should promise to live
abroad on the understanding that there would be no renuncia-
tion of her title or rights, which would be recognized by British
diplomatic agents abroad. Brougham must have indicated that
this went beyond the Government's offer and expressed the
belief that they would be willing to bargain.

The Queen did not seem to be much interested, but she
expressed a desire to see the Government's proposal in writing.
On the morning of the 4th Brougham wrote to Hutchinson at
the Queen's command asking for a statement in writing, as
Brougham had informed the Queen that 'he had reason to
believe that Lord Hutchinson had brought over a proposition
from the King to Her Majesty'. Brougham expected the production of the memorandum which he believed to be in Hutchinson's room and Hutchinson believed to be in Brougham's pocket.
Hutchinson, thinking that Brougham was playing for time,
wrote in reply a long rigmarole saying that he was 'charged with
a proposition', but that before he could put it in writing he
would have to examine a number of papers, and that he would
be further aided by the arrival of a courier from Paris whom he
was expecting. The Queen at two o'clock commanded Brougham
to reply to this that she was surprised 'at His Lordship not being
ready to state the terms of the proposition of which he is the
bearer', but that to give him time to put things together she
would wait until five o'clock. Hutchinson then began to construct the memorandum from memory. He made two mistakes,
one of commission and the other of omission. But he did not
forget to give the Government's warning that if she came to
England all negotiation and compromise would cease, and that
the Government would start proceedings against her 'as soon
as she sets her foot on the British shores'. To Hutchinson's communication the Queen replied: 'It is quite impossible for Her
Majesty to listen to such a proposition.' That note was dated
five o'clock.

Lord Hutchinson immediately sent a reply saying that he

would send a courier to England to ask for further instructions if the Queen would indicate what she desired. This did not reach her in time. She had given them till five o'clock; she left at five minutes past five. Brougham heard the noise, went to a window and saw the horses starting. She had not sent for him nor given him the opportunity of seeing her into her carriage. She was off to Calais and to England, and to the cheering crowds and, almost inevitably, to the Queen's Trial. That 'ass and alderman', Matthew Wood, had outwitted Brougham from start to finish.[1]

Brougham and Lord Hutchinson remained on the best of terms. It is interesting to read Lord Hutchinson's comments on St. Omer. In a letter to the King's private secretary he wrote:

In my opinion Brougham has acted with great sincerity during the whole of our negotiation with him, but I am convinced at the same time that he possesses no real authority or power over the mind or decisions of the Queen. I do not think that he ever made the slightest impression upon her or that she ever listened to him for a moment with the serious intention of following his advice. Before our arrival she had organized every thing for stage-effect: her chief performer was that enlightened mountebank Alderman Wood. . . . He [Brougham] had practised concealment too much: he ought to have told her at once that I was coming with him and also the object of my mission. I suspect that dull as he is, the Alderman had given her some hints and raised suspicions in her mind not only against him, but against me.[2]

The ardour and exuberance with which the London crowds welcomed the Queen had been prepared by Brougham himself six and eight years before. The legend of the persecuted Princess again became an issue, 'Injured Innocence' as Ward had called it. And there were new enhancing circumstances. She was Queen. Nothing became her better than her unquestioned courage. And she had come to claim her rights, she had come to fight against a government bitterly hated by the people in the aftermath of Peterloo.

The newspapers were hardly needed to add fuel to the flames,

---

[1] For these St. Omer pages: Brougham MSS., Lord Liverpool's memorandum; Add. MSS. 38285, ff. 172 seq.; Yonge, *Liverpool*, iii. 65 seq.; *Letters of George IV*, ii. 339 seq.

[2] Add. MSS. 38285, ff. 172 seq.; *Letters of George IV*, ii. 339 seq.

but they did their best. Barnes spread himself on the editorial page of *The Times* on the day of the Queen's arrival in London.

There have been disembarkations on the British coast bringing war and producing revolutions in the state ere now. . . . What were the feelings of the people at those momentous eras we know but feebly, . . . yet we should be inclined to say that neither at the landing of William the Conqueror, nor at that of the Earl of Richmond, nor of William III, were the people's bosoms of this metropolis so much agitated as they were last night, when it was known that Her Majesty, the Queen of England, had once again—bravely, we will say—set her foot on British ground. The most important Parliamentary questions were adjourned, the King's Ministers fled to the council-chamber, the streets were crowded, everyone was inquiring 'When did she land? Where will she sleep? Where will she reside? How will she enter London?'[1]

'Is she not a brave woman?' he asked in conclusion, and the question must have been echoed very often by many people in the course of that day.

The crowds had gathered long before the Queen appeared. The road from Greenwich to Westminster Bridge was packed. Horsemen and conveyances of all sorts accompanied her carriage. Men shouted vociferously as she passed and women waved their handkerchiefs. And in the Queen's open carriage Alderman Wood shared the cheers of the crowd. 'That beast Wood sat beside her', said the King. As that meant that Lady Anne Hamilton, a duke's daughter, had to sit with her back to the horses, the King must have been very deeply shocked. That night and for several nights to come, there was a great smashing of windows of those who would not illuminate them in honour of the Queen. Lord Sidmouth was kept out of his house for some time, and the crowd in its window-smashing did not over-look the carriage of the Duke of Wellington on his way home. All who refused to raise their hats in passing the residence of Alderman Wood, where the Queen stayed for a few days, were pelted with various missiles. It was not this effervescence that carried fear to the minds of those in high places, however; it was the angry talk against the Government, the hard temper of the people, and the known fact that the rank and file of the army were with the Queen.

[1] *The Times*, 6 June 1820.

Immediately after the Queen left St. Omer on the afternoon of the 4th, Brougham forwarded to her by special courier Lord Hutchinson's last note promising to try to get further proposals from England. Brougham accompanied the note with a letter of his own to the Queen in which he urged her to wait until she had heard whether the terms which he had suggested to her were acceptable to the Government.[1] These letters reached the Queen on the packet-boat before sailing, but they had no effect.

On his way to London Brougham's wrath increased, and on an angry impulse he wrote a letter to Denman and sent it ahead of him. He said that he was probably resigning as the Queen's Attorney-General, and that for all he cared Alderman Wood might take his place. He actually wrote out the resignation.[2] But when he arrived in the House of Commons, Castlereagh had brought down the Milan Commission evidence in a green bag and proposed to have it examined and reported on by a committee of the House. Brougham thereupon changed his mind and stayed in the fight. It was much more the war-horse scenting the signs of battle than an overwhelming desire to rescue a queen in distress. He spoke briefly in protest against the Government's action, and looked forward to throwing himself into the debate next day. Before the House rose a messenger arrived, so drunk that he could barely ask Denman to meet the Queen at Alderman Wood's house.

She had just arrived, and Denman found her very indignant at Brougham. Denman defended him. At last she agreed to see Brougham, and Denman went to his house in Hill Street. There Brougham had a number of things to say to him. 'In the most solemn and alarming manner, he laid open to me all his apprehensions on the subject of the Queen's case.' Brougham spoke of 'the most sinister reports' which he had received. Denman, whose conviction throughout was that he was engaged in a chivalrous defence of an innocent woman, believed that Brougham had been too credulous. We do not know whether Brougham told him from whom some of these reports came. But 'at the close of a long series of awkward statements', Brougham said: 'So now we are in for it, Mr. Denman.' Denman said that he would never

---

[1] *Memoirs*, ii. 362–3.
[2] Brougham MSS., Brougham to Liverpool, n.d.; Sir Joseph Arnould, *Life of Lord Denman*, 2 vols. (1874), i, p. 144.

forget the tone and manner with which Brougham said that. Canning was not so far out when he said that Brougham found it as difficult to convince Denman of the Queen's guilt as Denman did to convince others of her innocence. When they went to the Queen their discussion was a quiet one. As Brougham left the room, the Queen turned to Denman and said, 'He is afraid'.[1]

With the coming of the morning Brougham's gloom disappeared. 'He was all sunshine.' He was in the battle again. He presented to Parliament that day a letter from the Queen protesting against the Government's proposals, and he made a speech which Creevey was later to describe as 'the first of that series of incomparable speeches by which he so essentially served or rather saved both the Queen, the Lords, and the Constitution'. Castlereagh, who had preceded Brougham, said that the Government had expected bargaining over the proposals which Brougham had carried to the Queen. It had not been intended 'to preclude any negotiation'. But the Queen had been seriously warned that if she came to England negotiation would cease.

When Castlereagh sat down there was a call all through the House for Brougham. He said that before a select committee there would not be a single living witness but only papers in a green bag, gathered in Italy in a reprehensible fashion. He vehemently attacked the Milan Commission. The interests of the royal family, the peace, the tranquillity, and the morals of the nation were involved. There were those 'out of doors who were possessed of a greedy and diseased appetite for slander, and who only gave up their choice of vulgar private scandal on some such emergency as the present, where the allurement was increased by its affecting the most exalted individuals in the land'. It was true that at the moment the Queen wished for a public investigation, but he was prepared to advise her urgently against that and to counsel her to do everything possible to avert a national calamity.

If he might advise those who stood in a similar situation with regard to the King, he would say to them, 'Tender that counsel to your Sovereign which the case demands and do not fear that Parliament will abandon you or the country desert you; even party will

[1] Arnould, i. 144–7; *Journal of Henry Edward Fox, afterwards 4th Lord Holland*, ed. Earl of Ilchester (1923), i. 50.

not disgrace itself to the lowest level ... by taking advantage of your faithful and fearless discharge of a noble and disinterested duty'. [If they should be forced out of office and] if successors must be appointed to your places, be sure that they will not be formed within these walls (continued cheers).

He closed his speech with a repeated appeal to the House to do everything possible to avert the closing of the door for ever on negotiation.[1] Wilberforce, a Tory of course, supported Brougham earnestly in a speech urging negotiation. He moved an adjournment to which Castlereagh agreed, fearing to press his motion because of the feeling of the House. Thus the appointment of a committee was prevented and the way opened for negotiation. This was one of a number of occasions in which there was a marked recognition in Parliament of Wilberforce's moral authority.

Wilberforce agreed with Brougham in fearing the effect on the public of open proceedings against the Queen. And he had a large heart. He appreciated, though not in courtier fashion, the King's personal kindness and generosity to himself when the King had been Prince Regent. In his private diary he recorded his sympathy with the Queen because of the way in which she had been treated 'when she first came to this country', and he admired her in some respects 'though I fear she has been very profligate'. His principal reason for sympathizing with both was expressed in the statement that 'we marry our Kings and Queens contrary to the laws of God and of nature'.[2]

On the 9th (of June) Brougham wrote to his brother James: 'She [the Queen] is now reasonable enough. ... We shall negotiate.[3]' The Queen on the 12th, on Brougham's advice, offered to submit all matters to arbitration, subject to the approval of Parliament, and on the understanding that she would be recognized as Queen. It was proposed that there should be two arbitrators on each side. The Government replied that it could not arbitrate the matter but agreed that two on each side should carry on a discussion of all questions involved. Lord Castlereagh and the Duke of Wellington represented the Government, and Brougham and Denman the Queen.

[1] *The Times*, 8 June, Parliamentary report; *Hansard*, N.S., i. 928 seq.
[2] *Life of Wilberforce*, v. 57.
[3] Brougham MSS., 9 June 1820.

The discussions lasted from 14 to 19 June. They were based on the understanding that if agreement were reached on the points at issue, the Queen would consent to live abroad; and of course it was understood, though not specifically stated, that in that case no proceedings would be taken against her. If the Government had been willing at this time to include the Queen's name in the Liturgy, a settlement could have been reached. The Queen now became suddenly insistent about this. She saw it as a symbol of her honour. Brougham tried to introduce the matter to the four-man discussion in the most casual manner possible. Castlereagh cut in with, 'You might as easily move Carlton House'.[1] The Queen insisted that she must either have her name in the Liturgy, or the equivalent in a concession that would vindicate her honour. Brougham had suggested to her at St. Omer recognition of her as Queen in European courts, and that suggestion was now made again. The Government would go as far as designating her as Queen of Great Britain to the government of the country in which she chose to live, but they accompanied this with the reminder that European governments always made their own decisions in regard to reception at court.

The Queen was not satisfied, though she would have been glad to reach a settlement which she could accept with dignity and honour. On the day the discussion began, William Brougham had written to James Brougham that the Queen had every inclination to leave the country and Brougham had informed James that she was then 'reasonable' and 'manageable'.[2] Wilberforce thought he saw a way out. He moved a resolution which regretted the failure of the late endeavours to frame an arrangement, and urged the Queen, purely in the common interest, not to press matters beyond the concessions which the Government was now willing to make, and that the House understood that this forbearance on her part did not indicate any wish to shrink from inquiry; it would be accepted simply as a desire to submit her own wishes to the authority of Parliament.[3] The resolution was passed by the House, and a deputation, headed by Wilberforce, was selected to wait upon the Queen. On the night of its passing Brougham wrote to Wilberforce: 'She will accede to your address, I pledge myself.'[4] He did his best, but he was over-

---

[1] Arnould, i. 154.
[2] Brougham MSS. [14 June 1820].
[3] *Hansard*, N.S., i. 1213 seq.
[4] *Life of Wilberforce*, v. 65.

confident. The Queen would tell no one of her decision until almost the last moment. Brougham prepared a speech for her if she accepted the suggestion of the Commons, and Denman wrote one to be used if she rejected it. Brougham was not permitted to read his own speech, but was required to read the speech of rejection. When the disappointed delegation left the Queen, they were met by a hostile mob. Wilberforce took comfort in the fact that no stones were thrown; we do not know what was hurled at them, but the Queen's servants were glad to get them away safely. The crowds had found in the Queen a symbol of all sorts of enthusiasms and hatreds and hopes which they could not define to themselves.

On 5 July Lord Liverpool introduced the Bill of Pains and Penalties in the House of Lords and formally the Queen's Trial had begun. The preamble of the Bill charged the Queen with adultery with Bergami, and the enacting clauses deprived her of the title of Queen, with all the rights and privileges pertaining thereto, and declared her marriage with the King to be null and void. Formally it was to pass as a bill through three readings in the House of Lords and then three readings in the House of Commons. Actually it was a trial of the Queen for adultery, with counsel for the prosecution, counsel for the defence, submission of evidence on oath, direct examination and cross-examination. The hearing of evidence was to begin on 19 August.

For weeks Brougham had had to contend with the efforts of Alderman Wood, Lady Anne Hamilton, and others of the Queen's entourage to poison her mind against him. It has been said and generally believed that even after the introduction of the Bill the Queen was persuaded to drop Brougham as her leading counsel and to put Scarlett in his place. That is a misapprehension. The proposal was to add Scarlett to the list of counsel. As he enjoyed the reputation of being the best advocate in England, Scarlett would not wish to take second or third place, nor as Vizard, the Queen's solicitor, pointed out to him, would Brougham. He suggested therefore that they should take it in turns. One day Brougham should lead, supported by Denman, and the next Scarlett should lead, supported by another lawyer.[1] After thinking it over for a few days, Scarlett declined. By the end of the month the list of the Queen's counsel

[1] Vizard MSS.

was complete. The Queen's lawyers were all relatively young men. Brougham was 42, Denman 41, Williams 46, Lushington 38, Tindal 44, and Wilde 38. Brougham and Wilde (later Lord Truro) were to become Lord Chancellors, Denman Lord Chief Justice, Tindal Chief Justice of the Common Pleas, Lushington a judge of the High Court of the Admiralty, and Williams a Baron of the Exchequer. Four of Brougham's five colleagues became active in the anti-slavery movement, Lushington and Denman playing important roles. This was no coincidence, for Brougham used the friendship developed during the Queen's Trial to carry them into the movement (with the exception of Denman who had already been active).

In Denman, high principle, a sincere moral approach, devoted energy, and passionate eloquence, made up for the fact that he was neither brilliant nor learned in the law. Williams never missed anything; he mastered detail to the last degree and took evidence apart in a speech as skilfully as he took witnesses apart in cross-examination. Dr. Stephen Lushington was an accomplished and learned lawyer, a thorough-going liberal, with a likeable personality and an ardent humanitarianism. Tindal was the learned lawyer *par excellence*. He appeared to roam at will through the history of the law, and in later years his own judgements made a considerable amount of legal history. Two years before the Queen's Trial Tindal had announced to an astonished court room that his client would make his defence by trial by battle and then proceeded to prove that trial by battle had never been abolished and was still a valid legal process. That moved Eldon for once to favour a change in the law. Brougham had been a student in Tindal's chambers for a short time before he was called to the English Bar.

Counsel on the other side, five in number, were of course led by the Attorney-General, Gifford, who although he made one good speech seemed to be sadly outclassed. Brougham's real opponent was Sir John Copley (later Lord Lyndhurst), who was Solicitor-General. Lacking the oratorical gifts of Brougham and Denman, he was always complete master of his material. As Brougham was to write of him later: 'He possessed the gift of unfolding the subject in such a manner as to carry conviction by mere strength of exposition.' There was nothing showy about him, no flourishes. But there was frequently a keen subtlety behind his apparent directness. In cross-examination he was as brilliant as Brougham or Williams. He was to precede and to succeed Brougham as Lord Chancellor and during Brougham's Chancellorship he was a spirited political opponent. In later years they were to be companions in law reform as in many other respects, and a deep friendship developed between them. In Lyndhurst's last illness Brougham visited him every day, and after his death, when Brougham's mind became clouded, he called for his carriage and asked to be driven to Lyndhurst's; it was hard to persuade him that his old friend was no longer there. So much for the future. Now they were the great antagonists of the Queen's Trial.

In the interval of six weeks between the introduction of the Bill and the hearing of evidence Brougham made various preparations, carried on anxious correspondence in regard to the Bill which he had introduced to provide a national system of education, and went the Northern Circuit as usual, having an extraordinary amount of business on account of his connexion with the Queen. Tremendous as Brougham's energy always was, it was not quite inexhaustible. Nine days before the real opening of the Queen's Trial, Vizard, the Queen's solicitor, wrote with concern to the Queen, enclosing a letter from Brougham's doctor which said: 'If he now recommences his professional exertions in London before his health should be more recruited than it yet is, the consequences may be very serious to his constitution.' In any case he should remain in the country, to the last moment possible.[1] When the great day came Brougham went ahead with 'such a cough as I never had either before or since', but he was 'more than half well'.[2]

Gifford in his opening speech for the Crown, begun on Saturday, 19 August, and continued on Monday, impressed more by his matter than by his manner. The evidence which he outlined promised a strong case. His first witness was Theodore Majocchi, who had been a servant of the Queen. When the Queen saw him she raised her veil, looked fiercely at him, sprang up 'with the rapidity of lightning', advanced two or three steps, looking 'more like a Fury than a woman', shrieked out in a loud and

[1] Vizard MSS., 7, 8 Aug. 1820.
[2] Add. MSS. 34114, Gladstone MSS., ff. 143-4, Brougham to Gladstone [probably 1860].

angry tone 'Theodore', and rushed out of the House.[1] No one
ever explained this incident, but speculation was easy.

Majocchi's evidence was so extensive and so damning that
everybody recognized that if it stood the Queen was condemned
out of hand. The Queen was ill that night and was 'copiously
bled'. While she was being bled her counsel were going about
in a state of great uneasiness. Brougham, who always tried to
work others as hard as he worked himself, had already laid down
a rule that all of the Queen's counsel must meet after the end of
proceedings each day and before the beginning of proceedings
the next day to discuss everything relating to the case. But on
that day Tindal and Wilde were not satisfied with the meeting.
They woke Brougham up twice in the night with further suggestions for his cross-examination of Majocchi next day.

Early in that cross-examination of Majocchi someone in the
audience, who had been at Salamanca, said that at a certain
point Brougham seemed to grow taller and looked just as
Wellington had when he saw an opening in Marmont's line.
We cannot say exactly when this was, but after he had received
the reply 'Non mi ricordo', which the interpreter translated 'I
do not remember', to several questions, Brougham, although he
proceeded cautiously for a while, must have scented a possible
opening. Then he succeeded in getting *non mi ricordo* in answer
to an amazing number of questions. It is true that some of
them related to matters of which Majocchi could have had no
knowledge. Brougham threw those in for good measure. But it
was quite evident that a number of these answers related to
matters that Majocchi must have remembered if he really knew
the facts related by him in direct examination, that a number of
others were evasions when he did not wish to answer the questions, and that others referred directly to evidence which he had
given on the preceding day. Brougham had all the physical
qualifications, face, form, and voice, to frighten his victim when
he sought to do so, and in the course of time poor Majocchi was
saying *non mi ricordo* out of sheer fear. He got badly confused and
then he began to contradict himself. By the time Brougham got
through with him his evidence had been pulverized and he was

---

[1] Accounts of eyewitnesses. *Journal of Henry Fox*, p. 41; Hardcastle, i. 385.
Letter of Jack Campbell, which is misdated 9 Oct. and was obviously written on
21 Aug.

discredited as a witness. In sixteen pages of solid print recording Brougham's cross-examination of Majocchi, 'I do not remember' occurs eighty-seven times.[1]

The phrase *non mi ricordo* passed into the history of the next half-century. It was said a generation later that an appropriate use of the phrase could always raise a smile in a London drawing-room. At the time everybody heard the story of Majocchi, and the 'common people', who were all for the Queen and hated Italians anyway, enjoyed it immensely. It occasioned a number of songs of which the following may serve as a sample.

> To the House so large I went,
> Which put me in a stew,
> To tell a tale I was bent,
> Of which I nothing knew.
> There was a man stood there,
> My precious brains he bored–O.
> To what I couldn't swear,
> I said Non mi Ricordo.

The first of the Crown's two star witnesses had been laid flat. When the turn of the other, Louisa Demont, came, Williams's cross-examination was as skilful and almost as devastating though not as sensational. Of course there was other evidence. We have no space here for a description or an analysis of the evidence, and that would not be desirable. All that we can do is to discuss Brougham's handling of his case, some of the more important developments, and some of the striking incidents.

As the Crown's case proceeded, Brougham and his colleagues noticed that much of the evidence that had been promised in the Attorney-General's opening speech was not being produced. He had obviously based his speech on the depositions taken by the Milan Commission. The Queen's counsel also observed that their opponents could not always hide their surprise and embarrassment when they did not get the answers they expected. To give unsworn testimony, not subjected to cross-examination, at Milan was one thing; to give evidence on oath with the Queen's lawyers ready to cross-examine was something very

[1] *Trial of Queen Caroline*, ed. J. Nightingale, 3 vols. (1821), is a verbatim record of the Queen's Trial. There were also full reports in the newspapers, particularly *The Times*. References for evidence and speeches are not given in these notes as the passages can easily be found in these sources under the given dates.

different. The writer of this book has been able to make a comparison and can assert that the witnesses at the trial omitted a considerable amount of the evidence they had submitted to the Milan Commission.

The Queen herself did not attend regularly but only when her counsel deemed it to be desirable. On those occasions Lady Anne Hamilton was always with her, wearing the thickest veil to hide her blushes. The Crown lawyers concluded the presentation of their case with a brilliant summing up of their evidence by Copley, which altered the opinions of many and did something to re-establish their position. The House adjourned for three weeks until 3 October to facilitate the preparation of the case for the defence.

Out of doors in the meantime the excitement was mounting. Greville wrote in his diary: 'Since I have been in the world I never remember any question which so exclusively occupied everybody's attention, and so completely absorbed men's thoughts and engrossed conversation.' Littleton said that in the pubs throughout the country toasts to the Queen were accompanied by so vigorous and uproarious a thumping of the tables as frequently to break half the glasses. Lord Carlisle wrote from the north: 'The infatuation for the Queen prevails equally in the most secluded valleys of our moors as at Hampstead and Highgate.' The newspapers printed the fullest accounts, the details frequently reeking with indecency and obscenity. Most parents of Eton boys were against the Queen, but the townspeople at Eton were all for her; so there was a newer and grander occasion for town and school fights. Class lines were not drawn absolutely. The Queen had some opponents among the middle class. And while the upper class generally had never liked or respected her, the matter was becoming a party issue and the Whig aristocracy lined up enthusiastically behind the Queen. She had support among ladies of the upper class outside the Whigs, for some of them undertook to defend and justify her even if she was guilty; her husband, with his record, had no right to complain of her conduct. The moral outlook was not that of the Victorian age. And there were Whig families, like the Hollands, where the husband was all for the Queen and the wife was decidedly against her.

The crowds in London which greeted her every appearance

became larger and larger, and more carriages joined the impromptu processions. Troops were massed around the city, the soldiers became more outspoken in their enthusiastic support of the Queen, and fear mounted. A government which had given way to pressure from the King now faced in a more intense form pressure from the people. The Duke of Wellington had hitherto occupied a position all his own, not only in society but among the people; now for the first time he was hooted, hissed, and almost mobbed in the streets. The manager of a theatre at Brighton, where George IV was living, told Lord Darlington that he dared not permit the singing of 'God save the King', apparently for fear of a riot. Reports from everywhere indicated that the people were for the Queen whether she were innocent or not.[1]

On 3 and 4 October Brougham opened the case for the defence with the speech that everybody talked about for months and lawyers and statesmen for years to come. There would be little merit here in filling a number of pages with the eulogies of those who heard it and wrote their impressions at the time. They all said the same thing—that it was the best speech they had ever heard. Brougham's colleague, Denman, was closer to it than the others. In his narrative written in the following year he said: 'The House of Lords . . . was on that day addressed by Brougham in one of the most powerful orations that ever proceeded from human lips. His arguments, his observations, his tones, his attitude, his eye, left an impression on my mind which is scarcely ever renewed without exciting strong emotion.'[2] Lord Minto wrote to his wife next day:

I wrote you a few lines from the house this morning but whether they are tolerably rational or not I have no guess, as I had not recovered the full use of my senses from the most extraordinary display of oratory ever exhibited at the Bar by any one man, for he really seemed to possess the varied powers & excellencies of all the best speakers I have heard. The effect of this speech upon the House was such as those who are accustomed to Parliament might expect

---

[1] For these two paragraphs: *Greville Memoirs*, i. 36–37; Hatherton MSS., Lord Hatherton's Journal, 21 Aug. 1820; Add. MSS. 41854, ff. 159–60, Lord Carlisle to Lord Grenville; Lord Malmesbury, *Memoirs of an Ex-Minister*, 2 vols. (1884), i. 16; Colchester, iii. 162; Lord Ilchester, *Home of the Hollands* (1937), p. 347; Creevey MSS.; Howick MSS. General statements in the paragraphs are, of course, based on many sources.   [2] Arnould, i. 169.

a great speech always to produce, but what those who see much of our proceedings know scarcely any speech ever does effect. I mean that it made a very decided and obvious impression upon the opinions & feelings of those who both in opinion & feeling were most unfriendly to him & his cause.[1]

And we must not overlook the tribute paid to it by Creevey, Brougham's severe critic. Creevey had missed a good deal of the first day, but Sefton had told him that the speech was the finest thing he had ever heard, and 'Grenfell says it is the greatest exhibition of the human mind, and that Majocchi, Demont and Sacchi are gone to the devil'. At noon of the second day Creevey wrote home:

Brougham has just finished his opening. . . . I never heard anything like the perfection he has displayed in all ways, in his criticisms upon evidence, his prodigious talents, his overpowering eloquence. Let me not omit too his undaunted courage in winding up his speech . . . which produced the greatest effect upon myself and those about me. . . . This last appeal was made with great passion, but without a particle of rant and with the greatest possible effect on all who heard it. For one, I consider myself infinitely overpaid by these two hours and a half of Brougham, for all the time and money it has cost me to be here, and almost for my absence from all of you. Damned fair, I think, that last observation and neatly put. [The editor of the *Creevey Papers* omitted this last sentence.]

The speech had shaken the House of Lords. And in commenting on the newspapers next morning Creevey wrote: 'It is most justly said by both the *Chronicle* and the *Times* of to-day that one of the greatest merits of this great speech was that it never displayed any personal vanity, any thirst for glory for the speaker. It related to nothing but the client, and certainly was the chastest as well as the most powerful piece of acting I ever witnessed.'[2]

It would be difficult to discuss the speech here without a complete description of the evidence. But it may be noted that in this speech, as well as throughout the trial, Brougham was producing evidence to show that fantastic sums of money had been promised to these Italian witnesses, enough to assure them that they would not have to work for years or for the rest of their lives. He impressed upon the peers the temptations to perjury

---

[1] Copy in Brougham MSS., n.d. [5 Oct. 1820].
[2] Creevey MSS., 3, 4, 5 Oct., published in part in *Creevey Papers*, i. 321.

involved in this, the fact that they had nearly all perjured themselves by denying that they had received such money or such
promises, and the obvious fact that they had not given the
evidence that the Attorney-General in his opening speech had
promised they would give. Consequently nearly all of them had
lied at Milan and had presented in London only the less
dangerous lies. Many perjuries had been revealed by cross-
examination. The whole Crown case was a tissue of perjury,
and no perjured witness could be believed in any part of his
evidence.

When we read it today on the cold printed page, it is difficult
to understand the eulogies that were heaped upon the peroration, which Brougham said he rewrote at least seven times. But
we must remember the circumstances, the excitement, the face,
figure, and voice of the speaker. Some of the explanation of the
effect probably lies in contrast. Brougham had spoken for hours,
with penetrating analysis, powerful argument, and entertaining
sallies of masterly sarcasm, but otherwise without flourishes and
without deep feeling. As he made point after point, the peers
sat forward anxious to miss nothing. Then suddenly there came
a flood of passionate feeling that swept them off their feet. In
the midst of that peroration hard-bitten Lord Erskine rushed
out of the House with his hands before his face and the tears
rolling down his cheeks, saying that he could not stand another
second of it. Brougham closed his speech, as he frequently did in
his more important efforts, with a prayer. 'The Church and the
King have willed that the Queen should be deprived of its
solemn service. She has instead of that solemnity the heart-felt
prayers of the people. She wants no prayers of mine. But I do
here pour forth my humble supplications at the Throne of
Mercy, that that mercy may be poured down upon the people in
a larger measure than the merits of its rulers may deserve, and
that your hearts may be turned to justice.' Brougham sat down,
then a dead silence. 'No one spoke or moved for a minute or
two.'

It was said that a number of the peers, who up to that time
had been favourable to the Bill, were turned against it by
Brougham's speech. Some said that he had won his case there
and then and that it was not necessary to produce evidence for
the defence.

The defence, however, ran into difficulties at the outset. They had promised to do much with the evidence of Mariette Brun, the sister of Louisa Demont, and the Countess Oldi (another mysterious title), the sister of Bergami. But they discovered that the former was not safe, and Brougham, after talking things over with the Countess Oldi, reported to his colleagues that she might tell the truth on some important matters, but that she was such a constitutional liar that she would have no value as a witness. And that was exactly what James Brougham and others had reported from Italy about Bergami, when the suggestion was made that he should be used as a witness. All of Brougham's colleagues were in favour of taking a chance with the Countess Oldi, but they deferred to Brougham's judgement and she was not put in. The Crown lawyers made a great deal of this.

The friends of the Queen were much pleased with the evidence of Lady Charlotte Lindsay, who as lady-in-waiting had been with the Queen for several periods in Italy and had resigned in 1817. But the King said angrily: 'I never thought that I should have lived to witness so much prevarication, so much lying, and so much wilful and convenient forgetfulness, as, I am sorry to say, both Lord Guilford [Lady Charlotte's brother] and Lady Charlotte Lindsay, have displayed in their late examinations.'[1] It may be seriously doubted that Lady Charlotte Lindsay committed perjury. We have seen what her real opinions about the conduct of the Princess had been, as expressed in her letters to Brougham, but of course no one else knew anything about that. She testified that she had never observed any improprieties. She told the truth when, questioned by a peer, she admitted that 'the reports were of so unpleasant and degrading a nature, that they did operate upon my mind in making me not wish to continue in her service'. But she had skilfully managed to give the impression that those reports were mere rumour and she had said nothing about whom they came from.

Things were going well and London was 'literally drunk with joy', when on 9 and 10 October disaster came suddenly and surely. One advantage of the defence was that they had *English* evidence, and they presented as their two best witnesses Lieutenant Flinn, an officer of the famous polacre, and Lieutenant Hownam, who had been in the Queen's service in Italy. For

[1] *Letters of George IV*, ii. 371.

what happened to Flinn under the merciless cross-examination
of Copley we do not need to go further than Creevey's account,
which is accurate and adequate: 'This cursed Flynn . . . has
perjured himself three or four times over, and his evidence and
himself are both gone to the devil. . . . He has fainted away once,
and been obliged to be carried out.'[1] 'I knew he was lying', said
Copley. 'I looked hard at him. He fainted away and was taken
out of court.'[2] Hownam's evidence seemed to be good until,
under cross-examination by Gifford, he cleared up *for the Crown*
a very important and very doubtful and mysterious matter
which, but for Hownam, would have remained in doubt and
mystery. In fact it was almost, if not quite, the worst evidence
against the Queen in the whole trial and it was undoubtedly
true. What a case! The Crown had had two star witnesses and
they had both been discredited in cross-examination; the defence
had four star witnesses, two of whom they were afraid to put in,
one who broke down under cross-examination, and one who
supplied damning evidence against the Queen.

Brougham scored heavily in relation to Restelli. He had
presented evidence to prove that Restelli had been an agent as
well as a witness for the Crown, that he had sought out evidence
for the Milan Commission and that he and others had suggested
to witnesses the evidence that they were to give. Brougham asked
to have Restelli brought back for further examination, and a
sensation was created by the information that Restelli was no
longer in the country but had been sent on a mission to Italy.
Brougham had known this and did his timing well. It is probable
that the agents of the Crown had commissioned Restelli to go to
Italy without any idea of what was going to happen, and that if
he could have been brought back he would not have added a
great deal to what the defence already had in hand. It was in
connexion with this that Brougham made a famous quotation,
the background to which was the fact that the King, who in his
youth had been very handsome and graceful, had become a
corpulent gentleman rapidly getting the better of his corsets.
Brougham was grilling Powell about sending Restelli to Italy,
and he insisted on knowing whose agent Powell was. Against
whom were they contending in this case? Was it the Govern-

[1] *Creevey Papers*, i. 323.
[2] Theodore Martin, *Life of Lord Lyndhurst* (1883), p. 187.

ment or the King? Brougham went at that question in his own
way. 'If I knew who the party is against whom I appeared . . . If
I am told who he is, I may then be able to trace his lineaments
. . . I know nothing about this shrouded, this mysterious being
. . . this uncertain shape,

> If shape it might be call'd, that shape had none
> Distinguishable in member, joint, or limb.
>
> . . .
>
> What seem'd his head,
> The likeness of a KINGLY CROWN had on.

The King's angry comment was: 'He might have left my shape
alone.'

On 24 and 25 October Denman summed up for the defence.
It was a good speech on the whole, but marred by two things.
He extravagantly compared George IV with Nero, with the
result that the London crowds were soon dubbing Carlton
House 'Nero's Hotel'—and he ended his speech with the words
of Christ to the adulterous woman: 'Neither will I condemn thee.
Go and sin no more.' Just before this he had said: 'Even when
guilt was detected and vice revealed.' He meant that in this
case, where there was no guilt, they should show the same spirit.
He was very tired and had used the unfortunate words before he
realized how they would sound. But at that, what a closing for
the defence! It occasioned, of course, the familiar lines which
reflected the attitude of many a year later:

> Gracious Queen we thee implore,
> Go away and sin no more.
> But if that effort be too great,
> Go away at any rate.

As the vote on the second reading[1] approached men looked
for a modification of the Bill. In addition to the feelings of the
populace and the activity of the Whigs there were the Bishops,
who would not finally vote for the divorce clause. Liverpool had
thrown out hints some time before that the divorce clause might
be dropped. Nearly all of the Bishops voted for the Bill on the
second reading on the understanding that the divorce clause
would be got rid of. On the second reading the Whig Lords
voted solidly against the Bill, and they were joined by a large

---

[1] There had been no vote on the first reading.

number of Tories who said that while they believed the Queen to be guilty, they were now entirely opposed to proceeding with the measure.[1] In the vote on the second reading a very large Government majority in the House of Lords was cut to twenty-eight. When the news of that small majority reached the streets there was wild rejoicing. A mob got hold of Brougham and bore him in triumph to Brooks's Club.[2]

After the second reading the Government brought in a motion to delete the divorce clause. In the debate that followed the Bishops insisted that since anyone else would have to obtain a verdict in an ecclesiastical court, in which recrimination was possible, this Bill was placing the King above the ordinary law; the jurisdiction of the ecclesiastical courts was being side-tracked. They were supported in this position by a considerable number of peers. But the division on the motion was a strange one. The ministers all voted for it because it was a means of saving the Bill, and the Whig peers all voted against it because the divorce clause placed the Bill in jeopardy. Many Tory peers, however, were all for the Bill as it stood. Consequently the motion was defeated by a substantial majority and the divorce clause remained in the Bill. Before the third reading Croker had come to the conclusion that the ministers were hoping for a very small majority so that they might have an excuse to drop the Bill altogether. The chances of getting the Bill through the Commons were slight.[3] The Government contemplated with great fear the Bill's going to the Commons. The Crown lawyers knew that Brougham intended to attempt direct recrimination against the King[4] and that he had in his possession proof of the King's marriage to the Catholic Mrs. Fitzherbert, with which they feared that he was prepared to launch a legal argument against the King's right to the throne in spite of the fact that the marriage itself was illegal. (Although Brougham believed that he was right in point of law, he said afterwards that his purpose in throwing out hints was merely to frighten.)

On the third reading the Government majority was reduced to nine. The Government decided to go no farther. Lord Liver-

---

[1] This is attested by any number of statements in the sources.
[2] Creevey MSS., 6 Nov.
[3] Croker MSS., Letter-book 10, 3, 9 Nov.
[4] The Vizard manuscripts contain briefs for that purpose drawn up at this time. Vizard MSS.

pool announced the abandonment of the measure. Brougham tried to break the news gently to the Queen, who was in an adjoining room. She took it quietly. In the general rejoicing around them Lady Charlotte Lindsay threw herself into Denman's arms 'in a paroxysm of delight' (Denman's words). Brougham, apparently fearing too much of a demonstration, saw that the Queen was taken quietly to Brandenburg House, after she had entered her carriage in tears.[1]

Fast-riding couriers carried the great news all over the country, and that night bonfires and bells proclaimed the joy of the nation. While a few discerning observers understood the interplay of political and ecclesiastical forces and knew that Brougham had not exactly cleared the Queen, the people cared only that the Queen had won a great victory and that Brougham had won it for her. Small busts of the Queen and of Brougham were sold in the London streets. A number of 'peasants and mechanics' subscribed a penny apiece, and purchased and presented to Brougham a splendid candelabra in grateful appreciation. The freedom of the city of London was bestowed upon Brougham, Denman, and Lushington, and Brougham was able to make a collection of gold boxes containing the freedoms of a number of cities throughout the kingdom. All over the country pubs were renamed 'The Brougham's Head'. Lord Campbell said that the next time Brougham went the Northern Circuit, attorneys besieged him with briefs for the sheer pleasure of being able to meet and talk with the great man. 'During one whole round of the assizes . . . crowds came from distant parts to see and listen to him, and the Civil Court and the Crown Court were respectively overflowing or deserted as he appeared in the one or in the other.'[2] Nor have the great lawyers been chary in his praise. Atlay spoke for all of them when he wrote in his *Victorian Chancellors*: 'Though Brougham was assisted by some of the most learned, the most eloquent, and the most courageous members of the English Bar, the main credit for Caroline's defence must always rest with him. There was no man then living, and, I think I may add, there has been no man since, who possessed the same union of qualities.'[3]

---

[1] Arnould, i. 179, Denman's narrative; Lord Campbell, viii. 321–2.
[2] Lord Campbell, viii. 324.
[3] J. B. Atlay, *Victorian Chancellors*, 2 vols. (1906), i. 260.

Some readers will, no doubt, wish to ask whether Brougham believed the Queen to be guilty or innocent. The question cannot be answered. In conversation with his friends he said that at first he felt sure that she was guilty, but that as the case proceeded he became convinced of her innocence. That is just what we might expect Brougham to say. He made a public statement in which he solemnly declared: 'If, instead of an advocate, I had been acting as a judge, I should have been found among those who, laying their hands upon their hearts, conscientiously pronounced her Not Guilty.' Brougham could always summon up a degree of solemnity that was very impressive. But that statement does not answer our question. He spoke the truth, no doubt, but what it amounts to is that if he had been sitting 'as a judge' on the case as presented by Henry Brougham, his colleagues, and his opponents, his verdict should have been 'not guilty'. He did not say, and he could have summoned up an equal solemnity while saying it, that before God, in all conscience, he believed her to be innocent. Perhaps he did; but we cannot be certain.

Canning had said of the Queen's Trial early in October: 'I do truly believe that there never fell upon a country an evil, so gratuitously mischievous, and so entirely without compensation.'[1] Canning was wrong in saying that there was no compensation. In the first place, it had acted as an excellent safety valve. Before it began the country was in a revolutionary mood, though that was tempered by the traditional British respect for law and order, and by the lack of anything like organization. The situation had been a dangerous one. But the excitement over the Queen's Trial took precedence over everything. The scandal in the royal family and the popular enthusiasm for the Queen eclipsed even Peterloo. As Wilbraham put it in a letter to Lord Colchester in mid-September: 'Radicalism has taken the shape of affection for the Queen, and has deserted its old form, for we are all as quiet as lambs in this part of England, and you would not imagine that this would have been a disturbed county twelve months ago.'[2] By the end of the Queen's Trial there were signs in the country of increasing prosperity.

More important was the fact that the Queen's Trial ended an

---

[1] Add. MSS. 38742, f. 29, Canning to Huskisson, 1 Oct.
[2] Lord Colchester's *Diary*, iii. 164.

epoch in British history and ushered in a very different one. Brougham has been called the liberalizer of the Whig party. His task was made a much easier one by the fact that in the excitement of the Queen's Trial the Whigs became a popular party. The people noted with enthusiasm how the Whigs solidly supported the Queen. The Whigs and the people were associated in a common cause. Instead of being hated as aristocrats the Whig leaders found that they were popular, and then they found that they liked that. And since the Queen's Trial lost them more than ever support from the King, they were bound to throw themselves more upon popular support. Those developments gave the liberal Whigs the upper hand within the party, and made it much easier for them to pass the Reform Bill in 1832. Brougham's great personal popularity in itself did much to popularize the party as a whole. The Queen's Trial also had a marked effect upon the Tories. They had at all costs to avoid the extreme unpopularity of 1820, and the liberal elements within that party had henceforth a much better chance. The 'age of reform' could be dated from the Queen's Trial. The traditional interpretation has been that it began then because Castlereagh committed suicide and Canning took his place. That greatly exaggerates Castlereagh's antagonism to reform and the part which Canning played in domestic reform. (In foreign policy it has, of course, been shown that Canning built on the foundation laid by Castlereagh.) It has been pointed out by Dr. Feiling that by 1822 Britain was far enough away from the war for the movements feeling their way toward reform to find encouragement and expression. If one is looking for a particular watershed, the Queen's Trial is more of one than is 1822.

For at least fourteen years after this Brougham was the most popular man in England. Among humble men who never travelled far from home, and who knew nothing about the King's ministers or the other leaders of the Opposition, more than a little was known about Henry Brougham. That was due not only to the Queen's Trial but also to worthier achievements. On the other hand, the fame which he won through the Queen's Trial gave him a commanding influence in the movements for the abolition of slavery, for popular education, and later for law reform, and it strengthened his hand in all his fights for human freedom.

CHAPTER XIV

Political and Personal, 1821–5

QUEEN CAROLINE lost in a few months the popular support which Brougham had built up for her in eight years. She acted frequently, if not consistently, against his advice, yet in one matter in which she accepted it, he blundered badly. He hoped for a Whig fund to rescue her depleted finances and made a show of refusing money from the Government. The fund failed to materialize and she accepted the Government money, which greatly weakened Brougham's position, while the Queen blamed him bitterly. The Government stubbornly continued to exclude the Queen from the Liturgy and was supported by a remarkable majority of 310 in the House of Commons. In arguing for the Queen's right to be crowned Brougham was strong on precedents, but a queen consort had no substantive right to be crowned. Brougham strongly urged her not to attempt to force her way into the Abbey at the Coronation, but she refused to listen to him. She wildly and foolishly flew from one entrance of the Abbey to the other in a vain effort to get in. There were no cheering crowds. When Napoleon died a court official broke the news with 'Your Majesty's greatest enemy is dead'. The King's reply was 'Is she, by God?' The Queen did not survive Napoleon very long. When she died in August 1821, Brougham and Denman left their Circuits to attend the funeral. Brougham accompanied the body as far as Harwich, and Lushington went on to Brunswick.

Immediately after the Queen's Trial, Lady Granville said that Brougham was fatigued and also that he was twitching his nose 'twenty times more than ever'. In February 1821 Croker said that he looked 'ghastly' and that he was 'evidently labouring under some strong mental depression'. In April illness forced him to leave the Northern Circuit.[1] In February 1822 his health broke again and he was 'suffering from a severe and

[1] *Letters of Countess Granville*, i. 192; Brougham MSS., Hutchinson to Brougham, 7 Apr. 1821; Croker MSS.

dangerous illness'.[1] In March and April he was apparently absent from Parliament for a period of six or seven weeks.

On 11 February (1822) Brougham made a long speech on the distressed state of the country and on the 15th he spoke particularly of the agricultural distress. On the former occasion Ricardo, the purchase of whose seat Brougham had arranged, attacked him from his own side of the House. Ricardo disagreed sharply with Brougham on the causes of, and the remedies for, the distress, rejecting emphatically Brougham's plea for reduction of taxes. On the latter occasion Huskisson attacked him from the other side of the House. Huskisson 'had never heard a speech more abounding in mistaken assertions, more fraught with erroneous principles and contradictory inferences and more pregnant with alarm, mischief and danger'. He said that it contained 'some of the most visionary doctrines of political economy, which he had ever heard, at least from a person of his [Brougham's] acknowledged talents and ingenuity'.[2] Brougham, who could hit much harder than that himself, never minded such attacks. Whether he ever realized that economics was not, generally speaking, one of his stronger suits, is another question.

On 8 May he discussed the Corn Law. He said that 'nothing could be more injurious in its consequences than the act in force' and that in general 'he had rigorously maintained the expediency of a free trade'. On 21 May he expressed strong approval of a government measure modifying the Navigation Laws. A few years before, he had 'alluded to the improvement of the Navigation Laws as a remedy. . . . On that occasion the very person who now brought forward the present measure [Wallace] had moved the passing to the order of the day.' He hoped that the relaxation of the Navigation Laws would continue.[3] It should be noted that this was before Canning had rejoined and before Huskisson had been taken into the Cabinet.

On 24 June Brougham spoke against the excessive influence of the Crown. There were, he said, eighty-seven placemen in the House. The Government spent large sums in purchasing the support of individuals at elections; it maintained the excessive number of 19,000 officers on full pay in order to increase its patronage.[4] Castlereagh said in reply that he could not find

---

[1] *Hansard*, N.S., vi. 444.
[2] Ibid. 220 seq., 400 seq.
[3] Ibid., N.S., vii. 449 seq., 720 seq.
[4] Ibid. 1265 seq.

more than forty-eight members of the House of Commons 'who held offices under the Crown in a sense to which influence could be fairly attached'.[1]

Within two months Castlereagh was dead. Like Whitbread and Romilly he took his own life while of unsound mind. Brougham, of course, was not prostrated as he had been by the deaths of his two close friends, but he felt clearly enough that a giant had departed. 'This is really a considerable event in point of size. Put all their [the Tories'] other men together in one scale and poor Castlereagh in the other, single he plainly weighed them down.' And since he had been pitted against him so regularly in Parliament, Brougham felt that it was 'like losing an old connection suddenly'.[2]

While the world was waiting to learn whether Canning would be brought back into the Government as the successor to Castlereagh or go to India, to which he was under appointment, an interesting correspondence took place between Brougham and Lord Grey.[3] Writing to Brougham on 30 August Grey said that he believed that the Government would go on well with Canning, but that without him and with Peel as the leader of the House of Commons it might break down. And he went on to discuss what he (Lord Grey) would do as leader of the Whig Party if he were called on to form a government. He would be ready, at last, to undertake Parliamentary Reform (which he had said that he would not touch until he believed that the country desired it).

I would stipulate for some plan on a moderate principle, with a pledge to resist anything more. But there is a difficulty behind. . . . How is a Government to be formed in the House of Commons, and who is to lead it? This question, I feel, can be answered by *you* alone; on *you* must depend, in the first degree, the efficiency of any Administration that can be formed, in whatever situation you might be placed; and it is upon this that I hope you will not be unwilling to state to me confidentially and explicitly what your views and wishes are. . . .

Brougham in his reply agreed with Grey that they should consider what policies a Whig government should adopt. They should move for Parliamentary Reform but he disagreed with

---

[1] Ibid. 1299 seq.   [2] *Creevey Papers*, ii. 44, 19 Aug. 1822.
[3] *Memoirs*, ii. 442 seq.

Grey's suggestion of a pledge not to go further in the future. In regard to the 'nominal leader' of the House of Commons, 'really I can't see why Tierney might not go on, taking it just as easily as he chose'. (Which of course would mean Brougham going on as the real leader and going as far as he chose.)

As for himself: 'I could on no account give up my profession.' Grey wrote back to Brougham: 'Your saying you will take no office is, in my mind, tantamount to saying no Whig administration can be formed.' He added: 'The *something* I should do on Parliamentary Reform would be a good deal . . . but the only chance you could have of carrying anything would be some assurance that the thing would be kept quiet afterwards.'

On 16 September Canning re-entered the Government as Castlereagh's successor in the two positions of Foreign Secretary and leader of the House of Commons. According to the traditional interpretation of this period that was the cause of the great liberal Tory reforms of the next five years. But there had been for some years a trend in the Tory administration towards a more liberal policy, resulting in part from an awareness of changing conditions, in part from the influence of public opinion, as well as from the increasing impact of the views of Adam Smith and the economists, the two former factors making surrender to the latter possible. The Queen's Trial had greatly strengthened that trend.

The men who put through the great liberal Tory reforms were, of course, Peel, Huskisson, Robinson, and Wallace. With the exception of Huskisson, they were already in the Ministry and Canning had nothing to do with placing them there. After Canning's re-entry there were only two changes in the Cabinet. Robinson was promoted from President of the Board of Trade to Chancellor of the Exchequer and Huskisson, who had been in previous administrations, took the Board of Trade. In all probability those changes would have been made if Canning had gone to India. And the great measures were already on the way. In the session of 1817 Robinson and Castlereagh had declared that in principle they were in favour of free trade and believed in substituting it to a large degree for the old protective system. In commenting on Brougham's strong free-trade speech at that time, Robinson had said that he agreed with him, but that Brougham did not seem to understand the difficulties that departure from the old system involved, or the time that it would take. In 1821 both Liverpool and Robinson declared for a more liberal economic policy. We have seen that early in 1822, before Canning came back, Wallace passed important changes in the Navigation Laws. In the reform of the criminal law, Peel reaped where Romilly and Mackintosh had sown, though his reaping was tremendous, and in prison reform Peel had a number of immediate precursors. The Prime Minister had already made his decision and had declared for a policy of economic liberalism. Liverpool was, however, in all matters greatly strengthened by Canning's strong personality and that unquestionably speeded up reform.

All of the great liberal measures were heartily welcomed by Brougham. He could make mistakes in the details of economics, but he had declared stongly enough for the main line of economic liberalism and he had supported the advocacy of criminal law reform by his friends, Romilly and Mackintosh. Now, in 1822, before the great reforms took shape, he wrote in December, as the Whig leader in the House of Commons (as he regarded himself and was regarded by many observers), to Lansdowne who had become, for the time being, the real leader of the Whigs in the House of Lords:

What say you to the problem we shall (I foresee) soon have to solve? Given Canning's hostility to [Parliamentary] Reform, Improvement and Liberty generally and Whigs personally, supposed his agreement with us on Irish [Catholic Emancipation] and foreign policy and the enmity of almost all his colleagues towards him,—to find the course we should steer in order to aid him on points of agreement, to increase his differences with his colleagues, and not to commit ourselves on points of difference with him? My solution is 'abstinence' from needless attacks for a while.[1]

Lansdowne, in his reply, expressed agreement.[2]

Brougham learned as time went on that Canning was *not* opposed to 'improvement and liberty generally'. The 'abstinence' which he proposed was not to be 'for a while' but for the whole of the remainder of Canning's life, and he was determined to afford him general support. This was the beginning of that line of action in which many of the Whigs co-operated, but in

[1] Lansdowne MSS., postmarked 18 Dec. 1822.
[2] Brougham MSS.

which Brougham undoubtedly took the lead, which resulted in Canning's coalition ministry of 1827, in splitting the Tory party, bringing the Whigs into power and the Great Reform Bill of 1832.

This policy effected a complete change in the relations of Canning and Brougham in the House of Commons. Canning was now the government leader and he and Brougham were incomparably the best speakers in the House. Previously Brougham's opposition had been ruthless and unremitting. He and Canning would concede nothing to one another and the one was always lying in wait for the other. It was said that frequently speaker followed speaker in a protracted debate because Canning and Brougham were each waiting for the other to speak first. Their rivalry was as striking as that of Gladstone and Disraeli in the latter half of the century. On one occasion Canning's cousin brought to him a quotation that would be very helpful in an approaching speech. Canning read it and noticed that the suggested quotation stopped before it reached a passage that could have been quite harmful. 'No', said Canning, 'I dare not. Brougham would find me out. Nothing ever escapes him.'[1]

Canning faced a vexatious opposition in the Cabinet. The real leaders of opposition sat with Canning on the Government front bench. Palmerston, still a Tory, went farther than the front bench when he said with characteristic good sense and clarity: 'The real opposition of the present day sit behind the Treasury Bench; . . . the stupid old Tory party, . . . it is by these that the progress of the Government . . . is thwarted and impeded. . . . The Government finds support from the Whigs and resistance from their self-denominated friends.'[2]

The first session of Parliament after Canning took office began on 4 February 1823. Ever since he had re-entered the House of Commons in 1816, Brougham had usually made the first Opposition speech after the moving and seconding of the address. Now for the first time he did so not to oppose but to support. Of the Government's speech from the throne he said: 'That communication, coupled with the commentary of the honourable mover of

---

[1] Sir Denis Le Marchant, *Memoirs of Viscount Althorp, third Earl Spencer* (1876), pp. 217-18. William Canning's statement to Le Marchant.

[2] Bell, i. 55.

the address, will be the tidings of joy and the signal for exultation to England, . . . will be a source of comfort to all other free
states.' This was Brougham's great speech on the Holy Alliance
(as it was popularly called; we need not discuss the correctness
of the term). It was an all-out attack on Prussia, Austria, and
Russia, and a condemnation of the invasion of Spain. He concluded:

> I will not look backward to measures on the nature of which all
> may not agree, . . . reserving . . . my co-operation for any faithful
> servant of the Crown, who shall, in performing his duty to his country,
> to freedom and to the world, speak a language that is truly British,
> pursue a policy that is truly free, . . . quarreling with none, whatever
> may be the form of their government, for that would be copying the
> faults we condemn, keeping peace wherever we could, but not leaving
> ourselves a moment unprepared for war, not courting hostilities from
> any quarter but not fearing the issue, . . . determined to maintain,
> amid every sacrifice, the honour and dignity of the Crown, the
> independence of the country, the ancient law of nations, the suprem-
> acy of all separate states.[1]

In later years Brougham, on attending a school prize day, was
pleased to find that a boy who had all the great orators ancient
and modern to choose from had selected for recital this speech
on the Holy Alliance.

On 14 February he spoke on the Spanish situation and said
that he agreed in the main with Canning's policy.

> He observed that when the Minister for Foreign Affairs [Canning]
> rose and uttered sentiments which, as an Englishman, a statesman
> and an orator, would surprise and delight the country, and which
> would crown him with the ardent applause of that country, he
> observed that while those expressions were heard with delight by all
> who sat on the Opposition side of the House, while the loudest
> expressions of gratification were heard . . . a death-like silence was
> preserved by the gentlemen opposite, that the faculties of those
> who administered the government and their various adherers and
> supporters appeared to sink into a 'dread repose', astonished, he
> supposed, at the liberality of the principles which they had so un-
> expectedly heard.

After another eulogy of Canning and his policy, he said that 'he
wished those sentiments were common to all his [Canning's]
colleagues and his supporters'.[2]

---

[1] *Speeches*, i. 651 seq.   [2] *Hansard*, N.S., viii. 899 seq.

All this was too good to last, and before the week was over Brougham's temper betrayed his judgement. Canning had indulged in a bitter, uncalled for, and scurrilous personal attack on Folkestone, who was a friend of Brougham. Brougham disliked that kind of thing when he was not doing it himself, and he was also impatient with what he regarded as Canning's stalling on Catholic Emancipation. The word 'truckle' employed by Canning provoked Brougham's irritation. He admitted later that he had been angry when, on the following day, he said that Canning had betrayed the cause of Catholic Emancipation when it was a question of India or office at home, and continued: 'If at that critical moment he who had said on the last night that he would not truckle to a noble lord [Folkestone], but who then had exhibited a specimen, the most incredible specimen, of monstrous truckling for the purpose of obtaining office, that the whole history of political tergiversation could furnish —.' He got no farther. Canning was on his feet in a fury, shouting out: 'I rise to say that that is false!' Dead silence in the House. The Speaker asked Canning to retract the expression he had used, which was a complete violation of the rules of the House. Canning said that 'he was sorry to have used any word which was a violation of the decorum of the House, but nothing, no consideration on earth, should induce him to retract the sentiment'.

The Speaker again asked Canning to retract and again Canning refused. The Chancellor of the Exchequer (Robinson) suggested that Brougham retract in order to facilitate Canning's retraction. The Speaker said that the propriety of Brougham's language depended on whether it was applied to Canning 'in his public capacity' or 'personally'. Bankes moved that Canning and Brougham be committed to the custody of the Serjeant-at-Arms. Several speakers tried to iron things out without much success. Sir Robert Wilson was supposed by some to have 'settled it' (Creevey's phrase), but he only repeated the distinction that the Speaker had made. Canning, however, eventually took the hint, saying that he had felt that Brougham's accusation 'was cast not on his official but on his private character. If that imputation should be denied, he was ready to avow that in his statement subsequently he was mistaken.'

Brougham, after several attempts, at last got the floor. He

said he would be the last man to wish to see Canning censured for his expression; Canning had heard only half of the sentence which he had intended to speak. 'He did not profess that his mind was capable of making a very nice distinction in the selection of phrases which should apply exclusively to the personal or to the political character.' He had formed a conclusion from facts which he had believed to be true. He would be happy if he were to learn that they were not true. He stated the facts again and why he believed them to be true, and he stated the conclusion that he had been bound to draw from them. So he repeated the substance of his previous speech and he repeated the obnoxious phrases. And he made some additions. He spoke of Lord Chancellor Eldon as being opposed not only to Catholic Emancipation but to Canning personally. 'All these things seemed to show a truckling to the Lord Chancellor.' 'He was aware that it was wrong to impute motives and he gathered from the right honourable gentleman that he had been wrong in doing so in this instance.' That was the only concession that Brougham made. He said that he had never known anything of Canning 'as a private individual' that 'did not do him the highest honour'.

Peel then stated that the House should be satisfied. Brougham, of course, had been misinformed. And Canning, of course, had done no truckling. Bankes withdrew his motion. Canning did not retract, but he said that he would think no more of the matter. Brougham then said that he would think no more of it either and added: 'He had frequently been embattled against the right honourable gentleman on political occasions; no personal ill will had ever remained in his bosom on any of those occasions and none would on the present.'[1] And he proceeded with his speech. The feeling of the House was against Canning because it was naturally jealous for its rules, but as we look back, having followed it in *Hansard*, we are bound to feel that Brougham caused the trouble by going out of his way to make a quite uncalled for insinuation, and then, in a speech that hardly constituted a withdrawal, he saw to it that the insinuation was repeated both in substance and in language. One's sympathies in the affair lie strongly with Canning. After the clash, the two men met whilst riding near Lowther Castle. Usually Brougham

[1] *Hansard*, N.S., viii. 1089 seq.

met a man with whom there had been a quarrel as though nothing had happened and they had always been friends. But he was apparently nervous about trying that on Canning. From their opposite directions they came to a gate which was locked. Over the gate they looked steadily at each other, then both burst out laughing. They apparently chatted for a while and shook hands before parting.[1]

John Williams, who had been Brougham's colleague in the Queen's Trial, introduced a motion on the Court of Chancery on 5 June and was strongly supported by Brougham. Williams cited some of the many cases of arrears. In one of these begun eight years before, in 1815, there had been sixty-four charges for attendances and the case was still undecided. Brougham said that the abuses were 'as old at least as the time of Dean Swift, who had described Gulliver's father as having been ruined by gaining a Chancery suit with costs'. But the arrears had greatly increased under Lord Eldon, whom Brougham, as usual, praised for being the most learned and painstaking of judges and most gentlemanly in his relations with counsel. Brougham cited the opinions of a number of eminent lawyers who had practised in the Court of Chancery in the present and the immediate past. 'All these great men had pronounced with one voice that that court was a great public grievance and the severest calamity to which the people of England was exposed.' While rich men frequently lost heavily on account of the situation in the Court of Chancery, its injustice was much greater to the poor. It was closed to the poor so far as actions for small sums were concerned in every case where the suitor was well advised. 'No man who ever put a forensic habit on his back would think of advising a suit in equity to recover 50 l., or 80 l. or 100 l.' He praised Lord Eldon's wisdom in dealing with appeals to the House of Lords from Scotland and from Ireland and noted the great improvement that had been made in the appointment of judges in Scotland which was now marked by 'liberality and fairness'.

Canning, anxious to compliment Brougham, said: 'Dry as were the details, he had never listened with greater interest to any debate and never had he been more amply rewarded by the manner in which it had been discussed.' At that point his speech

---

[1] Charles Knight, *Passages of a Working Life*, 3 vols. (1864–5), ii. 198.

was interrupted by a loud snore from one of the members and, of course, a burst of laughter.[1]

In December of this year (1823) Lord Holland sent one of his verses to Miss Fox. Since Brougham's name was pronounced 'Broom' and that, of course, is the point of the verse, there seems to be a difficulty in the first rhyme, but there probably would not have been for Lord Holland.

> There's a wild man the world doth roam,
> A giant wit.—They call him *Brougham*,
>   And well methinks they may.
> He deals, whene'er he speaks or acts
> With friends and foes and laws and facts
>   In such a *sweeping* way.[2]

A month later Daniel O'Connell wrote to Brougham suggesting that he should do some more sweeping for the Catholics. He outlined some plans. 'We are indeed desirous to conduct the cause in the manner which should meet the approbation of our *sincere* friends in the House, amongst whom *on every account* you hold the first place.'[3] On 31 May Brougham presented a petition on behalf of the Catholics in Ireland, entrusted to him by O'Connell, asking for a reform of the Irish Church, exclusion of Orangemen from juries, and speedy and unqualified emancipation of the Catholics. The language of the petition was extravagant, and Brougham said that he did not agree with all of it but in the main he heartily supported it.[4]

The Catholic Association had been established in Ireland two years earlier by O'Connell to protect Catholic interests and to further Catholic Emancipation. It had brought together the Catholic priesthood and laity most effectively and as a work of organization it was remarkably efficient. It had created apprehension in England even among the friends of Catholic Emancipation. On 22 December Brougham wrote to Lambton:

[We should] above all not be scared from holding our own principles on the Catholic question by any fear of its being unpopular and becoming more so before a general election. . . . I suspect . . . we may even be obliged to go further and to bring forward something. The Catholic Association have, as Parnell writes to me, finally decided on sending over two petitions, one to Burdett and the other

---

[1] *Hansard*, N.S., ix. 775 seq.   [2] Lacaita–Shelburne MSS.
[3] Brougham MSS.   [4] *Hansard*, N.S., xi. 954.

to me and no more, unless (which is probable) they also send two to Lord Grey and someone else, in the Lords. These petitions, I believe, are to be very moderate, Emancipation and abuses in the administration of justice. So that whatever the attitude of the Association and their great power and influence may do in the way of menace, their language and propositions will be inoffensive. Parnell seriously considers the Association can prevent them from immediately combining all the Catholic people and taking the first opportunity of separating entirely from England. Abercromby and all who know Ireland have the same idea and I am clear that O'Connell & Co. feel that it is so from the very moderate tone they are now taking. . . . In the meantime O'Connell & Co. are coming over, I hope not before I return to town . . . so that we shall hear their own account of the matter.[1]

At the opening of Parliament on 3 February 1825 Brougham as usual made the first Opposition speech after the address had been moved and seconded. It contained an eloquent plea for Catholic Emancipation. With that achieved no one would need to worry about the Catholic Association. The way to 'put down' the Catholic Association was the concession of just claims, not the despotism of coercive action. What had Canning to fear in acting as he would wish to in this matter? 'Backed as he is by public opinion on this question, backed by the honourable friends who fill the benches around me and on which he would have triumphed even if he had been obliged to have left office on such grounds.' Nor did Canning need to fear because of the possible resignation of colleagues. And that started Brougham off on a slashing attack on Eldon who had borne with such constancy 'the thwarts that he has lately received on the questions of trade. His patience under such painful circumstances can be rivalled only by the fortitude with which he bears the prolonged distress of the suitors in his own court.'

In this speech he began by referring to the Government's 'mercantile' reforms. 'He was afraid lest in bestowing any praise upon them, he should seem to be bestowing commendation upon himself.' He had urged the acceptance in practice of the principles of free trade when the Government had been hesitant and had hung back. He had also in 1817 proposed the very modifications of the Navigation Laws and the changes in rela-

[1] Brougham MSS.

tion to the silk trade which were now being adopted. The new economic measures should occasion great rejoicing.

Canning, in replying to Brougham, noted the latter's claims to having proposed at an earlier time the Government's economic measures.

The honourable and learned gentleman was not an infrequent speaker in that House . . . and he was not generally remarkable for being concise. Having in the course of his parliamentary life, proposed and supported almost every species and degree of innovation . . . it was not easy for ministers to do anything . . . without borrowing, or seeming to borrow, something from the honourable gentleman. . . . In the reign of Queen Anne there was a sage and grave critic of the name of Dennis who, in his old age, got it into his head that he wrote all the good plays that were acted at that time. At last a tragedy came forth with a most imposing storm of hail and thunder. At the first peal, 'That's my thunder' said Dennis. So, with the honourable and learned gentleman there was no noise or stir for the good of mankind, . . . but he instantly claimed it for his thunder.

In regard to Catholic Emancipation, Brougham had asked what a minister had to fear ' "with this House, these benches, all England at his back". To which he would propose another question. "What would a minister do with only those benches and with no England at his back" '.[1] He must reserve to himself 'how, when, at what period' he would act.

On 10 February the Government introduced a bill to amend the acts relating to unlawful societies in Ireland in order to outlaw and suppress the Catholic Association. The extent to which English opinion had been alarmed by the Association can be seen from the vote in favour of this bill, compared with a majority vote a few weeks later on a measure embodying Catholic Emancipation. It was feared that the Catholic Association so strongly organized would proceed later to advocate measures beyond Catholic Emancipation, including repeal of the Union. In its sessions it followed closely the forms of Parliament and appeared to many, although it made no such claim, to be operating as a sort of Irish parliament. It levied a 'rent' on the Catholic population, actually small in total returns and voluntary in form but associated with a great deal of pressure. It concerned itself with the administration of justice and, in addition

[1] *Hansard*, N.S., xii. 72 seq.

to instituting prosecutions, conducted inquiries and pronounced its own judgements prior to the trial of cases. Those in brief were the charges made against it.

The fourth night of the debate on this bill was considered by everyone as the most important. It would have been that for no other reason than because on that night Canning and Brougham spoke. Canning summed up the objections to the Catholic Association with power and smoothness. He took occasion to state his own position, favourable as it had always been to Catholic Emancipation, which he was free to do, as the Government had made it an open question. But he added his belief that the course of Catholic Emancipation had been injured in Great Britain by the existence of the Catholic Association and by attacks made in Parliament on the Protestant Establishment in Ireland.

Brougham said:

I, Sir, am the defender of the Catholic Association . . . and my frank opinion is . . . the more energetic their resistance, provided it be peaceful, the stronger the language they use, provided it be respectful, . . . the more conformable it will be to the high interests of those who have all at stake which can render life desirable or existence honourable, and infinitely more likely to succeed than any abject course.

As for the Association interfering in the administration of justice, it had instituted prosecutions in two cases which had resulted in acquittals. The Secretary for Ireland (Peel) had given an inaccurate account of these trials. 'I am not satisfied with the acquittal of those prisoners.' The judge had acted improperly and the trials had been conducted without counsel or cross-examination.

After this, Sir, am I to be told that justice is administered with the same undeviating rectitude . . . which distinguish the courts of justice in England. . . . There is one law for the rich and another for the poor. . . . Such is the opinion of my lord Redesdale who, while he was Lord Chancellor of Ireland, must have seen something of judges, prosecutions and verdicts. . . . The Catholic has no chance of justice if he comes single and unaided into court.

So the Association felt called upon to render assistance. He would tell them how to get rid of the Catholic Association.

'Remove the grievances under which the Roman Catholics labour, show them that you are at length determined to do them justice.' It was charged that the Association collected a 'rent'; so did the Methodists. It was said that the priests were very active in the Association. What would have been said if they had not been? That they disapproved of the Association.[1]

The second reading of this Unlawful Societies in Ireland Bill in the House of Commons was passed by a majority of 155. But Brougham kept fighting. He presented petitions from Ireland against the Bill and on the 18th moved for hearing the Catholic Association at the Bar of the House.

Good God! are you to resist the prayers of six millions of people who claim an opportunity of vindicating themselves from unjust aspersions? . . . They [the Catholic Association] authorize me to tell this House that they have a cloud of evidence, parole and documentary, with which they are ready to substantiate every particular of their most crying wrongs. . . . Here we are, the representatives of the people of England; there they are, the representatives of the Catholic community of Ireland. Let us for the first time become acquainted with each other's feelings . . . and I promise you, Sir, that the result will be to banish doubt and discontent, and to create better and much kinder feelings between the two countries. All that I ask is that the same favour should be bestowed upon six millions of Roman Catholics that was granted to the hawkers and pedlars of England.[2]

But the Catholic Association was refused the permission for which they had petitioned by a vote of 222 to 89.

Ten days later, speaking on Burdett's motion for a committee on the Catholic claims, Brougham asked with his usual vigour the obvious question in regard to Catholic Emancipation. Was there any ground in reason or in justice for continuing to exclude Catholics from public office and from Parliament?

Were not the entrances to the legislature barred? Had they any voice in making the laws which they were compelled to obey or in the imposition of taxes which were levied upon them? Were they not deprived of all share in the civil government of the state? And did they not endure all this because they dared to be honest and to worship God according to the religion of their ancestors and the religion of their own hearts?[3]

[1] *Hansard*, N.S., xii. 497 seq.   [2] Ibid. xii. 544 seq.
[3] Ibid. xii. 827 seq.

Burdett on 23 March introduced a Roman Catholic Relief Bill which embodied Catholic Emancipation, preserving the Protestant succession to the throne, reserving the offices of Lord Lieutenant of Ireland, Lord Chancellor of Great Britain, and Lord Chancellor of Ireland, and substituting a new oath for the old Oath of Supremacy which had to be taken by office-holders. The understanding was that it was to be followed by two other bills, one establishing some provision toward the maintenance of the Catholic clergy in Ireland, and the other raising the forty-shilling freehold franchise in Ireland (the same as that of the English counties) to a £10 franchise with the object of preventing Catholic voters from outnumbering Protestant voters in Ireland in the election of members of Parliament, since the Relief Bill was to throw Parliament open to Catholics. Brougham was strongly opposed to this change in the Irish franchise. He was apparently out of London at the time and wrote a strong protest to Mackintosh who was one of the group in conference with Burdett. Brougham presented and spoke in support of several Catholic petitions and spoke strongly for the Relief Bill on its second reading in the Commons when it was passed by a majority of twenty-seven.[1]

The House of Lords now remained the only hope of the opponents of Catholic Emancipation, who were customarily called 'Protestants', while the friends of Catholic Emancipation were called 'Catholics'. The Duke of York, who was heir to the throne, went to the Lords and made a speech in which he opposed the measure as passionately as Brougham had supported it in the Commons. He threw in a bit about the royal veto and declared 'so help me God' that if Catholic Emancipation were staved off until he came to the throne, there was nothing that he would not do to prevent it. The Duke's speech was literally set up by the 'Protestant' press in *letters of gold* (gilt)[2] for the edification of 'loyal' 'Protestant' families, whose cosiness was fortified by the thought of a Royal Duke who stood on the steps of the throne saving the country from the Catholics. The speech stirred Brougham to angry protest. And as usual he lost no time. Next day in the House of Commons he said that since he was not permitted to allude to what took place in the House of Lords

[1] *Hansard*, N.S., xii. 1366 seq., xiii. 13, 68, 121 seq.
[2] K. G. Feiling, *Second Tory Party* (1938), p. 338.

he would deal with it only as 'a matter of history'. He said that he could hardly believe his ears when the news was brought to him that morning. 'That a prince of the royal family should promulgate to the world that, happen what would, when he came to fill another situation —.' Brougham got no farther. Plunkett checked him with a point of order and added that he was trying to save Brougham from saying in a fit of temper what in calmer moments he would regret.

The Speaker warned Brougham that if he said what he feared he intended to say, he would be out of order. In calmer mood, Brougham reminded the House that scarcely a debate took place in which allusion was not made to what was happening in the House of Lords, the member simply saying 'another place which it is not allowed me to name'. As a matter of fact, in the House of Commons 'you may attack the bishops, the woolsack, the lords collectively or individually, if you will, but if you only glance at the heir presumptive to the Crown, privilege shall rise up against you, even before the words, which are to contribute the offence, shall be uttered'. As he went on with his speech he managed to say that he admired frankness but with men of great frankness, unless they were men 'of enlightened under-standing', 'all hope of recalling them from their errors, so help them God, [cheering and laughter] was but visionary'. The lesson of this to the House of Commons was that they should give Catholic Emancipation the largest possible majority and send the Relief Bill up to the Lords with 'an overpowering majority' on its third reading. In this speech Brougham was supposed to be discussing the Bill raising the Irish franchise to £10. Finally he got to it and vehemently opposed it.[1]

Brougham closed the debate on the third reading of the Catholic Relief Bill on 10 May. He urged, as he had so frequently done before, that justice to the Catholics was the way to secure loyalty and peace in Ireland. 'It was said that the principle of persecution was inherent in the Catholic Church.' That was nonsense. Historically there had been persecution in all churches. And he treated the House to a lecture on history, in which subject his knowledge was remarkable. 'Let there no longer be a spot in the empire [Ireland] on which foreign enemies, who hated this country, could suffer their eyes to dwell with malicious

[1] *Hansard*, N.S., xiii. 204 seq.

pleasure.' He pleaded urgently for a large majority.[1] The majority was 21. A week later the Bill was defeated in the House of Lords by a majority of 48, the bishops voting 24 to 2 against Catholic Emancipation. One of the two bishops who voted for the measure also spoke for it. He was Henry Bathurst, Bishop of Norwich, whose outlook was universally liberal. He was an admirer of Brougham, had given valuable support to the Lancasterian schools, had been associated with Brougham in the launching of the British and Foreign School Society, and had held office in that society rather than in the National Society. To finish the debate in the Lords and take the division, the House sat through the night of the 17th and divided at five o'clock in the morning because the 19th was Derby Day.

So Catholic Emancipation had to wait another four years. Whatever had been said of its pros and cons, the one thing that should stand out in a biography of Brougham is that once more he had given powerful leadership to a struggle for freedom. O'Connell was highly appreciative. In writing to Brougham about a small matter of detail he said: 'I can not conclude even such a note as this without expressing to *you* our deepest and lasting gratitude and saying even to yourself that our admiration of your powers, which I thought could not be increased, is beyond the means of expressing it.'[2]

On 20 May Brougham again referred to the Catholic question. He paid his compliments to several persons including a bishop who sought to make a hero of himself by comparing himself with the Seven Bishops in their anti-Catholic stand at the end of the reign of James II. The Seven Bishops, Brougham said, exposed themselves to the liability of going to the Tower; this bishop 'exposed himself only to the danger of further promotion'. Brougham urged Canning to swing the Government over to Catholic Emancipation and to carry it as a government measure. He dwelt as usual on the division in the Cabinet (in order to increase it) but expressed the confidence that Canning was too strong for his enemies in the Government. There was always, of course, the implication that if he failed Canning could join with the Whigs. Canning said in reply that he would not risk breaking up the Government. He still felt that 'the mind of the people of England was not sufficiently matured for the reception of the

---

[1] *Hansard*, N.S., lxxxiii. 552 seq.   [2] Brougham MSS., 12 May 1825.

measure'. But the cause of Catholic Emancipation had made great progress. The opposition was now passive rather than active and there was a greater unanimity in the demand for it in Ireland. The ground on which the Bill had been resisted in the House of Lords, the idea that Catholics did not make good subjects on account of a divided allegiance was, said Canning, 'quite untenable'.[1]

In the meantime Edinburgh had honoured her famous son by giving him a great dinner on 5 April, when he was in Scotland being inaugurated as Lord Rector of the University of Glasgow (see Chapter XVIII). Cockburn, who was chairman and pronounced a glowing eulogy, said later that more persons were present 'than had ever attended a public political dinner in Scotland'.[2] There is nothing notable in Brougham's speech, though it included a good summary of his own achievements given in vainglorious manner.

On 31 May he spoke on a favourite subject of his, delays in the Court of Chancery. He said that the Commission that had been set up to investigate the situation in the Court of Chancery had been unwillingly established as a sop to public feeling and constituted in such a way that nothing could be expected of it. 'Who was selected to superintend that Commission? Why, John, Earl of Eldon, who presided in the Court of Chancery.' A week later Brougham analysed the composition of the Commission and pointed out that nearly every member had owed his advancement to Lord Eldon. 'It was proposed to inquire into the conduct of the Lord Chancellor, and the learned lord said, "Let me name my judges". That was granted, and the first judge he named was himself.' He (Brougham) was reminded of a case in which he had acted. A member of the jury bore the same family name as the plaintiff. He asked him if he was related to the plaintiff and the reply he received was 'I is the plaintiff'. The judge, of course, removed him from the jury box in a hurry. But no one could remove Lord Chancellor Eldon whose way of doing things 'would render the decision as speedy and satisfactory to one party as his practice in his own court was unspeedy and unsatisfactory to all parties'.

Canning reminded Brougham that the Commission was not conducting a criminal investigation, but he did so with tongue

[1] *Hansard*, N.S., xiii. 875 seq.   [2] Cockburn, *Memorials*, p. 369.

in cheek. For once Canning's speech was feeble. He had no heart in defending Lord Eldon and had probably greatly enjoyed all of Brougham's many attacks on him. (This Chancery Commission reported in 1826. Its report, while strong in analysis, was weak in recommendation and reflected Eldon's hesitancy in regard to law reform. Some new rules resulted from it. Several bills of Copley's based on it, for one reason or another, were not passed.)

While in the midst of Catholic Emancipation and other parliamentary questions, and also in the midst of the anti-slavery movement, Mechanics' Institutes, and the launching of London University, Brougham continued to be one of the chief entertainers at the very exclusive Beefsteak Club, the Sublime Society of Beefsteaks, as the King had once been when Prince of Wales. Hobhouse entered in his diary on 28 May [1825]: 'Dined at Beefsteak. . . . Brougham in the chair. . . . Brougham sang us a song in French, "The Pipe of Tobacco". He was in high force. He told us he always gets up every morning at seven, let him go to bed when he will, and that he is a good sleeper. He is a most extraordinary man.'[1] A few weeks later he added another entry to his diary: 'Brougham appears to me daily a more extraordinary man the more I see of him.'[2]

---

[1] Lord Broughton, *Recollections of a Long Life*, 6 vols. (1910–11), iii. 104
[2] Ibid., iv. 51–52.

CHAPTER XV

Fighting to Free the Slaves, 1822–9

THE year 1823 is always given as the date of the beginning
of the movement for the emancipation of the slaves. As
a matter of fact it was begun in 1822 by James Cropper,
who has never been recognized in that role. The story given here
is gleaned mainly from the Clarkson manuscripts in the British
Museum. James Cropper was a Liverpool Quaker philan-
thropist. In that year 1822 he organized the *first* society for the
abolition of slavery, with its headquarters in Liverpool, and he
persuaded Zachary Macaulay to interest his friends, the constant
champions of the Negro, to organize a society in London and
work definitely toward emancipation.[1] That was the beginning
of the emancipation movement.

Cropper could never have launched such a movement without
the old leaders, and if he was its projector, Zachary Macaulay
was the real founder. The first evidence in Wilberforce's letters
or diaries that he contemplated a movement for emancipation
occurs in a letter to Buxton on 3 December, in which he expressed remorse that they had not acted sooner, and suggested
a 'secret cabinet council' before Parliament met.[2] In the meantime, Zachary Macaulay throughout the latter half of 1822 had
been contacting old friends, obtaining old lists of correspondents,
and making campaign plans.[3] He was also writing *Negro Slavery*,
an indictment of the whole system. Zachary Macaulay invited
to his house on 13 January (1823) William Smith, William Allen,
and Buxton, and, according to Allen, that remarkable Quaker,
they 'laid the foundation for the London Society for the Abolition of Slavery in our Colonies, agreed upon the persons who
are to form the committee', and made arrangements for the first
meeting of the Society.[4]

[1] Add. MSS. 41267A, ff. 102–27.
[2] *Life of Wilberforce*, v. 157.
[3] Add. MSS. 41267A, *passim*.
[4] Allen, ii. 105. Diary for 1st month, 13th, 1823.

It is difficult to believe that Brougham knew nothing of all this until the beginning of February or that he should have hesitated about coming in, yet the first mention of him in this connexion in the extant letters and diaries is in a letter of 8 February, in which Zachary Macaulay wrote to Wilberforce: 'I have had two long talks with Brougham, and have gradually opened to him our feelings and views. I cannot help hoping that we have gained him. He offered voluntarily to write an article on slavery for the very next *Edinburgh Review*.'[1] In a letter to Lord Grey eleven years later Zachary Macaulay said, truly enough, that his *Negro Slavery* was the first direct attack on slavery, and added that Brougham 'when the pamphlet was first placed before him was so impressed by its perusal that on the very day it met his eye he wrote an article upon it which appeared in the *Edinburgh Review* of that period and produced a strong sensation on the public mind'.[2] We do not know when the February 1823 number of the *Edinburgh Review* went to press, but anything written by Brougham for publication that was as brief as nine pages was so unprecedented that one is bound to think that Brougham persuaded Jeffrey to work it in at the last minute. A few scattered quotations may serve to illustrate the character of the article.

We hold it to be altogether impossible for any rational being to maintain the abstract right of one class of men to keep another in the state of slavery . . . the horrible attempt at making a property of men, . . . and treating them as cattle or as inanimate objects, the absolute property of the owners. . . . Why, then, it may be asked, did the Abolitionists uniformly disavow all views of emancipation? . . . As long as you permit the planter to have an unstinted supply of new slaves (it was argued), so long will he neglect his native bands, and so long will every kind of ill treatment accumulate upon their heads. Cut off the supply, and the treatment will naturally be amended, the condition of the Negro be improved. . . . It seemed reasonable to look for what had always been predicted as the inevitable result of the abolition, a reform in the laws of the colonies relating to slaves. They now looked earnestly, wistfull, but in vain, for these measures. Associations are already formed in London, Liverpool and elsewhere, with the view of improving and liberating the West Indian population. . . . Liverpool, once famous in the enormities of the slave traffick,

---

[1] *Life of Wilberforce*, v. 167.
[2] Brougham MSS., 2 May 1834.

has now stood foremost as the first to make amends for its horrid fruits. The venerable name of William Roscoe stands at the head of the body there associated, whose pious object it is to adopt all lawful and peaceable measures for mitigating the evils of slavery, and preparing its ultimate abolition. Every good man must pray for its success.

A considerable part of the article consisted of quotations from *Negro Slavery*.[1]

The *Edinburgh Review*, with a circulation remarkable both for its quality and its quantity, had tremendous influence: with the appearance of this article the emancipation movement gained a most important ally.

The Quakers had started their own movement for the abolition of slavery in 1822 and in the following year they decided on a petition to Parliament, which William Allen asked Wilberforce to present.[2] Wilberforce reminded the House that the first petition to Parliament for the abolition of the slave trade had also come from the Quakers.[3]

The next day Wilberforce wrote to Brougham expressing surprise that he had left so soon for the Northern Circuit. He had wished to discuss a number of things with him before that, especially 'by what specific measures we ought to endeavour to prepare for the universal emancipation of the West Indian slaves'. He suggested that liberal-minded slave owners, for instance Lord Holland and Ward, should be asked to declare themselves in favour of emancipation and to attempt to influence other West Indian proprietors.[4] Nothing came of the matter, but the letter is an interesting revelation of Wilberforce's mind at the time. It is in harmony with his tendency all the way through to gain his objects by directly influencing very important persons, in most cases Cabinet ministers. Brougham and Zachary Macaulay, on the other hand, relied more on popular appeal and consequent popular pressure on the important persons.

The 15th of May 1823 saw the first parliamentary debate on the abolition of slavery. Thomas Fowell Buxton had been selected by Wilberforce to make the following motion: 'That the state of

[1] *Edinburgh Review*, Feb. 1823.
[2] Allen, ii. 34, 103, 108. Diary.
[3] *Hansard*, N.S., viii. 624.
[4] Brougham MSS., 19 Mar. 1823.

slavery is repugnant to the principles of the British constitution, and of the Christian religion; and that it ought to be gradually abolished throughout the British colonies, with as much expedition as may be found consistent with a due regard to the well-being of the parties concerned.'[1] Buxton laid his principal emphasis on a proposal that all children of slaves born after a certain date should be free at birth. That would definitely mean the abolition of slavery at some time in the future. 'Now, for the existing slaves. Slaves they are. Slaves, I fear, they must too generally continue; but slaves, under a description of servitude considerably mitigated.' He then described the mitigations which he proposed, which would prepare the way safely for the gradual abolition of slavery. He embodied them in resolutions which he moved.

Canning, speaking on behalf of the Government, said that to some of Buxton's proposals he had 'not the slightest objection'. The Government would take charge of this matter. He moved resolutions which, stripped of verbiage, meant that it was expedient to ameliorate the condition of the slave population and to improve their character as a preparation for participation in civil rights and privileges. He added that the Government could put these proposals into operation in the colonies over which 'the Crown exercises immediate power'. In those in which there were colonial legislatures it would expect 'a full and fair co-operation'. If they refused to co-operate 'not of reason, but of contumacy', the Government would come to Parliament for counsel. Canning was undoubtedly sincere in the desires which he expressed, but it may be noted that he said nothing about emancipation, either in the near or distant future. And for all Canning's sincerity, the Government always had in the back of its mind the danger of antagonizing the West Indian interest in Parliament.

Wilberforce, who followed Canning, said that the colonial legislatures had invariably opposed ameliorative measures. But he showed an inclination to accept the Government's proposals as a step in the right direction. Ellis, as usual, made the best speech for the West Indians. He protested that the proprietors were not responsible for the creation of slavery or for the evils associated with it. In most cases they had inherited it and they

[1] For this debate, *Hansard*, N.S., ix. 257 seq.

wished to make the system work as well as they could. For the degraded condition of the slaves, emancipation was not the cure; it would be by far the most harmful of all attempts in that direction. The solution lay in religious instruction. That the Church had been recreant in that respect in the past was the fault neither of the present planters nor of the present clergy. The clergy were now turning their attention to that matter. It was essential that the colonial legislatures should be trusted. Any attempt to coerce them would be met by a resistance which would be disastrous.

Brougham, as he so often did purposely, spoke late in the debate. He expressed his scepticism about the West Indian legislatures co-operating toward any real reform and any progress toward emancipation much more strongly than did Wilberforce. He said it was 'a delusion'. One speaker had read a letter from the Governor of Dominica which appeared to attest the good treatment of the slaves. Brougham said:

I am curious to know how soon after his arrival in Dominica this letter from Governor Maxwell was written; and whether it was before or after his having been presented by the grand inquest of the island as a nuisance. . . . If written afterwards, it would only show how forgiving a character, what a good-natured creature, the governor must be. It must, however, have been written before. And why, let me ask, was he presented by the grand jury of the island as a nuisance? . . . It was only for wishing to put in force the laws of the island in favour of some unhappy Negroes who had been most barbarously ill-treated by their masters.

Could they have any confidence, he asked, in the sort of person represented by such a grand jury or in 'the legislative bodies in general, whose conduct has, on many occasions, been not a whit less strange'. Here, as so often, Brougham appealed to the British respect for law and the fact that slavery made full legal protection for the West Indian Negroes impossible.

There were plenty of stories, Brougham said, all emanating from the interested parties, about the happiness of the slaves and their good treatment. There were also a great many advertisements in the West Indian papers for the recovery of runaway slaves, and in nearly every case such an advertisement described marks or scars of both branding and flogging. Brougham's conviction was (as expressed on many occasions but not in this

debate) that the principal hope for the improvement of the
slaves lay in religious instruction, but that they would not and
could not get that from the Anglican clergy in the West Indies;
they would get effective religious instruction only from the
Dissenter missionaries, if the planters and overseers would permit it and withdraw their antagonism to the missionaries. In
this debate Brougham said only that he too had heard something
about increased religious instruction on the part of the Anglican
clergy. One West Indian clergyman had written a letter about
it.

This worthy person states, with great simplicity, that he had been
between twenty and thirty years among the Negroes, and that no
single instance of conversion to Christianity had taken place during
that time. . . . All of a sudden, however, light had broken in upon
their darkness so rapidly, that between 5,000 and 6,000 Negroes had
been baptized in a few days! I confess I was at first much surprised
at this statement; I knew not how to comprehend it; but all of a
sudden light broke in upon *my* darkness also. I found that . . . these
wonderful conversions were brought about, not by a miracle, as
the good man seems himself to have really imagined, and would
almost make us believe, but by a premium of a dollar a head paid to
this worthy curate for each slave whom he baptized. I understood,
too, that the whole amount of the previous religious instruction which
each Negro received, was neither more nor less than attending, on
one occasion, at the church where the curate presided. . . . If any
person thinks that any real practical good can result from such an
administration of religious instruction and of Christian baptism, let
him enjoy his hopes; I cannot agree with him.

(This heinous provision for making Christians by baptism at so
much a head which had been recently established was ended a
few years after Brougham's speech.)

Brougham said that he knew that many of the slave-owners
were humane in their attitude, but by far the greater part of
them were living in England. 'They are absent, and know
nothing of what is actually going on upon their estates. It is an
individual who has no real interest in the estate, who is placed
as their agent on the spot to superintend the whole concern.'
The agents and overseers, in their own interests, over-worked
the slaves and treated them in an inhuman fashion. 'If they are
not now ripe for actual emancipation, at least we are arrived
at the time when it will be safe to legislate with a view to that

consummation; it seems to me to be now the imperative duty of the legislature to pass some act with respect to the freedom of unborn children.' Parliament must act for the protection of the slaves, and legislate directly with a view to their emancipation. Trusting to the West Indian legislatures would get them nowhere. Brougham referred to the experience of himself and his friends with those legislatures, and, in closing his speech, said: 'With these recollections deeply impressed upon my mind, let it not be supposed that I can indulge a sanguine hope of any beneficial practical results from these resolutions [Canning's].'

However, Buxton withdrew his resolutions and Canning's were passed. Acting on the basis of Canning's speech, Lord Bathurst, the Colonial Secretary, sent a dispatch to the West Indian colonies urging the cessation of the flogging of females and the dropping of the use of the whip in the fields; the speech made by Canning was enclosed, indicating further reforms. On 9 July Bathurst sent another dispatch recommending a number of reforms including further provision for religious instruction, the abolition of Sunday markets, the removal of all unnecessary obstacles to manumission, a regulation that husbands and wives should not be separated in slave sales, the acceptance of the evidence of slaves in the courts, with certain exceptions, if it were certified that they understood the nature of an oath, the general establishment of legal marriage and restrictions on the flogging of male slaves. These dispatches were supposed to inaugurate a period of 'amelioration'. Sceptical as they were, the emancipationists gave the Government's policy a trial for three years until their patience broke down at the small extent to which it was implemented in the colonies.

All the West Indians who spoke in Parliament and the writers of their pamphlets predicted that this beginning of a movement for emancipation would inevitably create insurrection in the West Indies. Buxton's parliamentary emancipation proposals were made in May and what were regarded as the Government's partial concessions in the dispatches of 28 May and 9 July. The first dispatch reached Demerara on 7 July. A slave insurrection broke out in Demerara on 18 August. Many were then prepared to agree with the West Indians that the emancipationists were impractical fanatics who understood nothing of conditions in the West Indies. No doubt the emancipation movement would have survived in some way, although seriously retarded, but there were many at the time who believed that the movement to free the slaves would have been buried in the graveyard of the Demerara insurrection—if it had not been for the case of the missionary Smith.

Planters and overseers had talked about the orders from the British Government but had withheld them from publication. Many of the Demerara slaves concluded that the British Government had ordered that they should be freed and their masters were refusing to put the order into effect. The slaves had also heard, correctly enough in this case, that the use of the whip in the fields was to be discontinued. That was always regarded as the symbol of the master's authority.

The leader of the Demerara insurrection was a young Negro who was called Jack Gladstone because he was a slave on an estate owned by John Gladstone, that Liverpool merchant who had been the commander-in-chief of Canning's forces in the 1812 election against Brougham, the father of the famous statesman. (William Ewart Gladstone was to make his first speech in Parliament in defence of slavery.) The Demerara rising spread to fifty plantations. The slaves in revolt killed only one man (under aggravating circumstances) and destroyed very little property. Planters and overseers were seized and some were placed in stocks. The suppression of the revolt took three days. Two hundred slaves were killed in the fighting, forty-seven were executed, and a number of others were, in Brougham's words, 'torn to pieces by the infliction of the most merciless flogging'. Several were sentenced to a thousand lashes each by the terrible cutting whip of the West Indies.

With these feelings of revenge and cruelty succeeding the terrible fears of the three days, the planter–overseer population sought for anyone on whom it might wreak its vengeance. Some of the leaders of the insurrection had belonged to the chapel served by the missionary John Smith. Talk about his having known of the revolt in advance and having preached inflammatory sermons developed into stories that he had directly incited to revolt, and he was placed on trial before a military court on 13 October. He was convicted of the offences with which he was charged and on 24 November he was sentenced to death. While the Demerara authorities waited for a confirmation of the death sentence from the British Government, Smith, though suffering from tuberculosis, was confined in a room that Brougham described as 'a kind of damp dungeon, where the crazy floor was laid loosely over stagnant water, visible through the wide crevices of its boards'. He died on 6 February (1824).

The London Missionary Society received a full and detailed report of the trial from Smith's counsel, and published its record of the trial. But it was Brougham who took the lead in informing the British people of the horrible injustices of the case. He did so in a long article in the *Edinburgh Review* for March 1824 and in two parliamentary speeches in support of a motion which he made. Nothing on this earth could have prevented Brougham from obtaining all the information available, dissecting the trial, and condemning the perversion of justice in his most forceful eloquence. But whether the lead fell into his hands entirely from the spontaneous promptings of a generous heart or because his associates selected him as the man best fitted for the task we do not know.

It is difficult to compress the story that Brougham told and much that is significant must be omitted here. The London Missionary Society in 1807 established a mission in Demerara, an island where there were 78,000 slaves and one clergyman of the Established Church. In 1816 John Smith, who was a Congregationalist, entered the service of this mission, taking charge of a chapel with a Negro congregation on an estate whose proprietor always praised him in the highest terms. Brougham described his success in making converts, encouraging marriage, and in imparting religious instruction. Twelve days after Smith's death the *Demerara Journal* made this statement: 'If we expect to create a community of reading, moral, church-going slaves, we are woefully mistaken.' Brougham's comment in his *Edinburgh Review* article was: 'Father, forgive them, they know not what they do! Can a more frightful issue be imagined on which to put the question of property in slaves, and the stability of the West Indian system? If it cannot exist together with Christianity, then it is indeed condemned to swift destruction.'

In his opening speech in Parliament Brougham dissected Smith's trial ruthlessly. The court, he said, had paid no attention to any rules in regard to the admission of evidence against the accused. Hearsay evidence was 'three or four deep'. Yet when

Smith began his defence he was told, 'You must confine yourself to the strict rules of evidence; and hearsay evidence will not in future be received'. New evidence was introduced and new persons mentioned after the prisoner was forbidden to make any further defence. Smith's papers had been seized and his private diary recording his inmost thoughts had been placed in evidence against him. That was 'inadmissible by anything wearing the semblance of a court'. There was no evidence that Smith ever expressed publicly the sentiments which he recorded in his diary. Brougham, for his own purpose, published in his *Edinburgh Review* article the whole of the extracts from this diary that had been read in court. They revealed what this sensitive and conscientious missionary thought in his secret heart of the slave system and the sufferings imposed upon the Negroes. Brougham asked: 'Where else, but among men inured to the horrors that so harrowed up this poor missionary's feelings, durst a prosecutor have read such passages as the following pages contain, read them to enrage the hearers, not against the perpetrators of those enormities, but against him in whom they roused the common feelings of a man?'

Smith said in this private diary that the overseers were working the slaves to death. 'The laws are only known by name here.' He recorded how his heart was moved by a slave praying in the Sunday meeting that God might touch the hearts of the overseers who kept their slaves away from the House of God. Instances were given of the most inhuman treatment of the slaves. 'The rigours of Negro slavery, I believe, can never be mitigated; the system must be abolished.' There Brougham had material that could hardly be equalled for his indictment of slavery and for the movement for emancipation. And he employed it with his customary power.

Four charges had been laid against Smith: (1) promoting discontent and dissatisfaction among the slaves; (2) advising and consulting with Quamina (the father of Jack Gladstone) immediately before and after the outbreak of revolt; (3) that he knew of the revolt and gave no information to the authorities; (4) that meeting Quamina after the outbreak of the revolt, he had not 'secured' him. Brougham dug under all of them and blew them up. He admitted that a missionary who taught conscientiously the simplest messages of the Christian Gospel, but who did not relate them to the treatment which the slaves were receiving, might through the Gospel cause some discontent, but that was not a crime. As for Smith advising and counselling with Quamina the night before the revolt broke out, the evidence was very clear that he advised him that he must have nothing to do with any revolt against authority or any resort to violence. One witness declared that Smith had known about the revolt six weeks in advance, and yet the evidence in the trial itself showed quite clearly that it was planned only a day or two before it broke out. In relation to the confession of the slave Paris, which had implicated Smith, Brougham read to the House of Commons a letter in which the minister of the Established Church, the Rev. Mr. Austin, said that he had received 'the last confession of Paris, who stated that Mr. Smith was innocent, and he [Paris] prayed that God would forgive him the lies that Mr. — had prevailed upon him to tell'.

The evidence for the defence was impressive, in spite of the fact that unjust limitations were placed on Smith and his counsel. The Rev. Mr. Austin, the only Church of England clergyman on the island, had expressed both in and out of court his admiration for Smith's conduct throughout, declared his belief in Smith's absolute innocence, and deprecated the methods employed against him. As Brougham put it:

By the testimony of the clergyman, and even of the overseers, the maxims of the gospel of peace were upon their lips in the midst of rebellion, and restrained their hands when no other force was present to resist them. 'We will take no life', said they; 'for our pastors have taught us not to take that which we cannot give', which drew from the truly pious minister of the Established church the exclamation, that 'he shuddered to write that they were seeking the life of the man whose teaching had saved theirs'.

Brougham in his article and in his speeches in Parliament was doing more than clearing Smith and indicting the court which convicted him. He was appealing directly to the British public to rise up against the whole slave system and to sweep it away as soon as that could be done. And he was appealing especially to the religious forces of the nation. In the peroration of his first speech he said: 'It was necessary that the missionaries should be taught in what an undertaking they had embarked; that they should be warned that it was at their peril they preached the gospel; . . . and therefore it was that the court-martial deemed it expedient to convict Mr. Smith, and to sentence him to be hanged by the neck until he was dead!' And Brougham, referring to the planters and overseers, continued: 'They find leagued against them every shade of the African race. . . . And they must now combine in the same hatred the Christians of the old world with the Pagans of the new!'

Brougham's parliamentary motion declared that the House of Commons 'contemplated with the most serious alarm the violation of law and justice which had been committed' in the trial of the Reverend John Smith at Demerara; 'that it prayed his Majesty to give orders for the more impartial and humane administration of the law in that colony'. The debate which followed, most of which came ten days later, was an anticlimax. Brougham had convinced the nation and little interest was taken in those later speeches, which lay buried in *Hansard* while Brougham's opening speech lived for at least a generation. The Government took objection to the motion mainly because it was opposed to Parliament censuring a West Indian court.

Wilberforce said that in reply Brougham would be 'terrific' (using the word a century before our slang deprived it of its force). Brougham's closing speech, however, lacked some of the acumen of his first, though it did not lack scorn, passion, and force.

The right honourable gentleman [Canning] seems much disposed to quarrel with the title of martyr. . . . When through that zeal, a Christian minister has been brought to die the death, I would have his name honoured and holden in everlasting remembrance. His blood cries from the ground—but not for vengeance! He expired, not imprecating curses upon his enemies, but praying for those who had brought him to an untimely grave. It cries aloud for justice to his memory, and for protection to those who shall tread in his footsteps, . . . shall prove themselves worthy to follow him, and worthy of the cause for which he suffered. . . . We [in Parliament] are sovereign alike over the white and the black. . . . Yet a little delay; yet a little longer of this unbearable trifling with the commands of the parent state, and she will stretch out her arm, in mercy, not in anger, to those deluded men themselves; exert at last her undeniable authority; vindicate the just rights, and restore the tarnished honour of the English name.[1]

[1] This treatment, of course, is a putting together of statements made by Brougham

The interest captured, particularly the religious interest, was tremendous. The emancipation movement was saved and given a much more vigorous life. And it had in truth found its martyr. Men reminded one another of the martyrs of Protestantism, and suggested that John Smith had lighted a candle that in England by God's grace would never go out. Years later, when an anti-slavery song came from across the Atlantic, a comparison was drawn between John Smith and John Brown. The American author of *The Anti-Slavery Movement in England* has written: 'So strong was the feeling of revulsion against the anti-slavery party that the hopes of emancipation seemed shattered, until Brougham by his masterly handling of the case of the missionary Smith, revived the cause and dealt British slavery a blow from which it never recovered. Probably it is not too much to say that the case of this missionary produced the same effect in Britain that John Brown's execution did on Northern opinion in the United States.'[1] John Smith's 'body lay a-mould'ring in the grave, his soul went marching on'.

A lady who was in the gallery on the last day of the John Smith debate wrote to her sister-in-law, Mrs. Josiah Wedgwood junior, that Brougham's closing speech 'was the most incomparable thing that I ever heard . . . . He handled Scarlett and Canning to my soul's delight, tossed them about like a cat a couple of mice from one paw to the other, teased them and threw them into the air with equal grace and strength.'[2] In this debate Wilberforce made his last parliamentary speech. No one regretted so much as he did himself that his active participation in the movement for the emancipation of the slaves had been limited to a little over a year and a half. On 2 February of the following year (1825) he wrote to Brougham:

You have treated me with so much kindness ever since we first became acquainted that I don't like the idea of your first hearing from common rumour or seeing in the newspaper that I am about to retire from Parliament. My physician tells me that if I were to have such another attack as I had last spring I should probably not

in his *Edinburgh Review* article (Mar. 1824) and in his two parliamentary speeches which are given in *Hansard*, N.S., xi. 961 seq., 1294 seq.; *Speeches*, ii. 51 seq.; *Works*, x. 115 seq.

[1] Klingberg, p. 220.

[2] Emma Dawson, *A Century of Family Letters*, 2 vols., i. 156, Fanny Allen to Mrs. Josiah Wedgwood.

have strength to stand it. . . . I have to balance all the benefit and comfort I might derive from my continuance in life. . . .

But I am greatly comforted by the consciousness that happily I am not wanted in the House of Commons. In writing to any other man I should pour forth the effusions which are ready to force their way upon paper. . . . To you I will only say may God bless and prosper you, may He grant you a long course of usefulness and comfort, and suffer me, my dear Brougham to add, may you be endowed with a still better portion and after this short span of life shall have expired may you be admitted to the enjoyment of Glory and Honour and Immortality.[1]

Wilberforce could now do little but write the occasional encouraging letter and appear at times as chairman of a public meeting, lending the movement his great prestige. He did not possess the remarkable physical strength of Zachary Macaulay and Buxton, nor the elemental toughness which sustained Brougham in spite of his frequent illnesses. His vitality was exhausted, activity was impossible, he was a very old man at sixty-five. It has always been believed, at least for the last hundred years, that Wilberforce appointed Buxton in 1823 as the leader of the anti-slavery forces in Parliament and that Buxton held that position. He had written to Buxton in 1821, before the emancipation movement began, but when he hoped that the condition of the slaves would be brought more fully before Parliament, expressing the wish that Buxton would assume that leadership when he relinquished it.[2] He proposed that Buxton should introduce the motion that opened the parliamentary campaign for emancipation and took Buxton with him when he approached the Government. And at the time of his own retirement from Parliament in 1825 he wrote in his diary: 'I then [in 1823] devolved my advocateship of the negro slaves on him [Buxton] because it would have been wrong to have appointed an Oppositionist.' He wrote to Zachary Macaulay about 'the importance of keeping this great cause in possession of its honourable distinction of being one in which all party differences were extinguished'.[3]

While it may seem like sacrilege to suggest that Wilberforce

[1] Brougham MSS., 2 Feb. 1825.
[2] Memoirs of Sir Thomas Fowell Buxton, 3rd ed. (1849), pp. 103-4.
[3] Life of Wilberforce, v. 238.

took himself too seriously in this respect, one may at least ask if the other champions of the slaves ever, in this period, regarded Buxton as their leader. There is no suggestion in their extant correspondence that they did. And George Stephen who knew nearly everything that was going on, and was closely associated with Buxton in the matter of slavery in Mauritius, said definitely in his *Recollections* that Buxton was 'not then the recognized leader of the party'. He referred to the period after 1823 and his statement seems to be applicable to any time before 1830. He had in mind, of course, the fact that Buxton *was* the leader of the anti-slavery forces in Parliament in the years immediately preceding the Emancipation Act of 1833. George Stephen spoke of a parliamentary *team* and, as he gave the names, the team was made up of Brougham, Buxton, Lushington, and William Smith.[1] A careful study of the slavery debates confirms that the parliamentary burden was shared almost equally by the members of the team, with occasional help from Denman and others. It was a better team than the friends of the slaves had ever had, and George Stephen maintained that each member of it was an 'Ajax in battle'.

There was also a cabinet for the whole movement. A letter of Galt's which is preserved in the Clements Library, University of Michigan, and is dated 7 January 1828, states that Brougham, Lushington, Macaulay, and Buxton met regularly at Brougham's house to review every aspect of the anti-slavery movement.[2] We do not know how long they had been doing that, but it seems likely that they continued to do so until the autumn of 1830. The fact that they met at Brougham's house does not mean that Brougham was their recognized leader. Zachary Macaulay convened them and we may be almost sure that he laid their agenda before them. In April 1829 Buxton, though ill, assured Macaulay that he would be at Brougham's if Macaulay called a meeting and on 25 November of the same year he wrote to his wife that they were meeting at Brougham's on Friday.[3]

[1] Sir George Stephen, pp. 55 seq., 65.
[2] Seldon MSS., Galt to Seldon.
[3] Buxton, pp. 187, 195. One of the ideas that have held sway for a hundred years is that a great deal was done for the abolition of slavery by the 'Clapham Sect'. That is another result of the confusion between the slave trade and slavery. But none of the parliamentary team ever lived at Clapham except William Smith, who was a Unitarian. Of the leaders of the emancipation movement only Macaulay,

No one gave the anti-slavery cause more devotion, persistence, and religious drive than Thomas Buxton A graduate of the University of Dublin, he was elected to Parliament in 1818, and advocated prison reform, like his sister-in-law, Elizabeth Fry, and the reform of the criminal law. A big man, frequently referred to as 'Elephant Buxton', he was a good debater and he could be eloquent at times, though his eloquence was not nearly as powerful as Brougham's or as that of Wilberforce in his day. He was an Evangelical, though his mother and wife were Quakers and he was always in close touch with the Gurneys and the Frys. He had the Quaker love of simplicity and indeed we detect in Buxton himself a strong Quaker faith in the Inner Word, the Inner Voice.

Zachary Macaulay organized and directed the campaign throughout the country. According to an *Edinburgh Review* article in October 1824, probably written by Brougham, there were already by that date, within two years of the founding of the London Society, 220 anti-slavery societies, and 600 petitions had been signed in various localities. In 1825 Macaulay began the *Anti-Slavery Reporter,* which was published monthly, edited by him and a great deal of it written by him. It massed carefully sifted facts and embodied a dispassionate, relentless description of the evils of slavery. Men noted Macaulay's objectivity and it has been said that he seldom wrote subjectively and could never do it with effect. In that respect, as in others, he and Brougham maintained a good partnership, for Brougham, in this period at least, found it difficult to be objective and very easy to be subjective. There can be no doubt at all that Zachary Macaulay was the mightiest worker in the anti-slavery cause. He allowed himself very little sleep. He had business affairs to look after but he worked on slavery far into the night and rose to it early every morning. He drove himself like a slave to free the slaves.

Ladies' anti-slavery societies were organized. Wilberforce seldom offered criticism from his retirement, but he could not

---

Stephen, and Smith had ever lived at Clapham; none of them lived there at this time. In the parish church at Clapham the names of the members of the Clapham Sect are inscribed: it is stated that they 'rested not until the curse of slavery was swept away'. Half of those men were dead before the emancipation movement began. Two others played no visible part in the movement. Wilberforce's part was very small. With the exception of the two noted here, Macaulay and George Stephen, none of them had anything to do with the freeing of the slaves.

brook ladies' societies. They offended both his sense of the fitness of things and his conception of the Bible, and he felt called upon to tell Macaulay that he disagreed with him. 'For ladies to meet, to publish, to go from house to house stirring up petitions, these appear to me proceedings unsuited to the female character as deliniated in Scripture.'[1] The ladies went ahead and did good work, probably without giving a thought to St. Paul.

The Smith case was followed by other instances of injustice and persecution in the West Indies, which the emancipationists employed to win public attention and support, particularly religious support. In Barbados feeling ran high against Methodist missionaries in any case and was heightened by one of them, Shrewsbury, criticizing West Indian society in a report to his board which was published without his intention. At first white men walked in on his black congregation whistling. Then one Sunday a crowd entered the chapel armed with bottles containing various evil ingredients and threw them at the poor Negroes while a lawyer stood at the rail of the communion table and cheered them on. Shrewsbury complained to the Governor who suggested that he appeal to the magistrates; Shrewsbury asked to which magistrate he should go, the one (a chemist) who had supplied the bottles or the one who boasted that he would lead a crowd to destroy the chapel, or to another similarly disposed. He announced that there would be no service next Sunday. But there were plenty who went to the chapel on that day, to vindicate, as they said, 'true religion'. They wrecked the chapel and then, to make it a more memorable occasion, smashed up everything in the missionary's home. Shrewsbury, fearing for his life, left the island. A year later a celebration was planned for the anniversary of the day of liberation—from the Methodists. They were to destroy the home of a poor Negro widow where some of Shrewsbury's congregation had continued to worship. The Governor protected the widow. When the Methodist Missionary Society sent out a successor to Shrewsbury, he was not allowed to land on the island.

One need hardly comment on what Buxton, Brougham, and Lushington made of that in Parliament after the tale was complete, speaking of course to the people of Britain as well as to the House. Buxton related the facts with deadly accuracy;

[1] *Life of Wilberforce*, v. 264.

Brougham and Lushington did the rest. Brougham wrote or prompted an article on it in the *Edinburgh Review*. A little later Denman brought to the attention of Parliament, and through Parliament to that of the nation, marked injustice in the conviction of a group of slaves in Jamaica. He was supported by Buxton, Lushington, Smith, and Brougham, and Brougham played up the matter in the *Edinburgh*.[1]

Although the publicity given to the Smith and Shrewsbury cases helped greatly the emancipation cause, planters had not been involved in them and they are not to be taken as typical of the attitude of the planters toward the missionaries. In the main that attitude was antagonistic; the missionaries were regarded as a nuisance and the managers of plantations were more or less hardened against the idea of having Christian slaves or educated slaves. But there were notable exceptions. There were a number of cases in which resident planters, Anglicans themselves, gave land for the building of chapels for Dissenter missionaries, built the chapels or subscribed generously to their building and maintenance, while others praised and encouraged the work of the missionaries. Examples were reported in the *Methodist Magazine* and the *Baptist Magazine*.[2] Bitter persecution of the Baptist missionaries in Jamaica came later but not until after the terminal date of this volume and under changed conditions.

There were, of course, few resident planters and in some districts none at all. The great bulk of the proprietors were living in England.[3] Brougham frequently conceded that members of Parliament who owned slaves were humane in their attitude, and in his speech at the second anniversary of the Anti-Slavery Society he extended that judgement to other planters.

I know indeed many West Indian proprietors, who, I am persuaded, do all that those can do, by directions of lenity and charity and humanity, who are absent owners, who are living nearly 4000 miles from the unhappy objects of their compassion. . . . To some resident proprietors too I might express my obligation for their desire to

[1] *Hansard*, N.S., xiii. 1285 seq., xiv. 1007 seq.; *Edinburgh Review*, Aug. 1825, Feb. 1826.

[2] Particularly *Methodist Magazine*, 1826, pp. 202, 352, 496, 567, 569; *Baptist Magazine*, 1826, pp. 299, 540, 542.

[3] Richard Hill, *Lights and Shadows of Jamaica History* (1859), p. 68.

meliorate the condition of their unhappy slaves, which, so long as slavery exists, must prove very unavailing.[1]

By agents and overseers, however, the slave was regarded mainly as an agricultural implement. The agents were usually paid by a percentage of the profits, and at this time they and the English mortgagees were out to make quick returns.[2] They worked the slaves to death. There was a tremendous decrease in the slave population between 1817 and 1829 and in the main the figures showed that the decrease was greatest in the colonies where the production of sugar per slave was greatest.[3] This fact persuaded many who had thought of emancipation as something belonging to the remote future that immediate action was necessary.

There were some misstatements in the flood of emancipation pamphlets that spread into all parts of Britain, but Zachary Macaulay was very careful in checking his facts. The horrible things which he published in the *Anti-Slavery Reporter* and fed to his team of parliamentary speakers were things that really happened in the West Indies and most of them could not have been perpetrated, or perpetrated unpunished, except under slavery. The lady who had all of her slaves flogged every Monday morning because she thought that was good for them may have been somewhat unique in her habits, but many of the overseers had worse practices. After all allowances are made, the conclusion of Professor MacInnes, who made a careful study of the whole situation, seems clear enough: 'Life on a Jamaica sugar plantation was one of the hardest and cruellest that human beings have ever been compelled to bear.'[4]

The local legislatures who blocked so stubbornly amelioration as well as emancipation were not, strictly speaking, planter assemblies. They represented, for the most part, a piebald population of 'managers, overseers, self-created lawyers, self-education physicians, and adventurous merchants' of mediocre ability and less character.[5] Many of the judges were more ignorant than learned in the law.

[1] *Anti-Slavery Reporter*, i. 5. An account in *Quarterly Review*, Oct. 1825, quoted from *British Press*, 2 May, is slightly different.
[2] L. J. Ragatz, *Absentee Landlordism in the British Caribbean, 1750–1833* (1931), reprinted from *Agricultural History*, v, 9 Jan. 1931.
[3] The figures are given in Hill, p. 143.
[4] MacInnes, pp. 86, 120.   [5] Ragatz, *Absentee Landlordism*, p. 15.

In an *Edinburgh Review* article in February 1826 Brougham supported a pamphlet of Stephen's in suggesting a new line of policy. The time for public feeling to express itself effectively was at elections, and the friends of the slaves should vote only for candidates who were *pledged* to abolish slavery. That required organization. There was not time before the election of 1826, but a beginning was made in the election of 1830, and when the Emancipation Act was passed in 1833, it was not because of zeal on the part of Whig ministers (with the exception of Grey, Brougham, and a few others) but because of pressure from the constituencies, pressure not only of feeling but of *pledged* members of Parliament.

On 1 May (1826) Canning made a statement to the House of Commons describing the legislation passed by the West Indian legislatures since the British Government dispatches of 1823. Brougham followed on the same subject and the two speeches were so divergent that it could hardly be supposed that they were discussing the same situation.[1] Zachary Macaulay believed that Canning had been wilfully supplied with false information by Wilmot Horton, Under-Secretary for the Colonies, who was a slave-owner.[2] Two days later Brougham moved for a return of the provisions of acts passed 'by the legislatures of the slave colonies since 15th May, 1823'.[3]

The return was analysed by Zachary Macaulay in the *Anti-Slavery Reporter*, but Brougham's analysis in the *Edinburgh Review* for December 1826, following closely the proposals of the 1823 dispatch from the Colonial Office, was more satisfactory. It would have been improved if the return had been examined in the light of the slave population of each of the colonies affected. Proceeding in that manner, the following conclusions may be drawn. In relation to religious instruction, nothing had been done except for the abolition of Sunday markets by one colony, which benefited a little over 2 per cent. of the slave population of the colonies reported. On the admissibility of slave evidence, while there was some trifling legislation there was no compliance with the terms of the dispatch. One colony, however, passed legislation that was perhaps as good as that indicated in the

---

[1] *Hansard*, N.S., xix. 973 seq.
[2] Brougham MSS., Z. Macaulay to Brougham, 4 Mar. 1828.
[3] *Hansard*, N.S., xiv. 1082.

dispatch, benefiting a little more than 2 per cent. of the slave population of the colonies reported. Three colonies (including Jamaica) did something, though not enough, to establish legal marriage of slaves, which benefited 68 per cent. of the slave population of the colonies reported. The dispatch had called for the removal of all unnecessary obstacles to manumission, and with that there was no compliance, nor was there any in regard to the separation of husbands and wives. One colony complied with regard to the separation of children under fourteen from their parents which benefited less than 2 per cent. of the slave population of the colonies reported. There was no compliance with the careful provisions of the dispatch in relation to the punishment of male slaves, no abolition of the flogging of female slaves, and no establishment of savings banks for slaves.

On 10 May 1827 Wilberforce wrote to Brougham: 'We are in circumstances in which you, under Providence, have become our mainstay.' This was unfair to Zachary Macaulay, no doubt, but Brougham now sat among the mighty and Wilberforce hoped that he might be able to wield direct personal influence on ministers. 'I cannot but indulge the hope', Wilberforce went on, 'that Providence may have augmented your influence with the present administration for the very purpose of enabling you to counteract the fatal hostility which self interest is able to generate even in such men as those to whom I allude. . . . May it please God to bless you both in counsel and in action, and to render you the instrument of delivering such a mass of human beings from a worse than Egyptian bondage.'[1] But in a little over three months Canning was dead; the Goderich government could do little but hang on for a troubled four months and did not even meet Parliament. Then Wellington and his Tory government came in, and Brougham's influence waned.

Before Canning's death, however, Lushington, supported by Brougham, brought the disabilities of the 'people of colour' (the mixed race) in the West Indies to the attention of Parliament and at the same time Brougham had an article on the subject in the *Edinburgh Review* for June 1827. People of colour could not serve on juries, hold public office, or exercise the electoral franchise. In the following year the disabilities were removed in the Crown colonies by Orders in Council, and in 1830 and

[1] Brougham MSS., 10 May 1827.

1831 they disappeared in Jamaica, Barbados, Dominica, and Tobago.[1]

Brougham made another anti-slavery speech in Parliament on 5 March, again insisting that the island legislatures were doing next to nothing and that Parliament must act.[2] Then his health broke, and for much of 1828 Macaulay, Brougham, and Buxton were all incapacitated by illness. In July Zachary Macaulay wrote to Brougham: 'I fear from the tone of your letter that your health still droops. . . . If there be any prayer I am more disposed to prefer with fervour to Him with whom are the issues of life than another at the present moment, it is that He may restore to you your capacity of usefulness and strength for the various services to mankind which seem almost to hang on your influence and exertion.'[3] With many men the full sincerity of that might be questioned. But not with Zachary Macaulay.

---

[1] *Anti-Slavery Reporter*, v. 222, cited in Mathieson, p. 195.
[2] *Hansard*, N.S., xviii. 979 seq.
[3] Brougham MSS., 16 July 1828.

CHAPTER XVI

Political and Personal, 1826–9

IN the session of Parliament that began on 2 February 1826
Canning and Brougham got along like two affectionate
brothers. Canning did not fail to express to his friends his
gratitude to the Opposition for their support. 'Their conduct
and particularly that of Mr. Brougham has been in the highest
degree honourable and praiseworthy.'[1] Lord John Russell wrote
to Tom Moore: 'Brougham is not so brilliant as usual. Very
moderate and conciliatory. But a man who pounces and claws
like an eagle cannot coo like a dove.'[2]

The Corn Laws caused considerable discussion, though the
Government was averse to plunging into such a matter so late
in the session. Huskisson particularly emphasized the need of
study and careful thought and promised full consideration next
session. Brougham urged that immediate consideration would
have a steadying rather than a disturbing influence in the acute
distress of that year which had followed the crash of 1825.

The present system was never intended as a final arrangement.
. . . It was now time to get rid of what had been called the sliding
duties and repeal the prohibitions, permitting the ports to be open,
only laying on such a protecting duty as would enable the agricul-
turalist to grow his produce on such terms as to stand the conflict
with the foreign grower. . . . Repealing them [the Corn Laws] would
give permanent and steady prices, lowering rents but preventing
fluctuations in them.[3]

On 25 April Brougham gave vigorous support to a Bill
introduced by George Lamb to permit counsel to address the
jury in cases of prosecution for felony. The jury might be
addressed on behalf of those accused of a misdemeanour or
treason, but not in cases of felony, in which counsel might assist

---

[1] A. G. Stapleton, *Political Life of Canning*, 3 vols. (1831), iii. 44, quoted in
Aspinall, p. 137.

[2] *Early Correspondence of Lord John Russell*, 2 vols. (1913), 23 Feb. 1826.

[3] *Hansard*, N.S., xv. 367 seq.

the accused only by examining, cross-examining and arguing points of law as they occurred during the trial. As the law stood at that time, counsel for the prosecution addressed the jury but in so doing he was permitted only to make a statement of facts, and it was the duty of the judge to prevent him from going beyond that. In theory, counsel for the prosecution was to be equally fair to both sides of the case and it was the duty of the judge to give special protection to the accused; it was frequently said that the judge was the prisoner's counsel. The Attorney-General, in opposing Lamb's Bill, argued that the effect of allowing counsel to speak for the defence would be to convert the court into an arena where opposing advocates might meet in professional conflict, 'each fighting for a victory', as they did in civil cases. Tindal said: 'The first objection was . . . that the immediate consequence of this must be a change in the character of the counsel for the prosecution, who, instead of being, as now, a minister of justice, would become the advocate of a party. . . . He would naturally be induced to bring all his talents into play for the purpose of ensuring a conviction. . . . Men of the first talent in the profession could not, except in very few instances, be retained by the prisoner, because he could not go to that expense.' On the other hand, the accused would be faced by counsel of great ability, who would then be out to convict him. Scarlett, in supporting the measure emphasized the importance of obtaining an adequate interpretation of circumstantial evidence. Brougham insisted that practice was not, and could not be, in harmony with theory; in many cases prosecuting counsel *did* speak *against* the accused. There should be someone to 'unravel' the complexities of the prosecution counsel's speech. When the prisoner was poor, and particularly when he was both poor and uneducated, his chance of obtaining substantial justice was cruelly limited under the existing system. 'There was no man who visited our criminal courts, who did not see the fearful odds against a prisoner; a counsel speaking against him and no one who could speak for him.' The system left altogether too much to the personal element in prosecuting counsel and in judges.[1]

It was noteworthy that the two leading advocates of the Northern Circuit supported this measure, but on reading their speeches one is struck by a contrast. Scarlett was coolly con-

[1] *Hansard*, N.S., xv. 589 seq.

cerned with an efficient operation of the courts, while Brougham's approach, as usual, was strongly and directly humanitarian. The attitude of both was admirable but there was at least a difference of temperament and essential drive. The Bill was defeated in a thin House by 105 to 36. A similar measure was passed and the new system installed in 1837.

The general election of 1826 was a strange one. Many of the Whigs supported liberal Tory candidates or withdrew opposition to them, and liberal Tories acted in a similar manner toward liberal Whigs. Catholic Emancipation was an issue everywhere, irrespective of party. Palmerston would have failed to carry his Tory seat at Cambridge in the face of Tory candidates who ran against him and the opposition to Catholic Emancipation which he favoured, if he had not been saved by Whig votes. He managed to carry the second seat but his experience made him a stronger Canningite, and a few years later a strong Whig when the Whig–Canningite union was completed (1830). For some years the liberal Whig Canningite alliance had been in preparation but the marks of that preparation had never been as clearly in evidence as in 1826. Brougham had done more than anyone to bring it about, partly from his own sincere liberalism and partly from his design of splitting the Tory party.

Brougham in this election fought the Lowthers in Westmorland for the third time. Again the Westmorland election occupied a considerable amount of space in the news and editorial columns of *The Times*, partly because of Brougham's supreme popularity and the interest of the nation in everything he did, and partly also because of his influence on *The Times*. Frequent eulogies of Brougham in *The Times* editorials of this period are not quoted here because they were to a great degree inspired, directly or indirectly, by Brougham himself.

On 17 February 1827 Lord Liverpool suffered the apoplectic stroke that put an end to his political life. Speculation was feverish for nearly two months on the question of who would succeed him as Prime Minister and how the ministry would be reconstructed, while a great deal of political history hung on the answers. Professor Aspinall has given such full and convincing accounts of the events of the months that followed that we need not enter here on that long and complicated story, but rather content ourselves with a brief survey of the part played by

Brougham.[1] While the King and his ministers played for time, a number of the Whigs made their general attitude to Canning known immediately. Canning was from the beginning the favourite in the betting and there was a feeling that if he were Prime Minister a number of the ultra-Tories would not support him. Brougham saw the Canning–Whig coalition, for which he had been hoping and working for years, as an imminent possibility. Within two or three days of Liverpool's stroke there was a meeting of Whigs, probably those closest to Lansdowne in the Lords and to Brougham in the Commons. The consensus of opinion was conveyed to Littleton, the friend of Canning, in order that he might pass it on to Canning. They were prepared to support him even if he did not bring Whigs into his government or undertake to arrange a settlement of the Catholic claims. If Canning became Prime Minister it would be 'a great advantage to the principles they hold in common with yourself'. Brougham, according to Littleton's letter to Canning, 'was not able to attend, being engaged in court at the time', but he had been heard to express 'the same sentiments and feeling toward yourself'.

It is altogether likely, however, that Brougham had been very much more active than this statement would suggest. *The Times* was then strongly under his influence. On the morning of the 20th there appeared an editorial in *The Times* which was almost certainly inspired by Brougham and may well have been written by him. After urging the importance to the nation of Canning being Prime Minister, the editorial continued:

It is more peculiarly thought from the general liberality of principle evinced by Mr. Canning that an union with the Marquis of Lansdowne might be accomplished, that nobleman stipulating only for the ministerial support of the Catholic question, and not rendering the admission of many of his friends *a sine qua non*. His friends also, it is said, that is the Whigs as a body, are ready to make this sacrifice of personal aggrandizement to public principle.[2]

Before leaving for the Northern Circuit early in March,

---

[1] Articles by Aspinall in *English Historical Review*, 1927, pp. 201 seq., 533 seq.; Aspinall, *The Formation of Canning's Ministry* (1937). Since the brief account given here is based very largely on Aspinall's treatments and the documents published by him, and he cites authorities with great care, I am in this section giving authorities only in the few cases where I have used other sources.

[2] *The Times*, 20 Feb. 1827.

Brougham was assured that no selection of a Prime Minister would be made for some time. He had instructed his friend Sir Robert Wilson to assure Canning of his (Brougham's) support without expectation of office for himself, thus relieving Canning of difficulty with the King, who would be strongly opposed to the idea of Brougham in office. Five days after arriving at Lancaster, Brougham felt that he was in the dark and had become a little afraid of it. He wrote to Wilson on 18 March:

I have as yet heard nothing from you. Is it possible Canning can dream of *safety* for six weeks if he thinks of taking office with the Ultras and no arrangement? Or is it possible he could doubt of *our* entire and cordial support if he holds out? For my own part I will only say that I am ready to back him in whatever way he himself would deem most effectual. It is our duty and we shall all be found at our posts. But so should we [against him] if he were to give in and throw his good principles over.

There was no intention of *showing* that letter to Canning, and Wilson sent it to his son, who was an aide-de-camp to General Bolivar, because Brougham had included at the end of it a message to 'the Liberator', urging him for the sake of his fame and his country to enrol himself in the 'new order of Teachers of Mankind' and give his best attention to the forming of a South American branch of the Society for the Diffusion of Useful Knowledge. Lord Erskine had been established as an inter-mediary between Canning and Wilson, and Canning asked if Erskine might see Brougham's letter.[3] Since Wilson did not have the letter, he gave Erskine a very free translation of it, but what he said was in harmony with Brougham's instructions to him on leaving London; he did not fail to emphasize Brougham's 'disinterestedness'. Wilson consulted Lord Lansdowne before sending his letter off to Erskine, and Lansdowne after reading it said that Brougham had often expressed those sentiments to him and that they were 'in perfect unison' with his own. Wilson then asked Brougham to write him another letter which could be shown to Canning. Brougham did so on the 26th. The substantial parts of the letter ran as follows:

. . . Among those hopes [for a liberal government] the greater part

---

[1] The endorsement on Wilson's letter to Erskine, 25 Mar. 1827, Add. MSS. 30111, f. 284, indicates that the request was made 'by Canning's desire'.

are certainly at the time connected with Canning, in whom and Robinson and Huskisson I place very great confidence. . . . I can answer for the most cordial disposition toward him [Canning] by all he needs to care about, as soon as they are thoroughly convinced he is disposed to risk what he ought in order to do his duty and obtain his just rights. As to his difficulties on his own side, they are comprised in one word, Peel. . . . We may think him an ordinary man and far inferior to Canning, yet we respect him and value the victories he has gained over his prejudices. . . . In truth the Catholic Emancipation question (on which Peel has always been a fair adversary) is the only point of very great difference. . . . My support will be all the more effective that it will be wholly disinterested. . . . I know there are very unworthy, womanish prejudices in certain quarters [the King] and I dont wish to thwart them. But moreover I am far better pleased to be out of office. I have (I know full well) a very considerable influence in the country which would be injured by taking office, and I like to use it for purposes which you must in office rather laugh at than assist.

On the day Brougham wrote that, Lansdowne wrote to him:

C[anning] goes to the cottage to-morrow as I understand, to bring himself to the point. Whether he has brought himself to the point I do not know, but . . . partly in consequence of a letter of yours, the substance of which has been and was of course intended to be stated to C, . . . a great anxiety was expressed yesterday to ascertain my sentiments and probable line of conduct under certain contingencies. I have pledged myself to nothing . . . but took the opportunity of insisting as strongly as I feel it on the unequivocal recognition of power and the subsequent use of it with a direct view to the prosecution of those objects on which everything must ultimately hinge.[1]

The point to which Canning would or would not bring himself was, of course, to tell the King that so far as he was concerned, it was *aut Caesar aut nullus*. He did not see the King until the 28th, by which time he had received Brougham's letter and it had strengthened his hand. On the 20th, after discussing with the King various impossibilities, Canning made his plunge and with all the firmness in the world stated that he would resign if he were not Prime Minister or had 'the substantive power of First Minister'. On 10 April Canning was authorized to form a government with the request that all of the existing ministers

---

[1] Brougham MSS., 26 Mar. 1827.

should be asked to remain; Catholic Emancipation was to continue to be an open question. Canning had expected that Wellington, Peel, and Eldon would not serve under him, but he had not foreseen the resignation of half the Cabinet and, in all, over forty resignations of men holding government office. His party support in the Commons was so weakened that the new Government could be kept alive only by Whig votes. Canning immediately turned to the Whigs, as Brougham had always hoped that he would. Within a few days negotiations were opened with Lansdowne, who was then acting as leader of the Whig party. The negotiations encountered serious difficulty from the beginning and on 20 April they were broken off. Some of Lord Lansdowne's group felt that the Whigs should be admitted to a coalition government as a party and not as individuals, others that Lansdowne should be government leader in the Lords, and there were various other topics of dissent. Lansdowne himself insisted that the Government of Ireland must be 'Catholic', with both Lord Lieutenant and Secretary favourable to the Catholic claims. Since the resignations had carried good 'Protestants' out of the Cabinet and the reconstructed Cabinet had come to have a 'Catholic' preponderance of nine to three, the King felt that partially to restore the balance, Lord Lieutenant and Secretary should both be 'Protestants'. Canning stood by that and neither he nor Lansdowne would give way.

A few hours before the breakdown occurred, Brougham wrote to Althorp: 'A greater or more ruinous error never was yet committed, or one more fatal to the Catholic question, than by holding out on subordinate points and punctilios of honour, to throw open again the Cabinet to the ultra-Tories. If we drive Canning to it he must yield to *them*, and then what becomes of Ireland and liberal principles?'

Within a few hours of the breakdown and the apparent abandonment of a coalition, Brougham and Wilson hastily called a meeting at Brooks's Club. Although Brooks's was the great Whig club, the gathering does not seem to have been a meeting of the club and it was not a party meeting. It was simply a meeting of Whigs, some leaders and mostly rank and file who were brought together to consider the matter. It was said to be a meeting of 'angry men'. Certainly its leaders were angry.

Wilson tended to be hot-headed. Brougham's remarkable gift for anger was exceeded only by his gift for conveying anger to others. There is no adequate account of Brougham's speech but he was probably as powerful as in his best House of Commons speeches. When he sat down the coalition was saved.

A delegation was sent from the meeting to Lord Lansdowne. The Whig grape-vine must have been overburdened that night and 'the rebellion' spread. Many servants must have called at Lansdowne House with notes late in the night and early in the morning. Lord Lansdowne had to go to Bowood next day, but before he went he wrote to Lord Holland: 'I am overwhelmed with letters reproaching me in friendly, of course, but strong terms for making the difficulty I did about the I[rish] Govt.' But he was not prepared to make any concession. 'How can I write and retract? . . . I will support Govt. I will recommend those who think they can take office to do so, I will listen fairly to any fresh proposition that can be made, but I confess with an earnest wish to keep *out*.' He asked Lord Holland to come into town and defend the position he had taken and Lord Holland replied that he would do so. 'I think however that the negotiation will be, in spite of you, revived.' William Lamb (later Lord Melbourne) wrote to Canning that he had seen Lansdowne the previous night and that the latter had said the negotiation was entirely at an end. But after that he had gone to Brooks's and heard about the rebellion. 'It might have been different if he [Lansdowne] had taken a little more pains beforehand to ascertain the opinions of those with whom he was acting.'

So Canning was not surprised when the Duke of Devonshire and Lord Carlisle on behalf of the Whigs reopened negotiations with him on the 21st. Brougham wrote jubilantly to Creevey: 'The negotiation is on again to-day with a fair prospect of success. . . . My principle is—*anything* to lock the door for ever on Eldon and Co.,' the anti-Canning Tories. That same day Brougham said to Jack Campbell ('very truly', as Campbell remarked): 'My support in the House of Commons is of much more importance than Lansdowne's in the House of Lords.' Four days later Brougham said to Campbell in characteristic fashion: 'I shall hate the word *negotiation* for the rest of my life. I could have got better terms for them in half an hour than they have been haggling about so long.'[1] Brougham kept in close touch with the Duke of Devonshire. Since he had no part in the negotiation we have only to record its ultimate success, with Lord Lansdowne and two other Whigs joining the Cabinet and several Whigs being appointed to the ministry outside the Cabinet. Professor Aspinall, who has so carefully examined this whole subject, has written: 'But for Brougham's rebelliousness, the Coalition would certainly never have been formed.' It is difficult to say just what would have happened if Brougham had not headed a rebellion, but certainly history took a sharp turn at high speed that night at Brooks's.

Fortunately there was no break in the friendly personal relations between Brougham and Lansdowne, and, when Lansdowne died in 1863, Brougham could write of 'sixty-seven years intimacy in all relations publick and private without a single word of dissension'.[2] The sixty-seven years, of course, went back to the time when they were fellow students at the University of Edinburgh. In his *Memoirs* Brougham wrote: 'There was never a more amiable or virtuous man in any party, or any political station, than Lord Lansdowne; and I believe no man ever went through a long course of party strife with so little detriment to his principles and his feelings. He possessed great prudence and calmness of judgment . . . and was as thoroughly honest and humble as a man can be.'[3]

There is another significant aspect of Brougham's 'rebellion'. Lord Lansdowne had vetoed an earlier suggestion of a party meeting. Lord Holland spoke of 'the unjustifiable step at Brooks's' (on the evening of 20 April) and 'never was so scandalous a step as that of Brooks's'. Lord Duncannon thought that the discussion of such matters should be confined to Lansdowne House and Burlington House. And Lord Essex protested against a meeting '*at a club* to settle a business of this nature. . . . Devonshire House, Bedford House, and Lansdowne or Burlington House are the places where men of high principles and character should be assembled to form an endeavour to advise their sovereign of matters in which the country is so deeply involved'. To that attitude Brougham was irrevocably opposed. It must be

---

[1] Hardcastle, i. 440, 443, Campbell to his brother George, 22, 25 Apr. 1827.
[2] Lansdowne MSS., Brougham to Shelburne, 4 July 1863.
[3] *Memoirs*, ii. 490.

always borne in mind that, in the most literal sense of that phrase, he had no use for aristocratic government. He wished to broaden the basis of government in the nation and he had to work for that end in a party where, after Romilly's death, with the exception of Tierney, all the leaders except himself belonged to the aristocracy, and where, too, he had become personally fond of the heads of the great families. He felt that the basis of government must be broadened within the party as well as in the nation. He realized that negotiation must be *conducted* by a few men, but at the point where negotiation was being broken off and a critical decision was being made for the party, he called in the party to control the situation, in what everyone described as a 'rebellion'.

Tierney said (on 1 May) that Brougham was writing *The Times* editorials relating to the coalition project. It is very probable that he wrote an editorial in *The Times* of 16 April shortly before the negotiation had broken down. It assumed that Canning and the King were contending against the high aristocracy in the Tory party, and deprecated the part played by the great families in both parties. They should be made to realize that the government of the country was vested by law not in the great families but in King, Lords, and Commons. The meeting at Brooks's came four days later. Brougham may or may not have known that about a week earlier Canning had said to the King that his father had broken the domination of the Whigs (meaning the Whig aristocracy); would he endure that of the Tories? And the King had replied without hesitation: 'No, I'm damned if I do.' And that was before the Tory resignations had roused the King's wrath.

Canning's coalition government purported to be an alliance of the liberals of both parties. That fact in itself helped to hasten the day when the Whig–Canningite union became a permanent one, and it contributed to the liberal triumphs of the early thirties. But those lines were not drawn as sharply in the Whig party as in the Tory party. There were few Whigs as liberal as the Duke of Bedford and Althorp, but the Duke was opposed throughout and Althorp was doubtful for some time before he gave a hesitating support. There were other liberal Whigs who drew back, while among the mass of the Government's Whig supporters in the Commons there were many who could hardly be called liberals but were keenly interested in the share of patronage that would come to the Whigs. Lord Grey said that he would not 'go into opposition' but expressed himself strongly against the coalition as it actually took shape. He would not have served under Canning in any case. His prejudice against Canning was deep-rooted. On other grounds Grey commands our sympathy, though not our agreement. Admittedly he had turned over the active leadership of the party to Lansdowne, but he had been leader for so long that he should at least have been fully consulted. Ellice said that a letter went astray, but that in itself cannot excuse the manner in which Lansdowne, Brougham, and the others neglected Lord Grey throughout. Grey's position was that a *real* coalition, with the Whigs entering as a party with a recognition of equal rights, would have been justified, but that Canning, who had been at the mercy of the Whigs, paid a cheap price with three Cabinet posts and any-thing but equal treatment for the support of a great party and the almost solid array of Whig votes in the House of Commons. And much of Grey's blame fell on Brougham.

One of the things that irritated Grey was Brougham's talk of his 'disinterestedness'. Brougham wrote that word into practic-ally all of his letters to everyone and he saw to it that it was splashed across the editorial page of *The Times*. His offer of full support to Canning, though he would not expect office on account of the King's feelings, had strengthened Canning's hand and probably helped him with the King, though when Canning reported to him Brougham's letter of 26 March all that the King said was 'very well'.[1] Brougham knew that so long as George IV lived he would never admit him to the Cabinet, not so much on account of the Queen's Trial as because of the eight years that had preceded it. So in that respect the disinterested-ness was cheap. And Brougham hoped that the new government would give him a high legal appointment. Six days after Canning took office Brougham wrote to his brother that he expected to be Attorney-General.[2] He could take that and remain in the House of Commons. But the Attorney-General was in a special sense the legal adviser of the Crown, and the King would not have Brougham in such a position. Scarlett became Attorney-

---

General, and the position of Master of the Rolls, which Brougham
would probably have accepted (though he denied it), went to
Leach when Copley was appointed Lord Chancellor as Lord
Lyndhurst. So Brougham continued to talk about being 'disinterested'. And that in spite of the fact that his friends so
pestered Canning about doing something for Brougham that
Canning was said to have burst out with 'Damn him, he shall
have my place'.

Finally, in July, Canning offered to make him Chief Baron
of the Exchequer. It meant the headship of one of the three
great Common Law Courts and carried a salary of £7,000 a
year. Brougham was not making that much in his practice. But
it was said that Scarlett being made Attorney-General and
being removed from the Northern Circuit would be worth
£2,000 a year to Brougham, and in the few remaining years in
which he was a practising barrister he earned £7,000 to £8,000
per annum. If he were Chief Baron he would be moved from
the House of Commons. Canning and Lyndhurst tried hard to
induce him to accept. One or other of them said that from that
office he would be able to go to the end of the road of judicial
honours, which, of course, meant the Lord Chancellorship.
'That is all very well,' replied Brougham, 'but you do not leave
me the horses to carry me on.' Brougham's horses were in the
House of Commons.

The King had in May relented to the extent of allowing him
to acquire at last his silk gown, but that was possibly only
because Lyndhurst was Lord Chancellor in place of Eldon. The
situation had been an absurd one. There had been only one
King's Counsel on the Northern Circuit—Scarlett. Brougham
said that silk was of no use to him now. He had done too well
without it. He said that he accepted only for the sake of his
seniors at the Bar who could now act under his lead if he wore
silk. The King said that he was not to kiss hands, at which
Brougham fumed so publicly that Wilson rebuked him. After he
had his patent of precedence, at the opening of the Circuit he
wore his old stuff gown for a few days, which of course was a
petty piece of play acting.

Canning died on 8 August and was succeeded by Robinson,
who had become Lord Goderich. While there is much to be
said for 'Prosperity' Robinson in British history, there is little or

nothing to be said for 'Goody' Goderich, under whose incapacity
for such a post the coalition died a lingering death. Brougham
took the position that nothing should be allowed to endanger
the coalition, but he did not have much influence on the disastrous
course of the Goderich ministry.

Lansdowne in a letter of 6 September charged Brougham, in
a friendly manner, with having been inconsistent in regard to
the appointment of Herries as Chancellor of the Exchequer.
Yet Brougham's attitude was consistent throughout. The King
had been urgent about the appointment of Herries, and the
Whig ministers had been opposed to it because Herries was
anti-Catholic and leaned to ultra-Toryism. There were also
suspicions about the way he had made his money and rumours
of a dishonest use of a previous office. Brougham wrote from the
Northern Circuit to Wilson, the Duke of Devonshire, and Lansdowne, and said some harsh things about Herries, but there
was no suggestion in the letters that the appointment should
be opposed *at all costs*.[1] Certainly there is no indication that
Brougham would have approved of their resigning and destroying the coalition over the Herries affair. Yet that is precisely
what they decided to do and then suspended action until
Huskisson returned from the Continent.

On 1 September, on account of the Herries appointment,
Lansdowne presented his resignation to the King, but the King
persuaded him to withdraw it. Brougham wrote to the Duke of
Devonshire on the 5th, highly pleased that they had escaped
disaster and praising the conduct of the King. 'I regard the
present arrangement as essential to the good government of this
country and the peace of Ireland.'[2] And he wrote to Lansdowne,
probably in reply to the latter's charge of inconsistency in his
letter of the 6th: 'Many will be doubting whether you have
ground for resigning. . . . My objections to H[erries] were very
truly, as you said, great and strong. The stock business required
to be cleared up, and his hostility to the liberals, his Lowther
and ultra habits were very distasteful. But it is one thing to say
"Dont take H. if you can possibly help it" and another thing
to say break up the government rather than take him.'[3] He
wrote again to the Duke of Devonshire on the 11th: 'I perfectly

---

[1] The letters are quoted in Aspinall, pp. 156–8.   [2] Chatsworth MSS.
[3] Lansdowne MSS., 'Monday', probably 10 Sept.

agree with you that Lord Lansdowne and Huskisson must be urged to treat the King with as much confidence as he deserves, which is a great deal. . . . I know you are discreet as the Cavendishes are famed for being.'[1]

Canning had been dead a month. It needed only another three months and a half for the Coalition Government to break itself up not through any lack of agreement on policy but through blunders, tangles, and lack of competent leadership. The coalition had been built on Canning. In supporting Canning the Whigs, or most of them, had found an unaccustomed unity and now they reverted to their old disunity, dissatisfied with Lansdowne's leadership but finding leadership nowhere else and disappointed with their small share of patronage. The King made appointments and distributed patronage in an unusual manner, excusing himself for being his own Prime Minister by the utter incompetence of the man who was supposed to be Prime Minister. When Goderich finally went out the King looked around for a new Prime Minister who possessed strength of character and some conception of how government should be carried on. He chose the one man who seemed to him to be adequate to the situation. The Duke of Wellington took office early in January with instructions to form 'a comprehensive government' and to include two Whigs specifically, Lansdowne and Carlisle, who refused to act. There was again a Tory government with Canningites and Ultras or semi-Ultras sharing almost equally the Cabinet posts (and Peel who was neither).

Some time before this Brougham had had an unfortunate experience with 'Dandy' Raikes, a man who had walked into Brooks's where he was a member but seldom appeared, stood with his back to the fire and addressed Brougham. According to Creevey he said, 'Mr. Brougham, I am very much obliged to you for the speech you made at my expense. I don't know what latitude you gentlemen of the Bar consider yourselves entitled to, but I am come here purposely to insult you in the presence of your club.' According to Wilson, Raikes said 'that he meant to do all that he could to insult him out of [an illegible word] professional privilege, and that if ever Brougham spoke to him again he would insult him personally'. Brougham, who was eating a meal, said that Raikes had chosen a strange time and

[1] Chatsworth MSS.

place, but that he understood him and would see that he got his answer. Spring Rice (a prominent Whig and later a member of three Whig cabinets) hurried out and as fast as possible went to Bow Street police station to inform the police that they might take measures to prevent the duel. Brougham, without knowing that, left to find Ferguson and ask him to act as his second. Ferguson refused and he went to Sir Robert Wilson, who consented to act and sent the challenge to Raikes. Wilson waited some time for Brougham to return, which he did under custody of a police officer. Brougham had been arrested, had apparently been locked up for a few hours, and had been bound over to keep the peace. The Lord Chief Justice, to prevent them fighting in France, issued an order binding Brougham under heavy penalty not to leave the country.

The Times of 12 March said: 'We may here state that the speech which gave occasion to the quarrel was declared by Mr. Scarlett, Mr. Raikes's counsel, not to have exceeded the just limits of professional licence; and that Mr. Raikes himself is reported to have viewed the matter in the same light till a contrary conviction was impressed upon him by certain persons in whose minds Mr. Brougham's caustic vituperation of the morals of fashionable life had excited equal resentment and dismay.' That, of course, was Brougham's own defence and as such is subject to suspicion, but we may accept Wilson's statement in a private letter to Lord Grey that Scarlett had told him 'upon his honour that Brougham had said nothing in court that could justify any offence being taken and that the whole Bar would be of the same opinion. . . . He [Raikes] suffered twelve days to pass before he took this step.' Three days after the scene at Brooks's the club demanded that Raikes apologize to Brougham, which he did.[1]

A young barrister, Thomas Babington Macaulay, wrote to his father in September, giving an account of the contest for the lead of the Northern Circuit, now that Scarlett was no longer there. He was probably an admirer of Brougham at that time, but in any case, knowing of his father's friendship, he would be sure that Zachary Macaulay would wish to know of Brougham's success.

[1] Creevey Papers, ii. 106–8; Add. MSS. 30124, ff. 254 seq.; The Times, 12 Mar. 1827.

Perhaps you will be pleased to hear that Brougham has been rising through the whole of this struggle. At York, Pollock decidedly took the lead. At Durham, Brougham overtook him, passed him at Newcastle, and got immensely ahead of him at Carlisle and Appleby, which, to be sure are the places where his own connections lie. . . . If he continues to manage causes as well as he has done of late he must rise to the summit of the profession. I cannot say quite so much for his temper, which this close and constant rivalry does not improve. He squabbles with Pollock more than in generosity or policy, he ought to do. . . . The other day Pollock laid down a point of law rather dogmatically. 'Mr. Pollock', said Brougham, 'perhaps before you rule the point, you will suffer his Lordship to submit a few observations on it to your consideration.'[1]

Brougham was very popular on the Circuit. Younger men everywhere and always, unless they had crossed or been crossed by him in some serious manner, always liked him and were devoted to him. Here, on Circuit, their elders shared the feeling with what appears to have been a rare unanimity. He had been going the Circuit now for a good many years and they had got to know him well. He indulged his sarcasm in all directions and he frequently lost his temper in court. But they took him as he was and they liked him. Just after Macaulay wrote that letter they crowned Henry Brougham, at Lancaster, King Henry IX, and they knew no better than we do whether they were crowning him king of the Circuit or king of their hearts. It was a grand occasion. All the trappings of a coronation were prepared with glee, and all the functionaries were mimicked from an archbishop to the humblest official. After the king was duly crowned, chosen members of the Bar were knighted and invested in all the magnificence of a new Order, the Knights of St. Henry. An ode appropriate to the occasion and scintillating with the best humour that could be mustered was read by a poet laureate, and in all probability the king was the best entertainer of them all.[2] Next day they were back to the winning and losing of cases. Though Scarlett was now out of the running Brougham was still up against strong competition and according to Jack Campbell, Pollock was winning more cases than he was.

A celebrated remark about Brougham by Samuel Rogers was recorded by Greville in his diary on 2 January 1828.[3] The con-

[1] Sir G. O. Trevelyan, i. 169-70.   [2] Campbell, viii. 354.
[3] Greville, *Memoirs*, 1899 ed., i. 119 seq.

text, as given in Greville, is also well known and is an important part of what may be called the Brougham legend. It requires examination:

About three weeks ago I passed a few days at Panshanger, where I met Brougham; he came from Saturday till Monday morning and from the hour of his arrival to that of his departure he never ceased talking. . . . Brougham is certainly one of the most remarkable men I ever met; to say nothing of what he is in the world, his almost childish gaiety and animal spirits, his humor mixed with sarcasm, but not ill-natured, his wonderful information, and the facility with which he handles every subject, from the most grave and severe to the most trifling, displaying a mind full of the most varied and extensive information and a memory which has suffered nothing to escape it. I never saw any man whose conversation impressed me with such an idea of his superiority over all others. As Rogers said, the morning of his departure, 'this morning, Solon, Lycurgus, Demosthenes, Archimedes, Sir Isaac Newton, Lord Chesterfield and a great many more went away from Panshanger in one post-chaise'.

That, no doubt, was the impression made on Greville by Brougham's conversation. What Greville actually saw and heard he recorded accurately in his famous journals. But for the facts that lay behind, he is far from reliable.

'After all,' he went on, 'Brougham is only a living and very remarkable instance of the inefficacy of the most splendid talents, unless they are accompanied with other qualities, which scarcely admit of definition, but which serve the same purpose that ballast does for a ship.' Brougham lacked 'ballast', but in view of his great achievements the word 'inefficacy' is absurd. Greville continued: 'Brougham has prospered to a certain degree; he has a great reputation and he makes a considerable income at the bar; but as an advocate he is left behind by men of far inferior capacity, whose names are hardly known beyond the precincts of their courts or the boundaries of their circuits.' The latter statement is untrue. Brougham had run second to Scarlett on the Northern Circuit and at the date of that entry he, at the least, shared the lead with Pollock. Scarlett was the best advocate in England; who were the 'men of far inferior capacity' who had left Brougham behind? If Greville intended to include appointment to the highest judicial offices, which apparently he did not, the King's veto on Brougham's appointment, for purely personal reasons, is the answer, as it is also to Greville's next statement. 'As a statesman he is not considered eligible for the highest offices.' Five years before this Grey had said that no Whig government could be formed unless Brougham were in the Cabinet (see p. 266 above); Althorp was to make exactly the same statement when the Whigs went in three years after this. Greville, moreover, apparently knew nothing of the deep satisfaction which Brougham could feel at this time at the progress of education and of the anti-slavery movement, about which Greville, judging from his many-volumed journal, knew little and cared less. Brougham loved power, but he was quite sincere when he said that the power he most desired was the power of contributing to the welfare of his fellow men.

Brougham's great law-reform speech on 7 February 1828 will be the subject of a later chapter. The other outstanding event of that session was the repeal of the Test and Corporation Acts. It was said at the time and has been repeated in all the books to this day that that was important only because it prepared the way for Catholic Emancipation. From that view Brougham strongly dissented. It was true that for many years the law had been evaded by 'occasional conformity', Dissenters wishing to hold public office being permitted to qualify by taking the sacrament occasionally in the Church of England and by annual indemnity bills covering the breach of the law. But Brougham asked, on 26 February:

Is the *stigma* nothing? Is it nothing that a Dissenter, wherever he goes, is looked on and treated as an inferior person to a Churchman? ... Is it nothing even that the honourable baronet should say, as he has said this night, 'we will allow you to do so and so'. What is it that gives the honourable baronet the title to use this language any more than the member for Norwich[1] but that the *law* encourages and entitles him to use it? The only difference between them is that the honourable baronet conscientiously believes in one faith and my honourable friend, the member for Norwich, in another.

The adherents of one faith had, Brougham argued, no *moral* right to permit the believers in another faith to hold office and enter Parliament on the condition of evading the law, or to evade it for them by passing acts of indemnity. All through his

---

[1] William Smith, a Dissenter, prominent in the anti-slavery movement.

life Brougham hated the word *toleration*, which was an insult in itself. What he pleaded for passionately on all possible occasions was religious *equality*. He insisted that these arrogant Acts should be removed from the statute books, insulting as they were and inconsistent with any decent conception of human freedom.

But, Brougham continued, there was more to it than arrogance and stigma. The Acts constituted an actual barrier to freedom and to public service. They did not, of course, apply to Presbyterians in Scotland, but they did to Presbyterians in England. Did they resort to occasional conformity? 'Sure I am that not one Presbyterian in a thousand would on any terms take the Sacrament of the Church of England. A strict Presbyterian will not go into a place of worship where there is an organ; he will on no account kneel at an altar.' Men's consciences differed and they had no right to violate the conscience of any man. Many Dissenters felt that they could not conscientiously evade the law by occasional conformity or under the protection of acts indemnifying them for committing a crime. So they did not seek office or try to enter Parliament. If the Acts were repealed, a large number of Dissenters would take part in public life and the nation would be enriched thereby.

At an earlier point in his speech Brougham had expressed his indignation at the sacrilege of making the taking of the Sacrament in a particular place and form a test for office.

I would ask every man, particularly every serious man who has made religion an object of his contemplation and who values it a rush, whether there could, by possibility, be devised a greater impropriety, a more polluting, a more degrading indecency and impropriety, than to make the Sacrament a custom of the constitution and a test of office. It is the most holy rite of our religion, of the purest religion upon earth, of a religion which above all others that all time has seen . . . was the most abhorrent of secular ties, most alien from fleshly purposes . . . and this rite, the most holy of that religion, was by this statute . . . made the passport to the place of a common game-keeper.[1]

The Bill, which had been introduced by Lord John Russell, passed the House of Commons by a majority of forty-four and later passed the House of Lords.

[1] *Hansard*, N.S., xviii. 764 seq.

There had been among the Dissenters a continuous movement for this repeal for some years, delayed by hesitation about the right time to strike for freedom. William Smith was the chairman of their United Committee; Lord John Russell took the lead throughout among the members of the Commons and Lord Holland in the Lords. When the committee interviewed several members of Parliament each day, a whole day was reserved for Brougham, probably because of the importance of his speech in view of his dominant position in the House of Commons and because of his own desire to be as well prepared as possible. After the attainment of final victory there was a sumptuous Dissenters' dinner at which Dr. Cox, who played such an active part in the founding of London University, proposed the toast to the Established Church.[1]

Brougham was not in good health after his labours on the great law-reform speech, and in March there began an illness which lasted until October, though he got through his parliamentary and circuit duties in some fashion.

In the course of a much later correspondence with William Forsyth, the latter wrote in the year 1859 that he believed that he was suffering from an ailment which Brougham had described in writing about Dr. Johnson in his *Lives of Men of Letters*. Brougham in that passage had said: 'I speak with some confidence on a subject which accident has enabled me to study in the case of one with whom I was well acquainted for many years; and who either outlived the malady, which in him was hereditary, or obtained a power over it by constant watchfulness, diligent care, and a fixed resolution to conquer it. As in Johnson's case, it was remittent.' Replying to Forsyth, Brougham wrote: 'My dear friend and fellow-sufferer. I am myself the person alluded to.' This particular disease, as Brougham had described it, rendered every exertion distasteful and difficult.[2] Brougham told Forsyth that at first this affliction had troubled him in the odd years up to and apparently including 1821, but had shifted to the even years 1824, 1826, 1830 and so on. His memory may have become somewhat dimmed in the passing of time, but certainly he was slowed up by illness in 1815, 1817,

---

[1] Bernard Lord Manning, *The Protestant Dissenting Deputies* (1952), pp. 317–53.
[2] *Works*, ii. 317 seq.; *Letters from Lord Brougham to William Forsyth* (1872), p. 49, 13 Sept. 1859.

and 1821. While he included 1826, that was altogether too busy and full a year for such an ailment to have been operative. With *1828* it was different.

From March to October every letter about Brougham or to him speaks of his illness. He went about, he did the routine things that had to be done, and that was all. He wrote nothing for the *Edinburgh Review* after the January number. He was of no use to the anti-slavery movement after March, and he does not seem to have done anything for the Mechanics' Institutes, S.D.U.K., or London University. Depression, hatred of exertion, sluggish mental activity, everything he described in the letter to Forsyth probably was with him then, and what else beside?

On 27 July Denman wrote to James Brougham urging him to join Henry if at all possible. '[A letter] which I received from your brother at York is calculated to make his friends uneasy.' The greater part of Denman's letter is taken up with ordinary health advice. But he thinks that perhaps Brougham should leave the Circuit. 'Our friend Birkbeck thinks the frame has been overworked and that repose is essential. I am sure you might speak with authority at such an important crisis, while I firmly believe that the comfort of your presence would make its occurrence [a sudden breaking off of his work on the Circuit] highly improbable.'[1] Two weeks later, on 14 August, Pollock wrote a short note to Mrs. Brougham: 'I am sorry to disclose to you the very dangerous state of Mr. Brougham's health. He is unwilling to acquaint his friends in London of it and would be highly displeased if he was aware of my informing you. I should think it advisable for you if possible to come here to see him.'[2]

He finished the Circuit and should have had a complete rest at Brougham in September. But he asked Mathew Davenport Hill to come to Brougham to talk over S.D.U.K. affairs. Since he had given them no attention for months, he thought that that was essential. It was the only thing outside of routine that he had done since March. At the end of September it must have been a serious state of affairs and the strictest doctor's orders that kept him away from the opening of London University, something, in fact, that went beyond the Dr.

[1] Brougham MSS., 27 July 1828.
[2] Ibid., 14 Aug. 1828.

Johnson reference.[1] But he wrote the letter to the Council on King's College which he regarded as absolutely necessary. By the end of October he seems to have recovered.

Before his illness began Brougham had been caught out in one of his major lies. He had told Creevey that Lord Grey had said to Lord Cleveland (formerly Lord Darlington) at the Doncaster races that the reason that he had refused to support Canning's government was that 'it leaned too much to the people and against the aristocracy'. Creevey saw to it that Lord Grey was informed of this. Grey and Cleveland both denied that such a conversation took place. Brougham wrote to Cleveland a feeble statement to be forwarded to Grey; it included a reference to mischievous tale-bearers, meaning, of course, Creevey. That naturally aroused Creevey's wrath. Having seen the statement, Creevey in his anger called it 'low, lying, dirty, shuffling villany'.[2] So Brougham had quarrels with both Grey and Creevey on his hands. That was in February. If Brougham had been in a normal state of mind in the months that followed he would undoubtedly have endeavoured to restore his previous good relations with Grey. As it was he did not write to Grey at all until October, when in his usual manner after a quarrel he wrote to him a very friendly letter as though nothing had happened, telling Grey of the good things he had heard about the opening lectures at London University.

Lord Grey replied also as though nothing had happened:

I have received with the greatest pleasure your confirmation of the account I had previously read in the newspapers of the successful opening of London University. It must afford the truest satisfaction to everybody who thinks, as I do, of the public benefit likely to arise from such an institution. But to you it must be peculiarly gratifying for *you* have been the creator of this establishment, and your name will be forever united with the improvements which may spring not only from this, but from the rival college [King's College] which never would have existed but for the success of your exertions.[3]

Their relations were again on the old footing of friendship, and Brougham resumed his frequent visits to Howich. On one of these, we do not know when, they were fording a river on

---

[1] For Brougham's part in the founding of London University see Chapters XIX–XX.   [2] *Creevey Papers*, ii. 149–50.
[3] *Memoirs*, ii. 498–500, 4, 7 Oct. 1828.

horse-back, and Grey, turning in his saddle, shouted, 'Brougham, can you swim?' 'I never have swum', answered Brougham, 'but I have no doubt I could if I tried.'[1]

The passing of Catholic Emancipation in 1829 was inevitable once the Duke of Wellington had made up his mind that it was necessary in order to avert the danger of civil war in Ireland. Brougham spoke in its support with his usual vigour, but there was nothing new to say except to praise Wellington and Peel in the most eloquent terms. Wellington's courage was above all praise as he faced the volleys of bigotry that werc lct loose upon him. 'I have a duty to perform and God direct me in the right way.' One hundred and seventy-three Tory members voted against the Bill in the House of Commons, while Whig support gave it a large majority. Having lost his left wing when the Canningites broke away from him, the Duke now lost a good deal of support on his right. In the last chapter we shall describe the last year of Wellington's government and Brougham's last year in the House of Commons.

[1] G. M. Trevelyan, *Lord Grey of the Reform Bill* (1920), p. 191.

CHAPTER XVII

The March of the Mind: Mechanics' Institutes

ON 22 June 1820, before the beginning of the Queen's Trial, Brougham had introduced a Bill which, by establishing government schools where the number of existing schools was inadequate, would establish a national system of education. That was the goal towards which he and his Education Committee had been working since 1817. According to the terms of Brougham's Bill, the Government was to establish schools in any parish or chapelry in which complaints that there were 'none or no sufficient schools' were confirmed by the justices of the peace. The master of such a government school was to be a member of the Church of England and while he was to be selected by a meeting of ratepayers, the local officiating clergyman might veto the selection, could exercise some superintendance over the work of the appointee, and was required to report on it to the bishop. The bishops in person, or through their diocesan officials, were to exercise a right of visitation and might dismiss the master. The schools were to be supported in part by a local 'school rate'. The Catechism of the Church of England was to be taught in half of one day of each week and also 'at a school meeting on Sunday evening, not exceeding three hours', if the officiating clergyman desired such a meeting. Children might absent themselves from the teaching of the catechism with the permission of their parents or guardians. All pupils were to attend the parish church except those who at the desire of their parents or guardians attended some other place of Christian worship.

It is hardly necessary to comment on the novelty of this plan. It was thirteen years later that the British Government planned to pay its first shilling for education, in the form of grants to the two great school societies. That was to be Brougham's work. But now in 1820 we have him proposing a nation-wide education with government schools supplementing existing schools.

It was known that Brougham had something like this in mind but the linking up of government schools so strongly with the Church of England came as a shock to many persons and it was particularly surprising coming from Brougham. The sincerity and strength of Brougham's liberalism were unquestioned. And this was an illiberal measure which would impose an illiberal situation on the nation for decades to come. Brougham had always been the friend of the Dissenters. It was known that he felt deeply about their disabilities and was prepared whenever the time was opportune to translate that feeling into action. In this proposed plan the Dissenters were justified in stating that new disabilities were to be created.

The reason for Brougham's action was clear enough. The progress toward universal education was too slow. It would be a long time before the schools of the societies, British and National, could cover the nation. He felt that a nation-wide system had to be provided and he believed that no system of government schools was possible in his day if it were not linked up with the Established Church. His elaborate explanations that in practice the Church's control would be more formal than real were no doubt sincere enough, but they had no chance of convincing the Dissenters. For them the issue was clear; they were asked to support, financially and otherwise, a system of government schools which, according to the language of the Bill, were placed under the control of the Church of England and in which no Dissenter could teach.

This was one of Brougham's major errors of judgement and it confirmed what was coming to be a general verdict, that Brougham's judgement was not comparable to his ability, zeal, and energy. This Bill antagonized liberals, antagonized the Dissenters, and antagonized strongly the British and Foreign School Society which he had created. Fortunately for the Dissenters and the British and Foreign School Society, however, it was not long before Brougham was again championing them both and his services were once more fully appreciated.

Mill wrote to Brougham in January 1821, when the latter, having withdrawn the measure in 1820 out of deference to the Dissenter opposition, was contemplating appeasing amendments, that he had been trying to win converts among the Dissenters.

I said . . . that I could easily conceive your motives, that aware as you were of the deep rooted hostility of the clergy and their power over the decision of our ill chosen legislators, you might be reasonably afraid that the project would be exploded at the first moving unless something was thrown out to the clergy which would operate as a lure. . . . I said I thought I knew pretty well your inmost thoughts upon the subject of the Church and thought I could answer for you that one of the last things you would ever consent to, would be that of adding to the power of any corporation of priests.[1]

Mill would not need to add that Brougham had very little admiration or respect for the bishops to whom so much power seemed to be given in the Bill; that was apparent enough from his candid public statements.

From our point of view a notable feature of the Dissenter attack was the respect for Brougham that was expressed in almost every statement. A book written in 1820 by a Dissenter reflects the general and practically unanimous Dissenter attitude:

The luminous and comprehensive mind of the mover of this important measure, the independent spirit of his speculations, his contempt of old prejudices, his hostility to all dwarfish, restrictive, and antiquated systems of policy, and his admirable exercise and success in exposing the iniquitous management under which a multitude of institutions for education had become worse than useless, seemed to give a certain pledge that any plan which he would propose could not fail to be a model of liberality and equity. It must have been from some widely different quarter that we could have expected a scheme framed in conformity to those very prejudices, those insidious distinctions in the community, those principles of exclusive privilege and unequal advantage, of which it had not been supposed that there could be a more determined enemy.[2]

Not only had Brougham offended the Dissenters by his measure, but he had also failed to please the Church. Under Brougham's leadership, 'the march of the mind' was on its way, but most of the upper classes still feared universal education like children frightened of the dark. They felt that disaster threatened a society in which the majority could read. And there were many High Churchmen who, although they had some faith in popular education, felt that Brougham's Bill was not at all

[1] Brougham MSS., 22 Jan. 1821.
[2] John Foster, *An Essay on the Evils of Popular Ignorance* (1821), preface.

ideal. Education was traditionally the function of the Church. If government was to support it on a national scale, it should be controlled by the Church which was by law established as the national Church, with a much tighter and safer control than that proposed in Brougham's Bill.

One good came out of it, however. The proposal for a national system of education was a great challenge. Those who were, in the main, the more intelligent and the men of greater faith came to feel more keenly the urgency of the need. All later educational development owed something to that challenge. When a national system of education was established half a century later, it followed Brougham's policy of 'filling up the gaps' with government schools supported in part by local rates, although, of course, Forster's Bill differed widely from Brougham's.

This defeat did not lessen Brougham's interest in elementary education and he gave personal attention, hours squeezed out in a miraculous fashion, to the infant schools and to the Borough Road School, the parent school of the Lancasterians. At the latter he endeared himself to pupils, basked in the comradeship of a Pestalozzian master, and rejoiced in the boys' feats of mind rather than memory. But his more important contributions during this decade lay in adult and university education.

Adult education was not entirely lacking in 1820; there were a few literary, scientific, and philosophical societies for the classes who were privileged. What was in 1820 almost unheard of and unthinkable was adult education for working men. Five years before, in 1815, a self-educated London working man named Timothy Claxton, having been refused admission to a philosophical society, said to himself: 'I am a mechanic, and though that is the reason why I wish to be admitted . . . it is the very reason also why I am not.' Feeling that working men would have to shift for themselves in this respect, he gathered a group of like-minded workers and organized in 1817 a 'Mechanical Institution' which had some of the features of the later Mechanics' Institutes. It was closed after three years when Claxton left the country.[1]

There were a few similar institutions. The Professor of Natural Philosophy at the University of Glasgow, Jolly Jack Anderson, left in his will some property, a good library, and some very poor

[1] Timothy Claxton, *Hints to Mechanics* (1839), 1844 ed., pp. 22 seq.

apparatus for the establishment of what he described as 'Anderson's University', to consist of four faculties or colleges. The will provided that there should be a 'ladies course of physical lectures', in which the ladies would be given simple instruction but at the same time be spared the torture of mathematics and the acquirement of ancient languages which would spoil them by making them pedantic. 'Such a stock of knowledge will be laid in as will make them the most accomplished ladies in Europe.'[1] Not very much came of this, but in 1799 there appeared at the Andersonian Institution as Professor of Natural Philosophy young George Birkbeck, a recent graduate in medicine at the University of Edinburgh. Needing new apparatus the professor turned to the workshop of Glasgow, where he was surprised to discover among the mechanics considerable curiosity about scientific matters.

Birkbeck asked himself a question. 'Why are the avenues to science barred against them because they are poor?' That was the primary question behind the Mechanics' Institute movement a quarter of a century later. It was the question which Brougham, the great energizer of that movement, was to ask and to answer many times, in relation not only to science but to knowledge generally. Brougham had asked that question in regard to the universal education of boys and girls as early as 1810; it was the question which moved Brougham to start the British and Foreign School Society and later the Society for the Diffusion of Useful Knowledge. And as we shall see, Brougham believed that the greatness of Pestalozzi lay in his heroic efforts to get that question answered more even than in his educational method.

Birkbeck's immediate answer to the question was to announce a free course of lectures for mechanics on elementary science, to be expressed in simple language and profusely illustrated by simple experiments. Seventy-five working men attended the first lecture, 200 the second, 300 the third, 500 the fourth, and Birkbeck's 'Mechanics' Class' was on its way. Birkbeck was a quiet man without ambition who, far from regarding this as an historical event, thought of it as a purely local undertaking. He has been described as 'simple, unassuming and artless'.[2] Nobody

[1] J. W. Hudson, *History of Adult Education* (1851). Appendix A.
[2] Henry Clutterbuck, *Memoir of George Birkbeck* (1842), p. 11.

could have said that of Brougham, but the perfect co-operation between the two men in the Mechanics' Institute movement is another illustration of how Brougham could work with people very different from himself. Birkbeck after a few years left Glasgow and in 1805 he began to practise medicine in London. During the following eighteen years he said that he occasionally dreamed of repeating his experiment in London but he did nothing about it. His Mechanics' Class, however, was continued by his successor, a library was added to it, it declined and was revived. It ultimately seceded from the Andersonian Institute and the workmen who belonged to it established the Glasgow Mechanics' Institute in July 1823, when it immediately achieved parenthood, for it brought into being the London Mechanics' Institute.[1]

The proponent of the London Mechanics' Institute was Robertson, the editor of the *Mechanics Magazine*. In September 1823 he read of the establishment of the Glasgow Mechanics' Institute and its whole history going back to Birkbeck at the turn of the century. He and his assistant editor, Hodgskins, assisted by Francis Place, drew up 'Proposals' for a similar institute in London, which they published on 11 October in the seventh number of the *Mechanics Magazine*. Dr. Birkbeck was the first to answer the call and Brougham was not far behind him. A private meeting was held on 8 November, for which Place prepared the business, and Robertson and Hodgskins acted as secretaries with Birkbeck in the chair. When Brougham entered the room he walked up to Place who was standing beside the table and said in his loud House of Commons voice so that all could hear him: 'This matter will go on well, I see. You are always to be found where there are proceedings to be taken for the good of the people. Your presence is a guarantee that the society will go on well.'

The first public meeting was held on 11 November. After Dr. Birkbeck as chairman explained the purpose of the meeting a letter from Brougham was read and greeted with loud applause. It expressed regret at his not being able to be present and enclosed a financial contribution 'proportionate to my means and not at all to my zeal for the important object we have in

---

[1] The term employed in all the early history of the movement was 'Institution', but 'Institute' is used here in accordance with later practice.

view'. 'The plan will prosper in exact proportion to the interest which the mechanics themselves take in its welfare and ought to be left in their hands as soon as possible after it is begun.' A series of resolutions were passed all of which were prepared by Place; Brougham was to have moved the first one. Brougham's name was placed first on the list of donations, followed by that of Birkbeck. Burdett later made a princely gift and Birkbeck provided a substantial loan. On 2 December four trustees were elected of which Brougham was one, and a rule was adopted that two-thirds of the managing committee must be working men. 'Working man' was at first defined as one who earned his living by the work of his hands but later it was added that anyone who employed a journeyman was excluded from the concept. Such working men were the 'mechanics' not only of the London Institute but of Mechanics' Institutes generally.[1]

Robertson in his *Mechanics Magazine* expressed disapproval of relying on donations, opposed gratuitous lecturing, and waxed bitter in ridicule of what he considered the extravagance of building arrangements. The feud between him and Place began early and it came to involve Birkbeck and Brougham. With his magnificent though troublesome habit of insisting that everything should be done *his* way, Place marked out Robertson as an obstacle to success. Robertson refused to appear before the Institute to answer charges of defamation, pleading freedom of the press. According to their respective opponents Robertson circulated 'fabrications and falsehoods' and Birkbeck was 'rude and scurrilous'. Robertson alleged that the rule that two-thirds of the management committee should be working men was 'shamefully violated'. This was obviously fallacious because he included in his figures the President, Vice-Presidents, and Treasurer of the Institute to whom the rule did not apply. He refused to attend the laying of the corner-stone of the new building on 2 December 1824 and he was on the outside of the project which he had originally proposed a bare year after its start. In the course of his criticisms he had asked: 'Who is going to guarantee the rent?' Brougham answered that question by

[1] For these two paragraphs the first volume of the Minutes of the London Mechanics' Institute preserved at Birkbeck College; the *Mechanics Magazine*, vol. i, nos. 7, 8, 10, 12, 15; Add. MSS. (Place MSS.) 27823, ff. 240–51, 27824, ff. 14 seq.; *The Times* and *Morning Chronicle*, 12 Nov. 1823.

doing it himself, and what he sowed in generosity he reaped in financial difficulties twenty years later.[1]

Every time Brougham made a speech on Mechanics' Institutes, and he made scores of them, he extolled his old friend Dr. Birkbeck as the founder of the movement and also as the founder of the London Mechanics' Institute. And every time he did so Robertson became sorer. In Brougham's famous pamphlet *Observations on the Education of the People*, however, it was clearly stated that the original proposal for a Mechanics' Institute in London was made by Robertson and Hodgskins in the *Mechanics Magazine* and that Birkbeck responded to their appeal. But that left out Place. Here was this remarkable piece of propaganda for Mechanics' Institutes being distributed throughout every city and into every remote hamlet without a word about Francis Place. It was an unfortunate omission. Place, who was always quick to assign motives, said:

Mr. Brougham was angry at the time and could not forgive me for writing as he supposed some article in the *Westminster Review* which I did not write, and therefore on this as on some other occasions he hesitated not to act a very mean part. Such proceedings are not at all uncommon with Mr. Brougham who on several occasions has not hesitated to garble accounts and play tricks with his friends. Yet notwithstanding this there is not a man living who has a stronger desire to have the people instructed than Mr. Brougham, nor one who has exerted himself more than he has to promote that object.[2]

The controversy between Robertson and Brougham as to who was the founder continued until 1835, when they agreed to disagree and a long correspondence ended.[3]

Brougham attended many of the early lectures at the London Mechanics' Institute;[4] that he found time to do so is astonishing. But he took no direct part in its government nor in the formulation of policy. He had laid down the principle at the beginning that it should be governed by a committee two-thirds of whom must be of the working class (and the officers who were not of the working class). He probably influenced Birkbeck who,

[1] Add. MSS. (Place MSS.) 27823, ff. 255 seq., 283; First Minute Book of the London Mechanics' Institute; *Mechanics Magazine*, nos. 14, 31, 42, 47–56.
[2] Add. MSS. 27823, ff. 247–8.
[3] The correspondence is in Brougham MSS. It is described in part by Place in Add. MSS. 27823, ff. 379 seq.
[4] *Mechanics Magazine*, no. 36.

though elected annually, was a perpetual president. For the London Institute, Brougham was a patron rather than a leader. At practically every anniversary meeting he occupied a place of honour and spoke, sometimes exalting Mechanics' Institutes for their purely educational value and sometimes for their preparation for democratic government. He was one of the select few for whose entertainment on such occasions the committee voted annually six bottles of port and six bottles of sherry with cakes and biscuits, as was duly recorded in the minutes.[1] On one occasion, in 1825, the publishers Knight and Lacy presented each member of the committee with a copy of a portrait of Brougham,[2] which they no doubt duly appreciated on account of his fame and popularity. (These portraits of Brougham were presented in Mechanics' Institutes throughout the country.)

He was consulted occasionally on matters where decision was difficult. Various organizations rented rooms in the building for their meetings, but the use of the building for political or religious purposes was frowned upon, these topics being barred in the Mechanics' Institutes themselves. In 1830 lectures by Brougham's friend, Robert Owen, which presumably advocated socialism, brought this matter to a head. Brougham was consulted and he advised (in the words of the minutes) 'that meetings of a political or religious character in the Theatre are calculated to injure our valuable Institution and compromise its usefulness'. A motion was passed which put an end to the letting of rooms for such purposes.[3]

It was in the dissemination of Mechanics' Institutes throughout the country that Brougham assumed a position of vigorous leadership. He wrote any number of letters to individuals in various parts of the kingdom, stirring up their interest and soliciting their activity; he received letters of inquiry from many individuals and groups. Just how he wrote to them we do not know because the letters are not extant. But it all went back to his pamphlet, *Practical Observations on the Education of the People*, which was published in January 1825, a year after the London Mechanics' Institute began its activities, and became the Bible

[1] L.M.I. Minutes of Council, 24 Nov. 1830.
[2] Ibid., 13 June 1825.
[3] L.M.I. Minutes of Special General Meeting, 27 Apr. 1830, and of Adjourned General Meeting, 29 Apr.

of the Mechanics' Institute movement and of the Society for the Diffusion of Useful Knowledge. This pamphlet was a careful elaboration of an article which Brougham wrote for the October 1824 *Edinburgh Review*. It was widely distributed in every city of the kingdom and found its way into many obscure villages. In three months it ran through nineteen editions. Its price brought it within the reach of all, but in some places interested persons bought up a number of copies and gave them away. Brougham donated his share of the profits to the London Mechanics' Institute.

In this pamphlet Brougham began with the importance of *reading*. Throughout he insisted that lectures and classes would achieve little unless they were associated with reading. The first part dealt with what he had in mind for his Society for the Diffusion of Useful Knowledge (which he definitely projected six months later) and then he went on to discuss Mechanics' Institutes. Reading, he declared, was 'beside the present amusement the surest way to raise our character and better our condition'. It could not be expected that the working men would suddenly become a mass of people reading good books, but he expressed the hope that a number of them would gradually influence others. The two greatest difficulties were lack of money and lack of time. The first should be met by good cheap publications. He urged 'a repeal of the tax upon paper which is truly a tax upon knowledge'. 'The method of publishing in numbers is admirably suited to the circumstances of the classes whose income is derived from wages.' (And so, in time, the *Penny Cyclopaedia*, *Penny Magazine*, and the other cheap works issued by his Society for the Diffusion of Useful Knowledge.) He urged that as far as possible knowledge should be made equally available to rich and poor. This was to many an age of economic opportunity. Brougham was driven by his restless and dynamic energy to do what he could to make it an age of *intellectual opportunity* for the unprivileged. Other means of overcoming lack of money lay in book clubs and reading clubs.

As for the lack of time for reading of those who worked long hours, Brougham suggested that knowledge should be simplified in treatises that were clear and concise and did not assume too much to start with. The education of the people could also be achieved by lecturing, not alone but 'combined with reading and subservient to it', and, in scientific subjects, accompanied by 'experimental illustrations'. From this Brougham turned to the expenses and proper organization of a Mechanics' Institute with its lectures, reference and circulating libraries, reading-room, apparatus, buildings, and advertising. He appealed to the privileged to be active and generous in the establishment of Mechanics' Institutes, but once they were established, it was 'a fundamental principle to make the expenses be mainly defrayed by the mechanics themselves; it is another principle, in my opinion equally essential, that they should have the principal share in the management'. He told the Glasgow story and that of the Edinburgh School of Arts, with emphasis on the classes of the latter where the monitorial idea was combined with general discussion in small groups (what was known throughout the Mechanics' Institute movement as 'mutual instruction'). Brougham then described the establishment of the London Mechanics' Institute and referred to the Mechanics' Institutes at Newcastle, Kendal, Carlisle, Manchester, Leeds, and Aberdeen. 'It should seem that a little exertion alone is wanting to introduce the system universally.' All that was needed for a local start was the enthusiastic leadership of one man, generous donations by the wealthy, and the response of the working men.

This was an age of philanthropy and Brougham was anxious to channel that philanthropy properly. In this pamphlet he delivered himself again of his views on what was commonly designated as 'charity'. He believed in later years that one of the greatest of his contributions to popular education was in persuading people to turn their philanthropy towards education.

He challenged the middle class to 'devote themselves more to the pursuit of solid and refined learning; the present seminaries must be enlarged; and some of the great cities of the kingdom, especially the metropolis, must not be left destitute of the regular means within themselves of scientific education'. This was a reference to the idea of a University of London which at that time existed as a dream in the minds of a small group. And it went farther. This pamphlet envisaged for the first time a number of English universities of a democratic type and with a due emphasis on science. In that Brougham's mind travelled beyond his associates who were discussing with him the establishment of a university in London. The April (1825) number of the *Edinburgh Review* in discussing this pamphlet sharpened this reference to the University of London project.

In his closing paragraph Brougham addressed working men directly.

If these pages should fall into the hands of any one at an hour for the first time stolen from his needful rest after his day's work is done, I ask him to reward me (who have written them for his benefit at the like hours), by saving threepence during the next fortnight, buying with it Franklin's Life, and reading the first page. I am quite sure he will read the rest; I am almost quite sure he will resolve to spend his spare time and money in gaining those kinds of knowledge which from a printer's boy made that great man the first philosopher and one of the first statesmen of his age. Few are fitted by nature to go as far as he did. . . . But all may go a good way after him, both in temperance and industry and knowledge, and no one can tell before he tries how near he may be able to approach him.

At this time there were about fourteen Mechanics' Institutes in existence. With the publications and wide distribution of the *Observations*, Brougham's powerful mind and abundant industry gave the movement the driving power which he afforded to so many movements. Within three months of the publication of the pamphlet thirty new Mechanics' Institutes came into being.[1] And in the next three months, according to the *Edinburgh*, 'many similar establishments have been formed'. In that year, 1825, twenty Mechanics' Institutes were established in Yorkshire alone. An almost equal number may be counted in southern England and the total number started during the year may have approached a hundred.[2]

Speaking at the opening of the London Mechanics' Institute's new theatre in July Dr. Birkbeck said:

. . . His [Brougham's] valuable *Observations* have so effectually confirmed the wavering and instructed and animated the lukewarm

---

[1] *Edinburgh Review*, Apr. 1825.

[2] Thomas Kelly in his *George Birkbeck* (1957), says: 'The vintage year was 1825, in which about 70 new institutes are known to have been founded' (p. 209). But in a statistical table in the Appendix (p. 329) he gives 104 as the number existing in 1826. That may, of course, mean by the end of that year. Since there were 20 at the end of the 1824, the balance of 84 may represent two years' growth rather than one. But he admits in his text that there may have been more than 70 established in 1825.

that Institutions similar to our own have rapidly sprung up, in numbers far exceeding all calculation and in places where their existence could least have been anticipated. . . . Although the Bar and the Senate [Parliament] number him among the most active, laborious, and enlightened of their members, yet they who mark his efforts on behalf of education alone, would conclude that Infant Schools, Lancasterian Schools, Mechanics' Institutes and a London University must possess his undivided time and attention.[1]

In his speech on that occasion Brougham said that 'scarcely three days ever elapse without my receiving a communication of the establishment of some new Mechanics' Institution'. He continued: 'Some will tell us that it is dangerous to teach too much to the working classes, for, say they, it will enable them to tread on heels of their superiors. Now this is just the sort of treading on the heel that I long to see.' Which again was just the sort of speech which induced Whig borough-owners to look askance at Brougham. But Brougham knew that the future was on his side.

In addition to everything else Brougham 'devoted the summer' of 1825 to writing a course of lectures to be sent out to Mechanics' Institutes where they were to be read and discussed. He hit on the plan of what he called 'anonymous lecturing' because of the difficulty many of the Institutes had in finding lecturers. These anonymous lectures were to be 'perfectly simple, intelligible and plain descriptions, containing the elements of science in a way that would be readily comprehended by uneducated men'. His scientific knowledge was adequate to this simple anonymous lecturing and he possessed that essential which was too frequently lacking in the Mechanics' Institute movement, the gifts of the popularizer. He wrote lectures on Political Economy as well, and also induced others to write lectures for the Institutes. A later set of lectures on Political Economy by an unknown author was altered and adapted by Brougham in 1834.

Brougham's own lectures were used extensively throughout the kingdom. Their anonymity was rigorously guarded, though there were some correct guesses at their authorship. How many courses he prepared we do not know, but he continued to write them for many years. In 1839 a letter from Coates spoke of Brougham's lectures supplying 'political information divested

[1] *Mechanics Magazine*, no. 99.

of party politics'. In 1848 Hudson, then secretary of both the Yorkshire Union of Mechanics' Institutes and the Scottish Union, planned to send a course of Brougham's lectures to all the Mechanics' Institutes in Yorkshire and in Scotland. And, when he published his *History of Adult Education* three years later, Hudson said that manuscript lectures were widely distributed in the Northern Union, that spoken lectures of the formal type were at that time failing to attract interest, but that the members studied and discussed the manuscript lectures profitably.[1]

In September 1826, a year and eight months after the publication of his *Observations*, Brougham sent out a questionnaire to a number of Mechanics' Institutes. The answers represent, of course, their earliest experiences but some of them indicate a trend. The following were the questions and the general character of the replies:

What has been the effect of the depression of 1825 and 1826? The reply from Ayr expressed cogently the general verdict: 'We do not find that the pressure of the times has effected [*sic*] our Institutions by lessening its numbers, but it may have prevented its increase from those particular trades most depressed at present.' Devonport reported that the only unfavourable effect of the depression had been loss of funds caused by a bank failure. In some cases fear was expressed for the coming winter.

What was the present number of members? Has experience suggested any change in the regulations? There were various answers to this which Brougham appears to have passed on to others. Was the managing committee doing its work well and did the working men act in harmony with their superiors and with one another? The replies were strongly in the affirmative probably on account of initial enthusiasm; the later history of Mechanics' Institutes indicates a mixed situation in both respects. What was the average number of books taken from the library weekly and was that number on the increase in proportion to the number of readers? The answers were generally in the affirmative. Were scientific books or general books most read?

---

[1] *Speeches*, iii. 176–7; University College, MSS., Abraham Clarke of Newport to Brougham, 26 Feb., 12 May 1826, Wilbur Turner to Brougham, 7, 15 Oct. 1826; Brougham MSS., Coates to Brougham, 7 Sept. 1839, Hudson to Brougham, 11 May 1848; Hudson, pp. 187, 191.

In most of the cases where there were clear statements, a preference for general literature over scientific books was indicated; history was a favourite subject.[1] Here, very early in the general Mechanics' Institute movement, we have a definite swing away from Birkbeck's original conception towards Brougham's hope (shared by Birkbeck as the movement developed) that the Institutes should be for the general adult education of working men. It should be noted, however, that the majority of the lectures did not move away from science until the next decade. In spite of this development, Brougham always insisted that an emphasis on science must be maintained.

There were already members who were not working men (or honorary members by virtue of financial support). The secretary of the Devonport Mechanics' Institute wrote to Brougham that there was no library in Devonport except a bookseller's library (which presumably was expensive or difficult) and young men of the town who were not working men were joining the Mechanics' Institute because of its library.

The projects to which Brougham gave leadership always created a great deal of public discussion, partly because of their essential importance and not a little because of the admiration and malice which his previous activities had attracted. So far as influential groups were concerned, the men active in the Mechanics' Institute movement were pleased with the support they received. They said that the only aggressively hostile forces were a section of the Tory press and the High Church party, but that most of the political leaders were in favour of the movement. Of the public men who backed it, the majority were Whigs and Radicals, but Tory statesmen including Liverpool and Huskisson gave it quiet support. Hobhouse wrote to Place in December 1827 on the 'march of intellect' (a phrase applied to the movement which Brougham himself disliked): 'I find that all who talk with me find it no laughing matter at all. . . . Some, like Lord Eldon, call it the rogues march and think it a time to which, one day or other, a hundred thousand tall fellows with clubs and pikes will march against Whitehall. Others regard it as a very beneficial change.'[2]

---

[1] University College MSS. This collection of letters has been in the Library of University College, London, for many years. It is not part of Brougham MSS.
[2] Add. MSS. 35148, ff. 6–8.

There was certainly a feeling against the education of the working men that ran wide and deep. It was more akin to fear and uneasiness than to contempt and amusement. It was urged that 'the march of the mind' would unfit the working man for his work and it would break down class distinctions: society would be completely undermined. The workers would become 'impatient, fantastic and mutinous'. 'A scheme more completely adapted for the destruction of this empire could not have been invented.'[1] There were also clergymen who feared that the activities of the Institutes would not leave working men time to say their prayers.[2] At a meeting to organize a Mechanics' Institute at Southwark, a lawyer who was strongly opposed to the move presented his point of view neatly enough:

Was it not well-known that the most abstruse sciences were taught in these societies? Was it not notorious that algebra, the highest branches of mathematics, nay even botany, navigation and astronomy were taught to the working people? Reading-rooms were established which caused them to neglect their families and their homes. Their constitutions were weakened and debilitated by intense mental study, which would in time prevent them from pursuing with the same vigour their usual labour. . . . If they were to go on, the time would arrive when the higher classes must sweep the streets, groom their horses, and clean their own boots. Society would be uprooted, the marks which distinguished different classes thrown down, the government be over-turned, and a state of anarchy would be the ultimate result.[3]

Between such people and Brougham, of course, there could be no peace: indeed it was war to the finish. That scurrilous and entertaining paper, *John Bull*, which had dogged Brougham's footsteps ever since the Queen's Trial, frequently represented 'the march of intellect' as one of the Brougham menaces: 'To see Squire Brougham active is to know that mischief is busy, to see him associated as he is in the dirty work of inflaming the minds of the lower orders. . . .' There were others who were not likely to be influenced by *John Bull* who were suspicious of Brougham's motives. He was 'dictatorial' and also he was a 'revolutionary'. Much of that was insincere enough; it came

[1] *Bell's Weekly Messenger*, 16 Nov. 1823; *St. James's Chronicle* in May 1825.
[2] J. G. Godard, *George Birkbeck* (1884), p. 88.
[3] A newspaper clipping in Add. MSS. 27824, f. 107 (Place MSS.).

from men for whom any whip was to be seized to lash Brougham with. Where it was sincere it conveys to our minds some pathos but it was an essential part of the story of progress in an age when Britain was in so many respects breaking through into the light.

The antagonism of the Established Church was genuine enough and deserves a certain amount of sympathy. Education was the traditional function of the Church: adult education without religion was inevitably an offence to many good men, and to others no adult education could be anything but harmful unless it were controlled by the Church of England. High Churchmen particularly could not agree with Brougham and his co-workers that in that day of religious strife to include religion would have wrecked the whole enterprise. Failing to influence Brougham and his supporters, the Church established its own adult-education organizations. But they were distinctly inferior and, strange to say, though they were under the desired auspices they included very little religious teaching.[1]

Brougham's work for the Mechanics' Institutes after 1830 belongs to the second volume of this book, but for a moment we may move ahead to note the estimates of its importance formed by J. W. Hudson who came to know more about Mechanics' Institutes than anyone else, held a number of secretarial positions within the movement, and wrote the standard history of adult education in England in 1851, and Edward Baines, Junior, who gave to it much time and leadership in the midst of a busy life as editor of the famous *Leeds Mercury*. Hudson wrote to Brougham, 11 May 1848: 'It must be peculiarly gratifying to your Lordship to observe the progress of those adult educational societies which mainly owe their existence to your invaluable advocacy', and on 22 February 1861 Baines wrote: 'Though we allow you to rank Dr. Birkbeck as our founder, we all know that your influence did more than that of any living man to promote the spread of these admirable means of popular enlightenment.'[2]

While detailed description will have to wait until another volume, a few generalizations should be ventured here about the history of Mechanics' Institutes after 1830. Some of these

[1] Coates noted the latter fact in Brougham MSS., Coates to Brougham, 7 Sept. 1839.
[2] Brougham MSS.

conclusions differ from general beliefs.[1] The movement has frequently been described as a failure because it did not serve the class for which it was intended and the working men ultimately left the Institutes. Both of these statements are exaggerations; a great deal was done for a limited number of working men and there were very few Mechanics' Institutes without working men at any time (Mechanics' Institutes in intention and organization, not to be confused with general societies for adult education). The figures given in the appendix to the 1841 report are misleading because the report included various organizations for adult education, and the small proportion of working men sometimes means the few that were included in a society that was never intended for them. At a meeting in Leeds in that year Coates, who made the report, stated that there were 265 Mechanics' Institutes in England with 25,651 members, about four-ninths of whom were mechanics.[2]

It should be pointed out that the class which displaced the 'mechanics' to a considerable extent was also a working class; to use a later term they were 'white-collar workers'. Clerks of all sorts, warehouse men, small shopkeepers and their assistants, young men with little money and large ambitions, sometimes in a professional direction, they thought of themselves as belonging to the 'middle class', but they were quite as much unprivileged intellectually as the mechanics, and their wages and incomes averaged lower than those of the 'skilled labourers' among those for whom the Mechanics' Institutes were originally intended. For them the Mechanics' Institutes proved to be a great boon.

The best work was done by the classes and the libraries. Even when working men in the narrower sense predominated, books in general literature and history were preferred to scientific volumes and with the changing character of the membership, the clerk class demanded a broad range in both books and classes, which corresponded to Brougham's ideal. While novels were barred at first, that was only an instance of the great prejudice against novels at that date; later, all of the great novelists of the century were welcomed and the statement that the Mechanics' Institutes discouraged imaginative literature is

---

[1] For later history of Mechanics' Institutes, see Mrs. Mabel Tylecote's *Mechanics' Institutes of Lancashire and Yorkshire before 1851* (1957), and three chapters of Thomas Kelly's *George Birkbeck*. [2] Add. MSS. 29824, f. 197.

clearly disproved by lists of lectures and of books. Another fallacy, dear to those who pass hasty comment on Mechanics' Institutes, is the idea that there was a narrow utilitarian concentration on making the workers better at their jobs. That aim was one among many at the very beginning but it faded away.

Baines could write to Brougham in 1856: 'Mechanics' Institutes are still considerably on the increase in numbers and efficiency.'[1] Frequent statements that there were 700 Mechanics' Institutes in the United Kingdom in 1850 have been probably based on Hudson's book, but he listed *all* societies for *adult education*. There were something over 550 Mechanics' Institutes at that time and over 700 in 1863 with the number still increasing, so in the last eighteen years of Brougham's life, from 1850 to 1868 (from his seventy-second to his ninetieth year), the number of Institutes must have increased by between 25 and 30 per cent.[2]

Before mid-century all the cities and many small towns in the United States had Mechanics' Institutes. How much that owes to the British movement it is difficult to say, but the influence was considerable. Certainly there was a Mechanics' Institute in New York a few weeks at least before the establishment of the London Mechanics' Institute. The ideals go back to Benjamin Franklin. In fact Brougham knew much about Franklin's career and was probably influenced by him. The spread of Mechanics' Institutes throughout the British Empire was undoubtedly an expansion of the British movement. In Canada an effort was made to emphasize scientific instruction for the working men, and government grants were made to Mechanics' Institutes for that purpose, but as in Great Britain a swing took place toward the ambitious white-collar workers and general literature. A young man who was to become the founder of Canada's greatest newspaper chain had been obliged to leave school early and he continued his education in the evenings at the library of the Mechanics' Institute of London, Ontario, where it is said that he 'almost literally read it through'.[3] There must have been many stories like that, now forgotten, though few where the success was so marked. Many of the public libraries in Canada today were originally Mechanics' Institute libraries.

[1] Brougham MSS., 5 July 1856.
[2] Kelly, p. 329, gives the number in 1851 as 562.
[3] *Hamilton Spectator*, 29 Feb. 1932.

CHAPTER XVIII

Lord Rector of Glasgow: Society for the Diffusion of Useful Knowledge: the Schoolmaster is Abroad

IN the spring of 1825 a remarkable election took place for the honorary position of Lord Rector of the University of Glasgow. The nominees were Henry Brougham and Walter Scott. They were the most distinguished sons of Scotland in that generation, both graduates of the University of Edinburgh. Scott was at the height of his fame as the author of the *Waverley Novels*. For many years he had denied their authorship or brushed the question aside. When asked it again at the time of the Queen's Trial he had said that he must reply 'in the favourite phrase of the day, *non mi ricordo*'. But the veil had worn thin and in 1825 the Great Unknown was fully revealed.

The count was even and Brougham was elected by a casting vote. In his rectorial address he discussed the great orators, ancient and modern, comparing all others unfavourably with Demosthenes and calling him 'Old Man Eloquent', which he suggested was more fitting than Milton's application of the phrase to Plato. But his mind was full of Mechanics' Institutes and his dreams of a Society for the Diffusion of Useful Knowledge and a London University. From eloquence he passed to the proper employment of eloquence. The answer to that was the cause of liberty and from that it was easy to pass to a new unhampered liberty of the mind for men of all classes.[1]

Just at the time of this new honour at Glasgow Brougham was trying to start his Society for the Diffusion of Useful Knowledge. In April 1825 he brought together a group in which Lord John Russell, William Allen, and Lushington were prominent, and apparently founded a society with that name. But the depression interfered with their plans and no recorded progress was made.

[1] *Speeches*, iii. 69 seq.

On 6 November 1826 Brougham summoned another meeting which was regarded as the true inauguration of the Society. Those whom Brougham had gathered together included Abercromby, Denman, James Mill, and Matthew Davenport Hill. A prospectus was prepared and circulated privately. A more complete prospectus was published early in the following year and both the December (1826) and the June (1827) numbers of the *Edinburgh Review* gave further descriptions of the plans of the Society in articles probably written by Brougham.[1] The name of the Society was almost inevitable. At that time when knowledge was spoken of in popular circles it was customarily 'useful knowledge', and the spreading of it was nearly always 'diffusion'.

The prospectus stated:

The object of the Society is the imparting of useful information to all classes of the community, particularly to such as are unable to avail themselves of experienced teachers, or may prefer learning by themselves. The plan proposed for the attainment of this object is the periodical publication of treatises under the direction and with the sanction of a superintending committee. . . . Each scientific treatise will contain an explanation of the fundamental principles of some branch of science, their proofs and illustrations, their application to practical uses and to the explanation of facts or appearances.

The treatises were to contain thirty-two octavo pages each, with as much printed matter as would ordinarily appear in a hundred pages and each was to be sold for sixpence. One would be published at the beginning and one in the middle of each month. The following was given as a general outline: under Natural Philosophy 66 subjects (including Astronomy, Algebra, Geometry, Breeding of Cattle, Dairy Farming); under Intellectual Philosophy 6 subjects; Ethical Philosophy 4 subjects; Political Philosophy 8 subjects (including Objects of Government, Civil Jurisprudence, Criminal Jurisprudence, Political Economy); History of Science 9 subjects (including histories of Ethics, Religion, and Law); History of Art 6 subjects (Fine Arts and Useful Arts); History of Nations 22 subjects; History of Individuals (9 Patriots, 12 Warriors, 12 Discoverers, 6 Self-Exalted Men, 6 Moral Philosophers, 6 Navigators, and 6 Statesmen).

[1] A manuscript thesis on the S.D.U.K. by Miss Monica C. Grobel at University College, London, contains a great number of important facts, some of which are used in this chapter; Charles Knight, ii. 45; Add. MSS. 27824 (Place MSS.), ff. 115 seq.; *Edinburgh Review*, Dec. 1826, June 1827.

To which was added the following modest statement: 'The foregoing list is not to be considered as comprising every subject ... but principally those which it is intended first to be treated of.' That elaborate programme was never carried out in the form indicated, but most of the subjects were included in one form or another in the publications of the Society. Of the subjects proposed in this prospectus, 66 would be called by us scientific (related to natural science) and 92 were non-scientific. But it was all science to Brougham and his colleagues because it was all knowledge; 'science, which in its comprehensive sense means *knowledge*, and in its ordinary sense means *knowledge reduced to a system*'. It is with that terminology in mind that we must read all contemporary statements about the Society for the Diffusion of Useful Knowledge.

The article in the December 1826 *Edinburgh* was probably written by Brougham and certainly represents his view of the project. This work was to be for the nation not for a class. The article referred to the members of the Mechanics' Institutes and said that with them everything ultimately went back to books.

Elementary works that really answer the description are rare indeed. ... This is a want felt not merely by the working classes, but by persons of every rank in society. Even the young of the upper classes who are learners of any science, with every advantage of previous education, ... feel it. ... But those of more advanced years, who may have neglected the improvement of their minds by the cultivation of science ... most probably would be glad to learn if they could find the most interesting branches of knowledge expounded in a plain and purely didactic manner. With such helps, a man having the advantages of leisure which is enjoyed by the wealthier classes would often be led from step to step until he had learned the whole of a science; whereas he is now repulsed at the outset by seeing a mass of cramp [*sic*] statements in hard words ... unintelligible to the beginner. Design ... embracing all knowledge for its means, and the good, the highest good, the moral improvement of all classes, for its end.

The article on the Society in the June *Edinburgh* again emphasized its value for the upper classes as well as for the lower.

To carry out this plan a large committee was formed, which during most of the history of the Society had some fifty or sixty members. In the selection Brougham broke sharply with the traditional practice of loading every benevolent institution with aristocracy. There was here no lists of patrons, honorary presidents, honorary vice-presidents and presidents made up of lay peers and bishops with two or three commoners, who were really active, at the tail of the vice-presidents. For that sort of thing Brougham had no more respect than he had fundamentally for aristocratic government. There was a duke on their committee and a marquis, but Bedford and Lansdowne were not as ordinary dukes and marquises. The Duke of Bedford had displayed a very busy interest in education and a liberal outlook on public questions. Lansdowne had been active in the anti-slavery movement and very active in regard to infant schools. There were no officers at any time except a chairman, vice-chairman, a secretary, and a treasurer. Thomas Coates was secretary and William Tooke treasurer. After eighteen meetings had been held, at thirteen of which Brougham presided, a chairman was elected by ballot. Brougham received all of the votes and was returned at every subsequent election. Lord John Russell was elected vice-president. A feature of the committee that was obvious to all was that about half were members of Parliament, nearly all of whom were liberal Whigs. When Brougham later tried to obtain financial help for the Society from Peel's government, Peel did not neglect to remark that 'the Society . . . comprises the names of men of high distinction both in public life and literature, but almost without exception they are of different political connection from my own'.[1]

In November 1826 Brougham met Charles Knight, who was to be the Society's publisher throughout nearly all of its history. Matthew Davenport Hill, who in later years was closely associated with Brougham in many interests including the treatment of criminals and schools for juvenile delinquents, brought together these two as men who had dreamed the same dream. The son of a Windsor bookseller, Knight, as he expressed it himself, formed in his youth 'a desire to make knowledge a common possession instead of an exclusive privilege'. In 1812 he sketched out a plan for a cheap weekly series of books that would bring all sorts of knowledge within the reach of the poorest; in 1819 and 1820 he made an attempt, which left little behind it but an Essay on Cheap Publications. Of this first meeting Knight wrote:

[1] Add. MSS. 40528 (Peel MSS.), f. 326.

There was an image in my mind of the Queen's Attorney-General, as I had often beheld him in the House of Lords, wielding a power in the proceedings on the Bill of Pains and Penalties which no other man seemed to possess,—equivocating witnesses crouching beneath his withering scorn; mighty peers shrinking from his bold sarcasm; the whole assembly visibly agitated at times by the splendour of his eloquence. The Henry Brougham I had gazed upon was, in my mind's eye, a man stern and repellent; not to be approached with any attempt at familiarity; whose opinion must be received with the most respectful deference; whose mental superiority would be somewhat overwhelming. The Henry Brougham into whose chambers in Lincoln's Inn I was ushered on a November night was sitting amidst his briefs evidently delighted to be interrupted for some thoughts more attractive. After saluting my friend with a joke and grasping my hand with a cordial welcome, he went at once into the subject upon which I came. The rapid conceptions of the features of my plan; the few brief questions as to my wishes; the manifestation of a warm interest in my views without the slightest attempt to be patronizing, were most gratifying to me.... The foremost advocate of popular education made no harangue upon its advantages. He did not indoctrinate me, as I have been bored by many an educationalist before and since, with flourishes upon a subject which he gave Mr. Hill and myself full credit for comprehending.... So did Henry Brougham take for granted that he and I were in accord upon the subject of the diffusion of knowledge. He was then within a few days of the completion of his forty-seventh year,[1] full of health and energy, one who had been working without intermission in literature, in science, in law, in politics for a quarter of a century, but one to whom no work seemed to bring fatigue, no tedious mornings of the King's Bench, no sleepless nights in the House of Commons, able to 'stale his infinite variety'. From that hour I felt more confidence in talking with perfect freedom to him who worthily filled so large a place in the world's eye, than to many a man of commonplaces whose depths I had plumbed and found them shallow.[2]

In July 1827 Knight undertook the superintendance of the Society's publications. *The Library of Useful Knowledge*, with its sixpenny books twice a month, had been begun in March. The introductory treatise was written by Brougham. It was entitled *Discourse on the Objects, Advantages and Pleasures of Science* and it attained a sale of over 39,000 copies. Such an amazing sale (for

[1] He had, a few months before this, completed his forty-eighth year.
[2] Charles Knight, ii. 45–47.

that time) could be accounted for only by Brougham's name and fame, but it was an excellent introduction to the publications of the Society. The experts noted that the book contained errors. While recognizing that, the *Dublin Review* said that 'it was as clear as writing could be; it abounded in instances drawn from every corner of the universe and put together in such shape that interest never flagged'. Knight wrote of it later:

The sale of this work had been as extraordinary as its merits were striking and almost unexampled. Some called it superficial because it touched rapidly on many departments of scientific knowledge; but the more just conclusion was that it was the work of 'a full man' who had . . . poured it forth out of the accumulated wealth of his rich treasury of knowledge. No reader to whom the subjects treated were in any degree new could read this little book without feeling an ardent desire to know more or to know all.[1]

The title of this introductory treatise of the Society, though perhaps responsible for the persistent belief that the Society concentrated on science in a narrowly utilitarian fashion, strictly defined Brougham's own attitude towards knowledge. 'There is', he wrote at the beginning, 'something positively agreeable to all men . . . in gaining knowledge for its own sake', even if the knowledge may not 'ever be of the least use to yourself practically'. 'The mere gratification of curiosity; the knowing more to-day than we knew yesterday; the understanding clearly what before seemed obscure and puzzling . . . is an agreeable occupation of the mind; and beside the present enjoyment, elevates the faculties above low pursuits, purifies and refines the passions, and helps our reason to assuage their violence.' The greater part of the treatise discussed in detail the interest evoked by natural science, after which he suggested that a similar treatment might be accorded to other branches of knowledge, the intellectual and moral faculties, man's duties to society, political science, government, and law.

The object of 'science' was to make a man more useful in his work; its advantages were that it enabled a man to make discoveries that had a value for all men. The third benefit was, when rightly considered, 'just as practical as the other two, the pleasure derived from mere knowledge'. That extends to works

[1] Miss Grobel's thesis, p. 160, quoting *Dublin Review*, ii. 104 seq.; Charles Knight, ii. 55.

of imagination. 'Every one is amused by reading a story; a romance may divert some.' 'There is a positive enjoyment in knowing what we did not know before; and this pleasure is greatly increased when the information is such as excites our surprise, wonder or admiration.' Brougham loved the intellectual life for its own sake, and because of its 'giving a dignity and importance to the enjoyment of life'. In this treatise and in the Society he was founding he was trying, among other things, to pass that love on to as many as possible.

Brougham also wrote the 'Hydrostatics' in the Library's first series. It displayed a forthright clarity, but its slips were obvious. The Society had so many good scientists available that it should not have been necessary for Brougham to write on Hydrostatics, but it is well that public service should at times be sugar coated for the giver as well as for the recipient, and Brougham experienced, no doubt, a particular enjoyment in displaying his knowledge of natural science, which, at any rate, was the product of a sincere interest in it.

In September (1827) Mill wrote to Brougham that Black had informed him that the support of the country newspaper editors might be obtained. Brougham took up the suggestion immediately and Knight promised an analysis of the provincial press.[1]

It was at this time that Knight went to Brougham with the idea of publishing a good almanac; the many almanacs in existence were very popular and at the same time banal and tawdry, full of ignorant superstition, absurd and puerile predictions, old wives' tales, and thinly veiled obscenity. According to Knight, Brougham, 'the rapid genius of unprocrastinating labour', asked him if he could have the new almanac out before the end of the year. 'Yes, with a little help on the scientific matters.' 'Then tell Mr. Coates to call a meeting of the General Committee at my chambers at half past eight to-morrow morning. . . . You may have your choice of good men for your astronomy and meteorology, your tides and your eclipses. Go to work and never fear.' At 8.30 next morning 'the energy of the chairman swept away every doubt'.[2] 'In an hour the preparation of the new almanac was in the hands of different com-

---

[1] Brougham MSS., Mill to Brougham, 24 Sept., Knight to Brougham, 26 Sept. 1827.
[2] Charles Knight, ii. 62–64.

mittees and in a month thousands of it were in the shops.'[1] So
the British Almanac began its very long, successful, and popular
career, driving out many of the poorer almanacs. It was priced
at half a crown and sold 10,000 copies in its first week.[2] Thirty-
four thousand were sold in the year 1828 and 41,000 in 1829.[3]

Francis Place's manuscript diary for 1828 includes the following for 19 January: 'He [Brougham] has a capital project,
making school books and story books and books of science for
children and young people, than which nothing can be of greater
importance. I have promised my assistance.'[4] That was not
followed up immediately but the S.D.U.K. inaugurated a series
of children's books in 1833.

By the beginning of 1828 the *Library of Entertaining Knowledge*
was contemplated, although its first treatise was not published
until 1829. It was explained that the *Library of Useful Knowledge*
was 'addressed to those who having the habit of reading formed
are in want of proper works for their instruction'. This *Library
of Entertaining Knowledge* was intended 'to make men become
readers', lured by entertainment. 'As much entertaining matter
as can be given along with useful knowledge, and as much
knowledge as can be conveyed in an amusing form.'[5] The first
series of the new Library was entitled *Menageries*. It dealt with
the strange habits of animals, their structure and their capacities.

There were some protests against this development. One
somewhat ruffled correspondent wrote to Brougham that it was
a weak surrender to those who considered that the former
treatises were too scientific. 'If you are to find amusement for
those gentlemen pray form a . . . Society for the Diffusion of
Funny Knowledge and let those gentlemen have their fun to
themselves. . . . I do hope and trust that you who have written
on the porism of Euclid will not condescend to cater for such
lazy drones or incurable blockheads when tens of thousands are
ready to hail you with gratitude for furnishing them with what
is really beneficial.'[6] One is bound to regard the 'fun' with some
scepticism. 'Entertaining' was, of course, given a wide connota-
tion. There was a treatise on Insect Architecture. Brougham had

[1] *Edinburgh Review*, Jan. 1828.   [2] Charles Knight, ii. 62–64.
[3] *The Times*, 2 May 1830. Report of S.D.U.K.
[4] Add. MSS. 35146 (Place MSS.), f. 95 v.
[5] *Edinburgh Review*, Jan. 1828, Mar., Oct. 1829.
[6] S.D.U.K. Letters, William Bote to Brougham, 22 May 1828.

been fascinated by that subject for years. For a mind like his it was highly entertaining. But, even if Brougham had written it himself, would that treatise have been 'full of science and yet as interesting as a novel' to the readers at whom the S.D.U.K. aimed? One writer, after describing the agonies which he experienced in trying to make Cholera 'entertaining', complained that the committee went and deleted every passage in which he believed that he caught a distant glimpse of success in that respect.

There were two volumes in the *Library of Entertaining Knowledge* on 'Paris and its Historical Scenes'. The histories of various nations had been started in the *Useful Library*. Biography played a prominent part in both libraries. Lives of successful self-made men were, in that age of opportunity, always thought of as combining entertainment and high utility. A *Farmers Series* was announced in March 1828, but plans developed slowly and the first treatise (on the Horse) did not appear until October.

Knight said that he was exchanging letters with a number of men but with 'none more unremittingly' than with Brougham, and that even when Brougham was engulfed in his law work, 'contending in friendly rivalry for the leadership of the Northern Circuit with Mr. Pollock', his mind was always turning to 'thoughts of the society which he had founded and which was daily grown more important'. Brougham was writing about the Society to others beside Knight. The range covered in a single letter may be illustrated by one he wrote to M. D. Hill when the latter was on a visit to Edinburgh. Brougham enclosed a letter for Jeffrey and told Hill that he had arranged with Leonard Horner for two other letters of introduction. Hill was urged to find someone in Edinburgh to do an introduction to a book on Mechanics and another to write a book on Astronomy. He was to get Atkinson to put him in touch with Colquhoun and induce Colquhoun to do Dyeing and Bleaching. He was also to do everything he could for the *Farmer Series* and other practical treatises. Knight might well say: 'How could I let the grass grow under my feet with such an inciter to activity.' Brougham could not rest even in the short holiday at Brougham Hall which he had promised himself in the autumn of 1828 when, not yet recovered from the illness brought on by his great law reform speech in February, he had finished the arduous circuit and thought of seizing a breathing space before plunging into work again in London. He sent for Hill to come to Brougham and they sat down to making S.D.U.K. plans for years to come.[1]

By the autumn of 1828, within a year and a half of its first publications, it was felt that some of the 'little books' were too difficult for the contemplated readers to understand. A letter to Coates complained that the language was not sufficiently simplified and that 'nine-tenths of the labouring classes throughout the country cannot read them'. Brougham himself wrote with concern to Coates: 'My informants in Newcastle and elsewhere greatly strengthen the opinion I before had that *more easy* treatises are absolutely necessary.' Two weeks after writing that letter Brougham explained carefully to his old Edinburgh classmate, Anthony Thompson, under appointment as professor in the new University of London, how these treatises should be written.[2]

A series of very superior and useful maps was begun in 1829, and the same year Brougham urged that they should embark on a journal of education. The result was the *Quarterly Journal of Education*, which, although it lasted only five years, occupies an important place in the history of education. It was the first British periodical of its kind. The articles, including some by Thomas Arnold, were excellent; it established contact with Fellenberg and other continental educationists and it did much to improve the quality of education throughout the nation. Its emphasis on teaching method did something to console Brougham for the continued lack of the teachers' colleges on which his heart was set. In November 1830 just as the Whigs at long last came into office, with Brougham as Lord Chancellor, the Society made its first venture in working-class economics with the beginning of the *Workingman's Companion*, to be published occasionally at a shilling a copy. In December, after rioting had again broken out in the country, Knight wrote a volume for the new series entitled *The Results of Machinery*. It had a remarkable sale partly because of its topicality and partly because it was believed to have been written by Brougham. This

---

[1] Charles Knight, ii. 113–14; *Memoir of M. D. Hill* (1878), pp. 82–84.
[2] S.D.U.K. Letters, J. Millan to Coates, 8 Sept. 1828, Brougham to Coates, 11 Aug. 1828, quoted by Miss Grobel, p. 102; Brougham MSS., Coates to Brougham, 4 Sept. 1828; Add. MSS. 26053, ff. 23–24, 29 Aug. 1828.

volume and 'the march of the mind' campaign of which it was a part were blamed for having caused the riots, veen though *The Results of Machinery* urged restraint and deplored these outbreaks of violence. Lord Wilton said popular disaffection might be credited to 'the march of education, to the malign nastiness of the schoolmaster, to the spurious morality of the present day, and the dangerous influence of Mr. Henry, now Lord Brougham, and cheap libraries'.[1] In that neat summary Lord Wilton was almost as right as he was wrong.

The further publicity efforts of the S.D.U.K., the factors modifying its success, and Brougham's untiring leadership must wait for another volume. But in any attempt to estimate the success and failure of the S.D.U.K. it must be judged as an educational movement, and not because it did not function as an appendix or regulator to any social movement. It must be judged as part of a great movement which included much more than good cheap books, and at the back of it all stood the 'gigantic' figure of Brougham, to employ the adjective so frequently applied to him in the letters of the time.

While Brougham's educational activities in this decade were mostly associated with adult education, including the beginning of the University of London, he kept in touch with the remarkable development taking place in primary education. When Parliament opened in 1828 with the Duke of Wellington as Prime Minister, Brougham said that although he regretted that all patronage was controlled by a military man, he had no fear of military rule. 'There had been periods when the country heard with dismay that the soldier was abroad. That was not the case now. Let the soldier be ever so much abroad, in the present age he could do nothing. There was another person abroad. . . . The schoolmaster was abroad and he trusted to the schoolmaster armed with his primer more than he did to the soldier in full military array for upholding and extending the liberties of the country'.[2]

He made another 'schoolmaster is abroad' speech in that same year at the annual meeting of the British and Foreign

[1] R. K. Webb, *The British Working Class Reader, 1790–1848* (1955), p. 105, quoting *Fraser's Magazine*, Dec. 1830. See Webb's chapter on 'Agricultural Disturbances and Machinery' and *passim* on the S.D.U.K.

[2] *Hansard*, N.S., xviii. 57–58.

School Society. And to complete the picture, we import from a later date, 1835, another reference of Brougham's to the schoolmaster.

There is nothing which these adversaries of improvement are more wont to make merry with, than what is termed 'the march of intellect'. . . . It is a very absurd because a very incorrect expression. . . . The conqueror moves in a march. . . . His [the schoolmaster's] is a progress not to be compared with anything like a march, but it leads to laurels more imperishable than the destroyer of his species, the scourge of the world, ever won. . . . Their calling is high and holy. . . . Each of these great teachers of the world, possessing his soul in peace, performs his appointed course, awaits with patience the fulfillment of the promises, resting from his labours bequeathes his memory to the generation whom his works have blessed, and sleeps under the humble, but not inglorious epitaph, commemorating 'one in whom mankind lost a friend, and by no means got rid of an enemy'.[1]

This was probably the first public eulogy in Great Britain of the teaching profession as a whole. By 1828 Brougham's name and fame were such that anything he said was quotable. The phrase 'the schoolmaster is abroad' had a special appeal for those interested in popular education, and it became a slogan. The words of the 'schoolmaster is abroad' speeches were frequently quoted, and found their way into educational reports in Upper Canada.

[1] *Speeches*, iii. 602–4.

CHAPTER XIX

Launching London University, I

THE founding of London University was much more than the establishment of what has become one of the great universities of the world. It was the first English university that was free from barriers of wealth and religion, of privilege and pride. It prepared the way for all the free universities that followed. Its establishment in England put university education on a democratic basis and it was one of Brougham's greatest contributions to liberty.

Strictly speaking the present University of London dates from 1836, the year of its charter foundation. But in effect the history of the University of London began in 1826 with the founding of the institution whose official name was London University, which was frequently called the University of London, and which in 1836 became University College.

In 1826 Oxford and Cambridge were the only universities in England. Circumstances combined to make them privileged communities, regulations combined to bar from Oxford all but Anglicans, and no one could proceed to the more common degrees in Cambridge except Anglicans. The story of the beginning in London of something very different has been so well told by Professor Bellot in his *University College, London*, that all that can be attempted in these chapters is to supplement his account and, of course, call special attention to the part Brougham played in the great enterprise.

In 1820 Thomas Campbell, the poet, was in Bonn, and in conversation with the professors there he conceived the idea that there should be a university in London, which, he said, was the only European capital without one. In the following year after returning to England, Campbell talked about that in the narrow circle of a literary club to which he belonged. In 1824 he was speaking of this to a number of men, and ideas were forming in his mind of the kind of university that he desired, ideas drawn from Scottish and German universities. He said that he would make a public proposal.[1]

In December (1824) Brougham was writing his *Observations on the Education of the People*, in which he put forward a proposal for not one university but several, to make higher education possible for all. Brougham said afterwards that he and Campbell hit on the idea of the University of London at the same time but it is altogether probable that when he wrote the *Observations* he had heard something of Campbell's talk. There is at least one important difference. Campbell was thinking only of a university in London. Brougham from the beginning contemplated a start in London and then other universities of the same type throughout the country.

It was Isaac Lyon Goldsmid, a wealthy Jewish merchant, who introduced Campbell to Brougham. Goldsmid and Brougham had been associated in the anti-slavery movement and in Brougham's educational enterprises. After this they continued a long and affectionate association in many activities, including in later years the political emancipation of the Jews, for which, Goldsmid said, Brougham did more than anyone.[2] They were both apostles of liberty and both believed in action. It was said that Goldsmid alone of Campbell's friends promised assistance in turning dreams into deeds. He became a member of the first Council of the University and his interest and attendance were constant. He and his family made a number of generous gifts to the University over the years.

On the evening of 30 January (1825), shortly after the publication of his *Observations*, Brougham gave a calve's head dinner. There can be no doubt that its purpose was to discuss the university idea. Among those invited were Campbell, Joseph Hume, and James Mill. Campbell told Place next day that all who were at the dinner had promised him support for his project.[3] That discussion induced Campbell to write his letter to Brougham who sent it to *The Times* where it was published on 9 February. Very likely it was decided at the dinner that Campbell should write and publish such a letter, urging the establishment of a university in London. 'The plan I suggest

[1] H. Hale Bellot, *University College, London*, 1826–1926 (1929), pp. 1, 14–15.
[2] Brougham MSS., Goldsmid to Brougham, 2 June 1848.
[3] Add. MSS. 27823, ff. 418–19, quoted in Bellot, p. 19.

is a great London University for the middling rich'. Brougham
and his colleagues were later to insist that it was for *all classes*.
The letter was addressed to Brougham no doubt because of his
prestige, his popularity, and his recognized leadership in everything pertaining to popular education.

Two weeks after Brougham's dinner, on 14 February,
another dinner was held at the home of John Smith, M.P., with
the same persons present to discuss the project further. Other
meetings followed. In the April and July numbers of the *New
Monthly Magazine*, of which Campbell was the editor, he published 'Suggestions respecting the Plan of a University in
London'.

That was Campbell's last act of leadership. After that his
part in the movement was of secondary importance. Brougham
had apparently already taken the lead so far as getting things
done was concerned and from that time on his leadership was
unquestioned. Campbell's proposals were important but when
it came to taking practical steps toward the founding of a university, he did not possess the requisite gifts. He lacked the
tremendous application and industry of Brougham. Sam Rogers
said after Campbell's death that if they erected a statue of him
at Westminster they should set it on a firm pedestal, for 'all the
town knew that for the last fifteen years of his life Tommy was
seldom able to stand steadily on his own feet'.[1] C. E. Macfarlane in his *Reminiscences* told of Campbell's being taken home
when he was 'past speech'. His friend forgot the correct address,
and the coachman was assailed by an irate voice through a
window: 'Damn Mr. Campbell. This is the third time within a
week I have been knocked out of my bed in the middle of the
night on his account. He lives in *Upper* Seymour Street. This is
Lower Seymour Street.'[2] To which Macfarlane added: 'Drink
did not improve Tommy's temper. It made him impatient,
captious, querulous and uncommonly unpleasant.'[3]

At this point too the main stream was joined by a lesser but
very important one. For some years the Dissenters had talked
among themselves of a university for Dissenters which would
best be established in London. The sons of Dissenters could

[1] Add. MSS. 30776 f. 116 v.
[2] Add. MSS. 39775, f. 74 v.
[3] Add. MSS. 39776, f. 10 v.

not study at Oxford; conditions at Cambridge were invidious and young men who were intelligent as well as ambitious tended to keep away. To go to Scotland or Holland to study, as some did, was expensive and so for financial as well as ecclesiastical reasons Dissenters were deprived of a university education.[1] In the *Baptist Magazine* for May 1820 a detailed programme was put forward under the heading Protestant Dissenting College. References in the introduction to the universities of Scotland and of Holland indicate that it was to function as a university. It was to provide 'instruction of their [the Dissenters'] youth in the higher branches of languages and sciences'. 'I beg here to submit . . . the plan of a college which will secure to the students a liberal education and communicate to them such a course of instruction as will enable them to appear with honour in the learned professions or to adorn private life with literary pursuits.' The plan was presented in great detail.[2]

It was almost certainly the work of the Rev. F. A. Cox, Baptist minister at Hackney, who led the Baptists throughout in their discussion of a university for Dissenters. Cox was, like Brougham and Campbell, a graduate of a Scottish university. He had graduated from Edinburgh after Brougham had left for London. He was a scholarly minister, active in the Hackney Academy, who had written a life of Melanchthon, and for three years had been secretary of the general body of Dissenting ministers. Professor Lardner said in 1830 that 'the first notion of a university is said to have been suggested by a dissenting clergyman named Rev. Mr. Cox'.[3]

What the immediate reaction was to the publication of that plan we do not know, but by 1824 general talk had given way to very specific discussion. Bogue published a plan, meetings were held, Cox published another plan, in fact a prospectus. In April (1825) the Dissenters appointed a Provisional Committee, which immediately appointed delegates to interview Brougham, Campbell, and their friends. A number of conferences between representatives of the two groups were held in Brougham's

[1] Bellot, p. 21. As early as 1812 Rev. David Bogue suggested that if a university 'open to all denominations, Christian or Jews' were established 'in a central part of England' it would receive adequate support.

[2] *Baptist Magazine*, May 1820.

[3] Add. MSS. 37185 (Babbage MSS.), f. 115–16, Lardner to Babbage, 8 Apr. [1830].

chambers and before the end of April an agreement was reached that they would join to support a general *secular* university.[1]

Brougham was credited with bringing the Dissenters in. He persuaded them that neither group could succeed without the support of the other and that the teaching had to be purely secular because any attempt at a plan for religious teaching that would satisfy Dissenters would antagonize too many Anglicans, who would support a secular university but would not hear of any teaching of religion that did not conform entirely to the Anglican pattern. He believed that the only path to a successful university lay in a strong union of moderates. Both extreme Dissenters and extreme Anglicans must be circumvented. Much more was gained by Brougham's union than the financial support of wealthy Dissenters, Catholics, and Jews, without which there would have been no University of London. The Dissenters had a record of remarkable educational success with their Academies.

The union with the Dissenters effected, Brougham sought to obtain a charter for the proposed university. He approached two of the Ministers who said that the Government would refuse to grant a royal charter. When he suggested a parliamentary charter and said that he would introduce a Bill, they were non-committal.[2] In moving for leave to bring in a Bill on 26 May Brougham said: 'The object of the university was to bring the advantages of education within the reach of those who could not afford to send their children to the universities of Oxford and Cambridge . . . to render education come-at-able by the middle classes of society.' Later he said that it was not intended that degrees should be given. He refrained from adding 'as yet'. 'One great object would be to lay the foundation of a good medical school, a thing which could be accomplished only in the neighbourhood of a large hospital or hospitals.'[3]

In a few weeks Brougham had had time to size up the parliamentary situation. His reasons for not proceeding with his Bill were given in the August *Edinburgh Review*, probably in his own words: 'Though [the Bill] would have passed the lower house in spite of the Ministry, yet as they were resolved not to countenance it, the Lords would certainly have thrown it out and the bill was therefore, to save expense and delay, prudently dropt.'

[1] Bellot, pp. 21–24. [2] *The Times*, 6 June 1825.
[3] *Hansard*, N.S., xiii. 840, 1033 seq.

On 4 June a 'private' meeting was held, attended by 120 persons. Brougham, from the chair, explained the purpose of the meeting and the general character of the university project. He placed his customary emphasis on the university being intended for 'almost every class in society'. He said that a number of meetings had been held in his chambers and a plan which had been prepared would be laid before them, and that they would be asked to appoint a committee to consider it and to make any revision that seemed to be desirable. Cox read the plan and a committee of thirty-five was appointed.[1] The first public meeting was held on 1 July with the Lord Mayor in the chair.[2] Cox presented the project and made an eloquent speech. Brougham's speech was, according to Hobhouse, 'a good speech, amusing and much to the purpose, except when he talked about religion'.[3] Cyrus Redding, who did not like Brougham, gave the following as his impression: 'He commenced, all was stillness; he proceeded, all was satisfaction; he concluded, and all was applause; he entered into the merits of the question with his usual adroitness and skill.'[4] Mackintosh moved, seconded by Campbell, that the name should be 'The London University'. Other speakers were the Rev. Joseph Fletcher, a Dissenting minister, Benjamin Shaw, another Dissenter, Gurney, Goldsmid, Lord John Russell, Abercromby, and Denman. The first prospectus was published on 9 July.

The shares were sold for £100 each. The original objective was the sale of 1,500 shares. During that summer Brougham wrote (with pen and ink in his own hand) '150 long letters' to friends and acquaintances asking them to take up shares. He approached others, no doubt, in different ways. He sold at that time about 200 shares (more than an eighth of the number sold in 1825). Altogether in that year and the next he got fifty refusals.[5] Most of those who accepted took only one share but a few took large blocks, notably the Duke of Bedford[6] whose general outlook was liberal and who was for a number of years president of the British and Foreign School Society, of which he regarded

[1] *The Times*, 6 June 1825.   [2] Ibid., 2 July 1825.
[3] Broughton, iii. 113.
[4] Cyrus Redding, *Literary Reminiscences and Memoirs of Thomas Campbell*, 2 vols. (1860), ii. 13–16.
[5] A letter a year later, Brougham MSS., Brougham to Denman, 8 Aug. 1826.
[6] Ibid., Duke of Bedford to Brougham, 28 Aug. 1825.

Brougham as the founder. It should be noted in this connexion that the Duke of Bedford had passed by Oxford and Cambridge in sending his son, Lord John Russell, to Edinburgh for his university education. Brougham sold other shares to the members of the aristocracy including the Duke of Devonshire and Lord Tankerville.[1] In his reply to Brougham's letter, Edward Petrie, who was a Catholic, said: 'I am sure nothing is more congenial to my feelings than to contribute support to an institution founded on such liberal principles by the most enlightened men of the day. I trust the Catholics will always be found ready to support those institutions which have for their object the diffusion of a liberal education, the only permanent basis on which religious freedom can exist, or civil liberty flourish.' Petrie promised to induce others to buy shares.[2] At the same time Brougham was making a strong appeal for the university through the *Edinburgh Review*.[3]

At the beginning of August Cox, who was acting as secretary for the committee, was satisfied by a total sale to date of a thousand shares. Writing to express regret that he could not accept an invitation to Brougham Hall, he added to his report on the sale of shares: 'Some of our *Evangelicals* however are at work in another way, and I or you or some of us may expect an attack (besides the caricature shops) of which I am by no means sorry.'[4] On 26 August Cox reported to Brougham that nearly 1,500 shares had been sold but that he believed that they should press for another thousand. He sympathized with Hume's suggestion that they should ask 'large holders to reduce their number' in order to have a larger body of shareholders, but he evidently distrusted that kind of over-confidence.[5]

Early in August Brougham 'arranged' for the purchase of the land and for advertising for plans.[6] But the committee was not in a position to buy the land; John Smith, Goldsmid, and Shaw, liberal Whig M.P., Jew and Dissenter, took the risk of purchasing it themselves until the university could take it over.[7] A few

---

[1] Chatsworth MSS., Brougham to the Duke of Devonshire, 10 Oct. 1825.
[2] Brougham MSS., Edward Petrie to Brougham, 14 Aug. 1825.
[3] *Edinburgh Review*, Aug. 1825.
[4] Brougham MSS., 2 Aug. 1825.
[5] Ibid., 26 Aug. 1825.
[6] *Memoirs*, ii. 469; Brougham MSS., Brougham to Loch, 10 Aug. 1825.
[7] Bellot, p. 34.

days after advertising for plans Brougham was asking Samuel
Rogers, and others no doubt, what they knew about architects.[1]
Late in September Cox wrote to Brougham that the shares were
then going slowly, warned that their enemies would make the
most of any weakness, and suggested that Brougham should
write something for *The Times* that would make the most of the
progress to date. Cox hoped that a Council could be elected
soon. 'I do not greatly admire our present heterogeneous Committee, half of whom can never be got together.' He had several
things to say about it which he did not care to commit to paper.[2]

Cox's fear of trouble with the Evangelicals was fully confirmed
in the following months. Evangelicals as well as High Churchmen were strongly opposed to the idea of a university without
religion. The Evangelicals were opposed to a university not
teaching religion; many of the High Church were shocked at
the thought of a university not teaching the religion of the
Church of England. Brougham received a letter from Wilberforce, who was, of course, the greatest of the Evangelicals, on
1 October, shortly after his retirement from Parliament. 'It
cannot but be reluctantly that I avow so wide a difference of
sentiment from you on a subject on which I have so long admired
your persevering efforts.' He suggested 'a separate endowment
for lectures on the Evidences of Christianity' and begged
Brougham to 'reflect seriously on the consequences of imparting
to so influential a body of men . . . all branches of philosophical
knowledge, leaving them wholly ignorant of the grounds and
basis of Christian truth'.[3] But Brougham was persistently opposed to a course of lectures on the Evidences of Christianity
in a university that was open to all, including Jews.

The first Council was elected at a general meeting of shareholders on 19 December but it was not formally appointed until
11 February (1826) after another general meeting had approved
the deed of settlement. And so the university was founded. The
names of that first Council make an imposing list, but a university
cannot be conducted by imposing names. Few of the members
had had the kind of experience that would qualify them for the

---

[1] P. W. Clayden, *Rogers and his Contemporaries*, 2 vols. (1889), i. 420, Brougham to
Rogers, 20 Aug. 1825.
[2] Brougham MSS., 21 Sept. 1825.
[3] Ibid., 1 Oct. 1825.

tasks ahead; Birkbeck alone (and Cox, the secretary) had been associated with any educational institution except as a student. The list of twenty-four was fully representative of certain groups while others had scanty representation if any at all. There were four peers and one son of a peer. There were nine members of the House of Commons, six of whom were liberal Whigs and three were Radicals. There were four Dissenters and two others, James Mill and Goldsmid, who were not members of the Church of England. But Lord Dudley and Ward, a Canningite, was the only Tory, Zachary Macaulay was the only Evangelical. There was no clergyman, either Church or Dissenter, because they were barred by a rule which had been decided on as early as the middle of November.[1] It has been said that the men who undertook to conduct the University of London were those whom Brougham had gathered around him for the Society of the Diffusion of Useful Knowledge. But it was not until November of that year, 1826, that the S.D.U.K. got its real start and appointed its first Council. Then Brougham selected for it only a third of the Council of the University of London. In the case of the S.D.U.K. the selection was almost entirely Brougham's; in that of the University of London it was probably largely so.

Brougham had written to Samuel Rogers in August: 'The Monasters [Oxford and Cambridge] are howling, and the Bishop of Chester preaching already.'[2] The 'monasteries' did not howl very loudly officially. The howling was done by a number of loyal graduates. The privileges of the ancient universities as by law established were being infringed; a university was something whose teaching was 'universal' (a silly but common error in etymology) and since this institution was not going to teach religion it could not be a university; purely secular education was as dangerous to the state as it was to religion and it must be opposed on political grounds by any government that had a sense of responsibility for the defence of the faith.[3]

An established order of society was endangered, and because Brougham was leading this new movement old enemies stirred themselves. There were those who for what they believed to be patriotic motives feared Brougham and all his works. There were

[1] Ibid., Cox to Brougham, 16 Nov. 1825.
[2] Clayden, i. 420, 20 Aug. 1825.   [3] See Bellot, pp. 62 seq.

lovers of comfort who feared him because he was changing too much in England and the future was not safe in his hands. There were also the old implacable enemies who had been hurt in the past, the slave-traders, abusers of charities, and many individuals who had been the objects of his invective; they were at all times out for revenge. And now there were new enemies from the old schools and the ancient universities. Yet Brougham, of course, enjoyed a great popularity at that time in the nation at large. There were thousands who would be for anything with which he was associated, just as in the days of the passing of the Great Reform Bill six years later, to thousands the names of Grey and Durham, of Althorp and Russell meant nothing. When the Bill had passed, it was for them Brougham who had done it all, and a group of miners in Cornwall greeted the news with 'Three cheers for Henry Brougham'.

The friends of stability and safety and of standing still generally, could always expect support from the ridicule and scurrility that flowed so easily from *John Bull*. Now, and especially in 1825 and 1826, it was the 'godless university', 'the Cockney College', that was assailed in poetry and in prose. Professor Bellot has reprinted several passages. Here are some others:

> From 'The Cockney College, an Invitation to Stinkamalee' in
> *John Bull*, January 22, 1826:
> First of all discover (if you're able) where is Gower Street,
> The terrae incognitae of Alfred Street and Store Street,
> Get safely through Carmarthen Street, escape will be a mercy,
> And on the right, at number ten, you'll see the University.
> Run, sweepers, run, 'tis now the time for lecturing.
> Every man must learned be in these wise days.
> .   .   .
> When those days arrive, quite different from now, my friends,
> Reason, worth and learning will assert their claims;
> Duchesses will knead and wash, and Dukes will hold the plough,
> my friends,
> Fruitless will be titles then, and all high names;
> Marquises must clean their shoes, and Earls attend the stable, sirs,
> Barons stir the kitchen fire, and Viscounts wait at table, sirs.
> Come then boys, my shirtless boys, who have such gay diversity,
> No Church, no King, no 'nothing else' but Gower Street University.

And in *John Bull*, 26 March 1826, under the heading of 'The March of Intellect':

It happened on the 31st of March, *1926*, that the then Duke and Duchess of Bedford were sitting in the good but old house, 17 Liberality Place.

(Enter Lady Moira) 'Was Duggins in the assistants' drawing-room, my love?' said the Duke. 'I want him to take a message for me'. 'I'm sure, then, he cannot go,' said Lady Moira, 'because I know he is gone, to the House of Parliament. (There was but one at that time.) For he told the other gentleman who cleans the plate that he could not be back to attend at dinner, however consonant with his wishes, because he had promised to wait for the division.'

'Ah,' sighed the Duke, 'this comes of his having been elected for Westminster.'

At this moment Lord John Russell made his appearance, extremely hot and evidently tired, having under his arm a largish parcel.

'What have you there, Johnny?' said her Grace. 'My new breeches,' said his Lordship. 'I have called upon the worthy citizen who made them over and over again and never could get them; for of course I could not expect him to send them and he is always either at the Academy or the Gymnasium; however today I caught him just as he was in a hot debate with the gentleman who was cleaning his windows, as to whether the solidity of a prism is equal to the product of its base by its altitude. . . . Unluckily the question was referred to me, and not comprehending it I was deucedly glad to get off, which I did as fast as I could, both parties calling after me, "There is a lord for you, look at my Lord," and hooting at me in a manner which, however constitutional, I cannot help thinking deucedly disagreeable.'

At this period, what in former times was called a footman, named Dowbiggan, made his appearance. 'Dowbiggan,' said his Grace, 'I wish you would take away these breakfast things.' 'Indeed,' said Dowbiggan, looking at the Duke with ineffable contempt, 'you do, that's capital. What right have *you* to ask me to do any such thing?'

'Why, Mr. Dowbiggan,' said the Duchess, 'his Grace pays you, and clothes you, and feeds you, to . . . .' 'Well, Duchess, let his Grace show me his superiority.' [He told of how he had asked the Duke a learned question, the answer to which he knew very well, and the Duke could not answer it.] 'Now if it can be shown that I, who am perfectly competent to answer any question I propose, am . . . to be required to work for a man who does not know as much as I do myself, merely because he is a Duke, why I'll do it; but if not, I will resist in a constitutional manner any such oppression, even though I am transported to Scotland for it.' . . .

'John,' said the Duke to his son, 'go and ask Monteagle if he will be kind enough to let the horses be put to our carriage.' 'You need not send to Monteagle,' said Dowbiggan, 'he is gone to the Society of Arts to hear a lecture on Astronomy.' 'Then, John, go and endeavour to harness the horses yourself,' said the Duke to his son.

'You had better mind about those horses, sir,' said Dowbiggan. 'The two German philosophers have been with them to-day, and there appears little doubt that the great system will spread.' . . .

Lord John Russell re-appeared as white as snow. 'My dear father,' cried his Lordship, 'it's all over now. The philosophers have carried this thing too far. The chestnut mare swears that she'll be damned if she goes out to-day.'

The enemies of the new university also expended much solicitude on what a terrible thing it would be to bring young men to London as university students. The unhealthiness of London was discovered and at the same time the street-walkers suddenly came within the observation of a number of good persons.

For the most part the adventurers followed their vision without attempting to hit back. Any project of Brougham's would, of course, be supported in the *Edinburgh Review*, but the *Edinburgh* articles, with one exception, consisted of descriptions of what was being aimed at. It was not Brougham apparently who instilled ginger into the *Edinburgh* on this question and carried the war into Africa, but Macaulay (Thomas Babington) who was then a young man of twenty-five. His article in the February 1826 number was quite as much an attack on Oxford and Cambridge as a defence of London. Though there was exaggeration and too much sting in Macaulay's article, it was, of course, well written. 'We have observed that since Mr. Croker, in the last session of Parliament, declared himself ignorant of the site of Russell Square, the plan of forming a University in so inelegant a neighbourhood has excited much contempt amongst those estimable persons who think that the whole dignity of man consists of living within certain districts, wearing coats made by certain tailors, and eschewing certain meats and drinks.' Macaulay closed his article not with a purple patch but with a simple confession of faith, faith in the principle of which the University of London was the symbol and the embodiment. 'We entertain a firm conviction that the principles of liberty, as in government and trade, so also in education, are all-important to the happiness

of mankind. . . . We do, in our souls, believe that they are strong
with the strength and quick with the vitality of truth.'

In the newspaper press the *Morning Chronicle* alone gave the
new university strong support. On 19 July 1825 it published
Praed's lines which were put into the mouth of 'a college tutor'
(Oxford or Cambridge) at 'a supper party'.

> Ye Dons and ye Doctors, ye Provosts and Proctors,
>   Who are paid to monopolize knowledge,
> Come, make opposition, by vote and petition
>   To the radical infidel College.
> Come, put forth your powers in aid of the towers
>   Which boast of their Bishops and Martyrs,
> And arm all the terrors of privileged errors,
>   Which live by the wax of their Charters.
>
> Let Macintosh battle with Canning and Vattel,
>   Let Brougham be a friend to the Niggers,
> Burdett cure the nation's misrepresentation,
>   And Hume make a figure in figures;
> But let them not babble of Greek to the rabble,
>   Nor teach the Mechanics their letters;
> The labouring classes were born to be asses,
>   And not to be aping their betters.[1]

The depression which set in toward the end of 1825 hit the
university financially and when it called for the payment of
first instalments it found early in 1826 that on 300 shares no pay-
ments were made. It was decided to sell extra shares but they
came in slowly. John Smith and Goldsmid again came to the
rescue in the autumn of 1826, taking fifty shares each of 200
supplemental shares that had been created.[2] Brougham, writing
to friends again, disposed of twenty shares in the early summer
of that year.[3]

Out of that situation came another flare-up between Brougham
and Francis Place. Up to this time Place had not been active but
Brougham had suggested to his colleagues that he would be useful in the matter of selling shares. Early in July (1826) Place

---

[1] For the whole poem see *Morning Chronicle*, 19 July 1825, and W. M. Praed,
Poems (1864).
[2] Bellot, pp. 33–34.
[3] Brougham MSS., Brougham to Denman, 8 Aug. 1826.

proposed to one of them a plan whereby 'squads' of three persons each would go around 'in coaches' and ask those who had taken shares to add to their holdings and urge their friends to buy shares.[1] Two days later Place's plan was submitted to the Council. According to Place's diary, Brougham approved of the plan 'but objected that my name if mixed up with the college might be injurious on account of infidel opinions I was (he said) known to entertain'. Campbell opposed Brougham and others, and argued that Place's opinions had nothing to do with the matter, that the Council contained 'some notorious free thinkers and that if exceptions were taken they would go round'. Place said that he knew all about this an hour later and before nightfall recorded it in his diary, which continues: 'The conduct of Brougham is as usual that of a shuffling lawyer, his [sic] is much better known as an infidel than I am, and he is known too as I am not known and cannot be known to be a shuffler in politics. I will challenge him to go round with me to sell shares and I dare say he will do it.'[2]

Everyone who knew Place knew that he did not pretend to be a Christian and his religious attitude was frequently commented on. On the other hand, no one spoke of Brougham in that fashion, though some in private correspondence wondered what actually went on in his mind in regard to religion. Unlike Place, Brougham was a professing Christian and a regular attendant at the lawyers' church at the Temple. He was perhaps too fond of asserting his love for the Church of England, which he most frequently did when severely criticizing its clergy. Like Place, Mill, and Bentham, Brougham in his mind rejected many of the doctrines of historical Christianity, but he never adopted their anti-Christian attitude.

Place usually let many suns go down upon his wrath and the way in which he believed that Brougham had treated Campbell over London University owed much to his irritation. 'Brougham tricked Campbell, ousted him from the credit of being the originator and, as Campbell is a simple sensitive creature, made him very unhappy. Brougham played so many tricks and acted in such an unprincipled manner as no one can well imagine. . . . Campbell shall, if I can obtain it for him or in

---

[1] Add. MSS. 35146, f. 31, Place's Diary, 6 July.
[2] Ibid., f. 31 v., quoted in Bellot, pp. 30–31.

any way assist to obtain it for him, have the credit of being the original proposer.'[1]

How roughly Campbell may have been thrust aside when Brougham took the lead we do not know. We have only Place's word for it. Brougham was frequently lacking in tact and sympathy when he was pushing ahead, but he later conceded that Campbell was the 'original proposer', whether or not he did so at this time, and in the actual establishment of the University Place recognized fully that Brougham took the lead and that Campbell could not have done so. He said later that without the energy and activity of Brougham and Hume there would have been no London University.

In November (1826) Place recorded a story which Campbell had told him. Campbell succeeded Brougham as Lord Rector of the University of Glasgow in the spring of 1826. But before the election Brougham had told him he would have no chance because he would be opposed by Moncrief who was sure to be elected. Consequently, Campbell advised his friends to drop the matter because he was withdrawing, but on investigation the friends discovered that only one elector had been canvassed for Moncrief and that it was Brougham who had approached him.[2] No one who knew Brougham would believe that he did that out of spite toward Campbell, but a good many would believe that Brougham could act in that manner to wangle an office for a friend or arrange an appointment that was for some reason desirable. Campbell was still talking about Brougham's trickery in the following March. On the 27th of that month, Hobhouse entered in his diary: 'The other day T. Campbell, the poet, called on me, big with complaints against Brougham, and told me several traits of his character which I would fain think unfairly drawn.'[3]

Brougham and Place were, of course, reconciled as usual. Ten years later Campbell was a happy guest at Brougham Hall, after which he wrote to Brougham: 'May I ask you when you are at leisure some day, if such a day ever occurs, to send me the brilliant verses of Voltaire which you recited to me at Brougham

---

[1] Add. MSS. 35146, f. 5 v. Though this is headed 'Memorandum concerning Sept. 1825', it was written later.

[2] Ibid., f. 64, Place's Diary for 1826, 27 Nov.

[3] Broughton, iii. 178. Quoted in Bellot, pp. 31–32.

Hall', and added that he was sending Brougham his new poem which would be out next week.[1] When Campbell died Brougham asked to be a bearer. At the same time he spoke of Campbell as 'the greatest poet of our times'.[2] It may be doubted that Brougham knew much about the poets of his time. There is no evidence of it and it is difficult to think of Brougham reading Keats or Wordsworth. The poets he loved were cast in more rugged mould, Dante and Milton. Yet he may have happened on something of Campbell's which he enjoyed.

Early in 1826 the Council undertook the task of preparing a curriculum. Brougham wrote to Lord Lansdowne:

> The digesting of a proper plan for the course of instruction must be the work of some time, and we [the Education Committee] only began by discussing a number of general principles. . . . Upon most essential points there was a general agreement, as that examinations should in every branch be introduced, the method of mutual instruction as much as possible, certain branches often taught as parts of the sciences kept separate (e.g. minerology and geology . . .) . . . I suggested a number of these points to them and others suggested more, and I have since drawn up a statement of what was talked about and the general impression on each matter that seemed to prevail. This is now circulating . . . as the groundwork of further discussion on some points next Saturday. The only thing concluded was to move the Council at its next meeting to collect [an illegible word] information in several of the best foreign (chiefly German) universities, but this too is not decided, it is only to be discussed on Saturday, and I have not at all made up my mind, for one, that I incline to it. In the meantime Mackintosh has drawn up a kind of prospectus, which is also circulating and will be considered next Saturday.[3]

So Brougham had charge of the fundamental curriculum building and Sir James Mackintosh of the preparation of a prospectus. After the prospectus had been fully discussed in the Education Committee and the full Council, it went back to Brougham and Mackintosh for final amendment and approval, and was published on 8 May 1826. Two statements published later continued the description of studies. The proposal to study German universities was adopted as policy. Campbell visited the University of Berlin in the autumn of that year, Goldsmid

---

[1] Brougham MSS., 23 Dec. 1836.   [2] Add. MSS. 40482, f. 6.
[3] Lansdowne MSS., n.d., but shortly before 8 May 1826.

went to Germany to observe universities in the following year, and Austin, under appointment as Professor of Jurisprudence, working in Germany on his influential lectures on that subject, also made careful observations.

The German influence was, however, slight compared to the Scottish, though it apparently did something to strengthen the currents from the north. Brougham and Mackintosh were graduates of the University of Edinburgh, as were six of the Education Committee of ten, Birkbeck, Brougham, Lord Dudley and Ward, Lord Lansdowne, Mackintosh, and Mill. Campbell who was also on the Education Committee had studied mainly at Glasgow, but briefly in Edinburgh. Cox, who as secretary of the Council was close to the work of the Education Committee, was also a graduate of Edinburgh, and when a warden was appointed he too was a graduate of Edinburgh. In its shaping London University has the appearance of a New Edinburgh, an educational New Jerusalem let down from the north. Everything points to the fact that the Scottish influence was predominant both in outline and detail: as Professor Bellot put it: 'The extended range of the subjects of university study, the lecture system, the non-residence of the students, their admission to single courses, the absence of religious tests, the dependence of professors upon fees, and the democratic character of the institution were all deliberate imitations of Scottish practice.'[1]

In the spring of 1827 the laying of the corner-stone was delayed until Brougham was able to return from the Northern Circuit. The stone was laid by the Duke of Sussex on 30 April and at the dinner which followed Brougham was the main speaker. Charles Bell (later Sir Charles Bell), the University's first Professor of Clinical Surgery, writing to his brother, said: 'Brougham was exceedingly good ... first sawing with one hand, and then the other, and generally holding out his two fists straight before him. He delivers himself in a measured, slow, continuous flow of words, and excels in sarcasm. His description of a man sneering at the University, and continuing the joke when the laugh was (to him unconsciously) altogether at him and not with him, was felicitous, and made the fat fellows roar again.'[2]

---

[1] Bellot, p. 8.
[2] *Letters of Sir Charles Bell* (1870), pp. 295–6, quoted by Bellot, p. 37.

During the greater part of 1827 and 1828 much of the attention of the Council was engaged by the selection and appointment of the first professors. There Brougham's influence was supposed to be supreme and any applicant who had the support of both Brougham and Mill might feel relatively sure of his professorship. Brougham was particularly anxious to appoint men who could teach well. He wrote to Lord Auckland, a member of the Council, of one appointee: '. . . an excellent *teacher* of long experience and was very famous for making admirable scholars. . . . Next, his heart and soul are in the work and he will devote himself to it. I am a little sick of professors who either cannot teach or will not devote themselves to it and I look to zeal and experience of teaching as everything.'[4]

One appointment for which Brougham was certainly responsible resulted in an important historical development in another institution. Sir Anthony Panizzi, perhaps the most famous of all librarians, whose bust occupies the place of honour above the doors of the great reading-room of the British Museum, had been a young rebel in Italy, joining the Carbonari at the age of twenty-three. A few years later he was in London, a refugee from the Austrian government with a price on his head. How nearly he starved in London at first we do not know, but the Italian poet Foscolo gave him letters of introduction to Roscoe of Liverpool, writer of Italian history and political friend of Brougham. In Liverpool Panizzi made a living by teaching Italian. It is likely that Roscoe originally introduced him to Brougham, and that this was the beginning of the friendship which led to Panizzi's appointment as Professor of Italian in the University of London. It happened, however, that less than ten students a year wished to study Italian, and Panizzi, who was dependent on students' fees plus a very small salary, was much worse off than he had been in Liverpool. Five months after Brougham became Lord Chancellor he appointed Panizzi assistant librarian at the British Museum, on 27 April 1831.[2] What Panizzi did with the opportunity afforded him is a matter of history. He gave up his London professorship in 1839, but his

---

[1] Add. MSS. 34459 (Auckland MSS.), f. 434.

[2] The appointment was actually made by the Lord Chancellor and the Archbishop of Canterbury, who were two of the three trustees, any two having the right to make an appointment. Add. MSS. 36714 (Panizzi MSS.), f. 224.

friendship with Brougham lasted throughout his life; we often hear of them dining together.

A story circulated later to the effect that Brougham refused to appoint Thomas Carlyle to a professorship at this time and that as a consequence, years afterwards, Carlyle, then a trustee of the National Gallery, opposed unsuccessfully the hanging of Brougham's portrait while he was alive, which indeed had never been done in the case of any other man. Carlyle was certainly vindictive in regard to Brougham, but this story is open to serious doubt. The known facts are that Carlyle thought of applying for a professorship in the new university and after hesitating between English Literature and Moral Philosophy, decided finally on the latter. Jeffrey wrote to Brougham on his behalf, but Brougham was not enthusiastic. Probably on hearing that, Carlyle changed his mind and did not apply.

There was also the unfortunate Bowring case. Bentham wrote long letters to Brougham recommending his friend and disciple for the professorship of English Literature. Bowring had a good knowledge of European literatures and was a remarkable linguist, he said that he knew 200 languages and could speak 100 of them. He also wrote two famous hymns. Bentham believed that he would be very useful to the University as foreign correspondent as well as Professor of Literature. He was a Unitarian, but Bentham said that surely religion would have nothing to do with an appointment to London University. Nor would Brougham turn him down because he had been editor of the Radical review, the *Westminster*.

At first Brougham said that they would not find a better man and that he would support the recommendation. Then he said that the great difficulty would be the scandal over the Greek Loan, for Bowring had been secretary of the first Greek Loan Committee. There was another one, but many believed that both had been handled foolishly, to say the least. London University was getting so much criticism at this time that Brougham was no doubt on his guard. But when the Rev. Thomas Dale was appointed to the chair, Bentham did not believe that Brougham had rejected his recommendation because of the Greek Loan, but because Lord Dudley and Ward, who was a member of the Council, an old friend of Brougham, and Foreign Secretary in the Coalition Government with which Brougham was anxious to exert as much power as possible, urged the appointment of Dale. Since Bentham believed that, his anger expressed later in his *Boa Constrictor* and *Lord Brougham Displayed* is understandable. They were, however, published after 1830 and belong to our other volume.

The largest group among the professors appointed were graduates of Scottish universities. It should be noted that of the five men among the first appointees who enjoyed established reputations, three were graduates of the University of Edinburgh and had been members of the Speculative Society at the same time as Brougham. There was a goodly number of Cambridge graduates among the professors but not a single graduate of Oxford.

CHAPTER XX

Launching London University, II

A T the annual general meeting of the proprietors (shareholders) on 27 February 1828 Brougham strongly opposed a course of lectures in the University on the Evidences of Christianity. There was, he said, so much disagreement as to what Christianity was: 'It was not because they disregarded religion or religious education that the Council had omitted theological lectureships, but because they deemed the subject too important to be approached lightly or inconsiderately. Their object was to leave the religious instruction of the students to their parents and clergymen.'[1]

On 27 May three of the professors under appointment who were clergymen of the Church of England announced publicly that, with the approbation of the Council, at a place near the University 'a course of divinity lectures will be delivered during the academic session'.[2] Cox and another Dissenting minister, the Rev. Joseph Fletcher, then announced that they too would give lectures, also with the approval of the Council and outside the University, on the Evidences of Christianity, Biblical Literature, and Church History. In September the Council disclaimed both courses. The three Anglican professors then joined forces with the two Dissenters and were prepared to make a joint appeal to the Council in support of their rights. It was agreed, however, that before that was done Cox should write to Brougham. Brougham was ill but they hoped to get action through him. Cox said in his letter that in spite of the feelings of a few of the proprietors, 'ten to one are warmly in favour of us'. They had acted, 'at least as much as from other motives, out of regard to the Institution. We have received many testimonies since, proving that the objections of many to the university are materially diminished, not to say entirely removed by this very announcement.'[3] Brougham apparently agreed. They proceeded with the lectures.

[1] *The Times*, 28 Feb. 1828.   [2] Ibid., 27 May.
[3] Brougham MSS., Cox to Brougham, 5 Sept. 1828.

A letter which Brougham received from Althorp on this matter must have been particularly gratifying. They had been very close friends for some years and, though not at all alike, they shared certain fundamental liberal principles. Althorp was a wretched speaker, genuinely modest, with a mind as slow as Brougham's was quick. Only his conscience kept him in politics. He would have much preferred to spend his time in agricultural pursuits. Brougham sometimes began his letters, 'Dear Man of Cattle'. Within two years Brougham would be presiding in the House of Lords, and Althorp leading the House of Commons successfully by sheer force of character, common sense, and thoroughness. Brougham and Althorp carried on long discussions and a correspondence on Natural Theology. A small Bible always lay on Althorp's table and even in his Cabinet days he kept it close to him. He had told Brougham that he would not take a share in a university in which no religion was taught. He was a strong Churchman but he would actually prefer that the religion taught at the University should not be 'a Church religion'; there should, however, be some religion. Now, with the outside lectures being given, he wrote to Brougham to say that the only objection 'which prevented me then from assisting in what I consider a most useful and great undertaking on every ground' had been removed, and that he wished to be a shareholder.[1]

In 1828 King's College was organized under the auspices of the official leadership of the Church of England, as a college in which, in addition to receiving instruction in various branches of literature and science, 'the minds of youth would be imbued with a knowledge of the doctrines and duties of Christianity as indicated by the Church of England'. What was to be the attitude of London University to this rival institution? Brougham made his feeling very clear in a letter written in August or early September to Denman, by that time a member of the Council:

King's College is a nice thing to handle. There is a cry against it raised by the Hume, Carlile etc. school . . .; there is also a feeling of a calm but equally erroneous cast among some of ourselves, even in the Council. The more I reflect the clearer I am that it is (the K.C.) a *great good*, if not an unmixed one. It has given up already 9/10 of the exclusive notions it set out with, and it must end in giving them

[1] Brougham MSS., 25 Mar. 1829.

all up, and except as regards resident students, being exactly on our footing. . . . Then we have two London universities instead of one, both teaching the middle and even upper classes in the *light* of London. We have another, tho' lesser good, the stopping of all outcry against universities in great towns and carried on by shareholders, and for persons in trade, and Liverpool, Manchester and Birmingham may take the hint given by us and adopted by the High Church party. Again, we have a hold eventually on the Govt. and even the Church, for whatever may be done at any time for the K.C. must be done for us, unless we at once set ourselves up as enemies. In short, on principle and for our interest we should keep quite fair and amicable with them, not to say for our dignity and also as considering them in the light of our offspring. Of course we should not overdo it, but far from giving the least countenance to the cry against K.C., I would distinctly express satisfaction, qualifying it with saying that this is grounded on the assurance that K.C. cannot *hurt us now* and must further our common object.[1]

Brougham was, of course, thinking of the universities, similar in character to that of London, which should follow, universities in Liverpool, Manchester, Birmingham, and other cities, the vision he had had, and at that time he alone had had, when he first mentioned the new university.

Coates, then secretary of the Council, wrote to Brougham that at a Council meeting on 25 September it was 'agreed that it would be better not to refer either to King's College or the subject of religion. Various paragraphs were tried and no one could be devised to which grave objections were not stated.'[2] Brougham lost no time. He wrote a letter to Coates, which was intended for publication. It repeats, in part, the unpublished letter to Denman, but the wording is important; it was read, approved, 'loudly applauded', in the general meeting and given to the press. It then represented the official attitude of London University toward the projected King's College.

Brougham first explained that, because of illness, he would not be able to attend the meeting. He spoke of the progress they had made and continued:

That the means of complete academic education on the soundest principles of universal admission will now be secured to the inhabitants of London and its neighbourhood, can no longer admit of a doubt and I look forward to the establishment of another institution arising

[1] Brougham MSS., 'Tuesday'. [2] Ibid.

out of ours as increasing those means in the same way that the National schools have so greatly promoted the system of education begun by the British and Foreign Society. The rivalry of the two seminaries will be salutary to both and useful to the community, nor can any true friend to either regard the other with any unfriendly feeling.[1]

Brougham's published letter was the beginning of relations between the first London University, later University College, and King's College. Brougham took some pride in feeling that he had started both, one directly and the other indirectly. Nearly two months before his letter to the Council, the Dean of York had written to Brougham, telling him about the educational work he was undertaking at York Minster, and saying: 'You may justly be proud of the diffusion of education in London. If you had never set on foot the London University, nobody would ever have thought of King's College. You may honestly lay claim to have founded both.'[2]

Brougham missed the opening lectures beginning 1 October 1828. They were the opening lectures of the Medical School, but they were thought of as the grand opening of the University. It would have been one of the proudest occasions of Brougham's life. But overwork, particularly his labours in preparing his great law-reform speech in February, had proved too much; he must have been ill enough for the doctor to have rigidly forbidden his attending or he would never have missed the opening. He reached London two weeks later. Leonard Horner, the Warden of the new university, who was on a short holiday, wrote to Brougham: 'It has been a disappointment to me that I could not be with you when you paid your first visit on your return, when you saw for the first time your great machine at work. Your pleasure would be something like Watt's when he first saw the steady majestic motion of a great engine, and you may as confidently look forward as no doubt he did to the consequences that were sure to follow the new power he had created.'[3]

Professor Bellot's careful research has failed to discover any contributions to the founding of the College on Bentham's part, although he was interested and on his death he gave part of his

[1] University College Correspondence, no. 647, Brougham to Coates, 27 Sept. 1828; The Times, 1 Oct. 1828.
[2] Brougham MSS., 4 Aug. 1828.   [3] Ibid., 16 Oct. 1828.

library. Professor Bellot recognized Bentham's influence through his disciples, and the similarity of principles of education enunciated in Bentham's *Chrestomathia*, the project for a Chrestomathic school, and those put into operation in London University.[1] Bentham's Chrestomathic school, if it had ever advanced from theory to realization, would have been a superior high school. It might be added that what was intended was a superior Lancasterian school with higher standards and extended subjects, and that much in *Chrestomathia* goes back to Joseph Lancaster. We have seen that Brougham founded the Lancasterian British and Foreign School Society before he had met Bentham. After that there must have been frequent talks between Bentham, Mill, and Brougham, or any two of them on education, each influencing the other. There is a similarity in several respects between Bentham's *Chrestomathia* published in 1815 and Brougham's *Observations on the Education of the People* published in 1825. How much did Brougham owe to Lancaster? What did he bring with him from Scotland? It would be impossible to separate the answers to those questions. But undoubtedly the Scottish influence was the stronger.

With the opening of the University came fears without and fights within. The quarrels were commenced by the professors but the Council provided them lavishly with material. The personal storm centres were Pattison, Professor of Anatomy, who was incompetent and attacked by professors and students alike in the Medical School, and Horner, Warden of the University. Leonard Horner was the younger brother of Francis Horner, and he undoubtedly owed his appointment to Brougham. They were not close friends but their families had been associated in Edinburgh and they had kept in touch with each other. Brougham had been impressed by Leonard Horner's successful founding and leadership of the Edinburgh School of Arts, which indeed appears to be the only justification, and that a partial one, for the appointment. He was for a time an underwriter at Lloyds and was active in a family business which was going down hill. He was not as unread as the professors liked to think, and he knew a good deal about geology. But he was not a scholar, and his educational experience had been brief and in a very different kind of institution. To place him over the heads

[1] Bellot, pp. 25, 12.

of the professors was regarded by the latter as an insult. And he was given what looked like a princely salary to the professors who were receiving what they considered very small salaries and fees doled out parsimoniously by a Council which treated them, they said, as mere employees. Horner had insisted on the salary and also on the office and title of Warden with authority over the professors similar to that of a Principal, whereas the original intention had been to appoint him Secretary of the University.

Under those circumstances, and they must mainly be blamed on Brougham, Horner did not have a chance from the beginning with a group of sensitive, financially embarrassed, and somewhat baffled professors. There can be little doubt that he was arbitrary and intolerably meddlesome. He was not so much a brazen dictator as a bureaucrat constantly prodded by the urge of his own importance and a tireless conscience, which invaded the exertions and the consciences of the professors. The Brougham manuscripts suggest that he made some efforts to change his ways and make it clear that throughout his tenure of office Horner was ill and very nervous.

One professor believed (and the belief was probably shared by others) that the appointment of Horner was a 'job' on the part of 'Brougham, Warburton and other Councillors' in the interest of a friend who was doing badly in business, that it had to be Warden and not Secretary in order to provide Horner with a large salary, and that to facilitate that there had been another 'job'; Cox had suggested 'the first notion of the university' and had been active 'during most of the preparatory meetings' and since he, Secretary to the Council at the time, considered himself aggrieved by the appointment of Horner, something had to be done for Cox, and he was appointed Librarian, although there was no library and he would be a mere book-buyer.[1]

Yet the librarianship had been suggested to Cox in November 1825, before the Horner appointment (in 1827) was thought of,[2] and a skilful purchase of books was one of the things the University most needed. There again Horner felt that he had to interfere. We have every reason to think that the scholarly Cox could select books with a fair amount of competence, and that Horner would be no good at it. But Horner read lessons to Cox

[1] Add. MSS. 37185 (Babbage MSS.), Lardner to Babbage, 8 Apr. [1830].
[2] Brougham MSS., Cox to Brougham, 16 Nov. 1825.

on how the job should be done and took a hand at the selection of books himself.[1]

The professors petitioned repeatedly for the dismissal of Horner and the abolition of the office of Warden. The Council was as badly mistaken in retaining Horner in his position as it was in appointing him. But it stood by him, whether from loyalty, pride, obstinacy, or sheer resentment. After the most acrimonious exchanges extending into the newspapers, the Council on 8 June 1830 passed resolutions which almost completely whitewashed Horner. The Council was divided, and Brougham, for all his friendship for Horner, did not approve. At a general shareholders' meeting on 3 July Althorp, not a member of the Council, moved, seconded by Lord Auckland, who was on the Council, for the appointment of a committee to investigate the whole situation. Brougham strongly supported the motion, saying that the newspapers 'had teemed with crimination and recrimination between the Warden and the professors', that the University was being seriously injured, and that a thorough investigation with the results reported to the shareholders could alone clear the situation. He was supported by Birkbeck, Hume, and Warburton, all members of the Council. But the shareholders defeated the motion by 94 to 60 and adopted the resolutions passed by the majority of the Council.[2]

Brougham's position was reported by Mill in a letter to Napier five days later: 'Brougham, with sincere friendship for Horner, did not conceal from me his wish and his hope that his friends would prevail upon him to resign.'[3] Horner resigned in the following March (1831), four months after Brougham became Lord Chancellor. Before leaving London he wrote to Brougham an angry letter saying that Brougham had not given him the support that he had counted on.[4] In later years their relations were externally friendly. When Leonard Horner published his memoirs of his brother, however, he studiously omitted Brougham's eulogy of Francis, while giving a number of others. Whether that was a carry-over from this situation or was caused by his feeling that Brougham had treated Francis badly we

[1] Ibid., Horner to Brougham, 27 Sept. 1828.
[2] Bellot, p. 203; The Times, 5 July 1830.
[3] Napier MSS. 34614 (Napier MSS.), f. 346.
[4] Brougham MSS., 12 July 1831.

cannot say. There was no reference to the latter subject in the memoirs themselves.

While the attacks of professors on Pattison and Horner were the most violent there was a strong undercurrent of feeling against the Council. Instead of appointing a principal from the faculty or bringing in a competent person from outside, the Council had not only retained Horner but had actually treated him pretty much as secretary and agent and, incredible as it seems, attempted to conduct the internal affairs of the University itself. Indeed there was no faculty at first. One was formed in the Medical School in 1828 and faculties were established elsewhere in 1832. The Council at first prohibited any joint action on the part of the professors and told them rather curtly that whenever there was any occasion for them to meet, the Council would make the arrangement. The Council might veto the books prescribed for students' use and members might investigate the teaching of the professors by visiting their lecture-rooms personally or by sending 'visitors' whom they had appointed. Professors were to pay out of their own pocket for any materials they might need for lectures and also for a substitute to be approved by the Council in the case of illness. In time the professors were successful in forcing the withdrawal of most of these stipulations;[1] but the vexed question of the guaranteed salaries and the proportion of fees which was to go to the professors continued to evoke a considerable amount of feeling. Some of the professors wrote individually to Brougham before approaching the Council, either because they felt that he would do them justice or because they believed that he would have the deciding voice in any case. On at least one occasion they took this action collectively after approaching the Council. Professor Lardner wrote to Brougham in April 1829:

We look up to you as the parent and natural guardian of this rising institution. . . . Our present object is to direct your attention to four points on which we are all sensitively alive and without the speedy adjustment of which we can scarcely hope that the consternation, which now prevails amongst the professors and which has paralyzed our daily exertions can be alloyed.

1st   Security for the possession of our officer.

[1] Bellot, p. 192.

2nd   Security against the arbitrary sub-divisions of those offices without our consent.

3rd   Security for the equitable partition of the sums paid by the students between us and the Council.

4th   Security for the moderate salaries in addition to our fees which are necessary to render us independent for the short period which must elapse before the University can be considered as fairly established.[1]

A few weeks before this Panizzi wrote a letter to a member of the Council, probably Lord Auckland, professing that the professors had been asked to consent to their own dismissal at any time without any cause shown (with an appeal within one month, to a general meeting of the shareholders). The general attitude of the Council to the professors was frankly described:

It is very hard for any man of education to see himself set down pêle mêle after the clerks, and with the workers and servants, as if before the eyes of the Council there was no distinction between a man of European reputation like Dr. Bell, for instance, and any beadle or porter of the University. . . . I shall also say fearlessly that every one of us has hitherto endeavoured to forward, to the utmost of his powers, the prosperity of the University, both within and without its walls. In this noble institution the professors have by far a greater interest than any proprietor.[2]

Panizzi followed this up two days later by a milder letter, still refusing to give his consent but adding: 'If I was certain, that you, My Lord, and Mr. Brougham with a few others who now belong to it [the Council] would always continue members of it, I should cheerfully and blindly subscribe any paper proposed for my signature.'[3]

Relations with the Professor of Political Economy, McCulloch, were to have important results in Brougham's later career. In the Napier manuscripts there is a series of letters from McCulloch to Napier, who had just become editor of the *Edinburgh Review*. He accused the Council of refusing to keep its promises to him in regard to salary and employed language that is not worth quoting. He stated that Brougham had misrepresented the situation in writing to Jeffrey.[4] Certainly we do not need to believe everything that McCulloch said in these letters; certainly,

---

[1] Brougham MSS., 1 Apr. 1829.   [2] Ibid., 24 Mar. 1829.
[3] Ibid., 26 Mar. 1829.   [4] Napier MSS., 6, 24 May, 25 June 1828.

too, Brougham was not very careful about the truth at times when he was giving a smooth account. The most certain thing of all is that McCulloch was as vindictive as he was bitter. Within two weeks of the last of these letters he was beginning a revolt against Brougham in connexion with the *Edinburgh Review*.[1] Brougham always blamed McCulloch for being the chief instigator of the concerted and venomous newspaper attack on him in 1834. So often in his later letters Brougham traced it back to this university clash.

When Brougham became Lord Chancellor in November 1830 the students of London University presented him with an address, signed by 'every student in the University'. The students say that if this were only a matter of great services 'to the welfare of the nation' being rewarded with public office and 'augmented influence', 'it would have been neither necessary nor becoming in them to do more than unite their voices in the general approbation.' But,

Collected within the walls of the University which is indebted to your Lordship for its establishment and defence, they assume a peculiar and a proud position, they cannot forget the benefits they owe to your indefatigable exertions. . . . They would be insensible to the just value of public honors, if they did not exult in the distinction which has been conferred upon him who was the founder, and has never ceased to be the champion of the Institution in which they have been happy to enrol themselves.[2]

It is doubtful whether any of the hundreds of congratulations which poured in upon him from friend and foe alike when he was appointed Lord Chancellor pleased Brougham so much as that address.

Brougham was to do much for the cause of universal education in primary schools after 1830, and for Mechanics' Institutes, for the S.D.U.K., and good cheap reading generally, and he was also to do a great deal for the University of London. But they were all well on their way, those projects for the education of the people in which he had pioneered and had worked tremendously, and some of which he had started. The University of London was the culminating feature of his planning, with the string of universities open to all and teaching many things which Oxford

---

[1] Napier MSS., McCulloch to Napier, 5 July 1828.
[2] Brougham MSS.

and Cambridge neither taught nor cared for, that string of free
universities that Brougham always associated with the University
of London from the time when he first gave it thought. In 1830
he merited already *Punch*'s tribute to him in 1851:

> The statesman who, in a less happy hour
> Than this, maintained man's right to read and know,
> And gave the keys of knowledge and of power
> With equal hand alike to high and low.

CHAPTER XXI

Law Reform Speech of 1828

O F Brougham's great law-reform speech of 7 February 1828 Atlay said in his *Victorian Chancellors*: 'This speech may be said without exaggeration to have led, directly or indirectly, to a greater number of beneficial and useful reforms than any other, ancient or modern.'[1] Atlay had in mind, no doubt, that it ushered in an epoch of law reform, that it resulted directly and immediately in the appointment of the two great law commissions on the Common Law and Real Property, that the commissions recommended most of the reforms which Brougham proposed, that most of its recommendations were implemented by Acts of Parliament, and that the commissions and the resulting legislation went beyond the limits of Brougham's speech, as did Brougham himself in his leadership of a law-reform movement in which other eminent lawyers co-operated, and which left Brougham vigorous and demanding in an old age that in some respects was never old.

There had, of course, already been a reform of the criminal law and there had also been attacks year after year on the defects and delays of the Court of Chancery, in which Michael Angelo Taylor, John Williams, and Brougham himself had spoken as persistently as had Romilly, Mackintosh, and Peel on the criminal law. Brougham in his great speech specifically excepted Chancery reform and the criminal law and initiated a more general and a broader reform.

As the speech itself indicated, as well as many of his later speeches, he was concerned with more than technical adjustments of the law. In fact technical adjustment in itself never appealed much to his mind. Lord Campbell was probably right when he said that Brougham knew very little about how to draft a statute. What electrified his mind and his words was the fact that the defects in the law meant injustice and human suffering. This was another example of the lifelong humanitarian

[1] Atlay, p. 285.

drive that carried him on in spite of defects in his own character that so often made him a mark for scoffing and sometimes for disgust.

It was not that Brougham did not believe that the law, in the main, was the greatest protector of human rights. He never spoke, as Bentham too often wrote, as though everything was wrong and everything could be put right by a new set of theories. Nevertheless, in law reform he was the disciple of Bentham, and five months before this speech he turned to the master for help in the preparation of it. In a letter written on 20 September and relating mainly to another matter, Bentham directed Brougham to parts of his works, with some of which he presumed that Brougham was familiar, while he might wish to familiarize himself more with others; he would send him something he had written on Evidence which Mill had been editing for him and an unpublished work on codification that Brougham might find valuable. 'As soon as may be after your return to town we should have a gossip. A dish of sweet [an illegible word], which for some time past has been known in the appropriate regions as *Mr. Brougham's pudding*, awaits and sighs for your embrace.' Four days later Bentham wrote another letter to 'my dearest best boy', said he was old enough to be Brougham's grandfather, and reverted to his best style of baby-talk. 'I could this moment catch you in my arms, toss you up into the air, and as you fell into them again, cover you with kisses. It shall have, aye that it shall, the dear little fellow, some nice sweet pap of my own making, three sorts of it, (1) IV, Evidence (2) Judicial Establishment (3) Codification Proposal, . . . all sent this very blessed day.' He informed Brougham that when 'the whole field of legislation is covered by an edifice . . . of statute law', he [Bentham] had an 'infallible patent method' to preserve it 'in all eternity' from being 'choked up . . . by a jungle of common, alias judge-made law'. In conclusion, 'kiss grandpapa again and accept his blessing' which, however, was conditional on his being a good boy. If he became 'naughty', though it was 'but in a parenthesis, the Bête Noir shall be set upon you and will gobble you up in a mouthful, all screaming and sputtering notwithstanding'.[1] Brougham was also helped in the preparation of this speech by Joseph Parkes of Birmingham, who in writing a recent

[1] Brougham MSS., 20, 24 Sept. 1827.

history of the Court of Chancery had increased his knowledge of the Common Law courts.

Brougham spoke for six hours and three minutes. One would have thought that half of that time would have been too much for any auditor on such a subject as law reform. Yet there was a good House to the end. And some members whose wives had invited guests for dinner could not tear themselves away from Brougham's speech, said good-bye to the dinners (or were very late), and risked the wrath of their wives. As Scarlett said in a later discussion of the speech in the House, in complimenting Brougham on his 'genius, learning and astonishing assiduity', 'he had spread through his progress a degree of vivacity which he alone could have introduced, to relieve the discussion of so many dull and uninteresting topics'.[1]

All through the six hours Brougham sucked oranges. He had a hatful of them beside him, supplied by Bellamy, who had become caterer to the House of Commons in 1790. (Legend had it that Pitt's last words had been: 'I think I could eat one of Bellamy's pork pies.') Brougham occasionally came across a bad orange. Then in a low voice he cursed Bellamy and in his speaking voice continued with the unnecessary complexities, delays, and expense of the law, the suffering involved and the remedies he proposed.[2]

The speech ran to 168 pages in Brougham's published speeches.[3] All that can be hoped for here is an indication of the scope and spirit of the speech, and some general idea of the way in which its proposals came to be enacted in later years.

Brougham urged that no aspect of government was as important as 'the pure, prompt and cheap administration of justice'. He first discussed defects and remedies in relation to the courts. The Court of King's Bench had, with the help of a legal fiction, drawn to itself actions which really belonged to the Court of Common Pleas. A certain amount of business was excluded from the Court of Common Pleas because of the early stage at which it required the payment of fees and the restriction of practice to sergeants. (That monopoly was abolished in 1832.) In the Court of the Exchequer only four privileged attorneys were allowed to

---

[1] *Hansard*, N.S., xviii. 904.
[2] T. H. S. Escott, *Club Makers and Club Members* (1914), p. 64.
[3] *Speeches*, ii. 319 seq.

practice. (That restriction was abolished in 1830.) The result
was that in the Court of King's Bench there was a great accumu-
lation of arrears, and delays caused distress, while in the Exchequer 'judges do not sit more than half an hour some
mornings'. (Thanks to Lord Lyndhurst's efforts during the next
decade, as many cases came to be entered in the Exchequer as
in the King's Bench and the delays in the latter court disappeared.)

It was said that the judges did not have time to do their
business. It was not lack of time so much as the way that it was
distributed, as in taking bail and chambers business. A better
arrangement of chambers business was proposed. (That was
effected within ten years.) There was, however, need for more
judges. There was so much more business than in the days when
Coke was fascinated by the peculiar properties of the number
twelve. Brougham suggested fourteen for the number of judges.
'I cannot quote fourteen Apostles nor fourteen Tables [a reference
to the Roman twelve Tables]. Though neither so divisible nor so
beautiful nor so classical as twelve it [fourteen] contains two
more digits than twelve . . . and that superiority recommends it
for my purpose.' (Two years later, in 1830, the number of judges
of the great courts was increased to fifteen.)

Brougham dealt next with *party* appointments to judgeships.
'The great object of every Government, in selecting the judges of
the land, should be to obtain the most skilful and learned men
in their profession' and the men whose character fits them best
for the position. 'I almost feel ashamed, Sir, to have troubled
you with such a truism. . . . Sorry am I to say that our system of
judicial promotion sins in both these particulars. . . . True, no
law prevents such a search for capacity and worth. But there is
a custom above the law . . . that *party*, as well as merit, must be
studied in these appointments. One half of the Bar is thus
excluded from the competition; for no man can be a judge who
is not of a particular party.' That might be going too far, for
there was the rare exception, but that was the general situation.
'Nowadays [when, with exceptions of a few months' duration,
one party had been in power so long] whenever a question comes
before the Bench, whether it be upon a prosecution for libel or
upon any other matter connected with politics [there is a leaning
toward the Government]. . . . The Judges have this leaning,

they must have it, they cannot help having it, you compel them to have it, you choose them because of their notoriously having had it at the Bar; and you vainly hope that they will suddenly put it off when they rise by its means to the Bench.' (The reform proposed by Brougham in this matter was not one of those effected within a few years of this speech, but the situation was long ago remedied to a great degree in Great Britain. In Canada, however, the practice in this respect is backward and reprehensible, and Brougham's words in 1828 are still to a large extent applicable.) He also pointed out the defects of the separate Welsh judiciary which should be abolished (as it was in 1830).

Brougham passed to appointment of judges in the ecclesiastical courts, 'who determine . . . the questions of marriage and divorce and may decide on the disposition by will of all the personalty in the kingdom. Is it a fit thing that the judges in these most important matters should be appointed, not by the Crown but by the Archbishop of Canterbury and the Bishop of London, who are neither removable nor responsible, who are not lawyers, who are not statesmen, who ought to be no politicians, who are indeed priests of the highest order but not, on that account, the most proper persons to appoint judges of the highest order?' (In 1832, under Brougham's Chancellorship means were taken to abolish that feature of episcopal patronage.) An appeal lay from the ecclesiastical courts to the Court of Delegates, which Brougham described as 'one of the worst constituted courts that was ever appointed'. 'The course of its proceedings forms one of the greatest mockeries of appeal ever conceived by man.' (Brougham abolished the Court of Delegates and transferred its appeal jurisdiction to his newly created Judicial Committee of the Privy Council in 1833.)

The Privy Council was next discussed. It was the court of final appeal for the whole of the overseas empire. At that time the appeal was to the actual Privy Council, which was, of course, not a body of men learned in the law. Those who exercised this appeal jurisdiction were members of the Privy Council who 'are chosen without much regard to legal aptitude, for you are not to suppose that the business of those nine days [in a year] upon which they sit is all transacted before lawyers; one lawyer there may be but the rest are laymen'. The Privy Council had 'neither a regular Bench nor a regular Bar'. 'The appeals have amounted to but few in number. I marvel that they are so few, and yet I marvel not, for . . . you have no adequate tribunal to dispose of them.' Brougham continued:

The Master of the Rolls alone is always to be seen there, of the lawyers; for the rest, one meets sometimes in company with him, an elderly and most respectable gentleman who has formerly been an ambassador, and was a governor with much credit to himself in difficult times; and now and then a junior Lord of the Admiralty, who has been neither ambassador nor lawyer, but would be exceedingly fit for both functions, only that he happened to be educated for neither. And such, Sir, is the constitution of that awful Privy Council which sits at Westminster . . . [and] is the supreme tribunal which dispenses the law to eighty millions of people and disposes of all their property.

Brougham said that he once saw property worth £30,000 per annum disposed of in a few minutes by 'the learned members of the Privy Council', who reversed a sentence pronounced by all the judges in the colony 'upon no less than nineteen days' most anxious discussion'. He spent some time on the consequent denial of justice and the dissatisfaction among the subject peoples of many races. He made a particular appeal for justice for India, whose natives should also be given an important part in its administration.

Brougham urged the creation of a real court of appeal for the overseas empire, with real judges of the highest ability. 'The judges should be men of the largest legal and general information, accustomed to study other systems of law beside their own. . . . They should be assisted by a Bar limiting its practice, for the most part, to this appeal court and the court should sit frequently and regularly at all seasons.' (Brougham effected that by his own creation of the Judicial Committee of the Privy Council, five years later, in 1833. He preserved the *formal* jurisdiction of the Privy Council by having four very able judges (four at first) appointed to the Privy Council in order that they might sit as the Judicial Committee of the Privy Council, which acted as a remarkably able court of appeal for the overseas empire.)

In his discussion of justices of the peace, he exaggerated their defects and failed to give recognition to their real merits. But there again we recognize his humanitarian outlook. He was harsh with justices of the peace because of his hatred of the game laws, their severe treatment of poachers, and the commitment of many who should have been discharged by the magistrates, particularly boys. 'Eighteen hundred and odd [boys], many of them mere children, have been committed in the Warwick district, during the last seven years. Nor is this a trifling evil. People do not come out of gaols as they went in. A boy may enter the prison gate merely as the robber of an orchard; he may come out of it, "fit for", I will not say "treason" but certainly "strategems and spoils".'

He dealt with 'the inconvenient differences in the tenures by which property is held, and the rules by which it is conveyed and transmitted, in various districts of the country'. In that connexion he said, in regard to wills: 'In one manor a devise is not valid if made longer than two years before the testator's decease; so that it is necessary for wills to be renewed every two years; in another one year; in a third, three years are the period; while in many there are no such restrictions.' (Uniformity in respect to wills was achieved by the Wills Act of 1837.)

'It is commonly said that the Crown and the subject come into court on equal terms. Lawyers of the present day do not, I am aware, profess this, but that eminent dealer in panegyric, Mr. Justice Blackstone, has spoken as if the King had no greater advantage in litigation than any of his people. . . . The Crown never moves by itself, but through the medium of the King's Attorney-General. No proceeding can be taken against the Crown without the *fiat* of the Attorney-General.' (That remained the law for over a century, until in fact the Crown Proceedings Act of 1947, when the change urged by Brougham was effected.)

He discussed the question, 'by what means unnecessary litigation may be prevented'. He would 'remove the encouragement given to rich and litigous suitors by lessening the expense of all legal proceedings; and I would put an end to all harassing and unjust defences by encouraging expedition'. He urged the permission of a declaratory judgement (which was effected in 1852). 'I would abolish all obsolete proceedings which serve only as a trap to the unwary, or tools in the hands of litigous and dishonest parties.' (Those evils were largely removed by the Judges' Rules provided for by Brougham in 1833.)

'I would abolish at once the whole doctrine and procedure of

Fines and Recoveries', which meant doing away with a complicated and expensive machinery for conveyancing, including the barring of entails, with the help of legal fictions and gallant service on the part of John Doe and Richard Roe. Brougham would get rid of all the long and expensive mummery by passing legislation that would provide simple and direct methods for achieving the same thing (which he effected by his own Act of 1833). 'Why in ejectments should *two* processes [one to obtain possession and the other to recover *mesne* profits] be required to give the plaintiff his remedy?' (That defect was corrected within the next ten years.)

He inquired 'how you may best shorten the suits brought by disposing of them in the shortest time and with the least expense'. 'Whatever brings the parties to their senses as soon as possible, especially by giving each a clear view of his chance of success or failure, and, above all things, making him well acquainted with his adversary's case at the earliest possible moment, will always be for the interests of justice, of the parties themselves, and indeed of all but the practitioners.' (Provision was made for that by the Judges' Rules of 1833 and the provisions for discovery.)

Brougham urged the abolishing of the arrest of a debtor on *mesne* process. 'In the first place we assume the defendant to be in the wrong, and not only so but to be meditating flight from his country or his home; we therefore arrest him immediately and cast him into prison or compel him to find bail.' For the well-to-do it was comparatively easy to find bail. 'He . . . would send for his butcher and his baker and get bailed; but a gentleman could not, after that, complain so well of the meat or the bread or the bills during the next half year. . . . But how does such a proceeding operate on a poor man, or a tradesman in moderate circumstances? He has no facilities for obtaining bail; if he does, he pays in one way or another afterwards for the favour; and if he cannot procure it, he must go to prison. Perhaps no man ever holds up his head, or is the same man again, after having once been in prison, unless for a political offence.' Brougham insisted that there should be no arrest or imprisonment for debt at any stage except in cases of fraud, gross extravagance or refusal to give up property to creditors. (Arrest on *mesne* process was abolished by an Act of Lord Cottenham in 1837, and all arrest for debt was abolished by Brougham's

Acts of 1844 and 1845. He did more than anyone to put an end to the whole horrible business of imprisonment for debt with its trail of human suffering, hopelessness, and degradation.)

The intricacies, technicalities, and verbosity of special pleadings with their piling up of delay and expense were discussed at some length. (They were remedied to a large extent by the Judges' Rules provided for in 1833.) Turning to the subject of Evidence, Brougham said: 'First of all we are met by the question,—ought the testimony of parties to be excluded.' He urged that it should be accepted, as should be the evidence of any interested person, on the understanding, of course, that it should be weighed in view of the situation. (Lord Denman in 1843 carried an Act abolishing the objection of interest to the competency of a witness, which prepared the way for Brougham's Act of 1851 which made the parties in civil suits competent and compellable to give evidence.) He referred to his own earlier Bill for permitting evidence of the truth in actions for criminal libel (which was effected in part by Lord Campbell's Act of 1843). He urged the acceptance of a Quaker's affirmation in criminal cases, as it was already accepted in civil cases. (That disability was removed by the Quakers and Moravians Act of 1833.) He urged the abolition of Real Actions 'sinning as they do against all sense and justice'. (All Real Actions except *Quare Impedit* were abolished in 1833.) He urged, in relation to imprisonment for debt, that all existing restrictions on seizure of property should be abolished but the *person* of the debtor should be spared except in certain flagrant cases.

Brougham's concluding words came to be known by nearly everyone in that period:

It was the boast of Augustus . . . that he found Rome of brick, and left it of marble; a praise not unworthy a great prince, and to which the present reign also has its claims. But how much nobler will be the Sovereign's boast, when he shall have it to say, that he found law dear, and left it cheap; found it a sealed book—left it a living letter; found it the patrimony of the rich—left it the inheritance of the poor; found it the two-edged sword of craft and oppression—left it the staff of honesty and the shield of innocence.

And then:

I move you, Sir, 'That an humble Address be presented to his

Majesty, praying that he will be graciously pleased to issue a Commission for inquiring into the defects, occasioned by time and otherwise, in the Laws of this realm, and into the measures necessary for removing the same'.

This motion was amended at the suggestion of the Government and called for the establishment of two Commissions, one on the Common Law and the other on Real Property. Brougham's letters of the previous year had indicated that the existence of the Coalition Government and the fact that he himself was out of office would afford him the time to initiate law reform and the advantage of doing so with the favour of the Government in power. Certainly he could not have done so before Eldon was removed, but the speech on which he had been working came one month too late for the Coalition. Yet the new Tory government was willing to support his proposals, largely because of the attitude of Lord Chancellor Lyndhurst and the fact that Peel had become a criminal-law reformer and looked with favour on law reform in general.

Brougham's speech was greeted with many eulogies and also with adverse criticism. It was said to contain inaccuracies, which were inevitable in anything covering so much ground (and the full scope of it could only be suggested in the account given here). Those criticisms, however, all said that there were a *few* inaccuracies. It was also stated that much of it was 'trite' and dealt with defects in the law that had often been the talk of lawyers. But that was one good reason for the making of the speech. Lawyers might have talked of those matters for at least another generation, and if it had not been for Brougham's courage and enterprise, nothing would have been done. As Sir William Holdsworth has said, applying to Brougham's work for law reform what had been written by some one else about another aspect of his activity: 'He led the way and others followed, who without him would not have moved at all.'[1] It was said that the speech was superficial. Of course it was. Dealing with so many topics it could not have been other than superficial. As Scarlett, who highly praised the speech, said in the House of Commons, in the part of it which he had heard Brougham dealt with twenty-nine topics 'each of which might

[1] Sir William Holdsworth, *History of English Law*, 13 vols. (1903–56), xiii. 646.

well employ the House during an entire session of Parliament'.[1] Brougham might have refused to be superficial; he might have written a book on each of his topics and all those books put together could not have effected what the speech did. What Brougham was after was legislation; legislation could be passed only by Parliament, and the attention and interest of Parliament could be captured for a general reform of the law only by a comprehensive speech in Parliament. And as a result approximately three-quarters of Brougham's proposed reforms were adopted in the next ten years. While Brougham had to be superficial in some respects, the two great Commissions which were set up by Parliament following the speech had time to be thorough. John Campbell, who was appointed chairman of the Real Property Commission, wrote in mid-century as Lord Campbell: 'His [Brougham's] suggestions were rational and practicable. . . . Without his exertion, the optimism of our legal procedure might have long continued to be preached up, and Fines and Recoveries might still have been regarded with veneration.'[2]

The most severe critic of the speech was Bentham. He said that Brougham's mountain had brought forth a mouse. A long introduction on the basis of the philosophy of Bentham would have been more to Bentham's taste, followed by fulminations against the common law, an appeal for the admission of all sorts of evidence, including hearsay evidence, and for an over-all code which everyone could understand and other matters that seemed very important to Bentham, but were quite impracticable. Bentham was the great basic theorist; Brougham the practical reformer. Even so it does seem strange, in view of how much his speech owed to Bentham, that Bentham's name was not mentioned in the whole six hours of it. It would have been more tactful and generous if Brougham had incorporated some small part of the long eulogy of Bentham as 'the father of law reform' which he wrote in the introduction to the speech when it was published after Bentham was dead.

In this matter, however, a layman in the law must yield the floor to the greatest historian of the English law. Sir William Holdsworth wrote in his last volume:

---

[1] *Hansard*, xviii. 904.
[2] Campbell, viii. 359–60.

Brougham had done more than any other person to forward the cause of law reform. We shall see that his great speech in 1828, in which the long list of abuses urgently needing reforming were set forth, made it impossible to shelve the subject of law reform, and so inaugurated the period which gave practical effect to many of Bentham's proposals. And yet in *Lord Brougham Displayed* which was published in 1832, Bentham fiercely attacked Brougham because Brougham did not see eye to eye with him on the form which the reforms of the Court of Chancery and the Bankruptcy Court should take, because he preferred bit by bit reform to the adoption of Bentham's impracticable measures. Brougham, he said, had not tried to further the two reforms on which all effective law reform depends ... and so Bentham represented him as given up to 'sinister influence, interest-begotten prejudice, and interest-begotten sympathy'. It was not until the very end of his paper that Bentham had the grace to acknowledge Brougham's professional and private virtues, and his kindness to himself, and thus to get as near to an apology as he ever got.[1]

And that in spite of Holdsworth's sincere and highly justified admiration for Bentham.

Another quotation from Sir William Holdsworth may be appropriate:

They [English lawyers] have preferred to build upon the stable foundation of the concrete facts of life and the needs of human beings, rather than upon the shifting sands of the conflicting theories of ingenious philosophers. . . . The solution was not, as he [Mill] and Bentham thought, to reform it [the Law] root and branch by the wholesale adoption of Bentham's suggestions, but to adopt the expedient which English lawyers in fact adopted, of using the talents of lawyers who were masters of the system, to make gradually the reforms which were needed, in such a way that the changed rules were harmonized with the existing system.

And finally in regard to this speech of Brougham's, Holdsworth wrote: 'There is no doubt that his speech was the most learned and thorough criticism of the many defects of the common law that had ever been made since the Commonwealth period.'[2]

---

[1] Holdsworth, xiii. 103.
[2] Ibid. xiii. 127, 306.

CHAPTER XXII

The Year 1830

IN January 1830 the Marquis of Cleveland (formerly Lord
Darlington) decided to give his support to the Duke of
Wellington's Tory government. He informed Brougham
that there need be no difficulty about the latter's continuing to
sit for his borough of Winchelsea. Brougham, it had been always
understood, was to enjoy absolute freedom. He might continue
to oppose the Government in the Commons while Lord Cleveland supported it in the Lords. But Brougham felt that for himself that would be an embarrassing situation. Indeed it would
inevitably produce adverse criticism. So the Duke of Devonshire
came to the rescue and offered Brougham a seat for his borough
of Knaresborough, which Brougham accepted. For the moment
Lord Cleveland was offended, but their many letters throughout the remainder of Lord Cleveland's life reflect a close friendship.

On 29 April Brougham introduced his Local Courts Bill, with
the object of bringing the law to every man's door in an inexpensive form and with simplified process, where small amounts
were involved. These local courts were to sit once a month under
judges who were to be sergeants or barristers of ten years'
standing. In the assize courts held in each county twice a year,
considerable expense was involved in the travelling of parties
and witnesses, the delay was oppressive, and the procedure was
such that it was almost impossible to sue for a small amount
without incurring an expense much greater than the amount
involved.[1] (This Bill could not be proceeded with in that session,
was reintroduced by Brougham in 1831, in 1833, when it was
defeated in the House of Lords by two votes, in 1837, and in
1842. Local courts of this nature were finally established by an
Act of 1846 under the Chancellorship of Lord Cottenham.)

A Jewish Relief Bill reached its second reading on 17 May.
Brougham made the outstanding speech in favour of the Bill.

[1] *Hansard*, N.S., xxiv. 287 seq.; *Speeches*, ii. 489 seq.; *Edinburgh Review*, July 1830.

'He did not wish to put this measure upon the footing of state necessity, nor of sound policy. . . . He put it as a case of justice to an assembly of just men.' He spoke of 'that chorus of Christians, whom he had heard that night cheer, and roar and howl forth their applause of the most anti-Christian doctrines and feelings'. He had heard something about Julian the Apostate and the obstruction of the decrees of Divine Providence. But what were the true decrees of Divine Providence? 'To do unto others as they would be done unto, to show justice and love mercy, and in following these precepts, to believe that they were promoting, not obstructing the decrees of Divine Providence.'[1] The Bill was defeated by a majority of sixty-three. The struggle for Jewish Emancipation was to be a long one. Goldsmid's tribute to Brougham's later efforts has been quoted in another chapter (see p. 360).

On 30 June Brougham called the supporters of the Government 'the mean fawning parasites' of the Duke of Wellington. Peel, who knew very well that Brougham had a considerable liking for him, asked if he meant that to apply to him. Brougham replied that that would be absurd. Peel said that he did not suppose that Brougham meant to apply it to him or in fact to apply it to anybody, and that Brougham had been carried away by the warmth of the debate. Brougham supposed that he had been warmer than usual and so backed down in rather humiliating fashion. It was said that, as on some previous occasions, the Opposition lost votes in the ensuing division on account of Brougham's intemperate language.

Brougham wrote for the July *Edinburgh Review* a slashing attack on the Government. A secondary theme was praise of the Canningites. Peel's position was accurately assessed with full appreciation of his liberalism. The hope of a Whig–Canningite alliance was playing a large part in Brougham's thoughts.

In the meantime the anti-slavery movement was becoming more demonstrative. Though the parliamentary movement had lagged because of the illness of the leaders in 1828 and the Catholic Emancipation crisis of 1829, Zachary Macaulay's work of educating and organizing public interest had been achieving marked success.

A great public meeting of the Anti-Slavery Society was held

[1] *Hansard*, N.S., xxiv. 807 seq.

on 15 May. Wilberforce had been invited to take the chair. His presence and his effort to speak roused enthusiasm though he could not be heard. Buxton moved a resolution favouring the entire abolition of slavery. But he said that he was not in favour of immediate emancipation. The slaves would have to be prepared for freedom by means more effective than any yet taken, but the children still to be born could be freed immediately. He proposed a resolution looking toward that, to which Pownall moved an amendment to the effect that Parliament should pass a measure by which every Negro born after the first of January next should be declared free. Brougham pointed out that that was not practicable. Parliament on the eve of dissolution would not welcome such a proposal when there was no time for adequate discussion or for implementation before so early a fixed date. He was heartily in favour of the amendment except for the fact that it named 'too near a day'. Buxton then read a resolution which substituted the words 'an early day'.[1] Sir George Stephen's *Recollections* give the impression that this became a turbulent meeting with demonstrations of impatience with the veteran leaders. The newspaper accounts do not confirm that, but there was no doubt that impatience for sharper action existed. His account may have reflected faithfully the feeling of the part of the large crowd that was nearest to himself. Since some immediate parliamentary action was called for, Lushington said that that must be committed to Brougham. 'He spoke the truth, lamentable as in itself it was, that scarcely a decent hearing could be obtained in that House by any other member on this subject. He alone was possessed of that power and that influence which Parliament did not seem capable of resisting.'[2]

Brougham on 1 July presented a petition from 'a meeting that was equalled by none that I ever saw', but postponed his speech until 13 July. Then he made another of his superlative speeches, of which only an inadequate impression can be given here.

'I am aware that on the threshold of the scene and to scare me from entering upon it, there stands the phantom of colonial independence resisting parliamentary interference. . . . But when those local assemblies utterly neglect their first duties' Parliament was bound to do its duty. The constitutional aspects of the

---

[1] *The Times*, 17 May 1830.
[2] Quoted in Mathieson, p. 196.

matter were fully discussed. Much had been said of respect for property. He had as much respect for property as any man. 'What is the right which one man claims over the person of another, as if he were a chattel and one of the beasts that perish? . . . I set up the law of the Christian dispensation, which holds all men equal and commands that you treat every man as a brother!' The defenders of slavery said that the slaves were happy. Yet the slave population was declining and there was an amazing record of crime and punishment. 'In Trinidad I find that the slaves belonging to plantations, in number 16,580 appear, by the records printed, to have been punished in two years for 11,131 offences.' He told, in moving language, the stories of atrocities described in official documents that had gone unpunished by the West Indian authorities. He began with the Rev. T. W. Bridges, a clergyman of the Established Church, who had so vilified the anti-slavery leaders that a bookseller had been convicted by a British jury for publishing one of his pamphlets which had outrageously slandered Wilberforce. Yet in the West Indies this clergyman, whom nobody could respect or pretend to defend, had treated a slave girl with the utmost barbarity and, although a trial had been ordered by the Colonial Office, he had not been brought to trial.

He referred to the Missionary Smith case and spoke of his warning at that time that if the British Government and Parliament did not take the whole matter in hand there would be constant repetition of such injustice. 'I would to God that the facts did not so plainly prove me to have foretold the truth.' And he proceeded with stories of the persecution of missionaries and of crimes that had gone unpunished. In one case it was said that a slave girl had died of fever. Her treatment had been fully described in a Colonial Office dispatch. She had been beaten seven times in succession and pepper had been rubbed into her eyes to keep her fully awake to the pain. 'Then she had no sign of fever, she had caught no disease, she was all hale and sound and fit for the lash. At seven she was flogged, at noon she died. And those execrable and impious murderers soon found out that she had caught the malady and perished by "the visitation of God". No, no! I am used to examine circumstances, to weigh evidence, and I do firmly believe that she died by the murderous hand of man.' After he had completed his ghastly stories of persecutions and unpunished crimes he said:

Sir, I have done. I trust that at length the time is come when Parliament will no longer bear to be told that slave-owners are the best lawgivers on slavery; no longer allow an appeal from the British public to such communities as those in which the Smiths and the Grimsdalls are persecuted to death for teaching the Gospel to the Negroes; and the Mosses holden in affectionate respect for torture and murder; no longer suffer our voice to roll across the Atlantic in empty warnings and fruitless orders. . . . Tell me not of rights, talk not of the property of the planter in his slaves. . . . There is a law above all the enactments of human codes, the same throughout the world, the same in all times. . . . It is the law written by the finger of God on the heart of man. And by that law, unchangeable and eternal, while men despise fraud, and loathe rapine and abhor blood, they will reject with indignation the wild and guilty phantasy *that man can hold property in man.* . . . The slave trade had been abolished. How came this change to pass? Not, assuredly, by Parliament leading the way; but the country at length awoke, the indignation of the people was kindled. It descended like thunder and smote the traffic and scattered its guilty profits to the winds. . . . The same country is once more awake,—awake to the condition of Negro slavery. The same indignation kindles in the bosom of the same people, the same cloud is gathering that annihilated the slave trade.[1]

In relation to the passage about the 'law written by the finger of God on the heart of man', it has been said that Brougham was 'speaking as a lawyer', with the implication that he was questioning the literal legality of a property in slaves. That, of course, is absurd. He was obviously speaking not as a lawyer, but as a theologian, if you will, and as a moralist. Yet the passage was to have a strange history. It was frequently quoted on both sides of the Atlantic. They made a great deal of Brougham in the American anti-slavery movement. Garrison dedicated a book to him. In 1829 Brougham had written to Garrison that an emancipation 'drive' was in preparation for 1830 and continued: 'I am intensely interested in your American plans. We should get results here soon and if slavery goes in the West Indies, it will be a great help to you also.'[2] Though this passage about the finger of God was quoted at first in its

[1] *Speeches*, ii. 131 seq.
[2] Clements Library, Madison MSS., Garrison to Madison, 18 Feb. 1829.

figurative sense, it is said that it had a considerable influence on the employment of the concept of a higher law in American courts.

Brougham's motion was 'that this House do resolve, at the earliest practicable period of the next session to take into its serious consideration the state of the slaves in the colonies of Great Britain, in order to the mitigation and final abolition of their slavery, and more especially in order to the amendment of the administration of justice within the same'. That seems to have about it an air of ambiguity. It was apparently designed to obtain the largest possible support in the House and at the same time to be capable of interpretation as a call to immediate action. It must have been framed by the anti-slavery cabinet that met regularly at Brougham's house: Zachary Macaulay, Brougham, Buxton, and Lushington. It was defeated, but had a good division.

The general election occasioned by the accession of William IV began at the end of July. Although Brougham would, in any case, be returned for the Duke of Devonshire's pocket borough of Knaresborough, the anti-slavery forces wished to run him for the seat in Yorkshire that had been held by Wilberforce up to 1825 and were ready to meet the expenses. But this is an over-simplification of Brougham's candidature. Professor Norman Gash, who has made a thorough study of this Yorkshire election, has, in two recent articles[1] carried us through its complexities. In the first place no one who was not a resident of the county had been elected to represent Yorkshire in Parliament since the Reformation and no lawyer since the Commonwealth: this must have meant something to Yorkshire and to Brougham. Professor Gash emphasizes the part played by money in the matter of candidates. A Yorkshire election had been an occasion to spend a fortune and now in 1830 willingness to meet the tremendous expense broke down. To induce candidates to declare themselves, both parties had to promise that they would be freed from expense. Since Yorkshire had four members, the nomination of two candidates from each party afforded a ready solution. On 14 July, the day after Brougham's great anti-slavery speech, the Tories selected one

---

[1] *Proceedings of the Leeds Philosophical and Literary Society. Literary and Historical Section*, vol. viii, part 1; *Essays presented to Sir Lewis Namier* (1956), pp. 258 seq.

candidate. At the same time the Whigs agreed on Lord Morpeth, and promised the West Riding industrialists the opportunity to select another, both candidates to be freed from expense. A meeting was to be held at York on 23 July.

It had been said on the 14th that the anti-slavery forces were already urging Brougham's candidature but the great move was made by Baines, the editor of the influential *Leeds Mercury* on the 17th. He was appealing for the support of the West Riding industrialists, and in the general cause of Parliamentary Reform. A great liberal interested in every aspect of reform, he was no doubt quite sincere when he wrote in his editorial proposing Brougham:

The honourable and learned member for Knaresborough stands without a rival among the public men of the present day in their claims upon the gratitude of their country and of mankind. He has no competition in the House of Commons either in eloquence, in statesmanlike talent and information, or in the good he has effected for his country, and for the human race. . . . There is no great cause involving the public interest, the rights of man, the reform of abuses, the redress of wrongs, the improvement of the law and of the Government in all of its departments, which has not found a ready and effective support in the mighty eloquence of Mr. Brougham.[1]

There was, however, opposition to Brougham's nomination. To many who were land proud it seemed a shocking thing to elect a member to represent the county who did not own a square foot of land within its borders. And there was also the opposition of many of the local magistrates to the liberalism of Brougham's politics. At the 23 July meeting to select two Whig candidates, Lord Morpeth was chosen unanimously as by previous arrangement. John Marshall, wealthy Leeds industrialist, proposed Brougham, whose seconder was Daniel Sykes, an ardent advocate of the emancipation of the slaves. An anti-Brougham speech brought to his feet the Rev. Thomas Scales, a Presbyterian minister, who said that it was not politics that had brought him to that meeting but religion and humanity, that Brougham had no equal among those who were carrying on the great work of freeing the slaves and that he would certainly be nominated with strong support no matter what that meeting did. On a show of hands Brougham was chosen as a candidate.

[1] Quoted in Aspinall, p. 175.

That is a very inadequate summary of Professor Gash's first article. The second was concerned with showing that the influence of the July Revolution in France on the election was less than has been supposed and that Brougham in Yorkshire paid little attention to it.

The Rev. William Shepherd, Brougham's close friend, wrote to Panizzi two years later that Brougham won Yorkshire 'against the wishes of both Tory and Whig aristocracy'.[1] The mercantile parts of the county were strong for Brougham. Empson, who was at the meeting of 23 July, wrote to Napier, then editor of the *Edinburgh Review*, that the Whig country gentlemen would (after his nomination) support Brougham, 'but coldly', and added: 'The influence of Brougham's *name* is wonderful.'[2]

In truth for the *people* of the county and the nation, Brougham's name by this time was almost as eloquent as the man himself.

He began on the 26th a remarkable speaking campaign through industrial parts of the county. It was really a double crusade for the abolition of slavery and immediate Parliamentary Reform. Professor Aspinall has written: 'Nothing quite like that triumphal progress was again to be witnessed in Great Britain until Gladstone went on his famous Midlothian campaign.'[3]

The Northern Circuit was at York during the whole of this tour. Brougham left each day when court rose, travelled 'as fast as four horses could go to the various towns', made his speeches, and was never back in York until nearly midnight. Then he sat down to the study of his cases for the next day. Many years afterwards he wrote in his *Memoirs*: 'This kind of life lasted nearly three weeks. . . . But good health, temperance and the stake I was playing for, carried me through. I not only survived but, during the whole of this laborious time, I never in my life felt better or more capable of even further exertion, had such been called for.[4]

At the time Brougham wrote to his brother James: 'You can have no conception of anything at all like the state of this county. For enthusiasm I never saw anything approaching to

<hr />

[1] Panizzi MSS., 4 Apr. 1832.
[2] Add. MSS. 34614 (Napier MSS.), f. 365, 24 June 1830.
[3] Aspinall, p. 177.   [4] *Memoirs*, iii. 40.

it. . . . 15,000 people in the Cloth Hall yard. I went to Hudders-
field, and every village and house turned out, my colour and
name in them all. . . . I concluded at Downsbury and met
20,000 people.'[1]

That speaking tour and the circumstances of his nomination
were his real victories. The election was practically an acclamation for the four candidates who were elected, a fifth obtaining
a mere handful of votes. The greater victories of this Yorkshire
election were to come. In his speech on nomination day
Brougham said that this election would carry the great question
of Parliamentary Reform, revision of the Corn Laws, and the
extinction of colonial slavery, as the County Clare election had
carried Catholic Emancipation. As we shall see, it was Brougham's fulfilment of his Parliamentary Reform pledge to Yorkshire that forced the Tories out of power, and brought in the
Reform Bill administration. In a sense this Yorkshire election
led straight to the Great Reform Bill of 1832. It also led to the
emancipation of the slaves. Immediately it gave leadership
to the election of a number of candidates who were pledged to
the abolition of slavery. (This pledging policy had been proposed by Stephen and Brougham a few years previously.)

Everyone said that his Yorkshire triumph 'intoxicated'
Brougham. And when Brougham was intoxicated in that
fashion something always happened. What actually happened
we shall see in a moment. Something that Brougham planned
to happen is of equal interest. There is a letter in the Brougham
manuscripts from Zachary Macaulay that can only mean that
Brougham, believing that the country was ready for it, planned
to introduce a measure for the immediate emancipation of the
slaves in the session of Parliament that was to commence in
November, to be followed apparently by a nation-wide popular
appeal. Zachary Macaulay wrote to Brougham on 1 September:

I entirely, unreservedly and [illegible] approve of your plan for
opening the campaign. If there be any one point on which I and my
parliamentary friends have differed more than another it has been
on the very point which you have now so justly and firmly seized and
resolved to act upon. I have always felt that no great question and
especially no great moral and political question can ever be carried
unless some master mind shall so manifest his sense of its importance

[1] Brougham MSS., 28 July 1830.

as to disregard minor impediments and move forward boldly and almost recklessly to the attainment of his object. If he feel its importance and act as if he felt it, all those weak spirits who would not have dared to come forward to try the fortunes of the field will joyfully range behind his aegis. . . . The effect would be electric. Only let us choose our ground with judgment, and victory in such a plan is sure. . . . I thank God that it should be suggested to you. . . . I do rejoice in this spontaneous movement of your own mind to the very point toward which I have sighed and prayed for years. And yet perhaps such a course at an earlier period might have been premature. We are now however most unquestionably in full ripeness for it, and it cannot fail.

I approve much also of the purpose being kept secret for the present. It will be necessary by and by to impart it to a few, but as you [illegible] observe, to produce all its effect it must burst on the House with something of the effect of an explosion. Wilberforce alone shall know it at present and he is secret as the grave. . . . In a day or two I will send you an able work which embraces a comprehensive view for popular use of the whole of our subject, and which will serve as a text book for many a lecture and for many a speech throughout the kingdom. This is the production of a Baptist minister of the name of Godwin who keeps an academy at Bradford in Yorkshire. . . .[1]

Brougham's other object, Parliamentary Reform, moved too fast for this plan. With a new government in November pledged to a large measure of Parliamentary Reform, and the supposedly revolutionary Reform Bill announced a few months later, no other matter could catch the attention of Parliament or people for another two years. But, of course, the Reform Bill did much for emancipation.

In the letter of Zachary Macaulay quoted above he said that his son Tom was off to Paris 'laden with kind introductions from you'. But in another two weeks his son and Brougham had begun their lifelong mutual antipathy. On 8 September Brougham wrote to Napier, the new editor of the *Edinburgh Review*: 'I must beg and indeed make a point of giving you my thoughts on the [French July] Revolution, and therefore, pray send off your countermand to Macaulay . . . . All our movements turn on that pivot, and I can trust no one but myself with it, either in or out of Parliament.' Macaulay (Thomas

[1] Brougham MSS.

Babington) had arranged with Napier some time before that he should write an article for that October number on the July Revolution. On the 16th he wrote to Napier a very long and (quite rightly) a very angry letter, of which the following are the most pertinent passages:

It is not very agreeable to me to find that I have thrown away the labour . . . of a month. . . . This would not have happened if Brougham had notified his intentions to you earlier. . . . I always knew that in every association, literary or political, Brougham would wish to domineer. I knew also that no Editor of the Edinburgh Review could, without risking the ruin of the publication, resolutely oppose the demands of a man so able and powerful. . . . The present constitution of the Edinburgh Review is this, that at whatever time Brougham may be pleased to notify his intention of writing on any subject, all previous arrangements are considered to be annulled by that notification. His language, translated into plain English, is this: 'I must write about this French Revolution and I will write about it. . . . If he [Macaulay] has written an article he may throw it behind the grate . . . I am a man who acts a prominent part in the world; he is nobody.'[1]

Brougham had campaigned in Yorkshire for Parliamentary Reform as well as for the abolition of slavery. The movement for Parliamentary Reform made great progress in this year 1830. In January a Political Union had been formed at Birmingham to advance the object of Parliamentary Reform and the Political Union movement spread rapidly. The successful revolution in France in July strengthened it. The people of France had effected an important constitutional change by an almost bloodless revolution. It was generally believed that when Parliament met in November, the Government, which had lost ground at the election, would bring in a very moderate measure. Brougham, who said that he was pledged to his Yorkshire constituents to keep the matter in his own hands, was determined to make a Parliamentary Reform motion of his own. In Yorkshire he had advocated household franchise, and triennial parliaments which went farther than the Reform Bill of 1832 was to go, but he did not go so far in respect to rotten boroughs, although he advocated the granting of seats to the great towns. At first he intended to lay a plan before Parlia-

---

[1] *Napier Correspondence*, pp. 88, 89 seq.

ment. Before doing so he consulted some of his fellow Whig leaders and, more indirectly, the Canningites, of whom Palmerston became the leader after Huskisson's death. On Monday, 1 November, immediately before the meeting of Parliament he wrote to Sir James Graham a letter which has been published inaccurately in Parker's *Life and Letters of Graham*.[1] Brougham's letter, which is in the manuscripts at Netherby, runs:

Hill Street, Monday. Althorp and Stanley and Denman dined with me yesterday after our meeting and agreed to come again next Sunday at ¼ before six, to talk over the Reform plan [not 'Reform Bill' as in Parker] in detail before calling another meeting, and we all wished you and Macdonald to join us, at that hour. Stanley and I accordingly went to Brooks's, as he said you would be there, but we found you not. . . .

We all agreed that it would be highly expedient if you could in the interval see any of the Palmerston folks, and ascertain how far they are prepared to go, the heads being: Great towns; expenses of poll etc.; non-resident voters in boroughs; Scotch cos. and boros; general rights of [illegible] householders; disfranchisement of rotten boroughs and small towns, such as Barnstaple and Cornish nuisances, to the extent of one member to make room for great towns. My hope is that they will only very much object to the fifth and perhaps the sixth.[2]

That, with the omission of triennial parliaments, was the programme of Parliamentary Reform which Brougham had advocated consistently throughout. It is noteworthy that he clung to household suffrage. The publication of this letter in Parker's *Graham* omitted entirely the Scottish counties and boroughs, numbered only five heads, and omitted Brougham's closing remark about the objections that might be raised by the Canningites. The letter, without numbering, listed *six* heads; so it was on household suffrage that Brougham expected Canningite objections to fall mainly.

Replying on the next day, 2 November, Graham promised to see Palmerston and his Canningite friends, urged Brougham to be willing to make concessions and advised him in his speech next day only to give notice of his intention 'to bring this vast subject forward in all its details'. 'Let the subject rest in your hands, the Giant's hands, and let the Public know that you

---

[1] C. S. Parker, *Life and Letters of Sir James Graham*, 2 vols. (1907), i. 96.
[2] Netherby MSS.

have grasped it, but do not bring it to discussion prematurely and give no time to digest, to conciliate and to arrange.'[1]

On the opening day of the session, 2 November, the Duke of Wellington made the speech in which he expressed complete satisfaction with the state of affairs. 'I am not only not prepared to bring forward any measure of this nature [Parliamentary Reform] but I will at once declare that so far as I am concerned, so long as I hold any station in the government of the country, I shall always feel it my duty to resist such measures when proposed by others.' At the same time Brougham in the Commons refused to go into detail, but gave notice that two weeks hence, on 16 November, he 'would bring the great question of the reform of the House of Commons fully under consideration'. After consultation with Althorp, Graham, and others, Brougham decided that his motion of the 16th would simply be a motion to go into Committee with a view to some measure of Parliamentary Reform. That, in view of Wellington's statement, spelled the ruin of the Duke's government. Wellington at first said that the Government would have a good majority against Brougham's motion but few others believed that. The Duke's declaration had propelled Palmerston and his Canningite followers to throw in their lot with the Whigs for some measure of Parliamentary Reform.[2] After an excited and turbulent two weeks, with the people demanding Parliamentary Reform and most members of the Commons in favour of some measure of it, the Government suffered an unexpected defeat on the Civil List, which did not in any way require them to resign. But they decided that night to make that an excuse to resign rather than face Brougham's motion on the morrow.

Lord Grey came in as Prime Minister, and then followed the Cabinet making. The only difficulty was Brougham. Brougham told everyone that he did not wish to be in the Cabinet. Here was his Whig–Canningite coalition on a permanent basis at last and he would not join it. What he wished for was to be Master of the Rolls, a top judicial appointment for life which would have permitted him to remain in the House of Commons. His determination was to continue in the Commons and be independent of the Government. With his strength there and

---

[1] This phrase is omitted in Parker, *Graham*, i. 96–97, Netherby MSS.
[2] Bell, i. 93–94.

his tremendous popular support he could have supported or opposed Government at will. He believed that he could do much good, and everyone else was at least sure that he would make much trouble. When he was asked to be Attorney-General it was said that he tore the communication into small pieces, threw them on the floor, and stamped on them. He denied that, but certainly he was angry at being offered a position that was not good enough for him. He was not offered the Rolls. Grey had wished to do so, but the King and Althorp dissuaded him. Brougham might have been offered the Chancellorship at the beginning if Lyndhurst and his wife had not been trying so hard to induce Grey to continue Lyndhurst in office. Althorp had always felt that Brougham should be Lord Chancellor. He had said that to the Duke of Devonshire early in the year.[1] Palmerston later believed that it was he who had been the first to urge it.[2]

Immediately after Wellington's resignation, Brougham had written to his friends and stated in Parliament that he would not consent to be a member of the new government. He would have nothing to do with the Government and after a short postponement he would press his Parliamentary Reform motion, no matter what government was in power. Several who were close to the situation said, as was said whenever Brougham did something startlingly unpredictable, that he was 'mad'. Hobhouse wrote in his diary: 'As to B[rougham]'s not being affected by the change of Administration, I presume he means that his motion will not be affected, yet his words do not convey that precise meaning. He is a strange creature, and has done more to turn out the [Tory] Ministry than any ten men besides.'[3]

'Strange' he was, no doubt, but we need not conclude that Brougham was mad or insincere. He had *frequently* spoken before of being able to do more for his great causes, slavery, popular education, law reform, and the others, outside a government than in it. He really believed it, he would have much preferred to proceed with all of them irrespective of party, and he wished to put through Parliamentary Reform himself, with government help, no doubt, but not as a government measure.

Althorp told Grey that he would not be a member of any

---

[1] Chatsworth MSS.   [2] Brougham MSS.
[3] Broughton, iv. 69, 10 Nov. 1830.

government that did not include Brougham and that left him free in the Commons, and Grey agreed that it would be hopeless to form a government without him. Brougham told the Duke of Devonshire, and probably others, that no office held any temptation for him except the Chancellorship.[1] Yet when Grey, freed from the Lyndhurst idea, asked him to become Lord Chancellor he emphatically refused. Then Althorp spoke to Brougham frankly. 'You take upon yourself the responsibility of keeping our party for another twenty-five years out of power, and the loss of the great questions which will follow instead of their being carried.' He said that if Brougham did not change his mind before two o'clock, Grey would go to the King and inform him that he could not form a government. An hour later Brougham accepted the Chancellorship. Althorp always said that Brougham made his decision for the sake of the country and that has been the general judgement.[2]

A cartoon of the time represented Grey encouraging Lady Holland who as Delilah was cutting the locks of Samson. The reference was obviously to the removal of Brougham from the Commons. But one thing that the correspondence indicates clearly is that Grey, before he was dissuaded by Althorp and the King, intended to make Brougham Master of the Rolls, leaving him in the Commons. And removing Brougham from the Commons was not at any stage a primary motive with Grey, though some people at the time believed that it was. Mary Wordsworth wrote to a friend: 'The state of the Country causes general apprehension—and what will become of it, when Men like Brougham are placed in such high stations, is awful to think of. It is thought that the motive for making him Lord Chancellor was merely to get rid of him in the House of Commons—a

[1] Chatsworth MSS.
[2] G. M. Trevelyan, pp. 240–5; Aspinall, pp. 84–87; Le Marchant, pp. 261–2. The account given here is Brougham's account in the main. While it is not fully confirmed by Grey and Althorp, everything said by them harmonizes with it. Althorp believed that he dissuaded Grey from offering Brougham the Rolls, and Brougham believed it was the King, prompted by the Tories. Croker, in 1857, declared emphatically that Wellington and Peel did not warn the King against making Brougham Master of the Rolls. (Croker MSS., Croker to Brougham, 8 Jan. 1857.) Croker may have had good reason for contradicting a different statement of his made at the time. But the earlier one may have been correct or Tory talk may have reached the King indirectly. Documents in the Brougham MSS. bearing on the whole matter, including notes by William Brougham made at the time and later letters of various persons, add very little to our knowledge.

worthy one, we must allow.'[1] Similarly, the common, almost universal judgement, that Brougham 'sank on the woolsack as on his political death-bed', is exaggerated and misleading. Certainly the acceptance of the Chancellorship and his leaving the Commons placed him in a position that was particularly dangerous for a man of his temperament and character. But there was no inevitable fatality. On the other hand, the role that Brougham had set for himself as king in the Commons without office would not have been as satisfactory or as productive as Brougham had believed that it would be. His career after 1830 was to be marked by great achievement, much of which would not have been possible if he had not been Lord Chancellor for a season and if he had not become in the minds of so many 'the great Lord Brougham'.

It was Thomas Babington Macaulay who paid the farewell tribute of the House of Commons to Brougham's ascendancy there. Immediately after it was known that Brougham was Lord Chancellor, new writs for Knaresborough and Brougham's Yorkshire seat were discussed. Croker, implying that Brougham could be very eloquent about keeping his promises to his Yorkshire constituents until the Chancellorship was offered to him, said that a man who made so much of political virtue 'should stand clear of all shuffling intrigue'. He expressed regret that Brougham had not stood by his determination solemnly expressed in the House, to remain in the House of Commons independent of any government, and able to render pressure on government in the interest of the nation. Macaulay replied that Brougham was fully justified by the circumstances for changing his mind.

As a member of that House, he [Macaulay] could not banish from his memory the extraordinary eloquence of that noble person within those walls, an eloquence which left nothing equal to it behind; and when he beheld the departure of that great man from amongst them, and when he saw the place in which he usually sat and from which he had so often astonished them by the mighty powers of his mind, occupied in such an exceedingly different manner this evening. ... Was that a time for a member of that House, who would sooner have burned his tongue than have made such an attack in the presence of the noble person, thus to attack him behind his back?

[1] *The Letters of Mary Wordsworth* (1958), edited by Mary Burton, pp. 131–2.

The Speaker called Macaulay to order and he got no farther.[1]
Lord Dudley and Ward wrote to Mrs. Stewart:

His [Brougham's] power of attainment is almost miraculous and I
doubt not that he will quickly acquire the only branch of human
knowledge of which he is at present wholly ignorant,—the Law of
Equity. [He had never practised in the Court of Chancery.] I do
not know what effect this appointment may produce now, but I am
perfectly sure that a few years ago it would have seemed like the
beginning of a revolution. . . . As it is I cannot but think that the
clergy in general and a large part of the landed gentlemen will regard
him with an evil eye.[2]

His inauguration was an unusual event, men of all parties
and foreign ambassadors crowding to do him honour. A week
later Charles Knight went to see him about S.D.U.K. affairs.
Brougham as he started down the corridor to preside in the
House of Lords, said 'Advertise Paley to-morrow morning'.
Knight continued: 'He rushed along nimbly . . . the panting
mace-bearer toiled after him in vain. . . . I ventured to say to
one of those solemn men in black, "Is that quite regular?"
"Regular, sir? Oh dear! the last [Lyndhurst] was bad enough,
but this one! Oh, dear!" '[3]

We cannot catch up with him now, any more than the mace-
bearer could, but in a few years we may be able to follow him
through another volume.

[1] *Hansard*, 3rd series, i. 633–48.
[2] *Letters to Ivy*, p. 357 [20 Nov. 1830].
[3] Charles Knight, ii. 158.

APPENDIX

Brougham's Articles in the *Edinburgh Review*

FROM the beginning the articles in the *Edinburgh Review* were anonymous and the rule of anonymity was observed probably as well as such rules usually are. Jeffrey, the first editor, laid very heavy emphasis on the rule. The most prolific of the authors of this period, however, Jeffrey, Brougham, and Sydney Smith, often revealed their own authorship in letters written at the time, and discussed speculatively other authorships. Moreover, the principal reviewers of the early nineteenth century all published selections from their articles. Sydney Smith did so in his *Works* in 1839, and Jeffrey published a four-volume selection in 1843. Cockburn prepared, with Jeffrey's help, a list of Jeffrey's articles for his biography of Jeffrey published in 1852. Sydney Smith lent his authority to a similar list of his articles published in *A Memoir of Sydney Smith* in 1855. These and similar publications suggested to Brougham and his friends that a selection of his *Edinburgh Review* articles should be published. The result was a three-volume work in 1856, which unfortunately excluded all articles on behalf of the movements against slavery and for popular education, as well as a number of political articles. Brougham said that those articles were so well known that publication was uncalled for. What he did publish was listed under the headings of international policy, economics, constitutional questions, physical science, and rhetoric. While this project was under consideration in September 1855, Lord Murray was visiting at Brougham, and William Brougham suggested that with his help they should construct a list of the authors of as many articles as possible in the 'early' numbers of the *Edinburgh Review*. That list was not intended for publication and has never been published. All of those *published* selections and lists were related to one author only. A general list ascribing authorship to a considerable number of articles in all of the first hundred numbers was published by Professor W. A. Copinger in 1895. He did a considerable amount of research, but there were many errors and the most irritating thing about his work was that he cited no authorities. So far as Brougham was concerned, many of Copinger's omissions and mistakes were related to the obvious fact that he was not acquainted with the details of Brougham's career, his activities at a particular time, and his House of Commons speeches. There has been speculation in a general way about where Copinger found his material, but none of it has been convincing. The list supplied by Longmans, Green & Co. to Professor Aspinall in 1926 was identical with the Copinger List as far as the latter went, and has independent value only after the hundredth number.

In 1938 a doctoral thesis was written for Yale University by Leroy Buckingham. It dealt with the authorship of the first twenty-five numbers of the *Edinburgh Review*. The work was carefully done and the results are on the whole convincing. The Brougham Manuscripts' List which I have employed in this Appendix was unknown to him. Some of his sources, as he apparently realized himself, were weak. These included the Joline Manuscript and the Silliman Manuscript, in which Professor Silliman showed altogether too much confidence in his informants. Buckingham employed a much better source in the Cockburn Manuscript, which is a list in Lord Cockburn's hand of ascriptions of authorships from the beginning of the *Edinburgh Review*. It was attested by Lord Cockburn in 1843, but it continued beyond that. Cockburn was careful not to make an ascription unless he were fairly confident. His comments, however, ranged from 'I believe' to 'Certain, Jeffrey told me'. The Cockburn Manuscript, a copy of which I have used, is now in the possession of Lord Rosebery.

In 1945 and 1946 a Temple University group (Schneider, Griggs, and Kern) published two very important articles in *Modern Philology*. They described and discussed the markings ascribing authorship in the first thirty-eight numbers of a set of the *Edinburgh Review* now in Temple University. The markings are in Trollope's hand, but the Temple group are undoubtedly right in believing that they were copied from an earlier list. They argued in a convincing manner that the list from which the markings were copied was the list which Lord Brougham, Lord Murray, and William Brougham made in 1855. They adduced a suitable amount of evidence which helped them to pass judgement on the accuracy of those ascriptions for which I am fully obligated to them in the ascriptions I have made below, although occasionally I have disagreed.

In 1953 Professor Fetter published in the *Journal of Political Economy* a very important article, embodying the results of a study of the authorship of the economic articles of the *E.R.* Brougham's were confined almost entirely to the earlier numbers.

When I first contemplated this Appendix I felt disappointed that I had met with so little bearing on this question of authorship when I went through the Brougham Manuscripts. Then, as recently as June 1958, the executors of the late C. K. Ogden kindly made available to University College Library some additional Brougham manuscripts which they had discovered in the course of clearing the estate. Amongst these manuscripts were a number of lists of *Edinburgh Review* articles which I have studied on microfilm. Some do not concern us here. But others are particularly important in relation to this Appendix. With the 1856 three-volume publication of Lord Brougham's *Contributions* in mind, a considerably longer list from which those selections were to be made was clearly indicated. That could only be done efficiently by Brougham himself or under his direction and his authorship of the articles in that list which were not published is attested as clearly by him as in the case of those which were. The most important of these lists are two which are closely related and which I have described below as Brougham Manuscripts Lists. The one which I have called a rough list consists of a number of sheets of paper, each containing several numbers of the *Review* with names, obviously of authors, put down opposite the numbers of many of the articles. While they are loose sheets, if they were put together in proper order they would constitute a list which carries us well beyond 1830. The numbers for the spaces to be filled in and many of the entries are in William Brougham's hand. The other list which I have called the neat list is in a clear hand resembling that of a copyist, and forms a continuous list of *Edinburgh Review* articles to the end of the 110th number. The differences between the two are nearly all in the form of corrections. The list from which the Trollope markings were made was, in nearly every case, similar to this neat list; occasionally the Trollope markings correspond with the rough list only, and a few notes are omitted. In comparing the Trollope markings with the first four numbers of the Brougham–Murray list as given by Brougham in his *Memoirs*, the Temple Group's case was even better than they knew. The one discrepancy which they could not explain was Brougham's Memoir list giving Jeffrey, and the Trollope markings giving Sydney Smith, for No. 2 article 22. Whatever Trollope copied from must have been copied from this Brougham Manuscripts List before a note was added to the effect that this article is not in the Sydney Smith list and was therefore probably written by Jeffrey. So the difficulty disappears. A question still to be answered is why the Trollope markings ended with number thirty-eight.

William Brougham's original proposal for a Brougham–Murray list was that they should endeavour to ascribe authors to all of the *early numbers*. In the few days spent by Lord Murray at Brougham in September 1855, William probably prepared forms and a number of entries were made in the rough list. Murray had some notes which he had previously made and, I believe, a list of his own. After his return to Edinburgh he looked up friends who knew something about the authorship of the articles. Apparently he received most help from Robert Graham of Redgorton, whom he twice commended in letters to William as being 'very accurate' in this matter. It is significant that Murray in sending a list to Graham for comparison with Graham's *E.R.* markings asked for a comparison for the *first forty-two numbers only*, which went four numbers beyond the list apparently used later by Trollope, but was still concerned only with 'early numbers'. Graham's full report, the document extant in the Brougham Manuscripts under the title 'R. G.'s Markings', did not reach Brougham Hall until November, about a month after Brougham had left and headed 'toward the sun'. Unfortunately R. G. reported authorship only where his markings disagreed with Lord Murray's list, but the influence of those markings on what I have called the Brougham Manuscripts List is evident by merely glancing at the list in its two forms. In many cases the correct ascription in the neat list differs from that given in the rough list but agrees with R. G.'s Markings. Sometimes the exact wording of R. G.'s Markings is repeated in the lists, as well as several fuller notes.

William Brougham's diary in Brougham Manuscripts indicates that he was busy on the list during the remainder of 1855. The neat list up to the last part affords an impression of decision and finality, and the earliest part of it was probably made after consultation with Lord Brougham when he returned to England that winter. In his *Memoirs* Brougham wrote that 'they put the names of the authors to all the early numbers, he [Lord Murray] and I being the last survivors of the first contributors', and 'they made a very full and correct list'. The *Memoirs* give the impression that this was completed in September rather than several months later, but it all sounds like the successful completion of a project and a work well done. Brougham's words about the early years and early contributors could apply to the first ten years, roughly the first thirty-eight numbers. They could not reasonably apply to the list as it stands, extending over thirty years and more. The original project was completed and what seems to have happened is that someone extended both the rough and neat list. The neat list as it stands and many of the entries in the rough list are in William Brougham's hand. This extension may be considered a second project. Lord Brougham may have been consulted about ascriptions, but it is impossible to believe that he was consulted in every case. In this part of the list (say from No. 39 to No. 99) there are a number of omissions of articles which Brougham had said in contemporary letters that he wrote and articles that, according to the Cockburn Manuscript, Jeffrey had told Cockburn that Brougham wrote beyond a doubt. The fact that one article published in Brougham's *Contributions* in 1856 is omitted from the list may be due to oversight in checking, but it is not so easy to explain the omission of a number of articles whose titles occur in the lists from which the selection (a space selection) was made and which Brougham had undoubtedly designated as his own. I do not believe that these cases of discrepancy can be accounted for by a failure of memory on Brougham's part, or by a desire to deceive in what in any case was a private list not intended for publication. I believe that most, if not all, of these cases were not brought to his attention. In spite of these occasional discrepancies, the list as it stands is (up to No. 100) a good list. On the whole it is well supported by other evidence where other evidence exists. (Where there is no evidence at all except an ascription in this list, I have given the ascription only C rating below.) With No. 100 the list collapsed badly. It apparently encountered the same difficulties as did the Cockburn Manuscript when Napier became editor. But the omission of all ascriptions to Brougham in the remainder of the neat list, which ran to the end of No. 110 (Brougham wrote seven articles for Nos. 102 and 103 beyond a doubt) and the inclusion of only a fraction of Brougham's articles (well attested) in the remainder of the rough list make it clear enough that at this point, certainly, Brougham was not consulted.

The following abbreviations are employed below:

Br.	Brougham
B.M.L.	Brougham Manuscripts Lists
B.	Buckingham's Thesis
C.'s J.	Cockburn's Jeffrey
C.M.	Cockburn Manuscript
Conts.	Brougham's published *Contributions* to the *E.R.*
Cop.	Copinger
E.F.	*Brougham and his Early Friends*
E.R.	*Edinburgh Review*
H.	Horner
H.M.	*Horner Memoirs*
J.	Jeffrey
L.S.S.	*Letters of Sydney Smith*
Mems.	Brougham's *Memoirs*
R.G.M.	Robert Graham's Markings
Si.	Silliman Manuscript
S.S.	Sydney Smith
S.S.W.	Sydney Smith's Works
T.Gr.	The Temple University Group

In the following ascriptions A before a number means practically certain, B, highly probable, and C, more likely than not.

No. I, October 1802

B. 5 Olivier's Travels. By Br. to himself in *Mems.* i. 256 seq. (Br.–Murray list) and i. 255 (his detailed account of his work on this number). B.M.L. where rough list says 'Hamilton' and more correct neat list 'Brougham'. B. on basis of C.M. and Joline (*Edgehill Essays*, p. 107) who described a copy of this number which apparently bore a dated autograph by Br. Opposite each article in the index there are initials ascribing authorship. But could Joline identify Brougham's hand and particularly by initials? Otherwise, of course, the ascriptions could have been made by anyone at any time. Cop. to S.S., but it is not in the S.S. list.

B. 6 Jointly with J. See joint articles below.

A. 21 Hornemann's Travels. By Br. to himself in *Mems.* as cited in 5, C.M., B.M.L. and B. Cop. and Si. to Horner, who, however omitted it from his own list of the 'only' articles he wrote for this number. (*H.M.* i. 202.)

A. 23 Wood's Optics. *Mems.* as in 5, C.M., B.M.L., Cop., Si., B.

A. 24 Acerbi's Travels. *Mems.* as in 5, C.M., B.M.L., Si., B. Cop., said Br. and S.S., not in S.S. list.

B. 26 Playfair's Huttonian Theory. *Mems.* as in 5, B.M.L., where J. is given in rough list and in the neat list J. is struck out and Br. substituted. Cockburn gave it in his J. list but obviously did not include it in his contemporary account of J.'s articles in this number. C.M. to Dr. Moton. B. to J. An unlikely subject for J.

A. 27 Stephen's Crisis of the Sugar Colonies. B. citing, *Mems.*, C.M., Si., Cop., *E.F.* ii. 5. Also B.M.L. and Fetter.

No. II, January 1803

A. 9 Politique de tous les Cabinets de l'Europe. B. citing *Mems.*, Si., C.M., Cop. Published by Br. in *Conts.* and *Works.* Also *Colonial Policy*, ii. 544, B.M.L., and R.G.M.

B. 12 Woodhouse on Imaginary Quantities. B. to Br. and Ivory as in Cop. But *Mems.* (Br.–Murray list), Si., and the neat list in B.M.L. all say Br., which *E.F.* ii. 31–32 also supports.

A. 15 Herschel on the New Planets. B., citing *Mems.* (Br.–Murray list), Si., C.M., Cop., Br.'s contemporary list in *E.F.* ii. 32, and *H.M.* i. 201. Also in R. G.'s Markings.

A. 17 Bakerian Lecture on Light and Colours. B. citing *Mems.*

(Br.–Murray list), Si., C.M., and Cop. Br.'s letter in *E.F.* also supports this. B.M.L. (neat list). Br. himself appears to have always acknowledged this article which drastically criticized Young's theory of light. The T.Gr. was misled in this respect by the fact that the list from which the Trollope markings were taken in this case gives the rough list reading, 'Robinson and Brougham'. That had been the ascription in a list which Murray had sent to be compared with R.G.M., which said Brougham. Murray's ascription was apparently entered in the rough list before the comparison was made and the later neat list said Brougham, apparently on the latter's initiative. It is also Brougham clearly in the *Memoirs'* account of the Br.–Murray list given in Br.'s *Memoirs*. Also Si., C.M., Cop., *E.F.* ii. 31–32.

A. 18 Young on Colours. All of the above in relation to 17 was the same for 18, except that the latter does not appear in the *Mems*. account of the Br.–Murray list. When that was written Br. for some reason did not care to publish his authorship of the second article. The change, of course, may have been made by William after Br.'s death, though that is improbable. In any case there can be no doubt that both of these articles were written by Br.

23 Jointly with J. See Joint Articles below.

No. III, April 1803

3 Shepherd's Life of Poggio.
Jointly with Percival. See Joint Articles below.
The following articles are all ascribed to Br. by B., and are attested by Br.'s letter in *E.F.* ii. 67, Br.'s *Mems*. list, Si., and C.M., and all except 11 by Cop., who said Horner. Also all in B.M.L.

A. 8 Wollaston on Prismatic Reflection.
A. 9 Wollaston on Oblique Reflection of Iceland Chrystal.
A. 10 Hatchett's Analysis of a new metal.
A. 11 Guineas an Encumbrance. In Fetter's list of economic articles.
13 Ritson on Abstinence from Animal Food. Jointly with J. See Joint Articles below.
A. 26 B. citing *Mems*. list, Si., C.M., and Cop. Also in B.M.L. [B. also ascribes 20 to Br. but on the authority of Si. and Cop. which is inadequate, as Br. did not include it in the list he gave Loch in his contemporary letter (*E.F.* ii. 67) or in his *Mems*. list.]

No. IV, July 1803

A. 6   Transactions of the Am. Phil. Society. B. citing Br. *Mems.* list,
Si., C.M., Cop. Also in R.G.M. and B.M.L.

A. 8   Dallas's History of Maroons. B. citing Br. *Mems.* list, C.M.
Also in B.M.L., Cop. said Br. and J.

A. 12   Walker's Poems, B. citing Br. *Mems.* list, Si., C.M., Cop. Also
in B.M.L.

A. 15   Davis's Trades. B. citing Br. *Mems.* list, Si., C.M. Also in
R.G.M. and B.M.L.

16   Fuseli's Lectures. Jointly with Parry. See Joint Articles below.

No. V, October 1803

A. 1   Dr. Black's Lectures. B. citing Si., C.M., Cop., publication
by Br. in his Cont. and Misc. Writings. Also in B.M.L. Br.'s
contemporary letters in *E.F.* ii. 86–87.

A. 7   Second Voyage to Louisiana. B. citing Si. and *E.F.* ii. 86–87.
Also B.M.L.

9   Barclay's New Anatomical Nomenclature. Joint Article, see
below.

A. 18   Wheatly on Currency and Commerce. B. citing Si., C.M.,
Cop. Br.'s *Conts.* and *E.F.* ii. 86–87. In B.M.L. In Fetter's list.

No. VI, January 1804

B. 5   Karamsin's Travels. B. citing Cop. alone. Also B.M.L.

A. 12   Izarn, Lithologie Atmospherique. B. citing Cop. and Br.'s
publication of it in his *Conts.* and Math. and Phys. Tracts.
Also in C.M. and B.M.L.

B. 17   Hatchett on the Gold Coin. B. citing Si., C.M., Cop. Also in
B.M.L. In Fetter's list.

A. 19   Substance of a Speech intended to have been spoken in the
House of Lords. Same authorities as 12 except that Si. ascribed
to Horner and also that Br. published it in his *Conts.* (Bishop
Watson on the National Debt.)

No. VII, April 1804

A. 3   Resources of France and Russia. In B.M.L. and C.M. The
argument of the Temple Group that this article was written
by the same hand as IX, 1 is sound.

A. 5   Morgan's Comparative View of Finances. B. citing C.M.
Also in B.M.L. and in Fetter's list.

B. 11   Chevenix on the Chemical Properties of Palladium. B. citing
Si. In B.M.L.

B. 16   Hunter's Travels through France. B. citing Si. In B.M.L.

No. VIII, July 1804

A. 8   Lord Lauderdale on Public Wealth. Well known to be Br.'s at the time and so indicated in many sources including a contemporary letter from J. (*Mems.* i. 266). C.M. and Cop. Also B.M.L. In Fetter's list.

A. 9   Lord Chatham's Letters to his Nephew. B. citing C.M. Attested by J. to Br. in *Mems.* i. 269. Br. MSS. indicate that Br. considered inclusion of this in his *Contributions*. In B.M.L. Cop. ascribed to Horner but is negatived by a contemporary letter of Leonard Horner (in *H.M.* i. 265 n.).

A. 11 Rumford on the Nature of Heat. B. citing Si., C.M., and Cop. In B.M.L. Published by Br. in *Conts*.

A. 12 Rumford on a Phenomenon in Glaciers. Same authorities as 11.

B. 13 McKinnon's Tour in the West Indies. In B.M.L. Br. wrote nearly all of the slavery articles and he linked this up closely in a later article. Although the references to slavery in this article are brief, they are powerful. See T.Gr.

No. IX, October 1804

A. 1   Plans of National Improvement. In B.M.L., C.M. In Fetter's list. T.Gr. cite Br.'s own statement about writing this article in *Mems.* i. 193 and argue soundly that it and VII, 3 were written by the same author.

B. 5   Kotzebue's Travels. B. citing Cop. In B.M.L.

C. 6   Knight on the Motion of Sap in Trees. In B.M.L.

A. 7   Young's Bakerian Lecture. B. citing C.M., Cop., Peacock's *Life of Young* and Young's *Miscellaneous Works*. In R.G.M. and B.M.L.

A. 8   O'Connor's Present State of Great Britain. B. citing Si., C.M., Cop. In B.M.L. and Fetter's list. Br. MSS. show that Br. considered it for inclusion in his *Conts*.

No. X, January 1805

A. 16 European Armies. B. citing C.M. Br.'s contemporary statement in *Mems.* i. 294. In B.M.L. Si. ascribed it to Playfair.

No. XI, April 1805

B. 2   Venturi, Sopra i Colori. B. citing Cop. In B.M.L. Br. wrote on Optics for the *E.R.*

    4 Jointly with Playfair. See Joint Articles below.

B. 6   Sur les Colonies, &c. B. citing Si., Cop. In B.M.L. In Fetter's list.

B. 8   Mems. de l'Académie de Turin. B. citing Cop. In B.M.L.

B. 10 Toulongeon, Sur l'Usage du Numéraire. In B.M.L. In Fetter's list.

C. 11 Voyage de Bory de St. Vincent. In B.M.L. B. ascribes to Muirhead citing Brighton Ref. Lib. MS.

C. 13 Chambrier, Henri IV. In B.M.L.

C. 14 San Martino, Sopra il Carbone nei Pianti. In B.M.L.

No. XII, July 1805

A. 2 Lord Lauderdale's hints to Manufacturers. B. citing Si., Cop. Editor's note at end of No. 9 of *E.R.* Also B.M.L. and Fetter's list.

A. 8 Examen de l'Esclavage. B. citing Si., Cop. Also B.M.L. Generally believed at time. Statements similar to Br.'s elsewhere.

B. 11 De Langes. Statici per i Tetti. B. citing Cop. Also in B.M.L.

C. 12 Carr's Northern Tour. B.M.L.

No. XIII, October 1805

A. 4 Leslie on Nature of Heat. B. citing Si., C.M., Cop. Published by Br. in *Conts.* B.M.L.

B. 15 Thiebault Mémoires de Frédéric le Grand. B. citing Cop. Also B.M.L. Written in Br.'s characteristic *E.R.* style at this time.

B. 16 Horrors of Negro Slavery. B. citing Si., also B.M.L. Br. regularly wrote the slave-trade and slavery articles.

No. XIV, January 1806

A. 1 Lord Liverpool on the Coins of the Realm. B. citing Si., C.M., Cop. Also B.M.L. Br. MSS. show that Br. considered this for inclusion in his publication of *Conts.* Fetter's list.

C. 9 Dutens, Sur l'Usage des Voûtées. B. ascribes to Lord Aberdeen, citing Cop. alone. It is simply a matter of accepting the authority of Cop. or of the B.M.L. and the latter is preferable in these early numbers. The T.Gr. rejected the ascription to Br. because he did not possess 'this sort of knowledge'. I find no knowledge in the article that Brougham could not have mastered.

B. 10 Kotzebue's Travels in Italy. B. citing Cop. Also B.M.L. The style sounds very much like Br.

No. XV, April 1806

B. 3 Rumford on Hayti. B. reported 'no Data'. B.M.L. Br. was expected to write the slavery articles. Temple University group argued strongly on basis of the references to Br.'s Colonial Policy. Brougham's style.

B. 5   Hatchett on Tannin. B. citing Si. In B.M.L.

No. XVI, July 1806

B. 2   Lemaistre's Travels. B. citing Cop. In B.M.L.

B. 8   Dutens, Mémoires d'un Voyageur. B. citing Cop. In B.M.L.

B. 16 Account of Quaker work among N.A. Indians. In B.M.L. The high praise of Quakers and the statement that they were 'the most meritorious' 'among our religious sects' sounds like Br. and Br. alone among *E.R.* writers. There is also a neat touch on slavery which is not called for.

No. XVIII, January 1807

A. 1   Gentz on the State of Europe. B. citing C.M., Cop. Published by Br. in *Conts*. In B.M.L.

A. 3   Pinckard on West Indies. B. citing Cop. and J.'s letter in *Napier Correspondence*, p. 2. Also B.M.L.

A. 5   Turnbull, Voyage Round the World. B., citing Cop. In B.M.L.

B. 11 Hunter's Reasons for not making Peace. B.M.L. Contains reference to the Gentz book reviewed by Br. in 1 of this number.

C. 13 A British Merchant on Guiana Colonies. In B.M.L.

No. XIX, April 1807

A. 13 Wilberforce on the Abolition of the Slave Trade. B. citing Cop. In B.M.L. Br.'s style. Under the circumstances it is almost impossible to think of anyone but Br. writing this.

No. XX, July 1807

B. 1   Thornton on Turkey. B. ascribes to J. or Br. citing C.M. for J. and Cop. for Br. Cockburn in J. list does not include it. In B.M.L. Br.'s style.

B. 8   Dumouriez's Character and Conduct of Bonaparte. B. citing Cop. In B.M.L.

B. 11 Burnett's Present State of Poland. B. citing Cop. In B.M.L. [I am omitting 13. B. cited Cop. and T.Gr. argued for Br. authorship. Not in B.M.L. I believe that Br. added two pages to an article written by someone else.]

No. XXI, October 1807

A. 1   Randolph and others on the Neutral Questions. B. citing C.M., Cop. Br.'s contemporary statement to Grey (*Mems*. i.

270) and his publication of it in his *Critical and Misc. Writings*.
In Fetter's list.
[I am omitting 2 which B. ascribed to Br. on the basis of
Alibone (under Southey) alone. Alibone obviously knew
nothing about Br.'s articles, and gives no authority for this
one, the subject of which was not at all a likely one for Br.]

B. 6   Semple's Travels in Spain. B. citing Cop. In B.M.L. Contains
reference to other travel writers whose books Br. often had
reviewed.

A. 9   Young and others on West Indian Affairs. B. citing C.M. In
B.M.L. In Fetter's list. Br. would take any West Indian subject if able to do so.

No. XXII, January 1808

A. 2   Byron's Hours of Idleness. B. quoting C.M. 'Certain, Jeffrey
told me', Sir E. M. Grant Duff. *Notes from a Diary. Gentleman's
Magazine*, 1850. In B.M.L. T.Gr. cites *Medwin Conversations of
Lord Byron, Table talk of Samuel Rogers*, Lord Holland, *Further
Memoirs, Notes and Queries*, 4th series, vi, vii, viii. Sounds like
Br.

C. 3   Barrow's Life of Lord McCartney. B. says 'no data'. Is in
B.M.L. One sentence reads as though the writer had reviewed
Barrow previously in *E.R. E.R.* VIII, 15 on Barrow was
ascribed by Cop. to Br. but to J. in B.M.L. Neither article is
in C.'s J.

A. 8   Davy's Bakerian Lectures on Electricity. B. citing Br.'s publication of it in his *Conts*. In B.M.L.

A. 14   The Orders in Council. B. citing Cop. In B.M.L. Fetter's list.
It is undoubtedly Br.'s preparatory article for his 1808 attack
on the Orders in Council and could hardly have been written
by anyone but Br. who was so full of the subject.

No. XXIII, April 1808

C. 7   Wollaston's Bakerian Lecture. B. ascribes to Playfair, citing
Cop. alone. Br. in B.M.L. Not included in Playfair's *Works*.
[I am omitting 12 which B. ascribed to Br. on basis of Cop.
Not in B.M.L.]

B. 14   Portuguese Emigration. B. had 'no data'. In B.M.L. T.Gr.
presented good argument for ascription to Br. based on his
relations with Portugal, his statements to Grey (*Mems.*) and
his *Colonial Policy*.

No. XXIV, July 1808

A. 3 MacGill's Travels in Turkey. B. citing C.M., Cop. In B.M.L. In R.G.M.

A. 7 Davy's Bakerian Lecture. B. citing C.M. and Br.'s publishing it in his *Conts*. In B.M.L. J. to Br. 25 July 1808 in Br. MSS. shows clearly that Br. wrote it.

A. 11 Whitbread's letter on Spain. B. citing C.M., Cop., Br.'s *Mems*. (Br. to Grey, 6 October 1808) and *E.F.* (Br. to Loch, 30 July 1808). In B.M.L.

No. XXV, October 1808

14 The Don Cevallos article. Jointly with J. See below.

No. XXVI, January 1809

A. 7 Pamphlets on West Indian Affairs. Cop., Fetter's list. In B.M.L. Stated positively by S.S. in *Letters*, i. 157.

A. 10 Davy on the Earth. Published by Br. in *Conts*. In B.M.L.

C. 13 Expedition against Copenhagen. B.M.L. Br. MSS. indicate that Br. considered its publication in his *Conts*. Cop. ascribed it to Hamilton, as did S.S. at the time ('I believe'). The T.Gr. points out that while it was not at all a subject for Hamilton, Br. was not in Constantinople at the time as the article states. They suggest that Hamilton drafted this article or part of it which was rewritten by Br.

No. XXVII, April 1809

A. 16 Vaughan's Siege of Saragossa. In B.M.L. Published by Br. in his *Conts*. *Mems*. i. 443 seq.

No. XXVIII, July 1809

C. 2 Jackson's Account of Morocco. In B.M.L. No other ascription.

A. 8 Ruhliere, Anarchie de Pologne. In B.M.L. Br. MSS. show that Br. considered it for selection for his *Conts*. Cop. ascribed to MacVey Napier.

A. 11 Lord Sheffield and others on Foreign Affairs. In B.M.L. Published by Br. in his *Conts*.

A. 12 Davy's Bakerian Lecture. In B.M.L. Published by Br. in his *Conts*.

No. XXIX, October 1809

A. 14 The Conduct of the War. In B.M.L. Published by Br. in his *Conts*. Referred to *passim* in contemporary Br.–Grey

correspondence in *Mems.* as Br.'s article. Also attested by
L.S.S. i. 178, 179.

No. XXX, January 1810

A. 14 The African Institution. B.M.L., C.M. B.'s interest in the
subject and the fact that he regularly reviewed reports of the
A.I. for the *E.R.*

No. XXXI, April 1810

A. 5 Erskine's Speeches. B.M.L., C.M., and Cop. Published by
Br. in his *Conts.*

A. 8 Rose on Influence of the Crown. B.M.L., Cop. Must be the
article ascribed to Br. by S.S. in *Letters*, i. 189.

No. XXXII, August 1810

A. 9 African Institution. In B.M.L. Br. was generally known to
have written all these A.I. articles.

No. XXXIII, November 1810

A. 3 Education of the Poor. B.M.L. In the circumstances, Br.'s
subject and Br.'s style. Quoted by Lancaster at the time as
having been written by Br. (Br. MSS.).

A. 8 Papers on the Stone. B.M.L., C.M., Cop. Br. MSS. show
that Br. considered this article for selection for his *Conts.*

No. XXXIV, February 1811

1 Parliamentary Reform. Jointly with J. See Joint Articles
below.

A. 9 Davy on Oxymuriatic Acid. Published by Br. in his *Conts.*
In B.M.L.

No. XXXV, May 1811

C. 5 Jacob's Travels in Spain. Cop., R.G.M., *L.S.S.* Not in B.M.L.
Some of the language and sentiments sound like Br. and the
subject is not an unlikely one.

B. 9 Wilson on the Russian Army. Cop., R.G.M., B.M.L.

No. XXXVI, August 1811

B. 2 Report of the African Institute. In B.M.L., C.M. Br. reviewed
the A.I. Reports. In this article there is adverse criticism of
Br.'s Felony Act, which in view of its being so well known
that the act was Br.'s, was probably an editorial touch of J.'s.

B. 7 Campaigns of 1809. R.G.M. and B.M.L.

[I am omitting 9 because at this point I prefer B.M.L.'s exclusion to Cop.'s inclusion.]

[I am omitting 11. It is ascribed in the rough list of B.M.L. and that ascription found its way into the markings in the Trollope set, but the later, more accurate, neat list leaves a blank. Br.'s *Conts.* included five of Davy's papers but omitted this one.]

No. XXXVII, November 1811

A. 1 Education of the Poor. Cop., B.M.L., C.M. Br.'s subject and style. A follow-up to XXXIII, 3.

A. 5 West Indian Slavery. Cop., B.M.L.

C. 8 Brande's Papers in Phil. Transactions. Cop., B.M.L. R.G.M. ascribed it to Allen as did William Young, in *Dulwich College*, ii. 418, but it is not in Allen's own list.

A. 15 West Indian Slavery. Cop., B.M.L., C.M. Br.'s views and style. The Hodge Report.

No. XXXVIII, February 1812

A. 2 Disputes with America. Cop., B.M.L., C.M., Fetter's list. Considered by Br. for selection in publishing *Conts.* (Br. MSS.). Just before Br. opened his final campaign for repeal of Orders in Council.

A. 4 Speeches of Lord Erskine. Cop., B.M.L., C.M. Published by Br. in *Conts.*

A. 7 Romilly on the Criminal Law. B.M.L., C.M. Published by Br. in *Conts.*

No. XXXIX, July 1812

A. 5 Report of African Institute. In B.M.L. See above for these reports. Br. gives this as one of his two articles in this number in a footnote in his *Mems.* (ii. 47).

A. 8 Parliamentary Reform. Cop., B.M.L. Considered by Br. for selection in publishing *Conts.* (Br. MSS.). Br.'s *Mems.* statement referred to above. Similarities to Br. Parl. Reform publication of 1811 (for which see *S.S.L.* i. 210).

C. 12 Roscoe's 'Of Peace'. Cop. Contains an eloquent reference to the repeal of the Orders in Council. Reads like one of Br.'s House of Commons speeches.

No. XL, October 1812

A. 8 Rights and Duties of the People. Cop. Listed by Br. for consideration in selections for *Conts.* (Br. MSS.). A direct and timely bid for political support in Westminster. Not in B.M.L. but we are now beyond No. 38.

No. XLI, January 1813

B. 3   Trial of the Slave Traders. B.M.L., C.M. A likely Br. article on account of his Felony Bill.

C. 5   Project for Creating a Vice-Chancellor. In B.M.L. only.

B. 9   Education of the Poor. B.M.L. Br.'s subject.

B. 10 Foreign Policy of England. B.M.L., C.M.

No. XLII, July 1813

B. 7   Erskine's Tour through Italy. B.M.L., C.M.

A. 11 Report of African Institution. B.M.L. See above on A.I. Reports.

No. XLIII, October 1813

A. 1   Bentham's Theory of Punishment. B.M.L., C.M. Published by Br. in his *Conts*.

B. 5   John George's Law of Libel. B.M.L., C.M. A subject of particular interest to Br.

A. 8   Kelsall's translation of Cicero. B.M.L., C.M. Considered in selection for Contributions. Br. MSS. S.S. seems to speak of this as Br.'s (*Letters*, i. 241).

A. 10 Brande on the Blood. B.M.L. Listed by Br. in articles from which selection made for *Conts*. (Br. MSS.).

No. XLIV, January 1814

A. 3   Appeal of the Poles. B.M.L., C.M. In *Conts*.

No. XLV, April 1814

B. 4   Norway. B.M.L. Bennet to Creevey in *Creevey Papers*, i. 185 (certainly written in 1814). C.M. says Br. ('I Believe').

A. 6   Revival of the Slave Trade. A spirited protest against the treaty revival of the French trade which could hardly have been written by anyone but Br. The subject and style are his, the feelings are those which he expressed at the time, and there are party comparisons in regard to the slave trade which are almost verbal repetitions of what he had written in previous articles. Not in B.M.L.

No. XLVI, September 1814

A. 7   Letters of Nelson to Lady Hamilton. B.M.L. Published by Br. in his *Conts*.

A. 10 Constitutional Character of a Queen Consort. B.M.L., C.M. Published by Br. in his *Conts.*

A. 11 Shepherd on Paris in 1802 and 1814. Br. said he wrote it in contemporary letters to Grey and Shepherd (*Mems.* ii. 80). Not in B.M.L.

A. 12 Davy on Iodine. B.M.L. In listing of articles for *Conts.* 'five articles on Sir H. Davy' to be revised.

No. XLVII, November 1814

C. 6 Revival of the Slave Trade. The article that caused the quarrel with Stephen. B.M.L.

A. 10 Carnot's Memorial. Cop., B.M.L. Br.'s letters to Grey and to Carnot in *Mems.* ii. 103.

No. XLVIII, February 1815

B. 6 Brande on Magnesia and Uric Acid. B.M.L. Apparently by the author of XXXIII, 8 who was Br. He had reviewed earlier papers by Brande.

A. 12 Journal of Mungo Park. B.M.L., C.M. Published by Br. in his *Conts.* Begins with reference to the *E.R.*'s (Br.'s) reviews of reports of A.I.

No. XLIX

[C.M. ascribed 5 to Br., but in view of the state of his health, it seems unlikely that he wrote anything for this number.]

No. L, October 1815

A. 2 [Stephen] on Registration of Slaves. B.M.L. Br. said that he wrote it (*Mems.* ii. 222).

A. 5 Huber on Bees, Vol. II. B.M.L. Br.'s statement in *Mems.* ii. 222 clearly implies that he wrote this article. C.M. makes another ascription which is not clear.

A. 8 Carnot's Defence. In B.M.L. Attested by Br. in *Mems.* ii. 222.

B. 11 France. C.M. says 'Brougham (as Lord Dudley says, *Letters*, p. 125).' See Letters to Ivy. In B.M.L. a blank in the rough list, and in the neat list, Br. followed by a question-mark. Embodies Br.'s policy in relation to France.

A. 13 Not in B.M.L. Br.'s statement in regard to an article which he had written for the *E.R.* and Lord Grey's reply (*Mems.* ii. 228, 230). They correspond exactly with Br.'s description of the article which he wrote before 5 December hoping to get it into this October number which was late.

No. LI, February 1816

A. 6 Br.'s Income Tax article. Not in B.M.L. Well known to be his at the time. Resemblance in content and style to his speeches on the subject.

No. LIII, September 1816

A. 6 Law of Libel. In B.M.L., C.M., and Br.'s published *Conts*. Very much Br.'s subject at the time. The article gives a description of Br.'s bill of that year and refers in detail to Rex *v.* Creevey, in which Br. was counsel for the defence.

A. 10 Dangers of the Constitution. C.M. ('I believe'). Published in Br.'s *Conts*. Not in B.M.L.

No. LIV, December 1816

A. 3 (with part by J.) Bentham's Defense of Usury, and Protest against Law Taxes. In B.M.L. and Br.'s published *Conts*. In Fetter's list. See C.'s J. ii. 145: 'It is the work of a much greater person and not one third of it is mine.' So J. had a part in it, but he himself would have ascribed it to Br.

A. 10 Columbus. In B.M.L. and published by Br. in his *Conts*. Cop. ascribed to Foscolo.

No. LV, March 1817

A. 3 History of the Alarms with review of Canning's speech, 29 January. B.M.L., published in Br.'s *Conts*. A likely subject for Br.

C. 5 Foreign Policy of England. B.M.L.

No. LVI, August 1817

B. 1 Franklin's Private Correspondence. B.M.L. Published by Br. in his *Conts*. Cockburn's J. list. Cop. says J. (following J. list).

B. 4 Present State of West India affairs. B.M.L. The opinions stressed are certainly Br.'s.

A. 11 Present State of Public Affairs. B.M.L. In Br.'s best *E.R.* and House of Commons sarcasm. Has Br. written all over it and in direct accord with his parliamentary speeches.

No. LVII, November 1817

A. 5 Junius. B.M.L. Published by Br. in his *Conts*. Cop. ascribed to Mackintosh.

C. 8 Russia's Power and Policy. B.M.L.

C. 11 Rome, Naples, and Florence in 1817. B.M.L.

No. LIX, June 1818

C. 4 Birkbeck's Notes on America. B.M.L.

B. 7 State of Parties. B.M.L., C.M. ('I believe'). Br. would be the most likely author of such an article in *E.R.* The criticism offered and the policies advocated repeat statements previously made by Br.

No. LX, September 1818

A. 3 Mélanges d'Histoire et de Littérature. B.M.L. Published by Br. in his *Conts*.

C. 8 Buonaparte and the Elba MS. B.M.L.

No. LXI, December 1818

A. 7 Fellenberg. B.M.L., C.M., Cop. Br.'s subject, his visit to Fellenberg, his interest and his evidence before the Education Committee.

No. LXII, March 1819

B. 12 Education and Abuse of Charities. B.M.L., C.M. The rough list says 'Br. except puff by J.' See also C.'s J. ii. 151.

No. LXIII, July 1819

A memo. which I found in a J. bundle in Br. MSS. begins 'July 1819 No. 63 pp. 75' and continues with date number and total pages to November 1823. It appears to be in Br.'s hand and is obviously a record of total pages supplied to *E.R.* by Br. in each of these numbers. The 75 pages in this LXIII were made up by adding article 5, which was based on material supplied by Br., and article 9 which Br. MSS. ascribe to William Brougham, to the following articles written by Br. He would consider that he had supplied No. 9 to the *Review* particularly as he would almost inevitably have helped William with a subject with which he himself was so familiar. I consider all the articles where the paging coincides as 'practically certain' and have marked them A.

A. 4 Dr. King's Memoirs. B.M.L. Published by Br. in his *Conts*. C.'s J. list, and Cop. were wrong in ascribing it to J.

A. 10 New French Law of Libel. The subject was very much Br.'s. Not in B.M.L.

No. LXIV, October 1819

With other authorships for certain articles firmly established there is no possibility of a group of articles by Br. totalling as they stand

the 48 pages indicated. The pages of the following articles ascribed
to Br. by B.M.L. total 52. Various suggestions could be made for
explaining the discrepancy. One is that some one else may have
written a small part of one of these articles.

B. 4   History of Painting in Italy.
B. 8   Marcet on Calculous Disorders.
A. 13   Fellenberg's Establishments at Hofwyl. C.M.

No. LXV, January 1820

The total number of pages in the following articles is 52, the
number indicated in the memo. (It is, however, difficult to understand the exclusion of article 6 which Br. did not write but for which
he supplied the material, when a similar article was counted in
in No. LXIII.)

A 8   Adulteration of Food and Culinary Poisons. No evidence, but
       it is the only article in this number for which there is no
       indication of authorship. Br.'s knowledge of chemistry is
       adequate for it and he wrote on similar subjects. B.M.L.
       ascribe it to J.
A. 10 The Present Alarms. B.M.L. Another political debating
       article in Br.'s style. The natural sequel to LV, 3, LVI, II,
       and LIX, 7.

No. LXVI, May 1820

A. 9   [Creevey's] Guide to the Electors of England. The only
       article in this number that has been ascribed to Br. (B.M.L.),
       it contains 23 pages, the number given in the memo. Contains
       much eulogy of Creevey and a discussion of the Droits of the
       Admiralty, a favourite Br. topic.

No. LXVII, August 1820

The following articles total 53 pages, the number given in the
memo.

A. 7   Hogg's Jacobite Relics. B.M.L., C.M., Cop.
A. 11 Education in England. B.M.L., Br.'s explanation of and his
       case for this Education Bill of 1820.

No. LXVIII, November 1820

William Brougham's article on Pendulums which C.M. ascribed
to Br. added to the following makes a total of 17 pages. The number
given in the memo. is 18.

A. 9 Brande on Inflammable Gases. B.M.L. Br. had written previous reviews of Brande on similar subjects.

No. LXIX, March 1821

The following articles total 82 pages, the number given in the memo.

A. 4 Naples. B.M.L.
A. 9 Mountains east of Rome.
A. 12 Education. B.M.L. Br.'s Education Bill.

No. LXX, July 1821

The following articles written by Br. total 37 pages, the number indicated in the memo.

A. 10 Tomline's Life of Pitt. B.M.L., C.M., Cop. Published by Br. in his *Conts*.
A. 13 Education. B.M.L.

No. LXXI, October 1821

The following articles, all ascribed to Br. in B.M.L., total exactly 67 pages the number given in the memo.

A. 2 Foreign Slave Trade. B.M.L. Embodies Br.'s opinions and stresses his constant advocacy of mutual right of search.
A. 5 Demosthenes. Published by Br. in his *Conts*. Cop. said Br. and Williams. It reflects fully Br.'s life-long enthusiasm for Demosthenes.
A. 8 Craven's Tour in South Italy (and the Late Revolution in Italy). B.M.L. S.S. wrote to J. 7 August: 'I shall proceed to write a review of Scarlett's Poor Bill and Keppell Craven's Tour' (*Letters*, i. 378). The *Gentleman's Magazine* list credits him with the Scarlett article, but not this Craven one. The authoritative but not infallible list of S.S.'s articles given in his *Memoirs* does not include either of these. (Smith frequently promised articles which he did not write.)

No. LXXII, February 1822

The total number of pages in the following articles (two of which are ascribed to Br. in B.M.L. and the other is on a favourite theme of his) is 55, the number given in the contemporary Br. MSS. memo.

A. 2 Supplément aux Mélanges d'Histoire, de Littérature, &c. B.M.L. Published by Br. in his *Conts*. Sequel to LX, 3.
A. 4 The Last Session of Parliament. Cop.'s ascription to J. is

almost out of the question in view of J.'s statement and the subject. Not in C.'s J. list.

A. 10 Tonbridge School. B.M.L. Discussion of a court conviction arising out of Br.'s attack on charities, and of the proper disposal of the misappropriated funds.

No. LXXIII, June 1822

When Article 9, a scientific article ascribed by B.M.L. to William Brougham, is added to the following, the total number is 76, the number given in the contemporary memo.

A. 4   Constitutional Associations (Ireland). B.M.L.
A. 7   Napoleon. Cop., B.M.L.

No. LXXIV, November 1822

Total paging of the following articles is 2 short of the memo.

A. 4   Trial of Williams. C.M. says: 'Brougham!! (certain, Jeffrey told me)'. Not in B.M.L.
A. 5   Mr. Canning and Reform. B.M.L. Published by Br. in his Conts.

No. LXXV, February 1823

The following articles total 55 pages, the number given in the memo.

A. 3   Grattan's Speeches, B.M.L.
A. 8   Negro Slavery. B.M.L. See pp. 283–5 above. Zachary Macaulay to Br. (Br. MSS.).
A. 11   Scottish Law Courts. C.M. Cop. ascribes to Cockburn which must be wrong. Would have to be Br.'s to make the exact number of pages in the memo.
[This leaves 5 to J. which Cockburn ascribed to him in C.M. and later in his J. list, and B.M.L. Br. Cop. said '[Brougham], claimed by Jeffrey.']

No. LXXVI, May 1823

The following articles total 66 pages, the number given in the memo.

A. 6   Travels of Williams. B.M.L.
A. 8   Infant Schools. B.M.L. Cop. to Basil Hart.
A. 10   Carnot. A probability for Br. who had already written two Carnot articles. Not in B.M.L.
A. 12   Napoleon, B.M.L.

No. LXXVII, October 1823

The following articles total 64 pages, the number given in the memo.

A. 5 The Bourbons. B.M.L.

A. 7 Negro Emancipation. B.M.L. C.M.

A. 12 Court of Chancery. B.M.L. C.M. 'I believe', but referred to Eldon's *Life* which ascribed to Sir John Williams.

No. LXXVIII, January 1824

B. 7 Court of Chancery. B.M.L., C.M. 'I believe'.

No. LXXIX, March 1824

C. 3 Quinn's Visit to Spain. B.M.L.

A. 10 West Indian Missions. B.M.L., C.M. 'I believe'. This is Br.'s Missionary Smith article. He had charge of the subject and this article is closely related to his later speeches in Parliament.

No. LXXXI, October 1824

A. 1 High Tory Principles. B.M.L., C.M. Published by Br. in his *Conts.*

A. 5 Education of the People, Mechanics' Institutes. The basis for Br.'s 'Observations'. B.M.L. Leonard Horner to Br., 2 January 1825.

B. 10 Abolition of Slave Trade and of Slavery. B.M.L., C.M.

No. LXXXII, January 1825

B. 3 Hazlewood School. B.M.L.: ascribed in the rough list, queried in the neat list. C.M. 'I believe'. (Add. MSS. (Place MSS.) 27, 823 f. 379 seq.)

C. 7 Ellis's Letters on English History. B.M.L.

C. 9 The West Indies. Slave Trade. B.M.L., with question-mark in both lists.

No. LXXXIII, April 1825

B. 6 Dangers of Popular Education. B.M.L. Reply to article on Br. and the 'Observations'.

No. LXXXIV, August 1825

B. 3 New London University. B.M.L. Brougham's project.

A. 10 Outrage at Barbadoes. B.M.L., C.M. Br.'s subject in circumstances.

A. 11 Mechanics' Institutes. B.M.L., C.M., Br.'s subject.

No. LXXXV, November 1825

C. 10 Mme de Staël. Lettres sur l'Angleterre. B.M.L.

B. 11 Supposed Dangers of Knowledge. B.M.L. Likely Brougham subject.

No. LXXXVI, February 1826

C. 1 C.M. says Br. 'I believe'. Sounds like Br. Contains a characteristic attack on Lord Eldon. Cop. to McCullough. Not in B.M.L.

B. 3 U. of London. B.M.L. to Br. Cop. to Macaulay. Not in M.'s Essays or in a list in Br. MSS. S.S.'s letter to Br. 28 May apparently rebuked Br. for writing it.

B. 8 Colonial Slavery. B.M.L.

No. LXXXVIII, June 1826

B. 4 Maitland's Narrative. Napoleon. Cop., B.M.L.

B. 5 Independence of Judges. B.M.L.

C. 8 Parliamentary History. Cop. Not in B.M.L.

No. LXXXIX, December 1826

A. 5 Pulpit Eloquence. B.M.L. Published by Br. in his *Conts.*

A. 7 West India Slavery. B.M.L. This is Br.'s analysis of the parliamentary returns for which he had moved.

A. 8 Diffusion of Knowledge. B.M.L., C.M. This was a reply to an article on Br. The concluding pages repeated a statement made in his Observations earlier in the year.

No. XC, March 1827

C. 6 Industrial Capacities of Negroes. B.M.L.

A. 11 Defeat of Catholic Question in House of Commons. B.M.L., C.M. ('I believe'), *L.S.S.* i. 465.

No. XCI, June 1827

C. 6 George III and the Catholic Question. B.M.L.

C. 8 Ellis's Letters on English History. B.M.L.

A. 9 West Indian Mulattoes. B.M.L. Generally assumed to be Br.'s at the time. Related to his parliamentary speech on the subject.

B. 10 Society for Diffusion of Useful Knowledge. B.M.L., C.M. This reviews Br.'s introductory treatise.

C. 11 The Present Administration. B.M.L. *L.S.S.* i. 467 has a blank and the editor as his own surmise ascribes article to Macaulay.

No. XCII, June 1827

A. 1   Buckle and Dr. Lawrence. Cop., B.M.L., C.M.
C. 3   Royal Society President's address. B.M.L.
B. 6   State of Parties. B.M.L. Likely subject for Br.
B. 11   Paley's Natural Theology. B.M.L. Favourite subject with Br.

No. XCIII, January 1828

C. 5   Scottish Marriages. Wakefield's Case. B.M.L. Br. was counsel in the Wakefield case. But does not read as though written by Br.
A. 6   Pestalozzi. Diffusion of Knowledge. B.M.L., Cop. Very much Br.'s subject.
C. 10   The only ascriptions are C.M. and the rough list of B.M.L., which has Br. with query.

No. XCIV, May 1828

B. 8   Denman's Inaugural Address. B.M.L. Close relation between Br. and Denman.

No. XCV, September 1828

C. 9   Travel Books. C.M. In rough list of B.M.L. queried.
B. 10   London University and King's College. B.M.L., C.M. Very much Br.'s subject at that date.
B. 11   Library of Useful Knowledge. B.M.L. It is difficult to think of anyone but Br. writing in the *E.R.* on either of these two subjects at this time. The only possibility of that would be afforded by Br.'s health at the time.

No. XCVI, December 1828

A. 9   Religious and Temporal Knowledge. B.M.L., C.M.

No. XCVII, March 1829

A. 2   Courier. Cop., B.M.L. Published by Br. in his *Conts.*
A. 6   Library of Entertaining Knowledge. Cop., B.M.L.
C. 8   Law of Legitimacy. B.M.L. (W. Br. in rough list, Br. in neat list).
        [9 is too doubtful to include. B.M.L., gives Br. in the rough list only. Cop to Empson.]

No. XCIX, October 1829

J. to Napier, October 17 (Napier Corr. p. 68) said that Br. would contribute three articles to this number and *Napier Cor.*, p. 70 n., gives four as follows:

A. 1 King's Life of Locke. B.M.L. The manuscript in Br.'s hand
is in Napier MSS. (Add. MSS. 34, 627 f. 1 seq.). C.M. wrong
in ascribing to J.

A. 2 Library of Useful Knowledge. *Napier Cor.*, p. 68, B.M.L.
ascribes to J.

A. 12 Ascent of Mont Blanc. Cop., B.M.L., C.M.

A. 15 The New French Ministry. Cop., B.M.L., C.M.

No. C, January 1830

[Br. probably wrote nothing for this number. See J. to Napier,
5 November 1829 (*Napier Cor.*, p. 69) for the suggestion of a reason
for that. None of the subjects seem to be suitable for him.]

No. CII, July 1830

A. 8 Law Reform. District Courts. *Nap. Cor.*, p. 80 n., C.M.

A. 10 Library of Useful Knowledge. *Nap. Cor.*, p. 80 n.

A. 12 State of Parties. *Nap. Cor.*, p. 80 n., C.M. The only article in
this number noted in B.M.L. and there is a question mark
after Br. in both rough and neat lists.

No. CIII, October 1830

A. 1 The Late Revolution in France. *Nap. Cor.*, p. 88 n., C.M.

A. 8 Allen on the Royal Perrogative. *Nap. Cor.*, p. 88 n., C.M.

A. 11 Galt's Life of Byron. *Nap. Cor.*, p. 88 n.

A. 13 The general Election and the Ministry. B.M.L. with a question-mark in both lists. *Nap. Cor.*, p. 88 n.

JOINT ARTICLES

C. I, 6. Baldwin's Egypt. Probably by Br. and J. R.G.M. Neat list
of B.M.L., amending rough list which said Hamilton, Br.'s
Mem. list. B. ascribed to Hamilton, citing Si. (weak) and C.M.
Cop. to S.S., but not in S.S. list. T.Gr. point out that C.'s J.
said that S.S. wrote seven articles for this number, and seven
others are clearly attested. *L.S.S.* i. 72 n. simply follows Cop.

A. II, 23. Transactions of the Royal Soc. of Edinburgh. By Br. and
J. jointly, though B., Si., C.M., and Cop. all ascribe the whole
article to Br. R.G.M. and the rough list in B.M.L. were more
accurate. Br. in his *Memoirs* account of the Br.–Murray list
claimed only the latter part of the article (on papers by Ivory
and Wallace) and published only that part in his *Conts*.

[I am omitting III, 1, Gentz's *État de l'Europe*, because of doubt whether Br. wrote enough of it to justify classification as a joint article. The fact that Br. thought so is, no doubt, responsible for the J. and Br. ascription in the Mem. list and in the neat list of B.M.L. Jeffrey apparently did not think so. At the time he said that he was writing the article, and he approved of its ascription to him in C.'s J. list. To J. alone by B., Si., C.M., and Cop.]

A. III, 3. Shepherd's Poggio. Percival and Br. jointly. Clearly attested by Br.'s contemporary letter to Loch (*E.F.* ii. 67) where Br. said that he wrote 'the cutting part'. R.G.M. said 'Perceval with additions by Br.' which is repeated in rough list of B.M.L. The later neat list has 'Percival and Br.'. Joint authorship supported by Br.'s Mem. list, B. Ascribed to Percival by Si., and Cop.

A. III, 13. Ritson on Abstinence from Animal Food. Br. and J. jointly. B. citing Br.'s Mem. list. Also R.G.M. and B.M.L. Ascribed to Br. alone by Si., C.M., Cop. Br.'s contemporary letter on 'what I did in No. III' does not mention J. S.S. certainly had a part in it but apparently in an editorial capacity.

A. IV, 16. Fuseli on Painting. Dr. Parry and Br. jointly, B. citing Br.'s Mem. list. Also R.G.M. and neat list in B.M.L., where the rough list says Parry, as does C.M. R.G.M. ascribed to 'Parry, well salted by Br.' which statement Br. repeated later in his *Memoirs*.

A. V, 9. Barclay's Anatomical Nomenclature. B. says, 'Br. and Reeve?' Si. to Reeve. Cop to Thomson. B.M.L. to Br. In his contemporary letter in *E.F.*, Br. said that he wrote part of it.

B. XI, 4. Education. Playfair and Br., B.M.L., B. to Br., citing Si., Cop.

A. XXV, 14. The Don Cevallos article. Br. and J. jointly. See pp. 46–49 above for J.'s various statements and his final 'It was a joint publication'. T.Gr. have a full discussion. B., citing C.M. R.G.M. gave joint authorship but B.M.L. to Br. alone. C.'s J. and Cop. to J. J. published it as his own but included only parts of it. Then Br. published it as his own in *Conts*. and what he included, about a half, was probably, with some changes, what he wrote. The C.M. entry reads 'Brougham and Jeffrey [about one half each]'. That was probably written in close to the time of publication, and was much nearer the truth than what Cockburn reported later.

A. XXXIV, 1. Parliamentary Reform. Br. and J. jointly. R.G.M., B.M.L. To J. by C.M., C.'s J. list, Cop. J. and Br. both published it in their contributions, but different parts. J. apparently wrote on general principles and Br. on specific proposals. His plan, in this year 1811, repeated verbally some of what he wrote in this article.

The totals for the above ascriptions to Brougham alone, graded according to degrees of probability are A (practically certain) 158, B (highly probable) 62, and C (more likely than not) 33. Of the joint articles, 7 are graded A, 1 B, and 1 C. Of course, many of the C ascriptions are bare possibilities and some percentage reduction should be made for total possibilities of error in the above. But two things are clear; Brougham probably wrote twice as many articles as Copinger ascribed to him and, including those of the following period, many more articles than Jeffrey, although Jeffrey wrote many parts of articles which could not be credited to him.

BIBLIOGRAPHICAL NOTE

SINCE Brougham was mentioned in nearly every book of correspondence, diary, &c., published during the period, as well as in nearly all contemporary biographies and has been noticed in the great majority of secondary works written about the period, its movements or its persons, a bibliography of Brougham would be gigantic, hopeless, and useless.

I have used the following collection of manuscripts:

At University College, London

The Brougham MSS. (Over 50,000 items. This collection is not yet arranged but I was permitted to work through it prior to arrangement and indexing.)

Bentham MSS.   S.D.U.K. Letters
U.C. Correspondence

At the British Museum

Aberdeen MSS.   Napier MSS.
Auckland MSS.   Peel MSS.
Babbage MSS.   Place MSS.
Clarkson MSS.   Russell MSS.
Gladstone MSS.   Wellesley MSS.
Huskisson MSS.   Wilson MSS.
Liverpool MSS.

At the Public Record Office

Ellenborough MSS.   Russell MSS.

At Birkbeck College

London Mechanics' Institute MSS.

Clements Library, University of Michigan

Croker MSS.   Seldon MSS.
Lacaita–Shelburne MSS.

Various British manuscripts including a British Statesmen collection.

In private papers

Althorp MSS.   Lambton MSS.
Chatsworth MSS.   Lansdowne MSS.
Creevey MSS.   Netherby MSS.
Hatherton MSS.   Vizard MSS. (now moved to
Horner MSS.   Windsor)
Howick MSS.   Wellington MSS.

Althorp MSS., Aberdeen MSS., Wellington MSS., Russell MSS. will be cited in the second volume only.

I have used British newspapers for certain dates at the B.M. collection at Colindale and at the Library of Congress. I have worked through *The Times* and *Hansard* through the period. I have also used the files of contemporary periodicals, notably the *Edinburgh Review* and the *Quarterly Review*.

Since a list of the secondary books which I have used would be out of the question, I have given a full bibliographical reference for every book cited in the notes the first time the title of that book occurs, and have prepared the following index of those pages in terms of the shorter designation which may thus be readily identified.

Bibliographical Index of Short Titles

General Index

PRINTED IN GREAT BRITAIN
AT THE UNIVERSITY PRESS, OXFORD
BY VIVIAN RIDLER
PRINTER TO THE UNIVERSITY